HISTORY OF
THE SCHOOL
CURRICULUM

HISTORY OF THE SCHOOL CURRICULUM

Daniel Tanner

RUTGERS UNIVERSITY

Laurel Tanner

UNIVERSITY OF HOUSTON

MACMILLAN PUBLISHING COMPANY
New York
COLLIER MACMILLAN PUBLISHERS
London

Macmillan Publishing Company
866 Third Avenue, New York, N.Y. 10022

Collier Macmillan Canada, Inc.

Library of Congress Catalog Card Number: 89-34120

Printed in the United States of America

printing number
1 2 3 4 5 6 7 8 9 10

Library of Congress Cataloging-in-Publication Data
Tanner, Daniel.
    History of the school curriculum / Daniel Tanner, Laurel Tanner.
        p.   cm.
    Includes bibliographies and indexes.
    ISBN 0-02-897411-5
    1. Curriculum planning—United States—History.   2. Curriculum
change—United States—History.   I. Tanner, Laurel N.   II. Title.
LB2806.15.T36 1989
375'.001'0973—dc20   89-34120
                                                      CIP

For
Lloyd Chilton,
our editor

CONTENTS

Part *II*   TRANSFORMATION AND REFORMATION—SCIENCE AND SENTIMENT

3   THE NEW EDUCATION AND THE DEMOCRATIC PROSPECT

4   CONFLICTING CURRENTS IN CURRICULUM THOUGHT AND PRACTICE

Part *III*   IDEAS AND IDEALS—CONFLICT AND CONSENSUS

5   THE CRISIS YEARS FOR THE CURRICULUM

6 THE CURRICULUM LEGACY 270

7 IDEALS OLD AND NEW 327

FOREWORD

The curriculum is the heart of schooling. The decisions made, consciously or unconsciously, in developing the curriculum greatly influence what is taught, what students learn, what teaching procedures are used, what learning activities students carry on, and how instruction is organized to facilitate continuous and integrated learning. As time goes on and teachers and other educators make these decisions, the options available to them are changing. New bodies of knowledge that could be used by students are being produced. New conceptions of conscious human learning are being formulated and tested. New understanding of what needs to be learned to be a participatory citizen in a democracy is evolving. New knowledge of the potential for learning in *all* children is emerging from experience and experiment. The social, economic, and political contexts in which schools operate are undergoing great changes that have profound effects on the curriculum. Curriculum development is a continuous and never-ending process.

Today we can benefit from the study of the earlier work of teachers and other educators as they planned, developed, and implemented the school curriculum. The history of the curriculum is not only an interesting story; it also makes clear some of the important sources of tension in the continuing debate among educators and the public over each of the major decisions that must be made in producing and operating an educational program. A few examples of the issues debated by previous generations may indicate their continuing existence.

What criteria should be used in deciding to admit a new body of knowledge into the curriculum? Can thinking skills be taught in isolation, or are they more effectively learned in solving real problems? When should teaching be focused on memorization, and what should be memorized? How can students be grouped for effective learning? How can theory and practice be connected to improve the education of teachers and other professionals? What are the values and limitations in educating students in lecture sessions, discussion sessions, laboratory assignments, seminars, independent study, field study?

By reviewing the past experience in dealing with these issues, we can not only identify the arguments used in support of and in opposition to the options considered, but we can also see some of the consequences of the steps that were actually taken. This does not serve as a definitive answer to the programs of today, when the conditions are not the same as in the past, but it informs us of the possible importance of factors to be given thoughtful consideration in making decisions in the present.

This book has been written by distinguished scholars in the curriculum field. Their familiarity with curriculum issues and developments during the past two centuries gives authenticity to this history. It is also thought-provoking and interesting; a real contribution to curriculum scholarship.

Ralph W. Tyler
Stanford, California

PREFACE

"History does not repeat itself, but in times past nearly every one of the issues that are so hot today has appeared in one form or another, and men and women have grappled with them, and have disposed of them in some fashion—for their time, or passed them on." So wrote Charles A. Beard in 1938.

Thus while each generation must grapple with its own concerns under its own conditions, each generation also inherits whatever has been accomplished or left undone in the past. Although it is fruitless to wait for cycles of events to repeat themselves, there is much to be learned from the experience called history. The struggle for educational opportunity, social justice, and economic equity is an unending one. It is as timely today as any time in the past, despite the very different conditions that mark our current history. In the same vein, throughout this century thoughtful educators have sought to develop through the curriculum a binding force to provide for a common sense of discourse, understanding, and competence for all citizens of a free society, while also providing for the diverse interests and pursuits of a polyglot populace. This effort has undergone renewal at various times, just when it appeared to be all but forgotten, and it has surfaced once again today as a principal concern for the school, the college, and society.

An absence of history is like an absence of memory, with the result that current curriculum events are destined to be treated as "this season's" sports scene or fashion scene. Our history reveals that far too many curriculum "reforms" have been painfully instituted and painlessly discarded because of their isolated character. Progress depends upon the progressive redirection of experience through prolem solutions. It does not derive from isolated or transitory events or fads, but from movement in a constructive direction. History should provide us with a sense of movement over time and a perspective to determine the nature, direction, and extent of our progress along with our setbacks. In short, the sense of perspective provided through history should enable us to gain a vision of prospect.

Our purpose in this work is to examine the history of the school curric-

xiii

ulum so as to make contemporary ideas and developments in the curriculum field more comprehensible. The sources and consequences of leading curriculum ideas and practices are identified with a view toward understanding our curriculum legacy. We have sought to trace the great struggle for a more complete realization of the democratic potential of American society through the transformation of the school and the reformation of the curriculum. The periodic movements for curriculum reform and retrenchment are examined in the light of wider sociopolitical influences, revealing the pluralism and contradictions that have characterized the American experience. Eac epoch of the unfolding story has been marked by powerful crosscurrents and countercurrents operating against the mainstream of events.

Twenty years ago, Gunnar Myrdal expressed his dismay at the emerging tendency for American social scientists to abandon their great tradition of supporting popular education. Since the 1960s, an increasing number of scholars in the foundations of education have assumed a profound negativism in their protrayal of the American experience in the struggle for popular education. In so doing, they have tended to embrace overarching and often monolithic theses concerning the character and motives shaping the directions and functions of our public schools. The fashion has been to focus on what has failed rather than what has prevailed—to look at the limitations rather than the possibilities in popular education.

As a consequence, insufficient recognition has been given to the powerful pluralism of the American tradition, coupled with the centrist tendency of our people to resist extremes of any ilk. In tracing the history of the school curriculum, we have sought to examine the nature and implications of this great pluralism, along with the common faith that finds its expression through popular education. The characteristics, conflicts, and contradictions that have marked the major movements in the curriculum evolution are examined in the light of emerging social, economic, and political forces.

This volume is organized into three parts. Chapter 1 of Part I explores the nature and uses of historical scholarship as seen by leading American historians and as related to the school curriculum. Dewey's warning against "losing a sense of historic perspective and of yielding precipitately to short-term contemporary currents, abandoning in panic things of enduring and priceless value," is cited as one of the signal shortcomings of the curriculum field. In Chapter 2 the early developments of the school curriculum are examined, revealing both our points of departure from the educational traditions of the Old World and our adaptation of certain progressive European ideas to fit the unique conditions and ideals of our new nation.

Part II focuses on the great transformation and reformation of the school curriculum, the formulation of a uniquely American theory of education to serve as a compass for the progressive redirection of our schools, and the emergence of a uniquely unitary school system as opposed to the divided system of European nations. The main currents in curriculum evolution are traced, along with conflicting currents in curriculum thought and practice. The ideas and influences of leading educators are examined in the light of the democratic prospect. The timeline in Chapter 3 presents a visual protrayal of the evolution of a distinctively American system of public education, the struggle for a more practical and comprehensive curriculum, and the battle for universal secondary education and the extension of opportunity for higher education. Chapter 4 reveals the many-sidedness of the progressive educational reforms. It is seen that those who were identified with the new education were sharply divided in ideas nad practices. At the same time, those upholding the old doctrines of mental discipline, transfer of learning, and schooling as privilege did not yield easily to the unfolding evidence in child development and the growing concern for social equity and mobility—pointing to the needed progressive redirection of the school and the curriculum.

In Part III the great curriculum conflicts are examined in the perspective of the dramatic social changes from the 1930s to today. Chapter 5 focuses on the crisis years for the curriculum in the face of the social emergency of the Great Depression. The diverse and often conflicting views of those associated with the new education are examined. At the same time, the notably creative efforts toward the progressive redirection of the curriculum are appraised. The story is told of the efforts to develop a sound research base and a sense of professional consensus for the emerging curriculum field, the struggle to make the elementary school a more suitable and stimulating environment in the light of the growing evidence concerning the nature of the learner, and the struggle to free the high school from college domination over the curriculum. The story is told of the efforts to develop a coherent curriculum to meet the common needs of a cosmopolitan population while also providing for a comprehesive curriculum to meet diverse needs—a story without end. Major events and conflicts leading up to the conservative assault against progressive education at midcentury, in the wake of the cold war, are traced.

Chapter 6 presents an in-depth appraisal of our curriculum legacy: What have we learned, and what can we build upon? What curriculum questions, wrestled with by reformers for more than a century, remain unanswered? Why are educators so vulnerable to curriculum fads and fashions, or to curriculum reform by reaction and counterreaction? Why are so many curriculum reforms undertaken segmentally, with the result that areas of the curriculum are not only disconnected but are set off in opposition to one another—despite the evidence amassed over many years pointing to the needed interdependence of areas of knowledge and the needed coherence of the curriculum? These are some of the questions addressed.

At the same time, focus is given to identifying the ideas and practices from the progressive curriculum reforms that continue to live in the schools and that serve as a sound foundation upon which to build. The closing chapter offers a critical appraisal of the conflicting ideals, old and new, affecting the curriculum—from traditionalism to progressivism. A timeline is presented portraying the main currents and countercurrents over the past century between traditionalism and progressivism in the curriculum evolution. Here the great watershed between the old education and the new might well be expressed in terms of whether the school and the curriculum are conceived to put the learner in control or under the control of conditions.

Several of the chapters close with a timetable of events in education and society to give the reader a sense of the wide range of developments in the stream of our modern history. Events in society do not always have a direct impact on curriculum, but they nevertheless are part of the wider social drama in which the schools are undergoing change. For example, there is a common cliché, "Those were simpler times," in referring to bygone eras. Was life really simpler when there were no protections against child labor, or when females were denied educational opportunity? Was life really simpler before it was known that germs cause disease; or before much was known about human nutrition, sanitation, and birth control; or before the advent of electrification and refrigeration; or before the development of scientific agriculture (which freed our population from the drudger of survival off the land)? The answers to these rhetorical questions seem obvious.

Finally, we are indebted to several individuals who offered helpful ideas and suggestions in the development of this book. The late Hollis L. Caswell, President Emeritus of Teachers College, Columbia University, and Arthur W. Foshay, Professor Emeritus of Teachers College, made invaluable suggestions for the earlier versions of sections of certain chapters that appeared in the second edition of *Curriculum Development: Theory into Practice.* Our wide-ranging discussions with Ralph W. Tyler, Director Emeritus of the Center for Advanced Study in the Behavioral Sciences, enabled us to test and distill certain ideas on the modern evolution of the school curriculum. We are grateful to Michael Knoll and Craig Kridel of the University of South Carolina for their insightful advice; to Regina Weade of the University of Florida, who reviewed the entire manuscript so constructively in its final phases; and to Kenneth J. Rehage of the National Society for the Study of Education, for his wise editorial counsel. Our editor, Lloyd C. Chilton, Jr., initiated the idea for this book and provided us with the needed support and guidance throughout our work. The resources of the Alexander Library of Rutgers University, the Teachers College Library, and the Regenstein Library of the University of Chicago were invaluable to us in this project. Appreciation is extended to Marion Ann Keller, who typed the manuscript with care and cheer. And we are grateful to our students, who tested many of our ideas with us all along the way.

Daniel Tanner
Laurel Tanner

Part I

PERSPECTIVES AND PROSPECTS

History deals with the past, but this past is the history of the present.

—JOHN DEWEY

Perspectives on Curriculum History

The story of the school curriculum, and the great leaders, ideas, and conflicting currents that shaped its development, is the subject of this volume. We were not there. And not having been there, we can never know for sure how it really was. But by staying within the evidence we can learn a great deal about the movement of the school curriculum through time (which has sometimes been cyclical), how conditions grew out of previous conditions, and how the present has come to be the way it is.

CURRICULUM HISTORY: CHAOS OR ORDER AND MOVEMENT?

Every written history—of an event, a professional field, a race, a nation, or the entire world—requires that events be recorded, organized, interpreted, and presented. The scientific method is essential in finding out what happened and in revealing the conditions that made the events possible. Although the absolute truth can never be known, the historian is guided by the conviction that more can be known about the movement of history. The historian then chooses the manner in which the results of the research are given to others. Since new insights are continually being revealed by scholarly objectivity, history is—and always must be—rewritten. In this sense, all serious histories are reconstructions.

However scholarly the inquiry, historical facts and events alone do not produce a history. They must be selected, interpreted, and arranged in order to communicate to the reader the excitement of discovery about what happened. Of course, readers of curriculum history are concerned about the "why" of what happened as well as the events themselves. The why is important if the history is to contribute insights into problems of present concern to educators.

Barbara Tuchman, a distinguished American historian, believed that one must first find out what happened and arrange the personalities, events, dates, and documents in some sequence: "to be exact, in sentences, paragraphs and chapters." She told us that the process of transforming facts into a narrative "forces the 'why' to the surface." One does not begin with a thesis and select the facts that suit one's system. Tuchman wrote that the "why" of what happened "will suddenly appear and tap one on the shoulder, but not if one chases after it first, *before* one knows what happened. Then it will elude one forever."[1]

In the 1960s and 1970s, radical revisionists in the field of education began with the thesis that progressive education was conservative in intent and outcome. In writing history, they left the contradictions out.[2] This is one of the disturbing developments that has recently influenced the writing of curriculum history. The point of importance here is that the purpose of history is to find out what happened and why. As Barbara Tuchman maintained, "Leaving things out because they do not fit is writing fiction, not history."[3]

Conceptions of History

Historians are no different from anyone else; they see things from their own perspectives, which determine for them the events that are related. However meticulous the scholarship, there is in the historian's mind a view of history that controls the selection and arrangement of facts. As Charles Beard pointed out in his presidential address before the American Historical Association in 1933, it is when the historian denies having a frame of reference, so that it comes in through the back door, that we have a pernicious situation.[4] Although conveying an image of objectivity, the researcher masks the valuations that have dominated his or her thinking and have determined the selection and treatment of events.[5]

In attempting to avoid bias, according to Beard, the historian must be aware of his or her conception of history and not run away from it. Indeed, Beard told the association, the historian should "proceed to examine his own frame of reference, clarify it, enlarge it . . . and give it consistency of structure by a *deliberate conjecture* respecting the nature of the vast movements of ideas and interests called history."[6] In other words, the historian should expose and use his conception of history to advance historical knowledge. In so doing, the historian is also avoiding the trap of hidden bias (hidden perhaps even to himself).

Three Views. At the association meeting of 1933, Beard argued that only three conceptions of history were possible: "History is chaos and every attempt to interpret it otherwise is an illusion. History moves around in a kind of cycle. History moves in a line, straight or spiral, and in some direction."[7] In the closing lines of his address, Beard indicated that his own view of history was developmental—that the world is moving progressively toward a better future and the historian's function is to accelerate the improvement: to improve our understanding of the past in the interest of improving the present. For Beard, historical scholarship has a pragmatic purpose—to help reformers avoid the pitfalls and defeats of the past by helping them to understand why they happened, and to build a better future by knowing and explaining the vast movements of ideas.

Making History. "History," Henry Steele Commager tells us, "embraces all that is put together artificially, by the historian."[8] Here Commager is not talking about history in its simplest form—history as a chronological recital of happenings—but about history as a reconstruction of the past. History is unavoidably interpretive. The statements and achievements of human beings long gone, the enormous body of documents and other original sources, must be transformed into an understood past. "If the historian expects his readers to make any sense of such statements he must explain them," writes Commager, "and as soon as he starts explaining them he is forced to reconstruct history."[9] The historian reconstructs history under a controlling idea of present concern—the expansion of educational opportunity or the evolution of the power of the media. As the historian breathes life into the historical record and gives it meaning, he or she is re-creating history. But as Commager emphasizes, "what is presented is not the past but a selection, an organization, an interpretation of the past."[10]

A Developmental View

The development of the school curriculum is the organizing idea that the authors of this book have applied to the recorded past. Our conception of curriculum history is developmental: Despite periodic setbacks, the school curriculum has moved and is continuing to move from primitive beginnings to a higher level and toward access to knowledge for increasingly wider populations in our society. This is not to say that there are no problems such as fads and cycles in education, but that for all of the setbacks and reinventions of old educational ideas and practices, each era has made its contribution to new knowledge about the curriculum and has provided greater access to the curriculum for societal groups that were previously excluded.

The Past-Present Connection. "Without coordination and consecutiveness," wrote John Dewey, "events are not events, but mere occurrences."[11] The past must be coordinated with the present if it is to have any meaning, but the reverse is also true: The present must be connected with the past. " 'News,' " Dewey argued,

> signifies something which has just happened, and which is new just because it deviates from the old and regular. But its *meaning* depends upon relation to what it imports, to what its social consequences are. The import cannot be

determined unless the new is placed in relation to the old, to what has happened and been integrated into the course of events.[12]

History, Dewey said, should be "brought down close to the actual scene of events."[13] History should help in the formation of policies about matters of public concern—and education is indeed a paramount public concern.

As Beard argued, since the historian who lives, after all, in the present is re-creating the past, it is a contemporary picture of the past. In this sense the connection between the present and the historical past (a past reconstructed from historical inquiry) is unavoidable. And since all history is unavoidably contemporary history, it might as well be written for the purpose of helping us with our current situations. This history of the school curriculum was written from that perspective, so that it might be useful in decisions concerning the school curriculum. Curriculum history is a form of knowledge about the curriculum—what has happened and taken place in the school in relation to society. Such knowledge is essential in deciding what is yet to be done. Problems arise in the schools when decisions are made as though the world did not exist before we came on the scene. Errors in judgment are almost certain when what happened in the past—previous efforts at curriculum reform—is ignored.

In sum, the history of the curriculum is a practical past, if we wish to make use of it.

The "Giant" Metaphor. "We see farther than they did because we stood on their shoulders" is the voice of modern science. The picture of a long succession of mighty intellects, with each generation working with more knowledge than its predecessors so as to build on their knowledge, is preeminently associated with science. The standing-on-the-shoulders-of-giants metaphor applies equally well to the school curriculum. Progress has occurred through the contributions of long-gone leaders and teachers who still have lessons to impart to us.

The very notion of progress is developmental and implies movement and growth from the past to the future. Progress in education (or in any field) requires knowing about the course of development, and it depends on building on the ideas of others. Without knowledge of curriculum history we would be left with incomplete knowledge of the present, which, after all, is the consequence of past experience. We need to understand and build upon the contributions of those before us if the present is to be made better than the past.

THE USES OF CURRICULUM HISTORY

Curriculum history is useful because of the enduring character of many of the old ideas. The problem method of investigation as a classroom activity runs through the course of development from Dewey to the modern teacher.

And the idea that teachers should be professionals (curriculum makers) and not technicians is even older, dating back to object teaching in the 1860s. The key ideas in the curriculum field must be communicated from one generation to another. Curriculum history should fulfill this objective.

Curriculum history is the collective memory of the field of curriculum. Without it we could not obtain full pictures of our contemporary problems; if no one could find out what transpired before, we would reinvent the pedagogical wheel without realizing that there are successful and unsuccessful educational models. But the mere existence of the records of our experience is no guarantee that these records will be consulted by contemporary curriculum reformers. Indeed, our cultural penchant for innovation often finds us ignoring related events and lessons from the recent as well as distant past. At the same time, sociopolitical shifts in successive periods find the schools under pressure to undo the very reforms that had been imposed upon them in a prior period, or to institute reforms they were forced to discard at an earlier time. In one period we have the "new math" and the discipline-centered curriculum; in another we have the open classroom and the learner-centered curriculum. In one period we have a great expansion of the curriculum; in a succeeding period we have curriculum retrenchment and "back to basics." "New" segmental reforms are instituted as antidotes to reforms that had been imposed segmentally during a predecessor period.

The record of the past reveals that segmental approaches are bound to fail because they create problems of curriculum imbalance and a lack of curriculum articulation. Periodically there is the rediscovery of the need for curriculum coherence and a core curriculum along with a comprehensive curriculum. But problems arise when there is failure to draw from our earlier efforts to create curriculum balance and synthesis. Similarly, there is the periodic rediscovery of the need for reflective thinking, while at the same time there is failure to learn the lesson of the past that the development of such thinking requires the curriculum to be infused with ideas and problem-solving methods that transcend subject boundaries. The isolation of studies remains a persistent curriculum problem.

Curriculum history has yet another function: It helps us to understand the traditions that have defined our professional and personal lives. This function is not just a practical affair—it is a matter of feeling. We develop a sense of responsibility to our predecessors and, perhaps, we are fired with ambition to continue their work. History provides models, whether we are talking about the fifth-grader's admiration for President Lincoln and interest in his boyhood, or the professional educator's sense of obligation to Horace Mann, who was one of the first to urge that teaching be professionalized.

The Potential Energy of Ideas

If curriculum history is to be useful, it must be constructive. As noted, in the 1960s and 1970s radical revisionism in educational history influenced research and interpretations of the history of the curriculum. Many revisionist historians generated negativistic research and rhetoric that looked to the limitations rather than the possibilities of schooling in connection with children's social and economic mobility. Americans have always believed strongly in education as a means of opportunity for the rising generation and for building a better future for the individual and society,[14] but radical revisionist historians have tried to marshal evidence showing the limits of schooling. By the late 1970s, critics of radical revisionist historiography found depressing evidence of systematic omissions and citations of nonexistent source material in revisionist books on the progressive past. Moreover, sentences were often torn from their settings to convey an entirely different meaning than the original writer had intended. Some revisionist studies on the effects of schooling were statistical, with vast amounts of codified data, but the American people were not about to give up their faith in education.[15] Their belief was not a mystical faith but was based on common sense and personal experience.

The Real and the Ideal. During the late 1970s, evidence began to accumulate that schools can help children overcome the effects of socioeconomic disadvantage. Nevertheless, not all children have optimum opportunity to learn in the schools. As Ralph Tyler has pointed out, access to the public schools does not guarantee equal access to a rich curriculum. Tyler writes: "The practice of grouping and tracking students in the elementary and secondary school has resulted in large numbers of children being denied access to such a curriculum."[16] Providing optimal access to knowledge is one of the unfinished tasks of American education.

We have not yet completed the task and may never fully do so. But if our society is true to itself, it must be committed to this ideal by effecting every means possible toward its attainment. One of the most striking facts about a great idea is that it contains the seeds of its own realization. "An idea contains potential energy in no mystical sense," wrote Charles Beard in his introduction to Bury's volume on the idea of progress, and "we often discover that an idea which is not in accord with historical facts may become true in practice, at least partially."[17] Beard provided an example:

> When Jefferson wrote that "all men are created equal," it was easy for his critics to point out obvious discrepancies in physical and mental endowment and in social position, but nevertheless, Jefferson's idea wielded a wide empire over the human spirit, worked for liberalization of institutions, and has become a reality in so far as all men (and women) are theoretically equal before the law.[18]

Directing the Force of Ideas. An idea, emphasized Beard, "is not a mere intellectual conception; it contains within itself a dynamic power to move individuals and nations, to drive them in the direction of effecting the ends and institutions implicit in it."[19] Educators are professionals when they base practice on principles and ideals, and this is one of the uses of history. Those who work in curriculum development must understand how the force of the democratic ideal influenced educational development over a period of more than two hundred years so that they can continue this progress by directing that great force. It must be remembered that a living ideal serves as a test for existing practice and direction. Present means must be ideals in the making; otherwise, the ideals are merely paper statements.

The Concept of Progress.   The idea of progress is surely the most influential idea in curriculum history. This is the idea that humankind has advanced in the past and is continuing to move in an improving direction. The history of the idea of progress shows that it profoundly influenced education. The dominant objective of progressive education was what its name suggests: to bring about progress. Following Dewey's educational theory, and that of Lester Ward before him, progressive educators were profoundly concerned with developing critical thinkers. They wanted to send individuals into society who could control the environment rather than be controlled by it, who could plan for and bring about a better life. They believed that the world moves, and the motion can be in the direction of a better life if it is directed by human intelligence. The story of their work, and its continuity with the present, is told in this volume.

The idea of progress has been denigrated in the writing of history, as Gertrude Himmelfarb points out,[20] and curriculum history is no exception. "One of the most important myths in education is that of progress," say two curriculum professors, and their negativism is all too typical.[21] But as Himmelfarb goes on to say, there is a powerful case for the concept of progress.[22] If this is true in history generally, it is even more true in education. Education is by its very nature positive and is utterly incompatible with pessimism. Belief in the improvability of people is inherent in education; it is what education is all about.

Throughout the history of the curriculum all of the valuable contributions have been made by people who are committed to individual and social progress. John Dewey's *Democracy and Education,* which attacked the aristocratic alliance between culture and class that was reflected in unequal access to the school curriculum (as well as in the curriculum itself), was the most brilliant study of pedagogical principles and practices in a democracy that had ever been written. The Twenty-sixth Yearbook of the National Society for the Study of Education (1927), which addressed the resolution of the conflict between the nature and interests of the learner and the demands of adult life, threw a flood of light on the key factors of the curriculum field. This constructive and critically important analysis represented the whole range of educational thought: from Harold Rugg to William Bagley to William Kilpatrick, with statements by other leaders as well. But it was Rugg who conceived of making a contribution to curriculum progress by attempting to reconcile the antagonistic philosophies—or, at least to arrive at a consensus regarding a direction for curriculum reconstruction. Benjamin S. Bloom's profound analysis, *Human Characteristics and School Learning* (1976), which presented the factors involved in the learner's growth as connected with the school curriculum—from home conditions to school conditions—is richly constructive, as are such diverse earlier works as Alexander Inglis' *Principles of Secondary Education* (1918), Boyd Bode's *Modern Educational Theories* (1927), Gunnar Myrdal's *An American Dilemma* (1944), the Harvard report *General Education in a Free Society* (1945), and Lawrence A. Cremin's *The Transformation of the School* (1961).

Such works, along with many others in the twentieth century, relate to the idea of progress and the American faith in public education as anything but a blind faith. As Dewey pointed out about the prospects for progress, "If we want it, we can have it—if we are willing to pay the price in effort, especially in effort of intelligence. The conditions are at hand."[23]

Does History Teach Lessons?

"Boundless energy has been spent in countless classrooms reinventing the pedagogical wheel."[24] So wrote Lawrence Cremin in a comparison of progressive reforms of the 1970s with the original progressive education movement. In the 1970s educators became particularly interested in studying curriculum history with the thought that such study was preventive: Knowing our history would keep us from repeating our failures. In the 1970s and 1980s many curriculum professors turned their energies toward developing courses in curriculum history. Awareness that curriculum history is an important part of professional knowledge is a recent development that has influenced historic investigation of the curriculum.

The implication of such study is that there are lessons to be learned from history; that is, contemporary workers can wrest lessons about what to do (or, more frequently, what *not* to do) from the great record of past experience. History, it is said, teaches. Thus the solution to the problem of cycles and fads seems simple: Study history. The prescription makes perfect sense. Curriculum history is an extension of the personal memory, an extension that educators can share so that it becomes the memory of a professional field. To the extent that it does, say its advocates, it can regulate and guide the activities of reformers. But they often stop short of the "how."

Then there are some in academia who hold that the study of history should be pursued for its own sake. Under such circumstances there is the danger that historical scholarship becomes a self-serving enterprise whereby historical developments are removed from their consequences.

Does history teach by examples? Certainly the American Founding Fathers thought so, as Commager pointed out. "It was on history that they drew to justify independence, to guide them along the path of federalism, to provide examples for every experiment and warnings against every danger that lurked in the shadows."[25] Nevertheless, in our own time historians have generally rejected the notion that history has specific lessons to teach. The reason is identified by Barbara Tuchman: "The trouble is that in human behavior and history it is impossible to isolate or repeat a given set of circumstances."[26] The distinguished Commager adds that historians "are on their guard against the false analogy."[27]

History as Analogy.   Nevertheless, the idea that history can teach us lessons is very much alive. Indeed, the use of history by decision-makers in considering courses of action has a growing number of champions. The idea of lessons from history is enjoying a revival in the social sciences. Neustadt and May, for example, who are professors at Harvard's Kennedy School of Government, have developed a set of guidelines for the use of experience (history) in making decisions. Granted that their concern is mainly with helping our government officials make "more reflective and systematic" uses of history, their suggestions are broad and sound, and they are applicable to those of us who must make judgments about current curriculum problems and issues.[28]

Reformers need to look at our experience if they are not to retrace our false steps. For example, in the early 1970s a "new" child-centered educational movement—the open (informal) classroom—swept the United States. However, the idea was adopted mainly as an organizational arrangement for differentiated and individualized learning activities. The original idea for the open classroom was the integration of educational experiences. However, the response was to build open-space schools or schools without classroom walls without appreciably attending to the need for curriculum synthesis. Years later many school administrators and board members looked back and asked, "Whatever made us do such a thing?"

In connection with governmental misadventures, Neustadt and May observe that in each instance, if historical evidence had been brought into the light, the "such a thing" might not have happened. There were parallels between the open-education and child-centered movement of the late 1960s and early 1970s and the earlier child-centered movement of Dewey's time. An understanding of how and why child-centered education went awry in the 1920s and 1930s would have helped educators decades later to understand its deficiencies and perhaps avoid a repetition of past mistakes. Had educators done their homework and taken a closer look at the earlier experience with romanticist child-centered education, their decisions might have been more prudent and the counterreaction that was sure to come could have been avoided. (Part of their homework should have been to read John Dewey's *The Child and the Curriculum* [1902], which constructively analyzed the conflict between the child-centered and subject-centered poles of the curriculum.)

Tuchman's observation that history never repeats itself exactly is, of course, indisputable. Although curriculum history may *seem* to consist of blind repetitions of pointless cycles of "back to basics" and "do your own thing," analysis of an analogy with a previous movement shows differences as well as likenesses. As a result of the interplay between social and economic forces and discoveries made by systematic investigation, no two situations at different points in the stream of time can ever be the same. Neustadt and May suggest that both differences and likenesses be identified, for an analogy may have limited relevance and offer little guidance about what to do and not to do. On the other hand, the analogy might be fully pertinent, such as in the timeworn shifts in successive epochs between the child-centered and subject-centered curricula.

Finding History.   As Neustadt and May point out, "Historical information is no different from any other kind. You just have to recognize that you need it."[29] What is implied here is a critical cast of mind, an inquiring attitude that makes the professional into a kind of detective. Where does the curriculum detective go to find historical evidence? Like other detectives, the historian may begin with people: University professors, teachers, and supervisors who have worked in education for a number of years (Neustadt and May call them "old hands") are sources with whom to confer about recent analogies.

For example, many educators can recall with clarity the back-to-basics movement of the early 1950s—they were there—and can offer useful comparisons with the most recent version of back to basics. The old hand should be asked to relate what happened, how it happened, and why it happened.

Nevertheless, as Neustadt and May point out about old hands, "none will know more than part of any story."[30] In order to obtain a full picture of an analogy, one must consult the literature of the curriculum field. If the issue or proposed reform has a recent history, *Education Index* can guide one toward articles in scholarly journals. Books and documents are the best sources for information about pieces of curriculum history that date back farther in time. Yet a cautionary note should be injected here. While one is inclined to view recent books as the most authoritative sources because they presumably encompass and attempt to replace earlier knowledge, this is not necessarily the case. A new book may not mark an advance over an older work. Curriculum detectives should check the book's sources—footnotes and bibliography. As Neustadt and May suggest, "If it doesn't mention earlier writings you know about or if it seems based on skimpy research, turn to something older."[31]

Of course, an author should use primary sources whenever possible, and so should anyone who wants to make a wise curriculum decision. By turning to the original document or piece of research itself, one is best able to avoid the possible misconstructions of others.

We have observed that when the reform tide is high, books about a "new" educational movement tend to be promotional rather than cautionary and analytical. To illustrate, the reader should place himself or herself vicariously in the early 1970s, when Charles Silberman's *Crisis in the Classroom* was a national best-seller. Silberman's book was instrumental in promoting the British model of the open classroom, which set pupils to find things out without proper guidance. This idea had been tried and found wanting in the United States in the 1920s and 1930s. Moreover, it was already being abandoned in British schools as unworkable at the time Silberman's book was published. Silberman's book fed upon itself; reviews of the book were mainly laudatory, and decision-makers felt that they had to adopt the model—without knowing why or even if open classrooms were called for. Adopting the British model was a nonsolution to a manufactured problem: a crisis in the classroom.

Years later a number of American educators looked back at the events that marked the early 1970s and wondered how Silberman's book happened to have exerted such a powerful influence. "Since *Summerhill* appeared in 1960," wrote N. L. Gage in 1978, "we seem to have been more than ever at the mercy of powerful and passionate writers who shift educational thinking ever more erratically with their manifestos."[32]

This problem is not necessarily a recent one. The voices heard when priorities shift in educational reform have always been promotional. This means that educators have an enormous professional responsibility to search the literature for previous experiences with an educational reform. They should also look for dissenting ideas from authoritative sources. What evidence is offered from the record of past experience and the body of scholarly research literature? Professionals are obligated to seek the best available knowledge bearing on a proposed reform by combing the relevant literature and investigating the proposed reforms when they can be observed in practice. This takes time and effort. Moreover, it means that the norm for the school or school system needs to be directed at substantive curriculum improvement, rather than at following whatever tide may be most dominant at a particular time.

Finally, reforms need to be built on constructive and pervasive evidence. As Neustadt and May advise, if an author "claims to have discovered some truth never before suspected, especially some dark conspiracy, try another book."[33] The work of Ravitch reveals that many of the books by radical revisionist historians are of this ilk.[34]

Analogies from the historic experience can provide valuable insights to those who are seeking problem solutions in contemporary educational practice and in evaluating the worth of adopting currently popular reform prescriptions.

Solving Curriculum Problems

Defensive Uses of History.   Examination of analogies is one effective use of history. The history that is selected is the history that helps us to know whether we have experienced an educational proposal before. This use of history is, in a word, defensive. If all did not go well in the past with a reform that is being presently proposed, knowing what happened and why can help us avoid almost certain waste and even disaster.

Countering educational cycles and fashions is the primary responsibility of the schools. What makes the schools' situation especially difficult is that reform proposals are often politically rather than educationally motivated. The reformers issue proposals but are not responsible for their implementation or consequences. Temporary commissions like the national commissions of the 1980s, which issued a foray of reform documents, suffer from the limits of time, and their purposes are likely to be political.[35] But the use of history should not be merely defensive.

Constructive Uses of History. Curriculum reform efforts are often, but should not be, mere reactions to the excesses of a previous era of reform. In the 1970s, open-classroom excesses (laissez-faire pedagogy in the name of "freedom" and "relevance") troubled the schools. Little wonder, then, that the counterreaction was to "reform the reform" through a retreat to an old and simplistic "remedy"—curriculum retrenchment through "back to basics." Both waves of reform, "do your own thing" and "back to basics," ran counter to the body of research in the curriculum field.

Curriculum improvement should begin as an attempt to solve a problem. One starts with the problem, not the innovation or proposal. In working on a problem, one has to find out what happened before, and in so doing one is using history. In addition to being our collective memory, curriculum history is the cumulative experience of the curriculum field. Its value for us in solving contemporary problems may be enhanced if we consider curriculum history as *historical consequences,* or *products,* and *historical processes.* Historical consequences are the research findings and concepts that teachers, principals, boards of education, and state departments of education should draw upon in considering curriculum alternatives. In other words, curriculum decisions should be consistent with these consequences (facts, evidence, and principles).

One illustration dating back to 1901 is Thorndike's monumental research, which refuted the idea that particular subjects should be included in the curriculum because they were believed to develop disciplined habits of thought. According to Thorndike, his findings meant that there must be identical elements from one situation to another in school learning, and opportunities must be provided for the use of the knowledge by learners outside of school. Thorndike's studies are discussed later in this volume, but the point here is that since the early years of this century, when the studies were published, thinking about the curriculum has changed profoundly. In looking back, we can see that Thorndike's evidence, which he interpreted as pointing to identical elements or specificity, could also have been interpreted to make a convincing case for generalized learning. In other words, the learner is more likely to transfer the material to new situations when it is meaningfully generalized. Subsequent studies revealed this to be the case, resulting in new approaches to curriculum articulation for general education through curriculum correlation, fusion, broad fields, and other designs. Thorndike's research and subsequent related studies are an example of a historical consequence or product having important bearings on contemporary practice.

As Dewey and others have emphasized, the fund of knowledge about the school curriculum is not a closed system.[36] As research illuminates curriculum problems and issues, portions of that fund may be reevaluated in favor of findings shown to be more valid. Of enormous importance here is the fact that curriculum history need not be out of the remote past; it is history in the making. The criterion is that it be a matter of record that adds to our sense of where we need to go in our curriculum development efforts. Research and theory regarding the school curriculum are nothing more or less than the living presence of history—connecting the present with the recent and remote past (so that the latter is no longer remote).

Historical processes are educators' experiences in gaining knowledge about curriculum matters and in developing the curriculum in "real" schools. Such records exist but are likely to be neglected. An illustration is the set of reports published in 1942 on the Eight-Year Study.[37] The problem central to that monumental study—the development of a curriculum designed to be useful to adolescents by freeing the secondary school from college dominance—is still with us and is, indeed, one of the most persistent and difficult problems of American education. There is a great deal to be learned from reading the reports of that experiment. Another illustration, more remote in time, is an account by two teachers of the Laboratory School established by John Dewey at the University of Chicago in 1896 as a means of testing his ideas about learning and education.[38] This account is important because it is concerned with Dewey's school work—how he put into action his ideas about the curriculum.

"It is hardly likely," wrote William Brickman, "that the theories and methods of Progressive education will ever cease to be an important influence in American education. There will be further modifications, of course, but there will also be constant references to the doctrines of Dewey."[39] Thus Dewey's own experiences in applying what he felt were fundamental principles are of enormous interest to us today.

Descriptions of curriculum reform in any era may throw light on present problems, but they vary enormously in their usefulness. Progressive ideas did not always work out in practice, although this was not necessarily the fault of the ideas themselves. In his study of the progressive movement in education, Cremin points out that Dewey's books were short on suggestions about how to put his theories into practice.[40]

Schools attempting to implement Dewey's suggestions for needed reforms did not always indicate the problems that they encountered or show how effective teachers dealt with them. A case in point is *Schools of Tomorrow* (1915), a report on progressive education as practiced in a variety of schools, which Dewey wrote in collaboration with his daughter, Evelyn. As Cremin notes, the book's approach is journalistic rather than critical; the Deweys maintain that the principles of progressive education are followed in each of the schools, albeit in different ways.[41]

But the descriptions did not indicate the problems in applying the theories (which may not have been evident to the Deweys when they visited the schools in person). An illustration is the description of the schools in Gary, Indiana, a city with 60 percent of its laborers foreign-born and employed in the steel mills. In Gary every child did "his share of the actual work of running and keeping in order the school buildings. . . . Distributing school supplies, keeping the school records and taking care of the grounds are done by the pupils under the direction of the school office."[42] This was the Deweys' account of children at work in what was regarded as one of the leading progressive school systems in America early in this century. Yet a later survey found that the "helper" system had its problems, and that the youngsters were far from adept at keeping school records. Nevertheless, the fact that such practices were going on and were recorded does provide us with insights and directions. As William Brickman suggested in his Introduction to *Schools of Tomorrow,* the descriptions of actual practices of progressive schools are of value "for the historical record as well as for contrast with the present."[43]

The Unrecorded Past. Our present is not always recorded, and in the case of the school curriculum this seems to us to be particularly unfortunate. There have been many valuable experiences in curriculum improvement that teachers never wrote about. The experiences of most of the teachers who followed the Deweyan ideal of encouraging children to identify problems of interest to them and importance to the community died with them. If there is a lesson to be learned here, it is that if teachers and other educators are to make positive contributions for others to build upon, they must record their own experiences in curriculum improvement—with particular attention to the practical problems they faced.

History as Story

For all the importance of using history selectively, drawing bits and pieces from it to get a full picture of a current problem, it lights up only part of our road to the present. The human motives, efforts, and achievements, the processes through which the school curriculum has undergone modification over time, remain obscure. What is missing is the story.

Historians are often asked what is the "good" of history. In the early

1930s historian Carl Becker discussed the matter in a letter to a friend. "History as story is an old business," he wrote. "All children love stories. All primitive peoples cherish stories of their past, of their heroes." History "is an evolution of these early stories, a more expert and sophisticated treatment of the subject." But, stressed Becker, it still met a basic human need: the "need of a conscious creature, who has memory and who can anticipate the future, to enlarge his present perceptions of things that happened in the past." History, he concluded, is "simply the instinctive and necessary exercise of memory, but of memory tested and fortified by reliable sources."[44] History as story, for Becker, was rooted in the nature of humankind.

American educators, too, have stories of their professional past, of their great men and women. Like creations out of Washington Irving or John Steinbeck, they walk before us, leaving real footprints. As we read the story of the school curriculum, the narrative moves to the present. We have a sense of the connectedness of events—a time stream. This sense of connectedness is missing when we simply draw bits and pieces from our past and try to relate them to contemporary problems.

Where there are lessons to be learned from the past, they emanate from the relationships shown between and among events—the story itself. As Barbara Tuchman described her work on the history of World War I, "lessons, if present and valid, must emerge from the material, not the writer. *I did not write to instruct but to tell a story.* The implications are what the thoughtful reader himself takes out of the book."[45] In this sense, the reader of history must join with the historian in bringing the significance of the story to life.

If curriculum history is treated simply as a chronological recital of events, it cannot tell the real story of the problems and struggles that were encountered, along with the progress that was made. As a consequence, the possibilities for relating the problems and accomplishments of the past to current problems will be severely limited. But if the story is told so that what has been experienced and learned in the past is connected to current problems, educators will be able to build upon past lessons. New situations do not derive from a vacuum; they are the consequences of conditions that link the past with the present. Hence most of our problems are not new. One of the chief lessons of our curriculum history is that curriculum improvement is dependent on teacher participation in identifying problems and in their intelligent and active engagement in seeking solutions. This lesson has not been well learned.

MAIN CURRENTS AND COUNTERCURRENTS

Labels of segments of history have a bewitching effect. An example is the era in American pedagogy that dates from the post–Civil War period to the years after World War II. Historians have bestowed life and character on that era by giving it a name: the progressive education era. But the era is a pure invention, designed to make sense out of events that have a connecting thread—an idea that runs through the events and gives them unity. In this case the organizing idea was American Progressivism—which, as Lawrence Cremin writes, was a "vast humanitarian effort to apply the promise of American life—the ideal of government by, of, and for the people—to the puzzling new urban-industrial civilization that came into being during the latter half of the nineteenth century"[46] Progressive education was the effort of progressives to use the schools to improve peoples' lives.

But Americans began this century unaware that they were approximately halfway through the "progressive education era." Moreover, although Dewey wrote at midcentury of the "good that has been attained by the progressive education *movement* and of the better that is yet to come," he did not call it an *era,*[47] for an era signifies something dead and gone. Decades are also invested with individuality: "passive" (the 1950s), "radical" (the 1960s), "give me" (the 1980s). The trouble is that the characterizations leave out the complexities. As one observer noted, the idealism of the 1960s was still flourishing in the 1980s in the form of grass-roots movements concerned with environmental pollution, world peace, and the like.[48] Countercurrents are always present, regardless of the dominant directions of the stream of events. (The tables of events in education and society, presented in later chapters, reveal that significant events are not always in the mainstream.)

In seeking simplicity, eras are given stereotypic labels that mask important countercurrents or distort significant events and contributions. For example, there has been the tendency to label as "progressivists" all of the educators who sought to use Deweyan ideas on how to educate children to grow in social intelligence and participation. However, under the broad rubric of progressive education there were the child-centered romanticists, who gave only passing attention to the need for systematic curriculum development; the reconstructionists, who sought to marshal the agency of the school for direct social correction; and the experimentalists in the Deweyan tradition, who viewed social improvement as emerging through the democratic prospect for school and society.

As Hollis Caswell, who pioneered in statewide programs of curriculum development during the 1930s, recounted years later, not all educators who attempted to use Dewey's ideas called themselves progressive educators. Caswell referred to himself as a "liberal educator," and he pointed out that he was not a member of the Progressive Education Association.[49] Yet the curriculum development programs initiated by Hollis Caswell and Doak Campbell, which were based on helping individuals understand and deal with social problems, were viewed at the time as having "had the largest influence on current projects in curriculum reorganization."[50] This means that they were far more influential than the child-centered programs, which were found mainly in private and country day schools and whose headmasters and teachers furnished a *large* portion of the membership for the Progressive Education Association. (In many of these schools, Dewey's social ideas were not reflected in the curriculum, nor did the administrators and teachers heed Dewey's warnings against the emptiness of the child-centered curriculum.) Yet the child-centered image is the one conferred most often on the curriculum programs of the 1930s by the label "progressive education era," and the one that has endured. This is understandable when we consider that the "era" is a creation of historians.

Caswell once commented that it was astonishing how the accounts by contemporary historians concerning curriculum reforms of the 1930s were at such great odds with the perceptions of those who had actually played a leading role in those reforms.[51] For example, some historians have concentrated on child-centered schools and have left the more influential programs in city and state school systems out of the picture. This is a common problem in curriculum history: Many writers take a monolithic approach. Special care must be taken in following the various threads that crossed or intermeshed in the history of the school curriculum, including the segment of history that is now known and no doubt will always be known, as the progressive education era.

There are countervailing forces in any era, even within the same movement, which should not be overlooked if we are to have a genuine understanding of curriculum history or any history. Many years of writing led Barbara Tuchman to conclude that "human conduct is a steady stream running through endless fields of changing circumstances, of good and bad always co-existing and inextricably mixed in periods as in people, of crosscurrents and countercurrents usually present to contradict too-easy generalizations."[52]

Crosscurrents

"Every history is particular," wrote Frederick J. Teggart in 1925, "for every history is a story unified by a specific interest in the mind of the historian."[53] One of the major problems in historical inquiry for Teggart, who taught history and political science at the University of California at Berkeley, was the need for a synthesis of the history of humankind. The study of science and the study of history were "carried on in different worlds, and without appreciation of their common relation to the study of change in the course of time."[54] As Teggart so clearly recognized, the histories of all human activities are interrelated.

Curriculum history can and should be treated separately, but it is enormously important that we be alert to the interconnections with other histories: Political history and the histories of the behavioral and physical sciences, technology (which rests on scientific knowledge), and philosophy have influenced the history of the school curriculum. From psychology, Dewey developed and tested his ideas about the relationship between interest and effort, child development and learning, and reflective thinking and other modes of thought. Dewey's experimentalist philosophy orchestrated the main currents in scientific and democratic social thought that challenged the old views of human origins and destinies.

Developments in the curriculum do not occur in a vacuum—nor should they. Changes in knowledge (including knowledge about learning) and political and economic developments have influenced the curriculum, as anyone knows who worked in education through the quarter century from the launching of *Sputnik I* to the report of the National Commission on Excellence in Education in 1983. In both the post-*Sputnik* era and the early 1980s, concern about foreign competitors led to proposals for reforming science education. Moreover, from time to time, usually when society has been faced with a social crisis, the schools have been more concerned with helping children to gain an understanding of the problems and issues in real life. The Great Depression of the 1930s is a striking example of such educational redirection, as shown in Chapter 5.

The striking lesson is that the division of the various kinds of human activity and ideas into separate histories is artificial, a matter of human invention—for necessity's sake. The history of the curriculum should not be isolated from these histories, and in a very real sense it cannot. The social, economic, and political issues at any time quickly become educational issues, and a new world view becomes an educational philosophy or a new way of working with children.

The Relatedness of Ideas. It should not be surprising that certain outstanding ideas mark segments of history, as revealed in educational movements, social movements, and political developments. During the period known as American Progressivism, both Jane Addams, who founded the famous social settlement Hull House in Chicago, and John Dewey faced the problem of social reform. Both believed that the value of knowledge lay in its use to improve people's lives, and both saw education as a social process through which the solution of the industrial problem could be found.

The key for both was participation. A settlement's "social relations are successful," wrote Jane Addams, "as it touches to life the dreary and isolated, and brings them into a fuller participation of the common inheritance."[55] "A society which makes provision for participation in its good of all of its members on equal terms," wrote Dewey, "and which secures flexible readjustment of its institutions through interaction of the different forms of associated life is in so far democratic."[56] The ideas were remarkably similar. Much has been made of the fact that Dewey and Addams influenced one another; Dewey was a visitor to Hull House even before the University of Chicago opened its doors to students for the first time. (Hull House was founded three years earlier.) Dewey wrote to Jane Addams that he "got a pretty good idea of the general spirit and method" used in Hull House as an educational institution, and it is probably true that it influenced (or perhaps reinforced) his ideas about the social nature of learning.[57]

Cross-Fertilization.   Jane Addams, too, learned from Dewey and applied what she learned to the developing field of social work. At a seventieth birthday celebration for Dewey she recalled:

> John Dewey's little yellow-covered book, *School and Society,* made so clear the necessity for individualizing each child that it is quite fair, I think, to say that his insistence upon an atmosphere of freedom and confidence between the teacher and pupil, of a common interest in the life they led together, profoundly affected all similar relationships, certainly those between the social worker and his client.[58]

Their close personal relationship and reciprocal influence are certainly fascinating, but what should not be overlooked is that two professional fields were also influenced: education and social work. There was a cross-fertilization of ideas; the histories of social work and the curriculum are connected, and we know how and why.

Both Jane Addams and Dewey were influenced by the widespread interest in social reform during the post–Civil War period. Their conception of educational method was enriched by the method of science and the new ideas swirling about them in their time, particularly the social nature of self and the concept of evolution. Both had faith in democracy as the leading force in education. As Charles Beard described the period, this was an "age of democracy."[59]

Dominant ideas mark every period and influence the curriculum. Although the 1960s are usually associated with hippies and social unresponsibility, the dominant idea of the decade, as revealed by social legislation and the War on Poverty, was social justice. Social ideas, political ideas, and educational ideas had a common focus: the need to produce fundamental social change. Michael Harrington's book *The Other America: Poverty in the United States* (1963) has been credited with starting the federal government's drive against poverty. The book called for civil rights legislation and better schools for poor children, so that they could break out of the "culture of poverty."[60] These children were not only neglected; they were "invisible." Changes in public policy were needed, argued Harrington, if black children were to attend adequate schools. Some steps had already been taken, including the legal commitment to desegregated schools, "but they are only a beginning," he wrote.[61]

Despite the exigencies of the cold war of the 1950s, the idea of social justice was not wholly missing at the time; indeed, social science data documenting the inherent inequality of segregated schools were an important feature of the 1954 U.S. Supreme Court decision requiring racial desegregation of schools (*Brown* v. *Board of Education of Topeka*). The decision itself is evidence that the society had already been prodded into action. Granted that Harrington helped to influence the Great Society programs of Lyndon Johnson, he reflected an outstanding and inspiring idea that was already in the wind. Neither writers, nor U.S. presidents, nor educators can escape the influence of an idea. The crosscurrent of social justice wrote an indelible chapter in American history, in the history of literature, and in the history of education.

Countervailing Forces

Main currents of thought that were born in times far removed from our own still press for change, and they have been neglected in new demands for curriculum reform and a more professional conception of teaching. The present concern about ensuring access to the curriculum for all children attests to the continuing vitality of the American Creed: Each person should have the opportunity to become what he or she is capable of becoming. Inequality of educational opportunity is periodically rediscovered, and often has resulted in reform. For example, in the 1980s, as a direct result of John Goodlad's study of schooling, some schools did away with ability grouping and tracking practices.

Nevertheless, as Goodlad writes, "For many people, tracking appears to be such a rational, commonsense solution to a vexing problem that arguments against it are often ridiculed as soft, progressive, fuzzy headed thinking." Moreover, "Schools mirror inequities in the surrounding society and *many people want to be sure that they continue to do so.*"[62] For a period of more than two hundred years (Beard's "age of democracy"), the ideal of equal opportunity has been gaining headway—but there are conflicting currents. Thus, although responses to Gallup surveys revealed that public attitudes toward racial integration of the public schools were considerably more liberal in the late 1980s than a decade earlier, almost one-fourth of those interviewed for the 1988 poll held that less should be done to integrate the schools. Despite this, a majority of the respondents felt that school desegregation had improved the quality of education for blacks.[63]

The main current of social thought has been equality of opportunity, which was a powerful factor in curriculum improvement in the late 1960s, particularly in our large cities. Calls for reform were concerned with following approved practices in the education of poor children—for example, educating parents so that their interactions with the child were more likely to promote the development of school learning, and providing a central library for schools that had no library. The idea was to provide poor and minority children with access to a rich and stimulating curriculum so that they would complete high school and become competent adults. The curriculum principles and methods were not new; they were just being more widely applied. It was believed that talent lay everywhere; it had only to be discovered and nurtured. There was a renewed commitment in linking social justice and educational opportunity. This was a time of hope.

But the optimistic 1960s were soon to turn into the pessimistic 1970s—a time of curriculum retrenchment. For example, the federal Report of the National Panel on High School and Adolescent Education, *The Education of Adolescents* (1976), recommended that the curriculum be reduced to "essential skills susceptible to school training," that the comprehensive high school be disbanded in favor of an academic high school, and that compulsory schooling be sharply curtailed.[64] Many high schools, especially those serving disadvantaged youth, proceeded to follow the retrenchment policy of turning the curriculum to training in the basic skills through mechanistic drill work. Such work was stripped of ideas that give meaning to learning. The results were disastrous as the rise in school dropouts threatened to reach epidemic proportions. As noted earlier, Dewey had emphasized the importance of shared knowledge in a democratic society, but the principle did not grow in the 1970s. Retrenchment was a conflicting current, a countervailing force in opposition to the increasing availability of the curriculum to all groups that has characterized the development of the American curriculum.

As the 1980s drew to a close, many states required more courses in English, history, science, and mathematics for high school graduation in response to reports dealing with problems in the nation's schools and the need to improve our country's competitiveness in foreign markets. But the changes were regulatory and usually did not deal with fundamental and more difficult problems of curriculum content and the quality of life in schools. As a former U.S. Secretary of Education pointed out, "Education is not receiving the support it must have—nor is there even an intense awareness of the massive failures, the hopelessness, and the despair that plague education in our largest cities where more than 50 percent of the high school population drops out before graduation."[65]

The Need for Historical Perspective.   We have gone through our dark ages, when the problems of schools in blighted urban areas were all but ignored, and along came a revival of concern. The movement toward greater access to the curriculum for previously excluded groups has been going on since the Revolutionary period. Is it so firmly rooted in our American traditions that it is inevitable, or is there a danger that the countercurrents of intense individualism and weak federal support for public education will cause the ideal of equal opportunity to lose its historic vitality? This is the concern of many thoughtful educators.

The works of Dewey may offer some guidance here. "There is danger," he wrote in *Liberalism and Social Action,* which he dedicated to the memory of Jane Addams, "of losing a sense of historic perspective and of yielding precipitately to short-time contemporary currents, abandoning in panic things of enduring and priceless value."[66]

A sense of history should lead to the understanding that inner-city educational problems are American problems; that any particular curriculum reform effort has reverberations throughout the curriculum; that any given reform effort, no matter how compelling it may seen at the time, should not be taken at the expense of other equally desirable needs and practices.

Conflicting Forces in the School Curriculum. Throughout history there have been contenders for the curriculum, but historians differ in the way they are identified. According to Kliebard, four major forces battled for control of the curriculum: the humanists (those who thought that the traditional ways of teaching and traditional subjects were best), the child developmentalists, the social efficiency educators, and the social meliorists. Kliebard wrote: "The twentieth century became the arena where these four versions of what knowledge is of most worth and of the central functions of schooling were presented and argued."[67]

As we have pointed out, a version of the past is a reconstruction, the creation of the historian. The conflicting-forces approach is useful and realistic, but there are problems with this particular mode of analysis. The category or pattern is imposed on the material. For example, Dewey was both a child developmentalist *and* a social reformer (meliorist). Moreover, the classification of curriculum forces into set categories raises the danger of using terminology in distorted ways. Hence, in much of the literature in curriculum history the term social efficiency is interpreted in the narrow and evil sense as subordination of individuals to the demands of the industrial system and the authority of a ruling class. For Dewey there was another side to social efficiency—a side having a far different and broader meaning. It had an economic meaning (being able to exercise intelligent choices in making one's place in economic society); a political meaning (being able to take a determining part in the political process and in the exercise of justice in daily life); and a sociopsychological meaning (complete development of personality—the recognition of the uniqueness of the individual as essential to the well being of a democratic society). "It must be borne in mind," wrote Dewey, "that ultimately social efficiency means neither more nor less than capacity to share in a give and take of experience."[68]

The point is that social efficiency was manifested in two opposing forms: that of the old order of social predestination and that of the democratic prospect of releasing human potential for social mobility and improvement. Kliebard did not distinguish between the two sides of social efficiency. More significantly, no set categories can portray the myriad and conflicting points of view about the curriculum held by different educational leaders. In seeking patterns, care must be taken not to force the fit of concepts, individuals, and events into neat categories. History never comes out as neat categories.

Another notable example of distortion by terminology is the notorious use of the label "life-adjustment education" in our educational history. In a chapter titled "The Road to Life Adjustment" in his book *Anti-intellectualism in American Life* (1963), Richard Hofstadter sought to impose the label of "life-adjustment education" as a movement stemming from the wide sweep of progressive educational reforms beginning before the twentieth century. However, the term was actually first used in 1945 by a vocational educator in connection with the neglect of the majority of high-school youth who do not go on to college. Life adjustment never became a "movement," yet the label was used by such historians as Arthur Bestor to denote a movement and to caricature that movement as though it was a leading force that shaped the school curriculum.[69]

PERSPECTIVE

If the main currents and conflicting currents that shaped and continue to shape the curriculum are accurately identified and evaluated, the result is more than a better understanding of our history. By revealing the consequences of past ideas and events for the present, history can provide us with both perspective and direction. Accomplishments and hopeful influences in the past can be differentiated from false turns and negative influences. The knowledge can be useful in distinguishing what needs to be built upon from what needs to be changed in the present situation, for the present is the consequence of the past.

History should provide us with a sense of identity and collective conscience. Not only does history show the connectedness of events in the stream of time, but it also shows the force of great ideas. The American Revolution had an educational significance as well as a political significance. The idea of equality of opportunity has led to increasingly greater access to the curriculum for groups in our society that were previously excluded. Yet if we accept the principle merely in its negative sense (to protect children from denial of opportunity in the form of ability grouping or tracking, for example), we may forget that one of the purposes of equal access to knowledge is to become a community of shared interests.

Another purpose of equal access to knowledge is to help children and youth think and behave as responsible self-governing citizens. This was the underlying reason that our forebears—Jefferson for instance, who was one of our first curriculum theorists—were so passionately committed to the idea of popular education. They understood that the working of the ideal of American democracy depended on making the idea of popular education a reality. Our highest and widest social ideals are intimately connected to our educational ideals. And these all come down to earth in the school through that experience we call the curriculum.

NOTES

1. Barbara W. Tuchman, *Practicing History* (New York: Knopf, 1981), p. 23.
2. Diane Ravitch, *The Revisionists Revised* (New York: Basic Books, 1978).
3. Tuchman, op. cit.
4. Charles A. Beard, "Written History as an Act of Faith," *The American Historical Review* 39 (January 1934): 221–29.
5. Gunnar Myrdal, *Objectivity in Social Research* (New York: Random House, 1969), p. 9.
6. Beard, op. cit., p. 229.
7. Ibid.
8. Henry Steele Commager, "The Discipline of History," *Great Ideas Today* (New York: Praeger for Encyclopaedia Britannica, 1972), p. 232.
9. Ibid.
10. Ibid., p. 233.
11. John Dewey, *The Public and Its Problems* (New York: Henry Holt, 1927), p. 180.
12. Ibid., pp. 179–80.
13. Ibid., p. 179.
14. Gunnar Myrdal, *An American Dilemma* (New York: Harper & Row, 1962; first published 1944), p. 709.
15. *The New York Times* (June 9, 1973), p. 32.
16. Ralph W. Tyler, "Progress in Dealing with Curriculum Problems," Chapter 12 in *Critical Issues in Curriculum,* Part I of the Eighty-seventh Yearbook of the National Society for the Study of Education (Chicago: University of Chicago Press, 1988), p. 273.
17. Charles A. Beard, "Introduction," in J. B. Bury, *The Idea of Progress: An Inquiry Into Its Origin and Growth* (New York: Macmillan, 1932), p. ix.
18. Ibid.
19. Ibid., pp. ix–x.
20. Gertrude Himmelfarb, *The New History and the Old* (Cambridge, Mass.: Harvard University Press, 1987), pp. 155–70.
21. Thomas S. Popkewitz and Allan Pitman, "The Idea of Progress and the Legitimation of State Agenda: American Proposals for School Reform," *Curriculum and Teaching* I (April 1986): 11–23.
22. Himmelfarb, op. cit.
23. John Dewey, "Progress," in Joseph Ratner (ed.), *Characters and Events,* vol. 2 (New York: Octagon Books, 1970; first published by Henry Holt, 1929), p. 823.
24. Lawrence A. Cremin, "The Free School Movement—A Perspective," *Today's Education* 63 (September–October 1974): 73.
25. Commager, op. cit., p. 285.
26. Tuchman, op. cit., p. 249.
27. Commager, op. cit., p. 288.

28. Richard E. Neustadt and Ernest R. May, *Thinking in Time: The Uses of History for Decision-Makers* (New York: Free Press, 1986), p. 2.

29. Ibid., p. 241.

30. Ibid.

31. Ibid.

32. N. L. Gage, *The Scientific Basis of the Art of Teaching* (New York: Teachers College Press, 1978), p. 41.

33. Neustadt and May, op. cit., p. 244.

34. Ravitch, op. cit.

35. Paul E. Peterson, cited in Fred M. Hechinger, "Critical Commission Is Criticized," *The New York Times* (February 28, 1984), p. C6.

36. John Dewey, *The Sources of a Science of Education* (New York: Liveright, 1929); Gage, op. cit.

37. Entitled *Adventure in American Education.* Series published by McGraw-Hill in 1942. See Wilford M. Aikin, *The Story of the Eight-Year Study;* H. H. Giles et al., *Exploring the Curriculum;* Eugene R. Smith et al., *Appraising and Recording Student Progress;* Dean Chamberlain et al., *Did They Succeed in College?;* and *Thirty Schools Tell Their Story* (participating schools provide an account of their involvement in the experiment, which assessed progressive methods at the secondary level and ran from 1932 to 1940).

38. Katherine Camp Mayhew and Anna Camp Edwards, *The Dewey School* (New York: Atherton, 1936).

39. William W. Brickman, "John Dewey's Life, Work, and Educational Influence," Introduction in John Dewey and Evelyn Dewey, *Schools of Tomorrow* (New York: Dutton, 1962; first published 1915), p. xxvi.

40. Lawrence A. Cremin, *The Transformation of the School* (New York: Knopf, 1961).

41. Ibid., p. 153.

42. Dewey and Dewey, op. cit., pp. 182–83.

43. Brickman, op. cit., p. xxiv.

44. Carl Becker to William E. Dodd, January 27, 1932, in Michael Kammen (ed.), *"What Is the Good of History?": Selected Letters of Carl L. Becker 1900–1945* (Ithaca: Cornell University Press, 1973), pp. 156–57.

45. Tuchman, op. cit., p. 24.

46. Cremin, *The Transformation of the School,* op. cit., p. viii.

47. John Dewey, "Introduction," in Elsie Ripley Clapp, *The Uses of Resources in Education* (New York: Harper & Row, 1952), p. xi.

48. Studs Terkel, *The Great Divide: Second Thoughts on the American Dream* (New York: Pantheon, 1988).

49. Hollis Caswell, in a conversaton with the authors of this book, April 9, 1979.

50. Henry Harap (ed.), *The Changing Curriculum* (New York: Appleton-Century, 1937), p. 91.

51. Hollis Caswell, in a letter to the present authors, May 1, 1976.

52. Tuchman, op. cit., p. 9.

53. Frederick J. Teggart, *Theory and Processes of History* (Berkeley: University of California Press, 1977; first published 1925), p. 43.

54. Ibid., p. 78.

55. Jane Addams, "A Function of the Social Settlement," *Annals of the Academy of Political and Social Science* 13 (May 1899): 55.

56. John Dewey, *Democracy and Education* (New York: Macmillan, 1916), p. 115.

57. Cited in Allen F. Davis, *American Heroine: The Life and Legend of Jane Addams* (New York: Oxford University Press, 1973), p. 97.

58. Jane Addams, "A Toast to John Dewey," *Survey* 63 (November 15, 1929).

59. Beard, op. cit., p. x.

60. Michael Harrington, *The Other America: Poverty in the United States* (New York: Macmillan, 1963), p. 21.

61. Ibid., p. 78.

62. John I. Goodlad, *A Place Called School* (New York: McGraw-Hill, 1984), pp. 151, 161.

63. Alec M. Gallup and Stanley M. Elam, "The 20th Annual Gallup Poll of the Public's Attitudes Toward the Public Schools," *Phi Delta Kappan* 70 (September 1988): 39.

64. National Panel on High School and Adolescent Education, *The Education of Adolescents* (Washington, D.C.: U.S. Office of Education, 1976), pp. 10–14.

65. Terrel H. Bell, "On the Need for National Leadership to Make American Education Work," *Phi Delta Kappan* 70 (September 1988): 10.

66. John Dewey, *Liberalism and Social Action* (New York: Capricorn Books, 1963; first published 1935), p. 3.

67. Herbert M. Kliebard, *The Struggle for the American Curriculum 1893–1958* (Boston: Routledge & Kegan Paul, 1986), p. 29.

68. John Dewey, *Democracy and Education,* op. cit., pp. 139–43.

69. Richard Hofstadter, *Anti-intellectualism in American Life* (New York: Knopf, 1962), Ch. 13; Arthur Bestor, *The Restoration of Learning* (New York: Knopf, 1956), pp. 79–82, 116, 132.

SELECTED REFERENCES

Addams, Jane. *Democracy and Social Ethics.* New York: Macmillan, 1902.

Bloom, Benjamin S. *Human Characteristics and School Learning.* New York: McGraw-Hill, 1976.

Bode, Boyd H. *Modern Educational Theories.* New York: Macmillan, 1927.

Bury, J. B. *The Idea of Progress: An Inquiry into Its Origin and Growth.* New York: Macmillan, 1932.

Cremin, Lawrence A. *The Transformation of the School.* New York: Knopf, 1961.

Dewey, John. *The School and Society.* Chicago: University of Chicago Press, 1915; first published 1899.

———. *Democracy and Education.* New York: Macmillan, 1916.

————. *The Public and Its Problems.* New York: Henry Holt, 1927.

————. *Liberalism and Social Action.* New York: Capricorn Books, 1963; first published 1935.

Harap, Henry, ed. *The Changing Curriculum.* New York: Appleton-Century, 1937.

Himmelfarb, Gertrude. *The New History and the Old.* Cambridge: Harvard University Press, 1987).

Inglis, Alexander. *Principles of Secondary Education.* Boston: Houghton Mifflin, 1918.

Kliebard, Herbert M. *The Struggle for the American Curriculum 1893–1958.* Boston: Routledge & Kegan Paul, 1986.

National Society for the Study of Education. *Curriculum-Making: Past and Present.* Twenty-sixth Yearbook, Part I. Bloomington, Ill.: Public School Publishing Co., 1927.

————. *Critical Issues in Curriculum.* Eighty-seventh Yearbook, Part I. Chicago: University of Chicago Press, 1988.

Neill, A. S. *Summerhill.* New York: Hart, 1960.

Neustadt, Richard E., and Ernest R. May. *Thinking in Time: The Uses of History for Decision Makers.* New York: Free Press, 1986.

Oakeshott, Michael. *On History.* Totawa, N.J.: Barnes and Noble, 1983.

Ravitch, Diane. *The Revisionists Revised.* New York: Basic Books, 1978.

Report of the Harvard Committee. *General Education in a Free Society.* Cambridge: Harvard University Press, 1945.

Silberman, Charles E. *Crisis in the Classroom.* New York: Random House, 1970.

Teggart, Frederick J. *Theory and Processes of History.* Berkeley: University of California Press, 1977.

Tuchman, Barbara W. *Practicing History.* New York: Knopf, 1981.

Tyler, Ralph W. *Basic Principles of Curriculum and Instruction.* Chicago: University of Chicago Press, 1949.

2

Early Developments in the School Curriculum

There is a continuity between past and present, and in any professional field that continuity should be developmental. However, as indicated in Chapter 1, many curriculum reform proposals pay little or no attention to previous efforts. Curriculum improvement is approached by each new group of reformers as though the problems they are trying to solve have never been recognized before. As a result, there is a failure to build on curriculum work done in the past. The continuity between past and present has too often been a tale of repeated mistakes.

Although avoidance of past failures is sufficient reason for the study of predecessor models and movements in the curriculum field, there are two other (not unrelated) reasons for such study: to provide perspective on current problems and to help us build on past experience with an ever-increasing effectiveness, so that the continuity between past and present is, indeed, developmental.

This chapter considers the conflicting theoretical ideas that arose as the public schools developed. Among the predecessor models and ideas examined are the infant school, monitorial instruction, object teaching (inductive teaching), active learning, curriculum diversification, curriculum differentiation, curriculum balance, piecemeal change, curriculum synthesis, pushing subject matter down (from upper to lower grades), thoroughness (mastery learning), individualizing education, and curriculum making by national committee. Before 1900 all of the foregoing had become part of our curriculum legacy.

THE NONFUNCTIONAL CURRICULUM

The foundations of the American public school system were rigorously laid in Massachusetts in 1647, only twenty-seven years after the landing of the *Mayflower*. Every township with fifty or more householders was required by statute to appoint a teacher of reading and writing. Townships with a hundred or more householders were required to establish a Latin grammar school, an institution brought over from England. The main curriculum objective was to produce God-fearing Christians. Hence, religious indoctrination was emphasized from the lower schools through the Latin grammar school. The curriculum of the latter was composed of the classics—Latin and Greek—as well as religious principles.

An additional curriculum objective, however, was to promote the welfare of the state by making citizens capable of self-government. In time, this objective was to attain ascendency as the public school became grounded in secularism.

The Massachusetts law of 1647 provided for an elementary (dame) school virtually at the door of every family, run rather crudely by a woman in her own home who taught some rudiments of reading and writing. Yet probably less than half of the whites in colonial America had any formal schooling, and an examination of the statute books in Massachusetts shows a subsequent relaxation in the effort to require compulsory education and a declining interest in public education until the late 1820s. One reason for the relaxation of early school laws was the decline of community solidarity. A wave of immigration from northern Europe during the first three-quarters of the eighteenth century brought Swedes, Danes, Dutch, Germans, and French, who were given freedom by the colonial legislatures to establish schools in their own language. Another reason for the lack of attention to education was the Revolutionary War. The period from the outbreak of the war in 1775 until the beginning of our national government in 1789 was calamitous for educational opportunity (which had been meager enough before the war). The closing of most schools resulted in a sharp increase in illiteracy. Also, the road to new educational ideas was effectively blocked by the war; the colleges were preoccupied with the problems of their own survival.

Yet there was another more fundamental reason for the decline of interest in the public schools: the curriculum. The schools had remained stationary while society continued to change. To say that the classical curriculum of the colonial secondary school had failed to meet the needs of a society undergoing rapid economic and social change is a gross understatement. There was a growing demand for bookkeepers and surveyors as well as navigators. But one could not learn a skill or a trade at a Latin grammar school, nor could one learn it at home. The only alternative was a school providing career education. The demand for a utilitarian education generated the academy movement.

The Approach to Reform

Rather than reforming the publicly supported secondary schools, men of means had decided it would be less trouble to build their own schools.

Moreover, state legislatures encouraged the idea by providing the academies with pecuniary assistance. As a result, the public schools could not assume leadership in the improvement of education. Indeed, there was some question as to whether the public school system would continue to exist. In 1824, James G. Carter, a teacher and an advocate of liberal educational legislation, observed that the free schools in Massachusetts had received almost no legislative attention for nearly four decades.[1]

Why was there no attempt to reform the Latin grammar school—an artifact of the Old World? According to Cohen, these schools were "circumscribed in content and aim by the humanistic tradition and college entrance requirements. Their functions were known and approved."[2] Hence, the earliest means for coping with the restrictions of college entrance requirements was simply to build another school—the academy. During its academy phase, the secondary school was unhampered in its effort toward fundamental reconstruction. The freedom to build a new curriculum continued during the early decades of the public high school but was sharply curtailed by the report of the Committee of Ten on Secondary School Studies in 1893. From that point the high school was dogged by college entrance requirements. The report of the Committee of Ten is discussed in detail later in the chapter.

Halting the Downward Course of Public Education

In a plea for public high schools, Carter pointed out that state support for academies had created additional educational opportunities for those who would have them even without the assistance of the state. But the state had not kept faith with its charge to provide an education for every citizen, rich or poor.

> Thus have we departed more and more widely from the principle assumed by our fathers in the establishment of Free Schools, viz. to provide as good instruction in all elementary and common branches of knowledge for the poorest citizen in the commonwealth, as the richest could buy with all his wealth. Advancement upon advancement has been made by the few, while the mass, who are less vigilant remain as they were, with only the unconsoling advantage of a little reflected light sent back by those who have gone before them.[3]

"Public Academies."   The academies, which began to make their appearance in the colonies around 1780, were called "public academies." Indeed, they were open to the public—but not free of charge. Most people could not afford to pay the tuition. (In his plea for public high schools, Carter argued that nineteen-twentieths of the population of Massachusetts was unable to attend an academy because of the tuition.)

Many children who might have obtained a secondary education in a Latin grammar school did not do so. In the first two decades of the nineteenth century, the opportunity to attend such schools rapidly declined. It was not (and still is not) possible for a community to maintain two competing school systems. In towns where academies flourished, grammar schools tended to deteriorate or die out entirely. By 1820, the tuition academy had all but replaced the tax-supported grammar school.

It should also be noted that where grammar schools existed coterminously with academies, a class distinction arose between them. Indeed, it was considered a reproach for a man who was moderately well-off to send his child to a public school.

The Stigma of the Public School.   In the early nineteenth century, to attend a public school was often to be stigmatized as a pauper. There was good reason: as late as 1830 in New Jersey and Pennsylvania, and even later in Maryland, Virginia, and Georgia, the use of public money for schools was confined "to the education of the children of the poor." Outside of New England, education had been left to incorporated school societies. With subscriptions and bequests from wealthy individuals, and small grants from the city and state, these organizations tried to provide the rudiments of the three R's for the poor in New York, Baltimore, Philadelphia, Washington, and other cities. Those who attended the schools were not left unaware of the charity involved. For these reasons the free schools repelled the poor as well as the rich (when indeed such schools were even available).

In 1827, the downward course of public education in Massachusetts was halted. Largely through the influence of James G. Carter, a law was passed that required every town having five hundred families to maintain a high school. The curriculum provisions of the Law of 1827 are discussed later in this chapter.

REVOLUTIONARY CURRICULUM PERSPECTIVES

If the Revolutionary War dealt blows to schools and colleges, it did not put an end to educational thought. On the contrary, intellectual and political leaders gave much thought to the role that education should play in the young republic. Education itself was an instrument of the Revolution. According to Cremin, the movement for independence was a direct outgrowth of the increasing availability of schooling and secularization, not to mention an increasingly literate population whose minds were open to new possibilities.[4] The Revolution fed the idea that all of the people must be provided with educational and cultural opportunity.

Thomas Jefferson saw the continuation of republican government as "absolutely hanging" on the hook of public education.[5] He saw more clearly than anyone of his time that a free society cannot survive unless the people in general are educated. In 1779, three years after he expressed the ideals of equality and democracy in the Declaration of Independence, Jefferson developed a proposal for public elementary and secondary education. But colonial orthodoxies won out, and Jefferson lost an early round in the battle for equal opportunity that is still being waged today.

Jefferson's Proposal

Jefferson proposed a state plan of education that would provide three years of elementary schooling at public expense for all free children in Virginia. Grammar schools were also included in Jefferson's plan, and the best boys from the elementary schools were to attend the grammar schools at public expense. The curriculum of the elementary school, which was secular in character, consisted of reading, writing, arithmetic, and history (substituted for religious instruction).

The grammar school curriculum was to include Latin, Greek, English, geography, and higher arithmetic. It was a typical college-preparatory program, and a blend of the utilitarian and the classical, but without religious instruction. Jefferson's proposal was rejected by the Virginia Assembly. In a sense it was defeated by the existing class distinctions and the established church. Virginia was not ready to give all children a chance at education.

Nevertheless, Jefferson was successful in his efforts to reform American higher education. When his plan for the University of Virginia materialized, he emphasized that the university should be both secular and practical. Although the University of Virginia was not chartered until 1819 (later than the state universities of Vermont, Georgia, and North Carolina), it was, as Jennings Wagoner points out, "truly in advance of the others."[6] The wall of separation between church and state was to be maintained; there would be no divinity professors and no affiliation with any religious group.

Other colleges and even state universities required students to attend chapel and Sunday services, but not Virginia. Further, Jefferson was deeply committed to the pursuit of truth and the application of knowledge, and these commitments resulted in his designing a curriculum that included not only the classics but "all the branches of science deemed useful at this day and in this country."[7]

Education of Girls

To say that educational opportunities for girls were limited during the colonial period is an understatement. The seventeenth-century school laws in New England did not acknowledge girls at all, stating that "the word 'children' is interpreted to mean 'boys.' "[8] Still, girls attended the dame schools, and most learned reading and a little cooking and sewing. Piety, modesty, gentleness, and household economy were considered to be the chief elements in a girl's curriculum, and these could be learned at home. Arithmetic, geography, and grammar were considered superfluous except in very diluted amounts. (What need for figuring since all "expected to obtain husbands to perform whatever arithmetical operations they might need beyond the counting of fingers?"[9]

There were exceptions—mainly the daughters of fathers devoted to learning. Cotton Mather's daughter Katherine "was 'mistress of the Hebrew tongue' and 'a good Latin scholar.' "[10] And in Philadelphia, Quaker leaders conducted Latin schools for girls as well as boys, which were patronized by the most favored class of citizens, and where poor children were taught free of charge. There is no evidence of curriculum dilution for girls. Throughout the eighteenth century a theme of Quaker humanitarianism was that women, blacks, and Indians should be educated on an equal level with whites and males. Nevertheless, prevailing opinion in colonial America held that girls were not fit to attend school with their brothers.

Certainly some men recoiled from the idea that their women might be in a position to criticize them intellectually. At Plymouth, a few years after the Revolution, an opponent of female education argued in the town meeting that the "world would come to a 'pretty pass' when wives and daughters would look over the shoulders of their husbands and fathers and offer to correct as they wrote such errors in spelling that they might commit."[11] But the report in favor of a female school was adopted.

Inevitably, the philosophy of the natural rights of man, which was popularized by the Revolution, was extended to women. The Revolution gave impetus to the environmentalist theory of human nature. Many liberal Americans believed that the differences in the mental accomplishments between the sexes were due to the more favorable opportunities offered to males. (Recently, this theme sounded once again in the women's liberation movement.)

But public sentiment about education for girls did not change until after the Revolution, and then not immediately. Girls were admitted to the district schools in New England, but some town fathers remained to be convinced that girls had a natural right to education at public expense. The town of Northampton, for example, voted in 1788 not to admit girls to its public schools. (They were admitted in 1802.) Most communities allowed girls to attend the schools within a decade or two after the Revolution.

Once they were given free access to schooling, girls eagerly sought its benefits—sometimes exceeding the expectations of school authorities. A case in point was a high school established for girls in Boston in 1826. The school was such an "alarming success" that it was closed after eighteen months.[12] Apparently school authorities were dismayed at the way the girls crowded into the new school. The Pandora's box of educational opportunity had been opened and then quickly (temporarily) shut.

The Curriculum Engine

"Every engine should be employed to render the people of this country national," wrote Noah Webster in 1789.[13] Although independence had been won, there was a need to knit diverse cultural background and regional affiliation into a new American nationality. Two basic ingredients of nationalism were a common language and a common past. Webster singlehandedly created both. As Commager points out, Webster's speller "went triumphantly from generation to generation until it came to be as familiar as the Bible, and as essential," and "under its benign guidance generations of young Americans learned the same words, the same spellings, the same pronunciations; read the same stories; absorbed the same moral lessons."[14]

Webster's "engine" for "rendering the people national" included grammars, readers, and eventually dictionaries. It was a curriculum in every sense of the word. It made elementary education possible at once. Not surprisingly, Noah Webster was a schoolmaster in his early days.

Nationalism is often equated with narrowness and bigotry. Webster's nationalism sprang from his devotion to national unity. But of particular interest are the democratic elements of Webster's nationalism. Speech betrays class. A common language without accents is a requirement for a classless society. In England, language was the mark of class. Webster saw this clearly and worked for a common *American* language. As Commager writes, "The United States, dedicated to the unprecedented experiment of republicanism in a vast territory, a heterogeneous population, and a classless society, could not afford differences of accent or of language."[15]

The issue is relevant today, and raises questions regarding the place of Black English in the United States. The problem is one of acculturation and mobility versus ghettoization. To this day, speech marks social class in England. One of the factors in the resistance against the comprehensive secondary school in England has been the fear on the part of the more privileged classes that their children will be influenced by the speech patterns of the less privileged.

However, learning itself may also be at stake: Some linguists have identified specific characteristics of Black English that interfere with a child's learning mathematics and science.[16] Nevertheless, the main issue of Black English rested on the inability of many poverty-stricken blacks to make language switches from Black English to standard English as the occasion arises. So delimited, there remains the question of the perpetuation of cognitive and social isolation through language. This harks back to Noah Webster's efforts to develop a common American language as an antidote to the language differences marking the class-divided society of the Old World, and as a vehicle for social mobility in America.

THE EMERGING COMMON SCHOOL—MORALS, METHODS, AND MENTAL DISCIPLINE

Colonial views on education were shaped by the theological outlook of Calvinism in New England and the Church of England in the South. The predominant objective and spirit of education was religious, and the view of the child was harsh. It is probable that the informal setting of the dame school with its very terminal curriculum (a child might attend for only a few weeks, until he had mastered the rudiments of reading) did not lend itself to severe discipline, but the more formal schools that became available in the early years of the eighteenth century did. The Calvinist concept that the child was innately evil provided the chief method for classroom control. Children were continually reminded, in school and out, of the terrible consequences of sin: death and damnation. They were regarded as miniature adults and expected to live up to adult standards of religious and moral behavior.

Reading was the staple of the curriculum. Then, as now, reading was considered the most important offering of the elementary school. It was taught via the alphabet method. The most extensively used textbook during the eighteenth century was the *New England Primer*. Pupils began by learning capital and small letters and gradually advanced to multisyllable words, most of which had a religious or moral connotation. In the 1830s the a-b-c method of reading instruction was condemned by Horace Mann, who introduced the whole-word method. Mann argued that the time (sometimes years) spent in concentration on single letters and meaningless two-letter syllables killed the child's interest in reading.

The Retracing of Studies

There was no doubt, however, that children learned to read from the *Primer* (just as they learned by Horace Mann's method). The problem was that it often took them several years to learn what they might have mastered in several months. The time wasted in going over the same material year after year with a progression of teachers, or waiting for a few minutes of attention from the same teacher, was at the heart of the problem. That children were spending years traversing the same educational ground seemed to bother no one until after 1820, when educators and statesmen suddenly took notice. Then it became a burning issue for educational reform. To some extent (but to a much lesser degree), this problem is still with us today.

Moral Education

In addition to reading, writing, spelling, and arithmetic, children in the colonial period were instructed in catechism. As the view of the child became more liberal and the interests of the people more secular, religious instruction gave way to moral instruction. As Butts and Cremin point out, religious and ethnic diversity made it necessary to develop a common base for instruction: a common language (English) and common principles of morality.[17]

Another reason for interest in moral education was a concern for the educational deprivation of the children of the poor; to many they seemed appallingly deficient in the principles of morality. By the 1830s, juvenile crime on the streets had grown to alarming proportions in the cities. By way of explanation, educational reformers pointed to the fact that the street waifs were growing up in ignorance and idleness.

Faculty Psychology.   In the 1830s and 1840s moral education permeated the entire curriculum. The subject matter of textbooks was heavily flavored with morality, and teachers gave lessons in morals and character building. The underlying rationale for the inclusion of moral education in the curriculum was not to develop a common base for instruction. Rather, its proponents were motivated by the doctrines of faculty psychology (the educational psychology of the day), which held that the mind consisted of separate faculties, or powers, that were developed and improved by exercise. "Enlarging the mind and training its powers" was the object of education. Thus, the development of moral powers was considered to be as much the teacher's duty as the development of intellectual powers. (A third faculty was physical powers. The powers of the body, however, were given slight attention by educators in comparison with the powers of the mind and soul.) Faculty psychology was the basis for the method of mental discipline in education and for giving top priority to the classical studies and mathematics in the secondary-school curriculum.

Education and Competency

Not only were educators and the lay public convinced that there was a link between ignorance and crime, but they also advanced the idea that education rendered one more competent—and, therefore, more productive. In addressing the relationship between education and competency, Horace Mann observed: "Individuals who, without the aid of education, would have been condemned to perpetual inferiority of condition, and subjected to all the evils of want and poverty, rise to competence and independence by the uplifting power of education."[18] The relationship between poverty and incompetence was discovered anew in the 1960s, during the War on Poverty. Oddly, it was advanced as a brand new idea.

Democracy and Social Control

Educational reformers and friends of the public school based their argument for educating the common people on enlightened self-interest: The common man was the future legislator, judge, and juryman. It was the common folk to whom the interests of people of substance were entrusted. However, further argument was often necessary to convince the economically dominant group. Educators attempting to win the support of commerce and industry argued that workers who had been imbued with obedience and honesty when they were children in the public schools could be counted on to work more cheerfully and productively than those who had been left to loiter in idleness and ignorance during childhood.[19] As Ponder observes, the justification for schools on the ground of social control included the argument that schools could "help create a national character" by the "intentional inculcation of conformity to certain norms and habits."[20] Both the industrial and nationalizing functions of social control were stressed by reformers as they attempted to persuade people of position and property about the need to provide schooling for the poor.

This was no easy task. The ideal of democracy was by no means universal in post-Revolutionary society. Conservatives who regarded the war as an insurrection against England, not as a social movement, still saw education and culture as their own exclusive natural right. They had no intention of sharing with the common people the intellectual and cultural values of which they viewed themselves the guardians. The problem of social control was (and still is) the problem of a curriculum that marks off one class from another. No one saw this problem more clearly than Dewey. "When social efficiency as measured by product or output is urged as an ideal in a would-be democratic society," he wrote, "it means that the depreciatory estimate of the masses characteristic of an aristocratic community is accepted and carried over." To Dewey, social efficiency in a free society is reflected in the opportunity for the development of individual capacities in the context of democratic social responsibility.[21]

The Common School Curriculum

By 1850, it was recognized in all northern states and some of the southern states that "common schools," that is, free schools for all children, not just for poor children, were necessary for the well-being of a society with universal manhood suffrage. That is something the Puritans knew in 1647; we had come full circle.

From the start of their campaign for state-supported common schools, reformers stressed that these would have to be good schools or else the pauper taint would remain. This would mean a more up-to-date curriculum and better methods of instruction than those offered by the private schools. There was no alternative if the public school system was not to be doomed before it even got started.

What was the appropriate curriculum for common schools? There was no more agreement in the 1820s on the question of what the schools should teach than there is today. As Philip Lindsley, president of Cumberland College, informed the class of 1826 in his graduation address, there was no easy answer to this question.

> But what is meant by a common school education? This question has never been answered; and it cannot be very satisfactorily answered. Some may think it enough that their children learn to read: others will be content with reading,

writing, and arithmetic. Others will add to the list, grammar, geography, history—perhaps practical mathematics, physics, astronomy, mechanics, rural economy—with several other branches of science and literature, or ethics, rhetoric, political economy, geology, chemistry, mineralogy, botany:—in short, where shall the limit be fixed? Who shall prescribe the limit beyond which a common school education shall never extend?[22]

What did the common schools teach? In 1838 the American Institute of Instruction, an association of educators who promoted the common school, offered a prize of $500 for the best essay on a "system of education best adapted to the common schools of our country." According to Thomas Palmer, author of the prize essay, the curriculum in 1838 consisted of reading, writing, orthography, grammar, geography, and history. He urged that it be broadened to include elocution, composition, physiology, botany, mineralogy, geology, agriculture (in country schools), vocal music, and drawing.[23]

Also in 1838, Henry Barnard, the first chief state school officer for Connecticut, conducted a comprehensive survey of the Connecticut schools. Teachers were asked to respond to a detailed questionnaire about their methods of teaching reading, penmanship, spelling, composition, grammar, arithmetic, geography, history, drawing, and music. Undoubtedly, many Connecticut schools did not offer all of these subjects. But we may be reasonably certain that Barnard and his state board of education felt that they should be offered in all schools.

Critical Factors

In discussing what the common school taught before 1840, the following should be noted: (1) children attended school irregularly, (2) teachers had no professional preparation and tended to look upon teaching as temporary employment, (3) teacher turnover was very rapid, (4) the length of the school year varied with the amount of money available to pay the teacher, (5) schools were ungraded; children of every age, who used every variety of textbook, were crowded in one room under one teacher, and (6) there was not professional supervision of teachers.

EARLY THEORETICAL IDEAS

One of the earliest educational journals, the *American Journal of Education,* observed in 1830 that the question of which school subjects are the most important in a system of public education was seldom asked. When this question had been put to teachers, their answers reflected "some peculiar notions, or partialities," which caused education to be "defective and distorted" and "destitute of symmetry, upon which, both that beauty of the mind and character so much depend."[24]

In other words, explained the *Journal,* if the teacher's favorite subject was geography, he or she pointed out that nothing was as important as knowing about the earth on which we live. If a teacher had, or thought he or she had, skill in arithmetic, the position taken was that there was nothing like arithmetic to discipline the mind, and that the knowledge of arithmetic was what distinguished the civilized from the barbarian state.[25]

The Goal of Thoroughness

A rather widely accepted curriculum principle throughout the nineteenth century was that children should "complete" the study of a subject, or "learn it thoroughly," before beginning a new subject. This principle effectively debarred new subjects from the curriculum. It also seemed to educators that the goal of thoroughness was the reason for so much review and so little progress in common schools. Referring to teachers who believed that reading and writing were all that children needed to be taught, the *American Journal of Education* commented pointedly: "Their schools must of course study the spelling book and dictionary, write copies, and read in the Testament, daily and yearly, til they 'complete their education.' "[26]

Curriculum Development and Faculty Psychology

The *American Journal of Education* based its answers to the question of what are the most important subjects in a system of popular education on the doctrines of faculty psychology. It pointed out that no curriculum, if it is complete, will fail to consider the "whole physical, intellectual, and moral nature of the subjects in it."[27] Faculty psychologists held that the vigor of each mental power depended on the vigor of the others; if one area was neglected, the others would also suffer. Thus all powers of the mind—judgment, memory, and imagination—should receive attention. In its final comments on the problem, the *Journal* suggested that natural history and the natural sciences be introduced into the schools. The reasons were intellectual, moral, and physical.

> Would they not quicken, invigorate, and develope juvenile, as well as infantile intellect? Might they not be applied to the elevation of the moral being of children? Might they not, through them, be led to comtemplate, with a kind of awful, but salutary and animating solemnity, the Being who made them, and placed them in the midst of so much that is beautiful, and grand, and designed for their use? Would not a knowledge of the works, the properties, and the laws of created objects, be calculated to make better farmers, better mechanics, better merchants, better teachers, better legislators, better citizens, better men, and better women?[28]

Although faculty psychology has been blamed for the emphasis on rote learning that characterized the common school, it is usually forgotten that faculty psychologists urged that education be practical and that the body be given attention as well as the mind.

It is interesting to note that Horace Mann based many of his educational ideas on the principles of faculty psychology. One such recommendation was that the study of physiology be introduced into the schools. This is mentioned neither in an attempt to resuscitate nor redeem faculty psychology, but merely to point out some of its lesser-known influences on the curriculum.

Expansion: The Approach to Curriculum Improvement

As indicated, the awakening of interest in public schools drew public attention to the problem of the retracing of studies. Nineteenth-century public officials and educators thought alike about the problem; they saw it as stemming from a curriculum that was entirely too limited. The solution they proposed was curriculum expansion. Among the most influential advocates of a broadened curriculum was Governor DeWitt Clinton of New York:

> Our system of instruction, with all its numerous benefits, is still susceptible of great improvements. Ten years, of the life of a child, may now be spent in a common school. In *two years* the elements of instruction may be acquired; and the remaining eight years must be spent in either repetition or idleness, unless the teachers of common schools are competent to instruct in the higher branches of knowledge. The outlines of Geography, Mineralogy, Agricultural Chemistry, Mechanical Philosophy, Surveying, Geometry, Astronomy, Political Economy, and Ethics, might be communicated in that period of time by able preceptors, without essential interference with the calls of domestic industry.[29]

A quarter of a century later there was concern on the part of some educators that this approach to curriculum improvement was leading to a proliferation of studies and fragmented learning. In 1861, George W. Minns, a California teacher who was later to become principal of the State Normal School, made the following comments in an address to the State Teachers Institute:

> We should carefully avoid having too many studies in our schools. Non multa, sed multum is a maxim of sound sense. Do a few things well, not many things poorly. It should never be forgotten that correct spelling, reading, writing, arithmetic, geography, grammar, and facility in expressing one's self in good plain English, are indispensable. They are the foundations of all future acquisitions; in fact, without them, there can be no superstructure. They are worth any quantity of heads full of mere smatterings of *ologies* and *osophies.*[30]

Before the close of his address, however, Minns had advocated the introduction of the sciences into the public schools of California. The schools, he said, must keep pace with developments in the physical and natural sciences. This was already being done in the East.

It was true enough that the schools had not kept up with the development of new knowledge. But it was also true that most pupils left school without becoming proficient in the skills that the schools did teach, limited though these might be. Thus, a child might spend ten years reviewing the rudiments of reading, but it did not follow that he or she could read with understanding and ease. More often, the child could not. Expansion of the curriculum to round out the empty hours in school was a unidimensional approach to a many-faceted problem. One facet that was overlooked by this solution was the quality of teaching and learning in common schools. That the additive approach to curriculum development only compounded the existing problems of the schools was soon discovered.

ROTE AND RECITATION

A law passed in Massachusetts in 1789 authorized towns to divide themselves into small school districts. In 1827 the districts were empowered by law to select school trustees who were empowered to certify, hire, and fire teachers. Districts elected new trustees every twelve months. Each new board of trustees proceeded to dismiss the teacher and hire a new one. The effect of this system on children's learning has already been described. The effect on the teacher was, to say the least, demoralizing. As Potter and Emerson pointed out at the time, "This practice makes him, in truth, little better than a vagrant."[31]

Under the district system, which was quickly adopted by other states, as many as eighty pupils, ranging in age from two or three to more than twenty, were crowded together in one room under the supervision of one teacher. The furniture was appropriate for neither the older nor the younger pupils; there was a great deal of physical discomfort in district schools, particularly for the younger children, who had to sit still with nothing to do for hours at a time.

The problem for younger children went beyond enforced inactivity—some teachers tended to give short shrift to beginning reading instruction. As Barnard reported in Connecticut, the "diversity and multiplicity of studies attempted to be taught to children of every age . . . had led to an alarming neglect of the primary studies, and of the younger children."[32] Why teachers were often remiss in the instruction of their younger pupils seems obvious. Because of the impossible instructional demands made on them, they must have had to rely heavily on rote methods and on older pupils to provide instruction for the younger ones.

Common School Methods

But the chief evil of the system was the approach to learning. Hard-pressed for time, the teacher raced through the multiple and diverse curricular circuit, using the same method for every learner and for every subject. Pupils were summoned to the stand in groups of two, three, or four (depending on how many had the same textbook). There they "said their lessons," words hurriedly repeated in rote fashion from a book. Within moments they were back in their seats. A more superficial learning experience can hardly be imagined.

A good record of the instruction in a one-room school in the early nineteenth century was left by the Reverend Warren Burton in his book *The District School As It Was.* The curriculum in the New England school attended by Burton consisted mainly of reading, writing, arithmetic, spelling, and grammar. Reading, which was taught from the *Primer* and Thomas Dilworth's *New Guide to the English Tongue,* was scheduled for both morning and afternoon school sessions. Classes that had sufficient mastery of reading ("adequate to words of more than one syllable") also read from the Bible.[33]

In 1782 Webster published his famous "Blue-Backed Speller" (titled pretentiously *First Part of a Grammatical Institute of the English Language*). Spelling quickly became an independent subject and the spelling bee a fad. The teaching of arithmetic, which entered the elementary schools in the latter half of the eighteenth century, was based on the question-and-answer (catechetical) plan of instruction. Burton wrote that his study of arithmetic consisted largely of copying unintelligible rules into a notebook. Despite the concern of educational reformers for a curriculum providing the skills and understandings necessary for responsible citizenship, the methods of instruction used in the one-room elementary school rendered much of the content virtually meaningless to youngsters. The rote and imitation reported by Burton was characteristic not only of New England but of those schools that did exist in other sections of the country during this period.

MONITORIAL INSTRUCTION—THE PURSUIT OF EFFICIENCY

An instructional plan in operation in the cities before the battle for state-supported schools was won was the Lancaster model for education. For a short period (1815–30) this system fired the imagination of champions of free schools for the poor. Its major appeal was that it was so cheap; pupil monitors were used in the instruction of a large number of youngsters (200–1,000) in one room. Only one teacher was needed because the monitors did all the teaching. Commenting on the teacher's role, Joseph Lancaster, the English schoolmaster whose name was associated with the system, explained: "The master should be a bystander and an inspector."[34]

The system worked as follows: bright pupils were selected as monitors. They were each assigned a row of pupils (usually ten in number) to instruct and to supervise. The teacher first taught each lesson to the monitors, who then took their "stations" by the wall and taught their charges what they had just learned. The Lancastrian school was organized, military fashion, down to the last detail, and teachers were required to follow every detail.

Mechanical Education and the Conventional Wisdom

At first the monitorial plan was confined to the teaching of reading, but it was soon extended to include writing, spelling, arithmetic, and geography. Later, monitorial high schools were organized in some cities, and the plan was actually suggested for the colleges. At the peak of its popularity, the monitorial approach was considered tailor-made for elementary instruction. This was because it was mechanical, and the conventional wisdom held that the elementary branches could only be mastered mechanically. It was felt that the faculty of memory was well-developed in children under ten. Thus, the children, it was believed, could commit rules and definitions to memory. They could not, however, be expected to apply the rules or to engage in the processes of reflection, analysis, or generalization. Interestingly, it was the mechanical character of the system that caused it to fall into disrepute and led to its rapid demise.

Advocates of monitorial instruction were quick to point out advantages in addition to the low cost. For instance, the plan seemed to solve the problem of the time wasted by pupils in doing nothing while the master was listening to other pupils say their lessons. Under the monitorial system, pupils were engaged in constant recitation, moving to a new lesson as soon as one was finished rather than spending their time in idleness or play. Independent study was not provided for; experience had indicated that pupils so engaged "wasted their time" and "wore down the mind of the teacher."[35]

Additional advantages of "mutual instruction," as the plan was called, were cited by its devotees. Two of the most significant, in view of recent educational trends, were that teachers were relieved "of the burden of the more mechanical parts of instruction and recitation" and were free to get on with the "intellectual departments" of teaching, and that pupils who had made the most progress in school were able to help those less advanced than themselves to learn.[36]

A Declining View of Elementary Education

Even when monitorial instruction was at the peak of its popularity, its superficiality was recognized. It consisted of much recitation but little or no reflective thinking or meaningful activity. As was pointed out, its devotees saw this as an advantage, since the purpose of elementary lessons was to "produce impressions on the memory." Also, as they put it, the "silent and close application of the mind should come on gradually, beginning at later stages of progress, and harmonizing better with the development of the juvenile intellect."[37]

But this view of elementary instruction clashed head-on with the new educational psychology developed by the Swiss educational reformer Johann Heinrich Pestalozzi (1746–1827), who labeled rote learning as mere "outward show." The monitorial system, where pupils "parsed" lengthy lists of rules and definitions, was based entirely on outward show. Thus, it was rejected by educational theorists in favor of another approach that seemed more appropriate for the needs of the child. Also, a state-supported school system was being developed. There was no longer a need in the cities to use the only system of instruction economically feasible in charity schools. "It was born in poverty, and poverty was ever its best excuse for being."[38]

Mechanical Education Today

Today "mechanics" (rote learning in reading, writing, and arithmetic) dominates schooling for many urban youngsters. Moreover, adjustment-type programs for high-school students with severe attendance or behavior problems are often geared to prepare the student to pass proficiency tests in reading, writing, and mathematics so that they can qualify for a graduate equivalency diploma. Students are not engaged in idea-oriented learning through which they can learn to use their skills as working power. They become bored with mechanical drills and repetitive exercises that are severed from application and meaning in their daily lives. As one student said when questioned, "It's the same old stuff, over and over."[39]

During the late 1980s, as an outcome of the failures of the curriculum retrenchment of "back to basics," the national reports on educational reform were calling for "teaching thinking skills."[40] Critical thinking had been one of the dominant themes in the progressive curriculum reforms earlier in the century. The trouble with the recent efforts in teaching thinking skills was that a mechanical-segmental approach was often taken—as if thinking could be taught as a separate skill subject rather than in relationships extending throughout the curriculum. And once again disadvantaged learners were treated as a kind of subspecies. "For at-risk students," suggests one program guide, "thinking should not be integrated into the curriculum until one or two years after training in thinking begins."[41] As Brookover points out, many educators "believe that differentiating policies and practices enhance the education of their students," but such programs "do not recognize that equality of opportunity is not facilitated by highly differentiated programs based on the presumed differences between lower-class and middle-class children."[42]

In many respects, the situation today parallels that of the early nineteenth century. In 1898, Hinsdale analyzed the rise and fall of the monitorial system. He concluded that

The vogue of the system was due to the invincible faith of men in machinery, combined with the promise of cheapness in education. But in this instance men soon discovered, what mental science and educational experience both teach, that good education can be neither mechanized nor made cheap.[43]

However far-fetched as it may seem, to this day there is an occasional call for a return to the Lancastrian or monitorial system as a cheap and efficient means of providing an education for the poor in our inner-cities.[44] Nevertheless, other forms of mechanical education, including programmed instruction and workbook exercises, have acquired a visible place in the teaching-learning repertoire of many classrooms.

THE INFANT SCHOOL—DOWNWARD EXTENSION OF THE CURRICULUM

At the same time, another innovation was imported from England, one that was to profoundly influence theory and practice in early childhood education. This was the infant school. It was invented to provide a pleasant educational interlude in the lives of poor Scottish three- and four-year-olds before they were put to work in the factories at the age of five. There was a great deal of singing and dancing combined with the instruction; the idea was to keep the children active and happy. Emphasis was placed on firsthand experience rather than learning from books. However, the plan was soon formalized, and book learning became an accepted part of the infant school curriculum.

In 1816 the infant school idea was adopted in Boston because children were not permitted to attend the city schools until they could read and write. Thus, there was a need for primary schools to prepare them for admission to the city (grammar) schools. The infant, or primary, school took children from the ages of four to eight and was the forerunner of the primary grades in the elementary school.

Early Education and Social Reform

Educational theorists saw the infant school as a momentous opportunity to bring about social reform through early education of the poor. They also sought to introduce the methods used in infant schools into the elementary schools, where the "intellect had been forced into arbitrary channels, and accustomed to mechanical influence and morbid habits."[45] In a lecture before the first convention of the American Institute of Instruction, William Russell, editor of the *American Journal of Education,* described the mode of instruction in the typical elementary school.

We see usually a number of little sufferers, confined to one uncomfortable posture, for hours in succession; enduring an irksome restraint, as the condition of escape from penalties; conning mechanically a memory lesson which they do not understand, or reciting it as mechanically; controlled in every look and action by the aspect of authority—the whole nature of little beings put under a discipline of repression and restraint.[46]

In contrast was the infant school approach, which Russell hoped would be adopted in elementary schools.

Looking into an infant school, we observe the children employed in healthful and pleasant recreation, or enjoying a temporary repose; listening to a story inculcating the virtues of childhood; admiring a picture, or joining in a song; yielding a cheerful obedience to affectionate management; asking the artless questions which are prompted by the natural curiosity of infancy, or listening, with deep interest and attention, to their instructor's answers.[47]

Problems in Pedagogical Practice

Russell admitted, however, that not all infant schools conformed with this model. Rote learning was still the prevailing pattern, and much of the instruction was catechetical. Furthermore, most of the music and poetry used in infant schools was bad. "Better," said Russell, "that the imagination should remain uncultivated, than become degraded or perverted."[48] Infant school education stressed the use of pictures in the study of objects. (This was a Pestalozzian method; the idea was to link language and observation so that real comprehension occurred and rote learning would be eliminated.) The procedure was being utilized in some infant schools. But there was a problem: The pictures that were used were inappropriate. Said Russell:

The subjects are very often badly chosen, presenting to the eye of infancy the exhibition, sometimes, of the most degrading and horrid crimes, instead of such objects as should shed a serene and happy influence on the heart. . . . But an objection more general exists in the gross inaccuracy of forms, and the inappropriate colors, in most pictures prepared for children.[49]

Russell saw the infant school idea as evidence of a new humanism. In what he called the "new order of things," the child was beginning to be viewed as potentially good. "The human heart," he said, "begins to be regarded as the native soil of virtue, which early culture is to keep free from encroaching weeds; and the intellect begins to be treated as a self-impelling power, which education is to aid, rather than to check."[50]

Theory and Practice

Russell's remarks were made in 1830. That same year a manual for infant school education was published in Massachusetts. Nearly every instructional procedure found objectionable by Russell was incorporated as recommended practice. Listed under a category entitled "General Principles" was the author's view of the child (and of human nature generally): "It is a melancholy truth that there is a tendency to evil in the human heart."[51] Instruction was catechetical. Discipline was approached through the medium of fear. The following brief excerpt from a moral lesson on obedience is illustrative. It should be noted that the teacher read the questions and the children recited the responses from memory.

> How would it be in school, if children did not obey their teachers?
> We should be rude, and noisy, and hurt each other, and could not learn any good.
> How would it be if children should not obey their parents?
> They would contradict, quarrel, and hurt each other, and make their parents so unhappy they would get sick and die.
> And what would become of such wicked children?
> They would be left without food, or clothes, or any one to teach them, or care for them, and must wander about without any house or home to rest in.[52]

Objective of Infant Education.   In his lecture of 1830, Russell recognized that instructional practice was far behind theory. The problem, as he saw it, was that teachers were still shackled by previous custom. They could not seem to conceptualize learning as something the child did, if left to himself or herself, as naturally as breathing. Infant school instruction should follow the tide of the child's natural tendency to learn, not go against it, said Russell. The object of infant, or elementary, education was not to study any branch of knowledge in depth but "to excite a general interest in the rudiments of knowledge . . . to create an inquisitive and discriminating turn of mind."[53] It is worthy of mention that this is still the objective of infant school education in Britain today.

The Infant School Curriculum.   Russell stated that the rudiments of reading, writing, and arithmetic should be part of the infant school curriculum. Of these, only reading should be taught to the youngest pupils, and this in a spirit of enjoyment rather than urgency. Natural science, drawing, and singing were to be included in the curriculum. Formal lessons in astronomy and geometry were to be avoided. But a few of the solids that correspond to the shapes of common objects could be used to convey elementary concepts in geometry. Pictures, stories, conversation, plants, and animals were to be the sources of instruction. But the most important requisite of all was a teacher with the spirit of infant education.

CHANGING CONCEPTIONS OF METHOD

Probably the most profound influence on educational theory was not the new humanism described by William Russell but a new method for thinking and acquiring knowledge—the inductive and scientific method. In the seventeenth century, when Francis Bacon described the inductive method of science in his *Novum Organum (New Method),* an intellectual revolution was launched. Based on direct observation of the natural world, the collection of facts based on observation, and generalization based on observable relationships among facts, the scientific method was a frontal assault on the traditional deductive method of thinking. For instead of starting out with an uncriticized statement written by a traditional (or religious) authority in the distant past, the generalization came at the end of the thinking process. Furthermore, the new knowledge was acquired by the individual through his or her senses rather than playing with words.

Influence of Empiricism on Method

As the scientific method began to pay off with new knowledge about the natural world, philosophers and educators became increasingly enthusiastic about learning by experience (empiricism). One learns through one's senses: sight, touch, hearing, smell, and taste. Was it not obvious, then, that this would be the most fruitful approach to classroom learning? According to Bacon, learning would be most effective if the teacher started with careful observation of nature and developed the powers of induction rather than mere rote and recitation. Comenius systematized this idea into a method. The teacher should begin with the observation of simple phenomena, leading to the complex. Moreover (and this *was* revolutionary) learning aids—pictures and actual objects—should be used for developing children's sense experience.

In Germany, realism in education became a reality when educators established schools *(Realschulen)* where emphasis was put on the use of actual objects and excursions to acquire firsthand knowledge of life. In Switzerland, Rousseau popularized interest in the idea of sense realism when he argued for the free expression of children's natural impulses and the substitution of play and observation of nature for books and the classical (linguistic) studies. In England, a number of proposals for educational reform were made, based on sense realism. Of these, the infant school was the most famous and successful.

Object Teaching

As shown earlier, object teaching at the elementary-school level came to this country by way of England with the infant school early in the nineteenth century. (The foundational idea of sense realism, however, reached our shores much earlier; Benjamin Franklin's proposed curriculum for an academy, published in 1749, was based on the principles of sense perception. Franklin's proposal is discussed later in this chapter.) But it was not until after 1850 that object teaching became popularized.

The Method. Object teaching required, first of all, an object—a flower, fruit, toy, tool, or animal (or a model or picture of the object). Through the use of his or her senses, the child gained ideas about the object. Through sense perception, he or she was able to develop concepts and basic ideas and translate them into appropriate words. The objectives of object teaching were to develop alertness, accuracy of perception, concepts and generalizations, and vocabulary. These goals fit strikingly well with the objectives of elementary education today. It is of great interest, however, that teachers in the nineteenth century described the goals of object teaching in terms of faculty psychology (to cultivate the faculty of reasoning, for example) rather than the development of a scientific frame of mind. This was because faculty psychology was the generally accepted pedagogical psychology of the times.

Criticisms of Object Teaching. As it became formalized into a method, a growing number of criticisms were associated with object teaching. In too many instances, lessons were unrelated because there was no overall plan. Also, what began as a lesson on fruit or flowers might end up as a lesson in religion instead of science. Another unfortunate ending could be (and often was) a senseless vocabulary lesson. Finally, some teachers insisted that appropriate responses were wrong because they were not couched in the teacher's terminology. Obviously, none of these problems was implicit in the method itself; all were abuses of the method and, hence, problems of teacher education.

Impact on Educational Thinking. Despite the abuses and criticisms, object teaching was a tremendously important reform because direct experience concerning an object was substituted for teacher verbalism about the object. And despite the fact that object teaching was all but abandoned by 1880, learning by experience was here to stay. Other lasting influences of object teaching on the curriculum were the concept of learning as inquiry, visual aids, and the field trip.

EARLY CURRICULUM PROBLEMS

Pressures for Expansion

Cultural change resulted in demands for a broader common school curriculum. With universal manhood suffrage came demands for courses in history, government, and constitutional law as "education for citizenship." An increasing spirit of nationalism led to demands for patriotic education. As early as 1820, a few scattered proposals were being made for agricultural and industrial education. By 1870, these had increased in seriousness and in volume. The demands on the school were heterogeneous and often conflicting. Some stemmed from partisan, personal, or professional interests; physicians called for greater stress on teaching the principles of health and physiology, lawyers for teaching about the law. The governor in one state went so far as to recommend to the legislature that the penal code be made a textbook in the schools.

Pestalozzian ideas on instruction also resulted in expansion of the curriculum. Pestalozzi believed that the educational process should be harmonized with the natural development of the child. Education must proceed by observation and experience; the way to develop the "faculties" of the child was through self-activity and the organization of "sense impressions." As indicated, this led to science instruction in the form of "object lessons." The introduction of music and drawing into the elementary school was also based on Pestalozzian principles.

Pressures Against Expansion

Although there was tremendous pressure exerted on the school for curriculum expansion as the nineteenth century wore on, there was also opposition to expansion. This came from those who thought that children should spend their time in school "learning the fundamentals more thoroughly." It also came from those who held that the rudiments of the three R's were all that should be given to the masses. Education, they said, was depriving us of American laborers and forcing us to import our artisans.

It gives us pause for thought that some of the curriculum areas we take for granted today caused a great deal of furor when they were innovations. When music, other than the singing of hymns, was introduced into the schools, it created a storm of protest. Music, said the protesters, would steal time from the three R's. The following excerpt from an 1894 editorial in the Chicago *Evening Post,* long after music was introduced, illustrates the bitter and sustained battle incited by the addition of music to the elementary curriculum in that city.

> Music leers at the infantile intellect while its intellection is mastering the old proposition that the sum of a and b is "ab"; music with its do, re, mi and its do, si, la, to stunt the nascent child-mind before it has grasped the collective fact that r-a-t is "rat"; music that eats up the time that should be devoted to spelling, and paralyzes the child-brain by opening to it a black, unfathomable cavern.[54]

The Problem of Priorities

There was general agreement that the common school should teach *common branches,* that is, knowledge possessed in common by all citizens. But the problem was the lack of agreement on what this knowledge should be. Faculty psychologists such as William Russell, Horace Mann, and James G. Carter held (as did Pestalozzi) that the physical, intellectual, and moral faculties should receive an equal share of attention; the faculties were inter-dependent, and the strength of one depended on the strength of the others. The result, in theory at least, was a balanced curriculum. Obviously, a rank ordering of knowledge according to value was not possible with this ap-proach to curriculum development. (As pointed out, however, there was a vast gulf between theory and practice; in practice, the "intellectual faculty" was given most of the "exercise.")

What Knowledge Is of Most Worth?   It was in 1860 that Spencer pub-lished in the United States his famous essay "What Knowledge Is of Most Worth?" (The essay had previously appeared in England.) He stated that the purpose of education was "to prepare for complete living," and that the only way of determining the worth of an educational program was first to classify, in order of importance, the leading activities of life, and then to evaluate the educational program on the basis of the extent to which it offered this preparation. Spencer's classification of life activities, in order of their impor-tance, was as follows:

1. Those ministering directly to self-preservation.
2. Those securing the necessities of life (ministering indirectly to self-preservation).
3. Those which aid in the rearing and discipline of offspring.
4. Those involved in maintaining one's social and political relations.
5. Those which occupy the leisure part of life, gratifying tastes and feelings.[55]

In applying his own test, Spencer found that science was the knowledge of most worth in educating for self-preservation, yet it received the least at-tention in the curriculum. As for educational method, Spencer held that chil-dren "should be *told* as little as possible and induced to *discover* as much as possible."[56] To this end he favored object-teaching. As a result of the publica-tion of Spencer's work, and the discussion that followed, the study of science gained a new stature and was more rapidly introduced into all levels of the curriculum.

The Demand for Thoroughness.   As indicated, one of the most com-monly heard arguments against the introduction of new school subjects was that children should gain a thorough knowledge of the studies already pur-sued rather than dissipate their time and energy in additional studies. A num-ber of educators were quick to call attention to a major fallacy in the demand for thoroughness: Thoroughness, they pointed out, is not an absolute but a relative term; what would be thorough for a child of six would be superficial for a child of twelve. These educators also felt that it was not thoroughness, in the sense of completeness, that was meant by the popular criticism but clarity of understanding. Obviously, if the demand were for completeness of the study of arithmetic, geography, and grammar, this would be tantamount to a permanent exclusion of any new studies from the curriculum.

The Hierarchy of Difficulty.   A second fallacy believed by educators to be at the heart of the demand for thoroughness was the idea that the various fields of knowledge constitute a series of subjects that vary in difficulty, so that one subject should be completed by the child before he or she attempts to master the concepts of other, higher subjects. This notion about knowledge was voiced in the last quarter of the nineteenth century by teachers, parents, and school officials who sought to keep science out of the elementary school. As pointed out in 1882 by John Gregory, who was president of the National Education Association, nothing could be more fallacious. All science begins with concepts that are so simple that young children learn them, and the sciences advance in level of difficulty until they reach the philosophical stage. As Gregory put it: "Like so many Jacob's ladders, they (the sciences) have their feet in the dust, and their first rungs are so low that the creeping child may reach them. Their sublime summits are lost in the heavens, where only the strongest can soar and the steadiest can stay."[57]

Curriculum Development by Accretion.   Be that as it may, there were some very practical problems involved in finding time in the school day for physiology, botany, zoology, physics, chemistry, and technology in addition to reading, spelling, penmanship, arithmetic, geography, grammar, literature, manners and morals, and the history of the United States, not to mention drawing, music, and physical exercises. Accretion had, by 1880, become the established way of curriculum development. Each time a new subject was added, the curriculum became more crowded because the old subjects maintained their places. By this is meant that the older subjects such as grammar were often taught for the same amount of time, with no culling of useless subject matter. Not only did each study compete with all other studies for time, but teachers were not competent to teach so many specializations. Two curriculum principles were yet to be developed: first, *unification* (in the sciences this would provide a single elementary science course), and second, *differentiation* (the idea that the curriculum need not be the same for every child). This latter principle came to be applied mostly with regard to aptitude and intelligence, rather than interest, in the elementary school.

Educational Theory and Curriculum Change.   As indicated, educators who sought expansion of the curriculum gave two reasons relating to the nature of knowledge and society. They pointed out that the growth of new knowledge in a rapidly changing society had created new demands on the individual and that knowledge begins with concepts simple enough for young children to understand. One of the first to conceptualize curriculum change as a continuing process was William Russell, who, in the second volume of his *American Journal of Education,* wrote: "No system of education, however perfect at the period of its first establishment can fully accord with the progressive improvement of society. If the pursuits of life change, in the course of ages, so ought education to change to meet the demands of the public."[58]

Increasingly, as the nineteenth century wore on, educators were also giving psychological reasons for the introduction of new studies. A case in point was the teaching of so many sciences in the elementary school. This was defended on the ground of child nature; every normal child, it was said, acquires many elementary facts in all sciences before he or she comes to school. The school curriculum should be designed to foster this natural learning and, thus, should offer every branch of science. The turning of educators to the child for the answer to the ideal curriculum is discussed in depth in Chapter 4.

EUROPEAN IDEAS

Until the second decade of the twentieth century, American educators imported most of their educational psychology and much of their curriculum theory from Europe. The ideas of three Europeans—Pestalozzi, Froebel, and Herbart—streamed into the educational field, forming the bedrock for modern educational theory. Yet the ideas of these European educators were to undergo adaptation and transformation to fit the American experience.

Pestalozzi

As shown earlier, the ideas of Pestalozzi had influenced educational thinking in America before 1830. It was not until after the Civil War, however, that the theories of this remarkable Swiss educator were really evident in educational theory and practice.

Pestalozzi did more than just write about educational theory; he established and conducted schools where he could put his theories into practice. Mention has already been made of Pestalozzi's conceptions of learning. What is important to note here is that, unlike other faculty psychologists, Pestalozzi viewed the young mind as an active mind, engaged in perception, analysis, and generalization as opposed to rote learning.

Froebel

Another great European educational figure whose ideas had a profound influence on post–Civil War American educational thinking is Friedrich Froebel. According to Froebel, the educative process should begin when the child is three or four years old. Froebel believed that play is the method of development and learning for children. This obviously entailed a far less formal and rigid school environment. Froebel called the school for young children the *kindergarten,* a garden where children grow. His emphasis on manipulating objects, exploration, and self-expression led to a realization of the importance of activity in learning.

Froebel was honored far more outside his native Germany; in fact, although the kindergarten was successfully transplanted to the United States, it actually was banned in Prussia in 1851.[59] The tale of the kindergarten is particularly fascinating; it was one of the educational practices brought home from Germany and France by American educators who had gone there to study pedagogical practices. As Commager relates, they "came home to apply the lessons they had learned to conditions in this country, particularly to elementary education."[60]

Conditions in the United States were particularly favorable to the kindergarten; indeed, it was the "foreign country to which this German idea was most successfully transplanted."[61] Why did the kindergarten find so much more support in the United States than in Germany? According to Allen, "in Germany the child-care institutions ... that were founded in the early nineteenth century were under church sponsorship and used custodial and pedagogical techniques that were firmly based on traditional religious views of the child's nature as innately depraved."[62] The kindergarten in America, on the other hand, was based on secular thought derived from studies of physiology and medicine: Human nature is not completely preformed at birth but is formed in great measure by the action of the environment on the individual. Given a carefully controlled environment like the kindergarten, human nature had great possibilities. The latter idea was nothing more or less than what Commager has called the "*first* American principle." He goes on to say:

> We can call it for convenience, the theory of environmentalism, or of change, or even of progress. It was this: man was not really either depraved or virtuous, but a creature of circumstances—a point of view which found support in the philosophy of "the Great Mr. Locke," and which seemed, besides, the common sense of the matter. Depravity, corruption, crime, vice, superstition, ignorance, folly—all these were products not of nature but of history, that is, they were man-made, not God-made. Granted that in the Old World man appeared corrupt and ignorant, was that not because for centuries he had been weighed down by the tyranny of rulers, the might of soldiers, the superstition of priests; because for centuries he had been ground down in poverty, misery, and ignorance?
>
> But in the New World all this might be changed.... Education was to be what religion had been in a less secular age—the chief instrument for the regeneration of the human race.[63]

Herbart

A famous German philosopher whose theories greatly influenced American educational thought from 1890 to 1910 was Johann Friedrich Herbart. For Herbart, the development of character was the main purpose of education. This depended on deriving interest from the program of studies.

Such interest could never stem from the three R's because of their mechanical nature. Hence, Herbart urged that history, literature, and science find a place in the curriculum at every educational level. Herbart stressed the importance of *concentration,* having a subject such as history or literature as the core of the curriculum, and the *correlation* of all subjects. The objective of correlation and concentration was unity in the curriculum. *Isolation,* or the failure to achieve unity, was, according to Herbartians, the great failure of traditional education.

Herbart's followers formalized his classroom method of teaching. According to this method, it was the function of the teacher to impart knowledge by utilizing previous learning. This meant, of course, that he had to know of the child's previous knowledge and interest. As long as the teacher kept this psychology in mind, he or she could follow the five formal steps:

1. Preparation—the teacher calls previous learning experiences to the learner's attention.
2. Presentation—the new materials are summarized or outlined.
3. Association—the new ideas are compared with the old.
4. Generalization—rules and general principles are derived from the new materials.
5. Application—the new generalizations are given meaning by relating them to specific instances.

The Herbartians brought intense attention to such general curriculum problems as the selection of content, grading of materials, and organization of presentation. Nevertheless, their ideas met with some vigorous opposition from defenders of the status quo. One opponent of the ideas of Herbart was William T. Harris, United States commissioner of education from 1889 to 1906.

CRYSTALLIZING THE STATUS QUO

In 1888, Charles W. Eliot, president of Harvard University, read a paper entitled "Can School Programs Be Shortened and Enriched?" at the NEA meeting in Washington, D.C.[64] The question was rhetorical, for Eliot, who had an extensive acquaintance with the curriculum problems of the schools, believed that the answer to this question was yes.

Eliot proposed that the number of grades in the elementary school be reduced from ten to eight. He suggested that the program in arithmetic, which was taking up to one-sixth of the school time for ten years, be contracted to six years, thus making room for algebra and geometry in the seventh and eighth grades. He stated that the amount of time devoted to the study of grammar was too long and should be limited by culling out the memorization of rules and precepts and teaching the use of English through practice. Eliot suggested that, beginning in the primary grades, children be taught natural science by means of demonstrations and laboratory experiences rather than only from books. Elementary physics, also taught by laboratory methods, would be introduced in the upper elementary grades.

Eliot argued that the idea that democratic theory implied an identical curriculum for every child and uniform tests for promotion was "fallacious and ruinous. Democratic theory," he said,

> does not undertake to fly in the face of nature by asserting that all children ... are alike and should be treated alike. Everybody knows that children are infinitely diverse.... Every child is a unique personality.... Hence, in the public schools of a democracy the aim should be to give the utmost possible amount of individual instruction, to grade according to capacity ... and to promote not by battalions, but in the most irregular way possible.[65]

This paper was followed by other appeals by Eliot and others for educational reform. The result was the appointment by the NEA of three committees: the Committee of Ten on Secondary School Studies, the Committee of Fifteen on Elementary Education, and the Committee on College Entrance Requirements. (Eliot was chairman of the Committee of Ten.) Their reports cast a mold for education for years to come.

As Cubberley observed, "the committees were dominated by subject-matter specialists, possessed of a profound faith in mental discipline. No study of pupil abilities, social needs, interest, capacities, or differential training found a place in their deliberations."[66]

The Committee's Report

Eliot's recommendation to reduce the number of elementary grades from ten to eight was endorsed in the report of the Committee of Fifteen, as was his plan to substitute the study of algebra for arithmetic in the seventh and eighth grades. Geometry, however, was left in the secondary school. At the outset of its report the committee stated that grammar, literature, arithmetic, geography, and history are the subjects in the elementary school with the greatest value for training the mind. Throughout the report, the committee held the line against the newer subjects, allotting them relatively little time in the school program. (See Figure 2-1.)

The committee "protested strongly" against the use of the scientific method in elementary science teaching. "It is important," they explained, "not to hasten the use of a strictly scientific method on the part of the child.... He is rather in the imitation stage of mind than in that of criticism. He will not reach the comparative or critical method until the era of higher education."[67] In light of this conclusion, one hour of "oral lessons" each week in natural science (which included hygiene) was recommended. Despite the fact that William T. Harris (who authored most of the report) was a

Figure *2-1.* The Elementary School Curriculum as Proposed by the Committee of Fifteen, 1895

Branches	1st year	2d year	3d year	4th year	5th year	6th year	7th year	8th year
Reading	10 lessons a week	5 lessons a week						
Writing	10 lessons a week	5 lessons a week		3 lessons a week				
Spelling lists				4 lessons a week				
English Grammar	Oral, with composition lessons				5 lessons a week with textbook			
Latin								5 lessons
Arithmetic	Oral, 60 minutes a week		5 lessons a week with textbook					
Algebra							5 lessons a week	
Geography	Oral, 60 minutes a week		*5 lessons a week with text-book				3 lessons a week	
Natural Science and Hygiene	60 minutes a week							
U.S. History						5 lessons a week		
U.S. Constitution								*5 lessons
General History	Oral, 60 minutes a week							
Physical Culture	60 minutes a week							
Vocal Music	60 minutes a week divided into 4 lessons							
Drawing	60 minutes a week							
Manual Training or Sewing and Cookery							One-half day each	
Number of Lessons	20 + 7 daily exercise	20 + 7 daily exercise	20 + 5 daily exercise	24 + 5 daily exercise	27 + 5 daily exercise	27 + 5 daily exercise	23 + 6 daily exercise	23 + 6 daily exercise
Total Hours of Recitations	12	12	11	13	16¼	16¼	17½	17½
Length of Recitations	15 minutes	15 minutes	20 minutes	20 minutes	25 minutes	25 minutes	30 minutes	30 minutes

*Begins in second half year.

Source: Committee of Fifteen, "Report of the Sub-Committee on the Correlation of Studies in Elementary Education," *Educational Review* 9 (March 1895): 284.

leader in the kindergarten movement, and the NEA had put its stamp of approval on the kindergarten, the kindergarten was not recognized by the committee as part of the elementary school.

Not surprisingly, there were some vigorous expressions of dissent by committee members on such points as "oral lessons" in science (telling by the teacher), the failure to include observation and experimentation in science instruction, and the inclusion of algebra but not geometry in the seventh and eighth grades.

Educational Theory and the Report. A number of the committee's recommendations bore directly on the issue of the "new (child-centered) education." One of the most significant was that the child's interests should be considered insofar as motivation for learning was concerned, but *not* in deciding what should be taught. Of paramount importance was the committee's coolness to the concept of curriculum synthesis. "Rigid isolation of the elements of each branch" was considered essential in elementary learning.[68] The problem of curricular segmentation continues to this day.

The Outcome

In his proposal for reform, Eliot had suggested a reduction in the time devoted to grammar and arithmetic so that the elementary-school program could be diversified and enriched. But the outcome of the committee's deliberations was to give these subjects even higher priority than they had before. Indeed, grammar now topped what had become the official list of the common branches. It may be said that the effect of the report of the Committee of Fifteen on the elementary curriculum was to crystallize the status quo.

It is also abundantly clear that agitators for educational reform do not always achieve what they hope for once they have set the reform machinery in motion. In fact, the final result may well be the opposite of what they hoped for! As a more recent case in point, one of the main reasons given for initiating reforms of the high-school physics and chemistry courses in the 1950s was the need to bring the physical sciences into closer relationship. Yet the final result was the production of new courses that were even purer than the courses they replaced.

THE BROADENING OF THE SECONDARY SCHOOL CURRICULUM—DINOSAURS VERSUS DEMOCRACY

In many respects the early development of the secondary school parallels that of the elementary school. The first ancestor of the high school, the Latin grammar school, was, like the elementary school, a publicly supported institution. The curriculums of both were narrowly limited in scope in the period of their infancy. For the first two decades of its existence (1820–40), the aims of the high school were virtually indistinguishable from those of the lower school: to prepare the rising generation in the common branches of learning. Indeed, some of the first high schools, especially in small towns, were simply higher departments of the common school; thus, from the earliest days of the high school, some persons, at least, must have been led to conclude that any distinction between these two levels is arbitrary.

During this period, however, the last few Latin grammar schools died out and the high school gradually filled the role of the old institution that included the preparation of youth for college. Consequently, well before the Civil War, the high school had a dual purpose: preparation for life activities and preparation for college. The entrance requirements of colleges furnished a definite framework for curriculum development, which conflicted from the start with the liberal view of the high school toward curriculum expansion. But until the report of the Committee of Ten in 1893, high schools were relatively free to develop an independent program without control and restriction by the colleges.

Despite the similarities in the various stages of development in elementary and secondary education, and the fact that the secondary school literally became an extension of the common school, there were significant differences as well. During one of the most crucial stages of its development, the secondary school was not a publicly supported institution. And when universal elementary education was a reality, universal secondary education was still a much-debated dream. The fact that the secondary curriculum expanded and diversified when it was not yet part of the common school made it that much more difficult to articulate the various levels of the school system later on.

The Latin Grammar School—A Curricular Dinosaur

Institutions must change in order to meet the changing social, political, and economic needs of society or they die. This is as true of the school as of any other institution. The curriculum of the Latin grammar school was virtually the same at the beginning and the end of the colonial period. Yet a new social and economic structure had developed in the intervening years that required a vastly different education for youth than that brought over from seventeenth-century England. In the new commercial centers and on the frontier, a school for learning Latin and Greek found no favor.

Beyond the fact that a classical curriculum met neither the needs of youth in the cities nor those of youth on the frontier, the Latin grammar school was an intrinsically undemocratic institution. It was the child of an ecclesiastical autocracy, and no provision was made for the education of girls. Given all of these conditions, and the absence of interest in reform, little effort was made to enforce the laws that required towns to establish and maintain grammar schools. As shown earlier, with the decline of the Latin grammar school came a decline in the ideal of free public education.

The Academy

The institution that contributed most to the character of the high school was its immediate predecessor, the academy. As indicated earlier, academies received aid and encouragement from the various state legislatures but were privately controlled. The result was a great variation in curricula.

Almost from the start, the academy was a dual-purpose institution, educating for the practical duties of life and "fitting" students for college. Some academies not only offered courses meeting college entrance requirements but offered many of the college courses as well. Academies taught English, French, Latin, Greek, geography, arithmetic, geometry, declamation, rhetoric, history, logic, astronomy, natural philosophy, and many other subjects. The academy provided instruction for girls as well as boys.

Franklin's Plan for an Academy.   Around the middle of the eighteenth century Benjamin Franklin, who had previously founded a reading club, library, and learned society, came forth, not surprisingly, with a detailed plan for a useful education. Franklin set forth his plan for a new kind of school, the academy, in his *Proposals Relating to the Education of Youth in Pennsylvania,* published in 1749. Franklin buttressed his arguments for an education that was secular and practical rather than religious and classical by citing the European empiricists and sense realists. (The influence of Bacon and Comenius on educational method was discussed earlier in the chapter.) Franklin was well aware that a secular education where the study of English rather than Latin was central would meet with opposition from the classicists and religious sources.

Throughout Franklin's curriculum proposal, practical educational experiences were stressed. The expert use of the English language was a primary goal. Art also was included as an aid to creative expression. Mathematics (particularly accounting) was another staple item in the proposal. Franklin devoted the most space to the social studies, which included modern history, geography, social history, political history, religious and moral history, and political science. French, German, and Spanish were offered for prospective merchants and Latin and Greek for those preparing for the ministry.

In Franklin's proposal, actual experience with machines was important in developing insights into the contributions of science to commerce, manufacture, and civilization itself. Similarly, practical experiences in agriculture were an important part of the study of natural history. In line with the realist view of the importance of concrete teaching aids, Franklin envisioned a plentiful supply of maps, globes, and scientific apparatus.

The idea that the aim of education is not to acquire knowledge for its disciplinary value but to improve conduct so that the individual can better serve others ran through the entire curriculum. Thus, Franklin's curriculum had a moral objective, but it was distinctly secular.

It was Franklin's hope to develop an education for practical living that was as respectable as an education grounded in religion and the classics and, indeed, more valuable. But Franklin was one hundred years ahead of his time. Because of the heavy hand of the Latinists in the academy, the English school was neglected in favor of the Latin school. (Indeed, the Latin teachers plotted the demise of the English school.) In 1789, Franklin demanded that the English school be separated from the Latin school and the corporation be dissolved. He had enough years of experience with the institution to pronounce a failure the first attempt to combine the values of a classical and a modern education. The classicists had won the first battle, but they had not won the war. Gradually they lost ground. (To this day, however, they have not admitted defeat.) Franklin's academy was not a failure, for it gave impetus to the academy movement which ultimately led to the universalization of secondary education through the emergence of the public high school.

Curriculum

The classical curriculum in the academies for college-preparatory students was determined by college entrance requirements. But there were no restraints on the curriculum for students who were not college bound. The academy strove to meet their needs with a program that was both practical and general. In 1815, the principal of Woburn Academy advertised:

> It is his humble and pleasing object to instruct young Lads in a regular and genteel behaviour, and in the various branches of literature, viz: Reading, Writing, Arithmetic, Geography, Bookkeeping, English Grammar, Rhetoric, Composition, and the Latin and Greek Languages. Likewise—Astronomy, Navigation or Surveying, to such as may wish to acquire a knowledge in either of these branches.... [69]

According to Cubberley, 149 new courses of study were offered in the academies of New York State between 1787 and 1870.[70] More than half of these new courses appeared between 1825 and 1828, the peak period of development of the academy. There was no philosophy or principle behind the multiplicity of courses; the curriculum just grew by addition. A broad program was good for the academy from a business standpoint; thus, the growth of the curriculum was, if anything, opportunistic, stemming from proprietary interests. Yet, haphazard as was its development, the breadth of the curriculum offered by the academies had an impact on college entrance requirements: Geography was recognized for college entrance in 1807 and algebra in 1820. The academies were often ahead of the colleges in recognizing the place of the sciences in the curriculum.

In 1817 the New York State Regents tried to change the curriculum of the state-aided academies back to that of the old Latin grammar school; the academies were ordered to offer only a classical curriculum. But there was such an outcry about this reversion to an aristocratic concept of education that in 1827 the legislature ordered the regents to change the regulation to include nonclassical studies.

It should be noted that the academy was a prime source of teachers for lower schools because of the advanced instruction offered in common school subjects. Occasionally lectures were given on pedagogy for those interested in elementary teaching, but seldom were these formalized into courses for the preparation of teachers.

Improved Methods of Instruction. Whereas the only teaching tool in the Latin grammar school was the particular book being committed to memory by the students, globes, maps, charts, laboratories, and libraries were used as instructional resources in academies. Thus, in addition to an enriched curriculum, the academy contributed improved methods of instruction to its successor, the high school. There is evidence of an experimental approach to instruction in some academies. This is not surprising, since the academy was unbound by tradition and aimed to meet student needs and interests. Such an experiment was described years later by Thomas Cushing, an instructor at Chauncy-Hall School, a boys' academy in Boston.

> About the year 1837 or 1838 the experiment was tried of introducing books of real literature for reading lessons in place of or in addition to the usual class books specially prepared for that purpose. It was more easily possible to do this as the school included in its quarterly charge all English books used in classes, and could change them or introduce new ones as often as seemed for the best interests of pupils, without extra expense to their parents. Though not included in my special department of Latin and Greek, the experiment was made by my suggestion, and the carrying it into effect was entrusted to me.
>
> The book chosen for the purpose was Irving's *Life of Columbus,* of which an edition of convenient size and reasonable expense had recently been published. The story was interesting and the style good. Some history also could be taught in connection with the reading lesson. A large class of boys was supplied with the books and showed much interest in their perusal. The experiment was decidedly successful, and, in subsequent years, led to the introduction for reading purposes of quite a range of the best literature, including selections from the works of Shakespeare, Scott, Longfellow and many other authors.
>
> This use of what may be called *real books* in place of volumes of disconnected selections has been followed in recent times in some of our public schools, and is another instance of Chauncy-Hall's taking the initiative in what has proved to be a very useful educational improvement.[71]

Opposition to Academies. Nevertheless, there were complaints from some quarters that academies were not as innovative as they might have been. Horace Greeley opposed academies because of their devotion to dead languages; he felt that it led to class distinctions. In his *Essays on Popular Education,* Carter wrote: "It is most deeply to be regretted that their [academies'] plans are quite so much tinctured with the notions of the last century, and that the systems of instruction and government which they adopt do not partake more largely of the modern and improved ideas of education."[72] Carter believed that it was difficult to bring about change in the academy because of the conflicting educational views of individuals on boards of trustees. Their struggles made teachers and principals reluctant to try new ideas; the "fear of innovation hangs like an *incubus* upon many, and paralyzes the efforts of all, even those who have thrown it off,"[73] he contended.

As noted earlier, however, Carter's main interest was in the development of a public secondary school that would meet the needs of all rather than a few. His comments about the failure of the academy to innovate were intended to lend support to his case for public high schools, not to improve the academy system. The decline of the academy during the last half of the nineteenth century was the result of a growing popular demand, aided by Carter and others, to extend the common school upward. The tuition-academy was unable to survive the competition with the high school, which, in addition to being tuition free, saved students the expense of living away from home. But more than that was involved in the eventual replacement of the academy by the high school; a growing spirit of democracy demanded a secondary school that was open to all. This battle was not to be won until we were well into the twentieth century.

The High School: Early Curriculum Patterns

Although they differed in character, the first high schools had one common objective: to provide a higher education than that offered by the elementary school. Some high schools were nothing more than an upstairs room in the local school where students were taught at an advanced level the same subjects they had in the elementary grades. The curricular fare of the first high school in Middletown, Connecticut, for example, consisted mainly of the higher branches of the elementary school. Other high schools had from the start a three-year program in academy-type studies that was later expanded to four years. This was true in Massachusetts, where the Law of 1827 mandated the teaching of United States history, bookkeeping, algebra, geometry, and surveying in high schools serving towns with five hundred or more families. In towns with four thousand or more inhabitants, instruction in Latin, Greek, history, logic, and rhetoric had to be added.

Parallel Curricula. The legislation in Massachusetts showed quite clearly that what was wanted in the high school was an academy-style education at public expense. This law greatly influenced the development of the high school in other states. Not surprisingly, the pattern for curriculum organization in the high school was the same as that of the academy: parallel courses. Students were permitted to select a course of study but not the subjects within the course. The practice of allowing students to take only the studies that made up a course led to the rapid addition of parallel curricula. By 1900 the number of parallel courses of study offered in high schools had grown to thirty-six, ranging from an ancient classical course to a manual training course for girls.[74] (It should be remembered that the first high schools started out with two parallel courses: classical and English.) The problem was that there was no flexibility through the election of studies. Nor did this become an issue until the 1890s. Nevertheless, some of the more liberal high schools in Michigan and other Western states provided for partial election of subjects before 1880.

Curriculum Expansion and Equality of Opportunity.   There was another more fundamental reason for the expansion of the high-school program. It was an attempt to provide equality of educational opportunity: to make it possible for every boy and girl to discover and develop his or her talents. An intense faith in popular education and a, perhaps fortuitous, lack of agreement on the functions and purposes of the high school led to the development of programs in classical, industrial, commercial, cultural, scientific, artistic, and literary fields. Not only did manual training programs appear, but separate schools were established for training in this field. Commercial education developed more slowly but followed the same pattern. It may be said that from the close of the Civil War to the report of the Committee of Ten in 1893, the high school was increasingly socially responsive. The expanding curriculum reflected the aim of the high school to meet changing social needs.

There was no theoretical framework for curriculum development beyond the objectives of meeting student and societal needs and realizing the promise of democracy. The approach to change was, as put by Kandel, "venturesome and daring ... innovating and forward-looking ... fumbling and empirical."[75] In a very real sense it was also based on the theory of probability: It was thought that the greater the variety and number of programs, the more chance the pupil would have of finding the areas in which his or her capabilities might lie.

An Educational Revolution.   It is often mentioned that nineteenth-century educators neglected to consider the "what" of a liberal education in their obsession with the "how" of equalizing educational opportunity. What should be remembered, however, is that in 1889–90 only 6.7 percent of the fourteen- to seventeen-year-olds were enrolled in high school. In 1899–1900, high-school enrollment had nearly doubled but was still only 11.4 percent of the age group.[76] Thus, even the idea of high-school attendance was "forward-looking." What we are discussing is an educational revolution, with equality of opportunity as its driving force. The revolution provided the rationale for the growth of subjects and more practical curricula.

The Problem of Articulation. As the high school grew, so did its problems. From the start there were questions concerning its relationship with other parts of the educational system. Some of these problems were the result of being plugged into a system that was already in operation.

In the early 1870s in Boston, for example, boys were admitted to the English High School at the age of twelve but were being held back by grammar (elementary) school masters until they were fifteen. On the other hand, girls were not admitted to the High School for Girls until they were fourteen years old and had to wait around for a couple of years. The question naturally arose as to whether they might not be getting dull in the interim (as well as forgetting what they learned in grammar school). In response to this problem, the Boston School Committee suggested that assistant superintendents "examine and readjust our school machinery at the points of contact between the High and Grammar Schools."[77]

Problems such as the foregoing were relatively common and relatively easy to solve. But the underlying question was much more fundamental: What should be taught at each level? It was raised by resistant taxpayers who hinted broadly that much of the work of the high school overlapped that of the elementary school. It was also raised by the colleges that would have liked the secondary schools to begin work in the higher branches much earlier.

What was hoped for in the upward extension of the public schools was an educational system that would make possible an unbroken series of learning experiences. Thus, the School Committee of Windsor, Vermont, stated in 1845: "The schools are so arranged that the children of the district will now be able to pursue a regular course of studies, beginning with the alphabet, and continuing as far as in our best Academies."[78]

Yet in the crucial formative years of the public high school, admission to high school was by examination. This implied complete separation of the high school from the lower school. Gradually, a certificate of proficiency in elementary school subjects took the place of the examination. But by this time the break had become institutionalized. (It continues to be ritualized and reinforced today with graduation ceremonies and diplomas from lower schools.) The institutionalized break between the high school and the lower school had mitigated against the development of an unbroken curriculum. It owes its existence in no small way to the fact that the character of the secondary school was formed when it was not yet a part of the public school system.

Another reason for problems in articulation is that, until 1930, most children completed their education in the elementary school. The concept of the elementary school as a terminal institution led to a terminal view of the elementary curriculum. In this connection, one of the questions discussed but never settled by the Committee of Fifteen was whether the elementary curriculum should be the same for high-school-bound and non-high-schoolbound children. (Some committee members favored the European dual system of education.) If the decision had been made to put elementary children on two parallel tracks, it is almost certain that there would be less flexibility and opportunity for experimentation than exist today in elementary schools. Furthermore, the relationship between the elementary school and the high school would be similar to that of the high school and college.

The growing interest in high schools focused on the articulation of high school and college. From 1870 until the report of the Committee of Ten in 1893, this issue overshadowed other problems of secondary education. According to Wesley, the college-preparatory function of the high school "gained almost a monopoly of the thought and attention devoted to high schools" at conventions of the National Education Association during this period.[79] In 1888–90, only 14.4 percent of those enrolled in high school were preparing for college.[80] Thus, the curriculum of more than 85 percent of the students was being ignored to discuss the program of fewer than 15 percent.

COLLEGE DOMINANCE OVER THE HIGH SCHOOL

Among the most powerful figures in the NEA was Charles W. Eliot, president of Harvard University. As mentioned earlier, the appeals of Eliot and others for reform led to the appointment of three committees in the 1890s by the NEA. The Committee of Ten was created in response to demands for uniform college entrance requirements. Leaders in the movement for uniformity included James H. Baker of the University of Colorado and Nicholas Murray Butler of Columbia University. Baker, a strong believer in the value of the classical subjects for mental training, was appointed to serve on the committee, which included five college presidents.

Krug holds that "much of the demand for uniformity in college-admissions requirements came from the secondary-school men themselves."[81] He explains that even though most students did not go to college, the variations in requirements from college to college included not only the subjects but specific material to be covered. This entailed the time-consuming job of filling out detailed forms for each student and forced counselors to neglect those who were not college-bound.

On the other hand, Wesley describes the period preceding the appointment of the Committee of Ten as a period of war between the high schools and colleges.[82] The opening battle, he says, had been won by the high schools; they refused to teach Greek even though the colleges demanded it as an admission requirement. Their refusal, however, was not based on any principle concerning the usefulness of knowledge. It was, rather, a matter of circumstances: Teachers of Greek were scarce, and so were students who wanted to study Greek. By 1878, colleges in Ohio and Indiana had waived Greek as an entrance requirement. Some college men were beginning to fear that the high schools would, by refusing to teach certain subjects, set college standards. The report of the Committee of Ten assuaged their fears for at least a generation after its publication.

A Curriculum Hierarchy

The committee selected nine subjects on which recommendations would be made: (1) Latin; (2) Greek; (3) English; (4) other modern languages; (5) mathematics; (6) physics, astronomy, and chemistry; (7) natural history (biology, including botany, zoology, and physiology); (8) history, civil government, and political economy; and (9) geography (physical geography, geology, and meteorology). The choice of these subjects and the omission of others from consideration was enough to set the course for secondary education, and it did. The committee's refusal to discuss the place of art, music, physical education, and practical courses in the curriculum was based on the theory that these subjects had no disciplinary value. According to some observers, the effect of the report was to retard innovation in these areas. Nevertheless, the committee did decide that each of the nine recommended subjects were of equal value in disciplining the mind and enlarging its powers. This gave the so-called modern subjects the same status in the curriculum as Latin, Greek, and mathematics. This was not a unanimous decision; Baker wrote a minority report in which he argued that subjects differ in value for the training of the various powers.

Pushing Subject Matter Down.   When educational reforms are made from the top, they usually include a recommendation to begin instruction at a much earlier age. Thus, it might be expected that the Committee of Ten would suggest that the nine subjects be taught sooner. This is exactly what happened; it was urged that each subject be begun earlier, and that all subjects except Latin and Greek be taught in the elementary school. (Latin would begin in grade nine and Greek in grade ten.)

Superior and Inferior Tracks.   The committee presented four tables based on the recommendations of specialists in the nine subject areas. The proposals in Figure 2-2 were intended as a source for program development. From this table the committee constructed four parallel programs: Classical, Latin Scientific, Modern Languages, and English. The Classical and Latin Scientific programs required four years of Latin. The Modern Languages program required four years of French and German, whereas the English program called for four years of either Latin, German, or French. Commenting on the latter two programs, which did not require Latin, the committee stated: "The

Figure *2-2.*   Range of Curricular Offerings (High School) as Proposed by the Committee of Ten on Secondary School Studies, 1893

1st Secondary School Year	2nd Secondary School Year

Latin . . . . 5 p.
English Literature, 2 p. ⎫
  "   Composition, 2 p. ⎭ . . . . . 4 p.
German [or French] . . . . 5 p.
Algebra . . . . 4 p.
History of Italy, Spain, and France   3 p.
Applied Geography (European
  political–continental and
  oceanic flora and fauna . . . . 4 p.
                                             25 p.
	Latin . . . . 4 p.
	Greek . . . . 5 p.
	English Literature, 2 p. ⎫
	  " Composition, 2 p. ⎭ . . . . . 4 p.
	German, continued . . . . 4 p.
	French, begun . . . . 5 p.
	Algebra,* 2 p. ⎫
	Geometry 2 p. ⎭ . . . . 4 p.
	Botany or Zoology . . . . 4 p.
	English History to 1688 . . . . 3 p.
	                                            33 p.
	
	*Option of bookkeeping and commercial
	arithmetic.

3rd Secondary School Year	4th Secondary School Year

Latin . . . . 4 p.
Greek . . . . 4 p.
English Literature,   2 p. ⎫
  "   Composition, 1 p. ⎬ . . . . 4 p.
Rhetoric,   1 p. ⎭
German . . . . 4 p.
French . . . . 4 p.
Algebra,* 2 p. ⎫
Geometry,2 p. ⎭ . . . . 4 p.
Physics . . . . 4 p.
History, English and American . . . 3 p.
Astronomy, 3 p. 1st ½ yr. ⎫
Meteorology, 3 p. 2nd ½ yr. ⎭ . . . . 3 p.
                                             34 p
 	
*Option of bookkeeping and commercial
arithmetic.
	Latin . . . . 4 p.
	Greek . . . . 4 p.
	English Literature, 2 p. ⎫
	  " Composition, 1 p. ⎬ . . . . . 4 p.
	  " Grammar, 1 p. ⎭
	German . . . . 4 p.
	French . . . . 4 p.
	Trigonometry, ⎫
	Higher Algebra, ⎭ . . . . 2 p.
	Chemistry . . . . 4 p.
	History (intensive) and Civil
	  Government . . . . 3 p.
	Geology or Physiography, ⎫
	  4 p. 1st ½ yr. ⎬ . . . . . . 4 p.
	Anatomy, Physiology, and ⎪
	  Hygiene, 4 p. 2nd ½ yr. ⎭
	                                            33 p.

Source: Committee of Ten, *Report of the Committee of Ten on Secondary School Studies* (Washington, D.C.: National Education Association, 1893), p. 4.

programs called respectively Modern Languages and English must in practice be distinctly inferior to the other two."[83] Thus the committee had created a track system, with two superior and two inferior tracks. Yet the committee intended all four programs to be equally acceptable for admission to college.

Every educational issue that stirs much controversy in its time is fated to be replaced by a new center of controversy. And so it was with the problem of the relative worth of classical versus modern subjects. As the American people continued to bring the school closer to life by introducing stenography, typing, and vocational programs into the curriculum, the center of debate shifted. As Diane Ravitch points out, the classical curriculum and the modern academic subjects became, simply, the "college preparatory curriculum." But she goes on to state that "what had once been a contest between the classical curriculum and the modern subjects became converted in a short span of years into a rivalry between a traditional curriculum and a practical curriculum."[84]

What Ravitch does not point out is how quickly the programs that did not require Latin became "traditional" (new traditions), thus attesting to the changing and more progressive character of the school. Thus, Latin was replaced by modern foreign languages. More importantly, what is traditional is determined by the public and the profession at any given time. Given a pragmatic people, practical studies (typing, for instance) became traditional. Moreover, laboratory methods in the sciences were advanced enthusiastically after 1900 and eventually became traditionally accepted. The clear applications of scientific and technical knowledge in industry, in addition to the enormous increase in scientific knowledge, could not help but influence the secondary curriculum—including the subjects studied for college entrance.

Differentiation and Destination. One of the questions considered by the Committee of Ten was whether subjects should be taught differently to pupils going to college. The committee decided that every subject should be taught in the same way and in the same depth to every pupil, no matter what the pupil's probable destination. When the report was attacked for this stand, Eliot defended the committee's position, arguing that the European system of classifying children into "future peasants, mechanics, trades-people, merchants, and professional people" was unacceptable in a democratic society.[85]

The report states without equivocation that "secondary schools do not exist for the purpose of preparing boys and girls for colleges."[86] Yet the only subjects discussed are those that colleges required for entrance. This statement is indeed paradoxical and has been regarded by many as pious hypocrisy. It is doubtful that any hypocrisy was intended. Clearly, the committee considered preparation for college to be the best preparation for practical life activities.

An Important Precedent for the Curriculum Field

The report came at a time when the theory of mental discipline was undergoing critical examination. Faculty psychology had had its day, and a new psychology was being born. A sizable number of secondary-school educators were beginning to look at Herbartian educational psychology in terms of the high school. Yet the conservative recommendations of this report perpetuated the traditional subjects and methods for the next quarter century. It is also clear that the report established an important precedent—that of subject-matter specialists as curriculum makers.

Unresolved Problem of Articulation. There can be little doubt that the report effected an improvement in the relations between high school and college. It led to the appointment in 1895 of the Committee on College Entrance Requirements. The report of this committee proposed that four units in foreign language, two units in English, two in mathematics, one in science, and one in history be required for college entrance, in addition to six units of free electives. The latter were to be selected from among the nine subjects recommended by the Committee of Ten.

It should not be assumed, however, that these committees resolved the problem of curriculum articulation between the high school and college. Indeed, this problem is still very much with us today.

New Curriculum Issues

At the close of the nineteenth century, the high schools were faced with a growing number of problems bearing on the curriculum. Many students dropped out, vocational education was too little and too late, and instruction was formal and unindividualized. In short, the curriculum ignored the needs of adolescents. The report of the Committee of Ten was a big setback in this regard.

In 1900, the number of public-high-school graduates was only 11.9 percent of those enrolled.[87] Among the reasons most frequently given by students who dropped out was a lack of interest in school, thus pointing to the need for a more useful curriculum.

As indicated earlier, most youngsters never even entered high school. Needless to say, educators were concerned about the failure of the high school to attract and hold the school-age population.

Many of the children who left school did so for jobs in mills and factories, jobs largely without promise of advancement. The fact that the schools did not provide a practical curriculum put them in a vulnerable position. Increasingly, they were blamed for child labor. By 1907, vocational education had become the dominant educational issue. This raised new curriculum issues. The question of what constituted a liberal education, always puzzling, was asked anew in connection with the separate schools being established for the teaching of manual training and commercial education.

Eliot's ideal education stressed free electives. He believed that this was the only way individuals could discover and develop their talents. Eliot's program was not endorsed by the Committee of Ten, but the question of free choices remained. How much of the student's program should permit the sampling of studies and how much should be devoted to the transmission of common learnings? This question loomed larger than ever as the nineteenth century came to a close.

One of the most perplexing problems plaguing the high school was the question of method. What was sought was a method "carefully differentiated from the elementary school, on the one hand, and from college method, on the other."[88] According to one observer, at the close of the last century the high school was "waiting confidently" for three reforms: (1) a reorganization of its curriculum content, (2) a new method based on psychological principles, and (3) a new spirit that would relate the curriculum more closely to life and the ideas of democracy.[89] The Revolution was still, in the words of Benjamin Rush, not over.

EDUCATION AND SOCIETY: A RETROSPECTIVE OF EVENTS (1642–1899)

Table 2-1 presents a chronological list, or timetable, of events in education and society spanning the years from the mid-seventeenth century to the end of the nineteenth century. The timetable of events in society illustrates certain developments in politics, daily life, science and technology, and the arts to give the reader a sense of perspective of the human past. Many of the societal events in Table 2-1 do not have a direct bearing in sequence or consequence on the educational events listed, but they provide us with a flavor of the times. For example, in the year 1654, when Comenius published the first picture book for children, Germany was just getting over the devastating impact of the plague, which had caused the loss of half its population over the preceeding three decades. In 1856, when the University of Iowa opened and admitted females on equal terms with males, Gustave Flaubert published the controversial and widely censored *Madame Bovary,* and Sigmund Freud was born.

Darwin's *Origin of Species,* published in 1859, the year John Dewey was born, was to exert a profound influence on Dewey, who viewed knowledge as dynamic rather than immutable, education as growth, and human nature as flexible. Incredible as it may seem, the battle against Darwin and science has continued to this day, with religious fundamentalists demanding the teaching of "creation theory" alongside evolution in the school curriculum.

The great advances in science and technology, coupled with the practical needs for national reconstruction after the Civil War, led Lincoln to sign the Morrill Act of 1862, which provided for the establishment of a national network of "people's colleges" of agriculture and the mechanic arts—institutions that were to become the great state universities. The advances in science and technology led to the beginnings of laboratory instruction in school science during the last quarter of the nineteenth century, despite great opposition by the traditionalists. The efforts of progressive educators to extend educational opportunity during the last quarter of the nineteenth century corresponded with the ideas in the novels and stories of Mark Twain concerning human potential and social justice.

At the end of the nineteenth century, the British Empire encompassed one-fifth of the world's population and one-fourth of the earth's surface. The old classical education was deemed appropriate for the privileged who were

TABLE *2-1* Timetable of Events in Education and Society: 1642–1899

YEAR	EDUCATION	SOCIETY
1642	Johann A. Comenius (1592–1670): *A Reformation of Schools*	All theaters in England closed by order of the Puritans (to 1660)
		Galileo Galilei dies (born 1564); forced by Inquisition in 1633 to recant his support of Copernican theory
1647	Massachusetts Law of 1647 required establishment of Latin grammar schools (English origin) to teach knowledge of the scriptures	English civil war
1654	Johann A. Comenius publishes first book for children	Germany loses more than half its population to the plague between 1618 and 1654
1749	Benjamin Franklin (1706–90): *Proposals Relating to the Youth in Pennsylvania,* calls for a new kind of school, the academy, to replace the Latin grammar school; first academy opens in Philadelphia in 1751, becomes University of Pennsylvania in 1777 (by 1820 the tuition academy had all but replaced the Latin grammar school)	Georgia becomes a colony; first settlement of Ohio Company; sign language for deaf invented; Henry Fielding: *The History of Tom Jones, a Foundling*
1762	Jean Jacques Rousseau (1712–78): *Émile*	First exhibition of agricultural machines (London, 1761)
	First British school for the "deaf and dumb" opened (Edinburgh, 1760)	
1779	Thomas Jefferson (1743–1826): *A Bill for the More General Diffusion of Knowledge* proposed establishment of a complete system of public education (secular) in Virginia including free elementary schools, secondary schools, and a state college. Jefferson's plan defeated (temporarily)	First children's clinic (London)
1781	Johann H. Pestalozzi (1746–1827): *Leonard and Gertrude*	End of all land engagements in the American Revolution with British defeat at Yorktown

TABLE *2-1*   Timetable of Events in Education and Society: 1642–1899

YEAR	EDUCATION	SOCIETY
1783	Noah Webster (1758–1843): *American Spelling Book,* the first distinctively American textbook (spelling and reading) supersedes the gloomily religious *New England Primer* and helps create a unified American language in contrast to the class-divided language in England	Great Britain recognizes independence of United States; Beethoven's first works published
1806	First Lancastrian (Joseph Lancaster, England) school opened in New York City, leading to monitorial instruction and mechanical recitation, which spread in popularity over the ensuing quarter of a century	John Stuart Mill born (died 1873); England prohibits slave trade (1807); street lighting by gas in London (1807)
1818	Boston appropriates funds for establishment of infant schools (originated in Scotland, 1799) to prepare children for the "grammar" schools; infant schools popularize Pestalozzian object teaching; infant schools absorbed into primary schools after 1850	Illinois becomes a state; Karl Marx born (died 1883); first steamship crosses Atlantic (*Savannah,* 26 days)
1819	University of Virginia founded by Thomas Jefferson	Napoleon dies (born 1769); Missouri becomes a state; Faraday discovers fundamentals of electromagnetism; population of Great Britain 20.8 million, France 30.4 million, U.S. 9.6 million
1825	Noah Webster: *The American Dictionary*	French law makes sacrilege a capital offense; opening of first passenger railroad line (England)
1827	Massachusetts Law of 1827 establishes public high schools mandating practical studies (no counterpart for this institution in Europe); replaces tuition academy toward end of 19th century	Beethoven dies (born 1770); Pestalozzi dies (born 1746); Karl Baedeker publishes his first travel guide

(cont.)

TABLE *2-1* Timetable of Events in Education and Society: 1642–1899

YEAR	EDUCATION	SOCIETY
1828	Noah Webster: *American Dictionary of the English Language*	Andrew Jackson defeats John Quincy Adams for Presidency; construction begins on first U.S. railroad for passengers and freight (B&O)
1836	William H. McGuffey (1800–73): *First and Second Readers,* the beginning of a series of graded readers; helps establish the graded school with its class organization	Davy Crockett killed at Alamo; Texas wins independence from Mexico and becomes a republic; Arkansas admitted to the Union; first botanical textbook published
1837	Horace Mann (1796–1859) becomes Secretary of the Massachusetts Board of Education, which he helped create; devotes career to democratizing and modernizing the public schools (universal, nonsectarian, and free); issues first of 12 Annual Reports	Michigan becomes a state; electric telegraph patented; E. P. Lovejoy, editor of abolitionist paper, murdered by Mob in Alton, Ill.; financial panic in U.S.
	Friedrich Froebel (1782–1852) opens first kindergarten (Germany)	
1855	Henry Barnard (1811–1900) establishes *American Journal of Education*	Walt Whitman (1819–92): *Leaves of Grass;* London sewers modernized after cholera epidemic; Florence Nightingale (1820–1910) introduces hygienic standards in military hospitals
	Herbert Spencer (1861–1947): *Principles of Psychology*	
1856	University of Iowa opens, admitting women on equal terms with men (all state universities west of Mississippi coeducational from the start)	James Buchanan elected President; Bessemer perfects process for steel making; Sigmund Freud born (died 1939); George Bernard Shaw born (died 1950); Gustave Flaubert: *Madame Bovary*
1859	Morrill Act to create land-grant colleges passed by Congress, vetoed by President Buchanan	Charles Darwin (1809–82): *On the Origin of Species by Natural Selection;* Charles Dickens: *A Tale of Two Cities;* John Stuart Mill: *Essay on Liberty;* first oil well drilled (Titusville, Pa.); first practical storage battery; work on Suez Canal begins

TABLE *2-1*   Timetable of Events in Education and Society: 1642–1899

YEAR	EDUCATION	SOCIETY
1860	Herbert Spencer: *What Knowledge Is of Most Worth?* published in U.S. First English-language kindergarten in U.S. (private)	Abraham Lincoln elected President; South Carolina secedes from Union in protest against Lincoln; first practical internal combustion engine constructed; primitive typewriter invented in U.S.
1862	President Lincoln signs Morrill Act providing land grants for establishment of national network of land-grant colleges and universities of agriculture and the mechanic arts (the "people's colleges," which evolve into the great state universities)	Emancipation Proclamation; Pasteur's research links microorganisms with disease (germ theory), beginning scientific medicine
1865	Federal government creates bureau to provide schools for freed blacks in the South, with hundreds of teachers from the North enlisted to help the effort Cornell, MIT, Purdue, University of Kentucky, University of Maine founded	U.S. Civil War ends; Abraham Lincoln assassinated; Thirteenth Amendment abolishes slavery; Atlantic cable completed; Joseph Lister initiates antiseptic surgery; first oil pipeline (Pa.); Ku Klux Klan founded (Pulaski, Tenn.); first railroad sleeping cars appear in U.S. (Pullman); Gregor Mendel (1822–84): *Law of Heredity;* Lewis Carroll (C. L. Dodgson): *Alice's Adventure in Wonderland*
1867	Henry Barnard becomes first U.S. Commissioner of Education U.S. Department of Education established without Cabinet rank (reduced to Office of Education in 1868; gains Cabinet status in 1979)	Nebraska becomes a state; Russia sells Alaska to U.S. for $7.2 million; Karl Marx: *Das Kapital,* Vol. 1; bicycle manufacturing begins
1873	First permanent chair in education established at the University of Iowa (became a department in 1890 and a school of education in 1907); in 1879 the Department of the Science and Art of Teaching created at the University of Michigan First public school kindergarten in U.S. (St. Louis) at initiation of Supt. William T. Harris	Tolstoy: *Anna Karenina;* Herbert Spencer: *The Study of Sociology;* James C. Maxwell; *Electricity and Magnetism;* Remington gunsmith firm begins manufacture of typewriters

(cont.)

TABLE *2-1*   Timetable of Events in Education and Society: 1642–1899

YEAR	EDUCATION	SOCIETY
	Laboratory instruction in school science begins to find a place in the curriculum	
1875	Francis W. Parker (1837–1902), superintendent of schools in Quincy, Massachusetts, develops "Quincy system" of progressive education, leading to his theory of curriculum concentration or synthesis based upon Herbart's theory of correlation and concentration	Mark Twain (1835–1910): *The Adventures of Tom Sawyer;* London Medical School for Women founded; London's main sewage system completed
1880	Child-study movement initiated by G. Stanley Hall (1844–1924)	James A. Garfield elected President; Auguste Rodin: *The Thinker;* Thomas A. Edison and Joseph W. Swan independently devise first practical electric light; New York streets are first lit by electricity
1883	Lester F. Ward (1841–1913): *Dynamic Sociology*	Reform of U.S. Civil Service begins (to 1901); Metropolitan Opera House (N.Y.) opens; Bismarck introduces health insurance in Germany; Northern Pacific Railroad completed; Brooklyn Bridge opens; first skyscraper (10 stories) built in Chicago
1884	Charles W. Eliot (1834–1926) introduces elective system at Harvard College	Grover Cleveland elected President; Mark Twain: *Huckleberry Finn;* Ilya Mechnikov: *Theory of Phagocytes;* discovery of tetanus bacillus
1888	New York College for the Training of Teachers formed with Nicholas Murray Butler as president (became Teachers College in 1889; Butler served as President of Columbia University, 1902–45)	Benjamin Harrison elected President; Edward Bellamy: *Looking Backward, 2000–1887;* George Eastman perfects box camera; pneumatic tire invented
1892	National Herbart Society founded in U.S. after the German society to study and advance the ideas of Johann F. Herbart (1776–1841). Departing from its original purpose, the society changed its	Walt Whitman dies; Tchaikovsky: *The Nutcracker;* Diesel patents his internal combustion engine; first automatic telephone switchboard; Jacob A Riis: *The Children of the Poor*

TABLE *2-1*   Timetable of Events in Education and Society: 1642–1899

YEAR	EDUCATION	SOCIETY
	name to the National Society for the Scientific Study of Education in 1900, and to the National Society for the Study of Education in 1909	
1893	Report of the Committee of Ten on Secondary School Studies (NEA); chaired by Harvard President Charles W. Eliot	Karl Benz constructs his four-wheel auto; Henry Ford builds his first car
1894	Francis W. Parker: *Talks on Pedagogics*	French army Captain Alfred Dreyfus arrested, convicted of treason, and imprisoned on Devil's Island (Dreyfus cleared in 1899; "Dreyfus Affair" eventuated in separation of church and state in France); plague bacillus discovered; George Bernard Shaw: *Arms and the Man*
1895	Report of the Committee of Fifteen on Elementary Education (NEA) proposes eight-year elementary school in place of ten	H. G. Wells: *The Time Machine;* Karl Marx: *Das Kapital,* Vol. 3 (post.); London School of Economics founded: Röntgen discovers X -rays
1896	The Dewey Laboratory School opens at the University of Chicago	Utah becomes a state; William McKinley elected President; Nobel Prizes established with death of Alfred Nobel (dynamite); discovery of helium; Niagara Falls hydroelectric plant opens; first modern Olympics held in Athens; Puccini: *La Bohème;* Klondike gold rush begins
1899	Report of the Committee on College Entrance Requirements (NEA) John Dewey (1859–1952): *The School and Society* College Entrance Examination Board founded	First Peace Conference at The Hague; first magnetic recording of sound; British Empire encompasses one-fifth of the world's population and one-fourth of the earth's surface

Sources: *Annual Register of World Events* (London: Longman's, Green); Bernard Grun, *The Time-tables of History,* rev. ed. (New York: Simon & Schuster, 1979), based upon Werner Stein's *Kulturfahrplan* (Munich, W. Germany: F. A. Herbig Verlagsbuchhandlung, 1963); *The New York Times.*

destined to govern the British Empire. It was not until the end of World War II, when the empire disintegrated, that the need for wholesale reconstruction of the British school system was recognized to provide for the extension of educational opportunity through the secondary school, along with the modernization of the curriculum and the expansion of state support for higher education.

Although the list of events in education and society (Table 2-1) is organized chronologically, the reader will recognize that the events are not linear but interrelated in a stream, with many currents and crosscurrents. The events selected are illustrative of the human experience over time.

PERSPECTIVE

Nowhere was the impact of the American Revolution more revolutionary than in education. The natural-rights philosophy and the environmentalist conception of human nature, which were popularized by the Revolution, led to demands for an American culture that is as inclusive as possible. Girls as well as boys should have opportunities to study. Schooling in public schools should be available to every citizen. The bright promise of America was opportunity. However, there was more at issue than the rights of man (and woman). As Jefferson so well knew, an educated public was an indispensable condition for the survival of a republic.

The awakening of interest in schools led to the early delineation of key curriculum problems. Before 1830, educators advanced the theory that the curriculum would always have to change to meet the constantly changing needs of society. The question of what subjects are of most worth in a public school system arose with the establishment of state support for education. Educators based their responses on the doctrines of faculty psychology: Worthy subject matter would enlarge the intellectual, physical, and moral faculties. In practice, however, attention was focused on the intellectual faculties.

Nineteenth-century educational reformers were concerned about the time, sometimes years, spent by children in reviewing and repeating what they had studied before. It seemed that there was motion but not much progress. The remedy that was most commonly proposed was curriculum expansion. Three widely accepted ideas about the nature of knowledge and how children learn mitigated against expansion: (1) the theory of mental discipline, which held that some subjects are better than others for training the mind; (2) the idea that the "fundamentals" should be "learned thoroughly" before beginning additional studies; and (3) the theory that the fields of knowledge constitute a series of subjects that vary in difficulty, so that one subject should be "completed" before the child attempts to master the concepts of other, "higher" subjects.

Nevertheless, pressures for expansion caused the curriculum to develop by accretion. Supported by tradition and the theory of mental discipline, the older subjects continued to maintain their dominance in the curriculum. In the 1890s, in response to agitation for curriculum reform, the National Education Association appointed the Committee of Fifteen on Elementary Education and the Committee of Ten on Secondary School Studies. Despite the profound influence of the ideas of Pestalozzi, Froebel, and Herbart on educational thinking, the reports of both committees were based on the theory of mental discipline.

The concept that education should be individualized was advanced before 1890 by Charles W. Eliot of Harvard. An influential leader in the NEA, Eliot called for the election of studies from elementary school through college. Only then would children and youth be able to discover and develop their talents. Neither this idea nor Eliot's advocation that elementary-school science be taught by laboratory methods was endorsed by the NEA curriculum committees.

The Latin grammar school died because it did not change its curriculum to meet the changing demands of society. It was supplanted by the tuition academy, which offered both a college preparatory curriculum and a curriculum for "life." Perhaps as a reaction to the schools that taught only Latin and Greek, the curriculum of the academy was broad and innovative. The academy led the colleges in recognition of the place of science in education.

The character of the high school was shaped by its predecessor, the academy. Like the academy, the first high schools were dual-purpose institutions, offering a classical curriculum for the college-bound and an "English" curriculum for the terminal student. The number of curricula rapidly multiplied for two reasons: there was no flexibility through the election of subjects, and the aim of the high school was to meet expanding social needs.

Other than the goal of equalizing educational opportunity, there was no theoretical basis for curriculum development in the high school. Many observers believe that nineteenth-century secondary-school educators gave short shrift to the "what" of a liberal education in their anxiety to develop socially responsive and attractive programs. Yet it must be pointed out that less than 7 percent of the fourteen- to seventeen-year-old age group was enrolled in high school in 1889–90. Thus, even the idea of high-school attendance was "innovative." The objective of the high school to make it possible for every boy and girl to realize his or her potential was not to emerge until the twentieth century was well under way. The high school was yet to become the focus of an educational revolution.

The Committee of Ten considered preparation for college to be the best preparation for life. Their report established the precedent of subject-matter specialists as curriculum makers.

By the close of the nineteenth century, a growing number of secondary-school educators had endorsed a third principle for program development, in addition to scholarship and preparing students for life activities. This principle or viewpoint was the growth and development of the student.

NOTES

1. James G. Carter, *Essays Upon Popular Education* (Boston: Bowles and Dearborn, 1826), Preface.

2. Sol Cohen, "The Forming of the Common School," in George F. Kneller (ed.), *Foundations of Education* (New York: Wiley, 1971), p. 8.

3. Carter, op. cit., Preface.

4. Lawrence A. Cremin, *Traditions of American Education* (New York: Basic Books, 1977), pp. 36–37.

5. In Andrew A. Lipscomb (ed.), *The Writings of Thomas Jefferson,* vol. 2 (Washington, D.C.: Thomas Jefferson Memorial Association, 1903), pp. 84–85.

6. Jennings L. Wagoner, Jr., "Honor and Dishonor at Mr. Jefferson's University: The Antebellum Years," *History of Education Quarterly* 26 (Summer 1986): 156.

7. Jefferson to Littleton Waller Tazewell, January 5, 1805. Cited in Merrill D. Petersen (ed.), *Thomas Jefferson, Writings* (New York: Library of America, 1984), p. 1151.

8. See Clifton Johnson, *Old-Time Schools and School Books* (New York: Macmillan, 1917), p. 138.

9. Warren Burton, *The District School As It Was* (New York: Arno Press and The New York Times, 1969; first published by Crowell in 1928), p. 114.

10. Colyer Meriwether, *Our Colonial Curriculum* (Washington, D.C.: Capital, 1907), p. 25.

11. Cited in Walter H. Small, *Early New England Schools* (Boston: Ginn, 1914), p. 281.

12. Johnson, op. cit., pp. 138–39.

13. Noah Webster, in Homer D. Babbidge, Jr. (ed.), *Noah Webster On Being American* (New York: Praeger, 1967), p. 101.

14. Henry Steele Commager, "Schoolmaster to America," in *Noah Webster's American Spelling Book* (New York: Teachers College Press, 1962), pp. 1, 5.

15. Ibid.

16. Eleanor Wilson Orr, *Twice As Less* (New York: Norton, 1987).

17. R. Freeman Butts and Lawrence A. Cremin, *A History of Education in American Culture* (New York: Holt, Rinehart and Winston, 1953), p. 74.

18. As quoted in Alonzo Potter and George B. Emerson, *The School and the Schoolmaster* (New York: Harper & Row, 1858), p. 114.

19. Merle Curti, *The Growth of American Thought,* 3rd ed. (New York: Harper & Row, 1964), p. 343.

20. Gerald A. Ponder, "Schooling and Control: Some Interpretations of the Changing Nature of the Curriculum," in *Perspectives on Curriculum Development 1776–1976,* 1976 Yearbook of the Association for Supervision and Curriculum Development (Washington, D.C.: The Association, 1976), p. 145.

21. John Dewey, *Democracy and Education* (New York: Macmillan, 1916), pp. 142–44.

22. Quoted in *American Journal of Education* 2 (April 1827): 243.

23. Thomas A. Palmer, *The Teacher's Manual: Being an Exposition of an Efficient and Economical System of Education, Suited to the Wants of a Free People* (Boston: Thomas H. Webb, 1843), pp. 12–49.

24. *American Journal of Education,* vol. 5 (March 1830), pp. 113–15.

25. Ibid., pp. 113–14.

26. Ibid., p. 114.

27. Ibid., p. 115.

28. Ibid., p. 117.

29. As quoted in Potter and Emerson, op. cit., p. 181.

30. John Swett, *History of the Public School System of California* (San Francisco: Bancroft, 1876), p. 126.

31. Potter and Emerson, op. cit., p. 203.

32. Henry Barnard, "Editorial Address," *Connecticut Common School Journal* 3 (November 1, 1840): 11.

33. Warren Burton, op. cit., p. 55.

34. Ellwood P. Cubberley, *Public Education in the United States,* rev. ed. (Boston: Houghton Mifflin, 1947), p. 131.

35. *American Journal of Education* 3 (May 1828): 288.

36. Ibid., p. 293.

37. Ibid., p. 295.

38. Cubberley, op. cit., p. 137.

39. Murry R. Nelson, "Issues of Access to Knowledge: Dropping Out of School," Chapter 10 in *Critical Issues in Curriculum,* Eighty-seventh Yearbook, National Society for the Study of Education, Part II, (Chicago: University of Chicago Press, 1988), p. 237.

40. John H. Chambers, "Teaching Thinking Throughout the Curriculum—Where Else?," *Educational Leadership* 45 (April 1988): 4.

41. Stanley Pogrow, "Teaching Thinking to At-Risk Elementary Students," *Educational Leadership* 45 (April 1988): p. 80.

42. Wilbur B. Brookover, "Quality of Educational Attainment, Standardized Testing, Assessment, and Accountability," Chapter 8 in *Uses of the Sociology of Education,* Seventy-third Yearbook, Part II, National Society for the Study of Education (University of Chicago Press, 1974), p. 162.

43. Burke A. Hinsdale, *Horace Mann and the Common School Revival* (New York: Scribner, 1898), p. 60.

44. John Chodes, "Public Education—Dump It," *The New York Times* (December 19, 1988), p. A17.

45. American Institute of Instruction, *Discourse and Lectures* (Boston: Hillgard, Gray, Little and Wilkins, 1831), p. 98.

46. Ibid., p. 104.

47. Ibid.

48. Ibid., p. 102.

49. Ibid.

50. Ibid., p. 97.

51. Mrs. Howland, *The Infant School Manual* (Worcester, Mass.: Dorr and Howland, 1830), p. 2.

52. Ibid., p. 54.

53. American Institute of Instruction, op. cit., pp. 114–15.

54. *Chicago Evening Post,* October 13, 1894, as quoted in *Educational Review* 7 (December 1894): 515.

55. Herbert Spencer, "What Knowledge Is of Most Worth?," Chapter 1 in *Education* (New York: Appleton, 1860), p. 32.

56. Ibid., pp. 124–25.

57. John M. Gregory, "Some Fundamental Inquiries Concerning Common School Studies," National Education Association *Proceedings* (Washington, D.C.: The Association, 1883), p. 121.

58. *American Journal of Education* 2 (February 1827): 67–68.

59. Ann Taylor Allen, " 'Let Us Live with Our Children': Kindergarten Movements in Germany and the United States, 1840–1914," *History of Education Quarterly* 28 (Spring 1988): 23.

60. Henry Steele Commager, *The Commonwealth of Learning* (New York: Harper & Row, 1968), p. 16.

61. Allen, op. cit., p. 23.

62. Ibid., p. 34.

63. Commager, op. cit., pp. 22–23.

64. Charles W. Eliot, "Can School Programs be Shortened and Enriched?," National Education Association *Proceedings* (Washington, D.C.: The Association, 1893), pp. 617–25.

65. Ibid.

66. Cubberley, op. cit., p. 543.

67. National Education Association, "Report of the Committee of Fifteen," *Educational Review* 9 (March 1895): 270.

68. Ibid., p. 275.

69. Emit D. Grizzell, *Origin and Development of the High School in New England Before 1865* (New York: Macmillan, 1923), p. 27.

70. Cubberley, op. cit., p. 249.

71. Thomas Cushing, *Historical Sketch of Chauncy-Hall School* (Boston: Press of David Clapp and Son, 1895), pp. 39–40.

72. Carter, op. cit., p. 24.

73. Ibid.

74. Isaac L. Kandel, *History of Secondary Education* (Boston: Houghton Mifflin, 1930), p. 458.

75. Ibid., pp. 460–61.

76. U.S. Office of Education, *Digest of Educational Statistics* (Washington, D.C.: U.S. Department of Health, Education, and Welfare, 1978), p. 44.

77. *Annual Report of the School Committee of the City of Boston: 1872,* p. 15.

78. Grizzell, op. cit., p. 233.

79. Edgar B. Wesley, *NEA: The First Hundred Years* (New York: Harper & Row, 1957), p. 67.

80. Commissioner of Education, *Report for the Year 1889–90* (Washington, D.C.: Bureau of Education, 1893), vol. 2, pp. 1388–89.

81. Edward A. Krug, *Charles W. Eliot and Popular Education* (New York: Teachers College Press, 1961), p. 6.

82. Wesley, op. cit., pp. 70–73.

83. National Education Association, *Report of the Committee of Ten on Secondary School Studies* (New York: American Book, 1894), p. 48.

84. Diane Ravitch, "Curriculum in Crisis: Connections Between Past and Present," in John H. Bunzel (ed.), *Challenge to American Schools: The Case for Standards and Values* (New York: Oxford, 1985), p. 72.

85. "The Fundamental Assumptions in the Report of the Committee of Ten," *Educational Review* 30 (November 1905): 330.

86. National Education Association, *Report of the Committee of Ten on Secondary School Studies,* op. cit., p. 51.

87. Commissioner of Education, *Report for the Year 1899–1900* (Washington, D.C.: Bureau of Education, 1901), vol. 2, p. 2122.

88. Frank Webster Smith, *The High School* (New York: Sturgis and Walton, 1916), p. 354.

89. Ibid.

SELECTED REFERENCES

Association for Supervision and Curriculum Development. *Perspectives on Curriculum Development 1776–1976,* 1976 Yearbook. Washington, D.C.: The Association, 1976.

Barnard, Henry, ed. *American Journal of Education,* vols. 1–32 (1855–82).

Burton, Warren. *The District School As It Was.* New York: Arno Press and The New York Times, 1969; originally published in 1928 by Thomas Y. Crowell.

Butler, Nicolas Murray. *The Meaning of Education.* New York: Macmillan, 1907.

Butts, F. Freeman. *Public Education in the United States From Revolution to Reform.* New York: Holt, Rinehart and Winston, 1978.

Commager, Henry S. "Schoolmaster to America," in *Noah Webster's Spelling Book.* New York: Teachers College Press, 1962, pp. 1–12.

Cremin, Lawrence A. *The American Common School: An Historic Conception.* New York: Teachers College Press, 1951.

———. *American Education: The Colonial Experience, 1607–1783.* New York: Harper & Row, 1970.

———. *Traditions of American Education.* New York: Basic Books, 1977.

———. *American Education: The National Experience, 1783–1876.* New York: Harper & Row, 1980.

De Garmo, Charles. *Herbart and the Herbartians.* New York: Scribner, 1912.

Dunkel, Harold B. *Herbart and Herbartianism: An Educational Ghost Story.* Chicago: University of Chicago Press, 1970.

Grizzell, Emit D. *Origin and Development of the High School in New England Before 1865.* New York: Macmillan, 1923.

Hinsdale, Burke A. *Horace Mann and the Common School Revival in the United States.* New York: Scribner, 1898.

Johnson, Clifton. *Old-Time Schools and School Books.* New York: Macmillan, 1917.

Kaestle, Carl F. *The Evolution of an Urban School System: New York City, 1750–1850.* Cambridge: Harvard University Press, 1973.

————. *Joseph Lancaster and the Monitorial School Movement.* New York: Teachers College Press, 1973.

Krug, Edward A. *Charles W. Eliot and Popular Education.* New York: Teachers College Press, 1961.

Meriwether, Colyer. *Our Colonial Curriculum 1607–1776.* Folcroft Library Editions, 1976. (Originally published in 1907 by Capitol Publishing Co.)

Monroe, Will S. *History of the Pestalozzian Movement in the United States.* Syracuse, N.Y.: C. W. Bardeen, 1907.

National Education Association. *Report of the Committee of Ten on Secondary School Studies.* New York: Arno Press and The New York Times, 1969. (Originally published in 1893 by the U.S. Government Printing Office.)

————. *Report of the Committee of Fifteen.* New York: Arno Press and The New York Times, 1969. (Originally published in 1895 by the New England Publishing Company.)

National Society for the Study of Education. *The National Herbart Society Yearbook 1–5, 1895–1899.* New York: Arno Press and The New York Times, 1969.

Pestalozzi, Johann Heinrich. *How Gertrude Teaches Her Children.* London: George Allen Unwin Ltd., 1894.

Spencer, Herbert. *Education.* New York: Appleton-Century-Crofts, 1894.

Vandewalker, Nina C. *The Kindergarten in American Education.* New York: Macmillan, 1917.

Wesley, Edgar B. *NEA: The First Hundred Years.* New York: Harper & Row, 1957.

Part II

TRANSFORMATION AND REFORMATION— SCIENCE AND SENTIMENT

When the American Creed is once detected, the cacophony becomes a melody.

—GUNNAR MYRDAL

Human interest and passion for human progress break down barriers centuries old.

—LILLIAN WALD

3

The New Education and the Democratic Prospect

In the second year of the twentieth century John Dewey read a paper at the National Education Association (NEA) meeting in Detroit in which he discussed the nature of educational theory and reform since Horace Mann. Dewey, then head of the departments of philosophy, psychology, and pedagogy at the University of Chicago, told the association that for a half century after the time of Horace Mann, theoretical activity had centered on the methods of teaching and the atmosphere of the school. So well had Mann and the disciples of Pestalozzi done their job that ideas once revolutionary had become commonplace in pedagogical literature and meetings.[1]

THE CHANGING FOCUS OF EDUCATIONAL THEORY

The last quarter of the nineteenth century, however, witnessed a decided change in focus, as educational theorists were giving greater attention to the curriculum. This was absolutely necessary, said Dewey, for three reasons: (1) the new methods were fundamentally incompatible with existing school materials and subject matter, (2) the curriculum was badly congested because of the addition of so many new studies, and (3) there was a fundamental conflict between new and old studies, a conflict over the intellectual and moral value of the traditional versus the new.

Moreover, the educational literature of the nineteenth century was predominantly concerned with the issue of instructional method. A preoccupation with instructional method is revealed in the literature from the 1830s, when Mann argued for the "word method" in reading instruction, to 1880, when reports indicated the children in Quincy, Massachusetts, were superior in reading and writing to children elsewhere in the nation as a result of the adoption of the methods of Colonel Francis W. Parker.

Method and Educational Theory

In effect, educational method was perceived by many to be the entire realm of educational theory. An illustration of this is an article published in 1882 in *Education* by Jerome Allen, principal of a state normal school in Minnesota, who asked if we have a science of education. The question was rhetorical; the discussion that followed was an affirmation of the existence of a science of education consisting of "fundamental propositions standing in the same relation to a human being that Newton's laws of gravitation and motion do to the physical universe."[2] What were advanced as scientific propositions, however, were principles for pedagogical procedure such as putting the real before the symbol and the known before the unknown. There was no mention at all of the "what" of the curriculum—only the "how."

The Educational Conservative

Dewey emphasized that although the methodological ideas of the reformer were no longer viewed as revolutionary, they had not had an impact on classroom practice because the conservative still controlled what actually happened in the classroom. The conservative "was there not only as a teacher in the classroom but he was in the board of education; he was there because he was still in the heart and mind of the parent; because he still possessed and controlled the intellectual and moral standards and expectations of the community."[3] Educational reform, Dewey concluded, must be viewed as a phase of social reform.

The educational conservative knew that without any significant change in how knowledge was viewed, there would be little threat of any real change in the classroom, despite the exhortations of reformers to follow the way of nature in helping the child to develop. And, as Dewey pointed out, the reformer was coming to the same conclusion.

The "What" and the "How"

"The what to study is an important as the how to study," wrote William T. Harris in 1880.[4] That Harris' article, the opening piece in the first issue of *Education,* dealt with materials rather than methods is significant. The theoretical battleground was beginning to shift from the methods of teaching to the course of study. The conservative felt more secure here, and for good reason: He was on the side of "eternal truths"—the intellectual treasures of mankind.

Harris' concern was that textbook instruction was being devalued in favor of object teaching and "original investigation" (the predecessor of Dewey's method of experience). An educator of great reputation, Harris strongly favored the textbook-recitation method of teaching elementary-school science over the laboratory method. To Harris, the textbook was both the method of teaching and the curriculum. Preservation of the method would leave the curriculum intact. The child's mind would continue to be occupied with traditional subject matter, with "what has been tested and found essential to civilization."[5] To Harris, ignoring the book was tantamount to ignoring six thousand years of human experience. In trying to re-create the ladder of human experience we would get only as far as the first generation, he warned.

However, another consideration is central here. There had been an enormous increase in the number of cheap newspapers and in their circulation. The Pulitzer and Hearst presses (and their imitators) were "educating" the public and shaping public opinion via the emotional appeal of sensational events. Harris sought to counter this influence with one that did not serve special interests—the textbook. As Cremin puts it, Harris saw the textbook "as the pedagogical tool par excellence in a newspaper civilization where public opinion ruled and where the entire community needed access to similar facts and arguments if harmony was to be achieved."[6]

Whatever their distinctive pedagogical properties, the decision to confine the teaching of science to textbooks was overwhelmingly conservative. Harris and other powerful conservatives viewed method as inseparably bound up with the textbook. This was at the heart of their refusal to endorse methods such as the laboratory approach to teaching science, in which original investigation is substituted for textbook accounts of the results of others. The purpose of education was not to learn a method of investigation, said the conservative; it was to occupy the mind with the recorded wisdom of the human race. For this, what was needed were books and not laboratory experiments or specimens.

THE IDEAS AND INFLUENCE OF FRANCIS PARKER

Although the name most closely associated with progressive education is John Dewey, the pedagogical pioneer who launched the movement was Colonel Francis W. Parker. Indeed, Dewey called Parker the father of progressive education. For more than forty years, Parker conducted a relentless crusade against unnatural methods of teaching and the isolation of subjects. "No truth is more striking than the essential relation of all subjects to each other," he wrote in 1894.

The Quincy Methods

Parker's impact on educational theory began in Quincy, Massachusetts, in 1875, when he was named superintendent of schools. His charge was to examine and improve education in Quincy. Two years before, on public examination day, the Quincy School Committee had made an appalling discovery. The graduates of the grammar schools were unable to spell, write, or speak effectively. When asked by committee members to read from an unfamiliar book, they were bewildered and lost. They had been trained only for examination and could not read with fluency or comprehension. Furthermore, questions about their studies revealed that the children had no understanding of the thinking process. All they could do was parrot memorized responses to memorized questions prepared in advance by their teacher.

Parker's Pedagogy.   Parker, who had studied pedagogy in Germany, where elementary-school methods had been influenced by Pestalozzi and Froebel, was charged specifically with helping the children of Quincy to develop the power of expression. Because Parker believed that methods of teaching should be patterned on the child's natural way of learning, he adopted the word method of teaching reading. This, after all, was the way children learned to speak the language. Grammar was thrown out of the school, and talking and writing were put in.

Conversation, which was one of the innovations in Quincy schools, was cultivated as an art. "What did you do last evening?" or "What did you see on your way to school this morning?" were questions being answered by children who previously had been mouthing words by rote, without understanding the ideas they represented. All writing was done to describe children's activities, experiences, and feelings. Spelling was taught through this meaningful kind of writing.

Parker was opposed to teaching geography via the disconnected morass of facts and statistics in geography textbooks. Instead, the children took field trips around Quincy and made mud models and sketches of the landscape. These methods were indeed revolutionary at a time when pupils in most schools were expected to remain in the same position throughout the day without turning their heads.

The novel approaches of the "Quincy system," as it came to be known, attracted national attention. Children were learning to read, write, spell, and think simultaneously. As Parker said, they were learning to "talk" with their pens, as they had learned to talk with their tongues, by using them.[8]

The reactions to these methods were mixed. There were those who called Parker a charlatan, as they would have called anyone who tried to teach children how to think before they had thoroughly memorized the implements (facts) for thinking. In the main, however, his methods were widely acclaimed in both the general press and professional literature. Typical was the statement of B. G. Northrup, secretary of the Connecticut State Board of Education: "In Quincy, the children write better *throughout all the schools of the town* than is the case in *all* the schools of any other town within my knowledge in our country."[9]

A London journal, however, was unimpressed, finding the developments in Quincy to be nothing more than Froebel's theories put into action.[10] A comment frequently heard in educational circles was that Parker's ideas were not original. This was true: They had been tried in various places in this country and abroad, and Parker was the first to say so. But he had brought them together as a set of ideas and given them flesh and blood in one New England town. Moreover, Parker was the first to attempt to systematize and adopt the "new education" on a district-wide basis.

An Educational Breakthrough. Parker viewed the developments in Quincy more as a "spirit of study," a *search* for the natural methods of teaching, than as a system or a method. Quincy was an educational breakthrough, Parker said, because of its rejection of traditional education and its penetration into the "very thick crust of conservatism and conceit."

Parker's Theory of Concentration

Parker's "Quincy system" was a milestone in curriculum development. It was his Quincy fame that brought him to Chicago in 1883 as principal of the Cook County Normal School. Here, Parker and his faculty worked out and applied ideas for the "concentration" or unification of subject matter. The results, along with the teachings of Froebel, the psychology of Herbart, and the theories of Darwin and Spencer, formed the basis for Parker's theory of curriculum concentration or synthesis. He unveiled his theory in a series of talks at the Chautauqua (New York) Teachers Retreat in the summer of 1891. The talks were revised and published in 1894 as *Talks on Pedagogics: An Outline of the Theory of Concentration.*

Curriculum Synthesis and Educational Power. In Parker's theory, content was unified into what he designated the central subjects. Unification was not only a more valid reflection of the nature of knowledge than isolated subjects, but it would also solve the problem of an overcrowded curriculum. This problem had resulted in the dissipation of educational effort. Educational power could come only from an economical use of educational energy. "Economy of energy," wrote Parker, "is the intrinsic mark and sign of all progress."[12]

Parker believed that traditional education put quantity above quality. The method of quantity was "word-cramming and word-recitation; of believing and conforming . . . the method that keeps the mind from looking outside of a certain definite circle; the method of implicit belief."[13] It was a method suitable for an authoritarian system of government, in which people were discouraged from reasoning based on exact data. It was not suitable for a democracy, in which clear thinking was absolutely essential. Clear thinking was being able to see relationships. This was hardly possible when each subject was isolated, seemingly as far as possible, from other subjects.

The Child and the Curriculum. "The child," wrote Parker, "instinctively begins all subjects known in the curriculum of the university."[14] The goal of curriculum developers should be to build on the child's instinctive learning activities. Parker described in detail universal learning activities of young children and their relationship to subject areas in the curriculum. For example, the child is a student of family life—the relation of father to mother, parent to child. This is his or her beginning of the study of anthropology. Motivation is implicit because of natural interest in one's surroundings.

The Central Subjects. The subjects with which the child came into contact in his or her environment were the inorganic sciences—geography, geology, and mineralogy. Physics and chemistry would be learned in relation to the continual change in the form and qualities of inorganic matter. The inorganic sciences would be studied in connection with the life sciences because a "tree, for instance, is as closely related to meteorology, geography, physics, and chemistry as a leaf to the twig or limb to the trunk."[15]

The life sciences began with simple life forms and evolved, like the evolutionary process itself, to complex biological organisms—to the human being. The study of anthropology, said Parker, should be approached by the same methods used to study the lower animals. Humans would be studied in relation to their physical and social environment. The latter was ethnology, the study of the influence of communities on their members. History would add to anthropology the printed and written records of the human race's evolutionary process. But history was relatively meaningless without a knowledge of geography—the "stage of human comedies and tragedies, the land itself."[16]

Parker stressed that the central subjects could be considered as one subject. They were synthesized through the interdependence of nature and were also united through the study of form and number. Knowledge of the latter two, including geometry, could be acquired through the study of the central subjects.[17]

Mathematics. Although mathematics was not a central subject, it was related to every central subject. Numbers entered into all intellectual progress, into every phase of practical life. The problem with arithmetic was that it had been taught abstractly. Yet abstract numbers meant nothing to the child; they were worth nothing unless they were applied.

Parker's ideas on the study of mathematics are as revolutionary today as they were in 1894, if not more so, for the study of mathematics in all levels of the school has largely moved out of the realm of practical affairs and into the realm of the mathematics scholar. This is not because of the nature of the subject but, rather, of the spirit and nature of the post-*Sputnik* curriculum reforms. In the late 1980s, national reports were calling for the reform of mathematics education, beginning in the elementary school, so that students could subsequently handle more demanding courses in high school and college. As in the post-Sputnik era, the concern was that American students were being left behind. Consequently the emphasis was on presenting students with realistic problems and on encouraging them to solve those problems cooperatively.

Unity in Method. In Parker's theory there was unity in the "how" of teaching as well as in the "what." All learning took place through the senses. Parker divided the modes of learning into two categories: attention and expression. The modes of attention were "observation," "hearing language," and "reading." The power of language, oral and written, was to be acquired through the study of the central subjects.

Whereas the modes of attention were mental, the modes of expression were physical. There were nine modes of expression—gesture, voice, music, speech, making, modeling, painting, drawing, and writing. Parker considered their function to be the achievement of the unity of thought and action.

Parker emphasized that the modes of attention and expression were to be taught simultaneously. For example, reading, a mode of attention, and writing, a mode of expression, should be learned at the same time and in connection with subject matter. Again, the purpose of teaching skills and subject matter together was twofold: economy of effort and an integrated, more meaningful educational experience.

Parker and Herbart

Parker's theory of curriculum concentration or synthesis was based on Herbart's principles of correlation and concentration. As Parker saw it, the most significant difference between his theory and Herbart's was the setting. In Germany, the schools, although more scientific in method than anywhere else in the world, were class–divided schools. The only free school was for poor people, and education was regarded as a means for maintaining the system of social stratification. What was not wanted was free thought; that would result in a demand for personal rights by the common people. Therefore, the Herbartian theory had to stop short of encouraging individual freedom through personal effort.

On the other hand, the United States had schools that were common to all the people. In a democracy the problem was to promote rather than to prevent free action of the mind. In one sense, Parker's theory went on where Herbart's left off. However, a more accurate assessment would be that the theories differed completely because of differences in form of government and the relation of social classes.

Another important difference was that Herbart made moral education the basis of his educational system. History was considered the organizing center for the curriculum because of the contribution it could make to moral development. One of the chief reasons why his doctrine became modified in Germany was that the curriculum was being pressured to become more practical. Parents wanted their children to be good people, but they also wanted them to be prepared to make a good living or attend the university. For Parker, nature was the paradigm for curriculum development. Although he insisted that there was no single central subject in his curriculum, science was obviously the center of educational gravity. This was a giant step beyond placing science on a par with the ancient classical studies and mathematics.

Parker took the idea of concentration from Herbart, but he was not a Herbartian. His ideas for curriculum and instruction were rooted in a conception of education that was progressive and essentially Spencerian. (Spencer's ideas of education were built on the work of Charles Darwin.)

Parker as Curriculum Theorist

Despite his child-centered conception of education, Parker saw no conflict between the child and the curriculum. Like Dewey, he saw the child and the curriculum as part of a unified evolutionary process.

Parker is remembered more as a champion of children and an exponent of child-centered methods of education than as a curriculum theorist. Yet his ideas on the nature of knowledge were translated into principles for curriculum organization that remain fresh and untried to this day. "Much of what he found good, we still find good; much of what he was reaching for, we still seek."[18]

The Correlation Controversy

The years from 1895 to 1900 were particularly significant for the field of curriculum. Faced with a vast increase in knowledge and a badly fragmented curriculum, educators proposed and debated various schemes for determining what the schools should teach. A number of plans involved correlation of studies: making the pupil aware of the relationships between subjects.

One of these plans evoked considerable discussion at the 1895 meetings of the National Education Association and the Herbart Society in Denver. This was Parker's theory of concentration. But the structure of the elementary school curriculum had already been determined. As pointed out in the previous chapter, William T. Harris, who authored the section of the report of the Committee of Fifteen dealing with correlation, literally ignored the concern of educators for establishing relationships between subjects. Harris' plan also was presented in Denver.

Interestingly enough, it was Parker who two years before had called for the appointment of an NEA committee to study ways of making apparent to the child the relationship among the parts of the curriculum. His request had been honored, but the outcome was a report that was an elaborate defense of the isolation of subjects. Parker's reaction to the report in Denver was bitter. He moved that a new committee be appointed to revise it.[19] But the die had been cast. The report stood as written.

Herbartians also gave spirited opposition to the report. They feared that the report conveyed the impression that reform was not needed or that it had already been made. Their arguments were not in defense of Colonel Parker's theory; leading Herbartians had authored their own schemes for correlation. Rather, they argued that for the sake of the child, the overcrowded and disconnected curriculum could no longer be perpetuated.

THE HERBARTIANS AND CURRICULUM INTEGRATION

Of considerable significance were the discussions on curriculum unification at the 1895 meeting of the National Herbart Society. Never before, or since, was this topic given so much attention by a body of educational theorists. In the twentieth century the problem of curriculum integration was approached from the vantage point of child experience. There were also attempts to combine logically related fields together in "broad fields" and "core curricula." But never again was there such interest in total unification of the curriculum based on the nature of knowledge.

Reactions to Parker's Theory

Herbartian reaction to Parker's theory, particularly with regard to the focus of the theory, became a matter of debate. Parker's followers, Parker himself, and later Parker's historians insisted that the pivotal point of the theory was the child. But as Charles De Garmo, president of the new Herbart Society, observed, the organizing principle was *not* the needs of the child "but at bottom the principle of philosophical unity that binds all nature into one."[20]

An examination of the theory makes this most obvious. But how is one to explain Parker's insistence that his theory centered on the child? Perhaps the answer lies in the fact that although Parker was motivated by the need to emancipate children from the bonds of traditional education, the dominating force behind his theory was neither the philosophy of Pestalozzi nor that of Froebel. It was, rather, a passion for a new curriculum synthesis that would accurately reflect the unity of man and nature. If one were to identify the single most powerful influence on Parker's theory of concentration, it would probably be the theory of Darwin.

De Garmo's Concerns.   De Garmo raised three concerns about Parker's theory. As might be expected of any Herbartian, he questioned the subordination of the humanities to science. He gave as his reason the recency of science on the educational scene. "Civilization," he said, "has been possible without science." On the other hand, the humanities had "nurtured all the races of the past."[21] His second concern was Parker's relegation of the three R's to means for education, rather than ends. De Garmo thought that these studies, which had been the mainstay of the curriculum, would be neglected. His third concern is perhaps the most significant: the practicability of the theory. De Garmo asked whether the concept of unification was understood even by scientists, much less by elementary school teachers.

> How many scientists have we that clearly comprehend this grand unity of nature, and not only of nature, but of nature and man? Will not the blind be leading the blind when elementary teachers make serious attempts to follow such a principle?[22]

The Isolation of Scholarship.   The answer to De Garmo's question of how many is not many. Most scientists, now as then, think in terms of their own narrow specialization and do not seek interrelationships with other fields.It is this kind of thinking that has shaped the curriculum. (This is true not only of the scientist but of all scholars.) As for the ability of teachers to teach by the theory of concentration, Parker had implicit faith in teacher education. The thing to do, he said, was "to move steadily and unfalteringly toward the ideal, along the infinite line of unrealized possibilities."[23]

Correlation and Concentration

It is probable that De Garmo's criticisms were at least partly motivated by self-interest; he had a plan of his own. De Garmo thought that correlation within subject-matter departments was a prior condition for correlation between departments. The principles that constitute the structure of a given subject were more important and constant than the relation between that subject and other subjects, which tend to be occasional, he argued. For example, geography was being taught as three or four isolated subjects: political, mathematical, physical, and commercial geography. He believed that these should be blended into one on the basis of unifying principles. But, he added, almost in rebuttal of his own position, in the development of leading ideas certain cross-relations with other departments, such as with history in the case of geography, were bound to become apparent.

De Garmo said that he was opposed to the concept of concentration and gave the following reason. When a subject becomes subordinate to another subject, it loses its identity and its own natural sequence or organizing principles will not be made apparent to the learner. Therefore, *correlation* was preferable to *concentration*. But even with correlation, there would be considerable danger of the loss of integrity for a given subject.

Another question raised by De Garmo concerned the nature of the interrelationships between subjects. There was a distinction, he said, between the superficial or artificial associations brought out by the teacher to enliven the lesson and the significant relations that unified knowledge. This seems to have been a spurious point, a problem for teacher education, rather than a weakness in the theoretical basis for seeking the unity that underlies the curriculum.

After raising so many objections to the subordination of one field of study to another in the form of "concentration centers," De Garmo proceeded to identify geography as the subject that the believed "most universally unifies the curriculum."[24] In so doing he blurred the distinction between concentration and his earlier definition of correlation. For if correlation could also be defined as the unification of the curriculum through one central subject, it meant exactly the same thing as concentration. In so doing, he eradicated most of his arguments against Parker's theory of concentration.

Herbart and the Herbartians

One would think that the tie that bound the members of the Herbart Society was the philosophy of Herbart. But this was not so. According to Dunkel, the lack of interest evidenced by members of the Herbart Society in Herbart and his ideas and writings was "little short of astonishing."[25] Therefore, it was not surprising that the society changed its name in 1900 to the National Society for the Scientific Study of Education. (It was changed again in 1909 to the National Society for the Study of Education.)

Specialists Versus Concentrationists

Nor is it surprising that the Herbartians were not of one mind on the subject of concentration. In his article on the subject in the first yearbook of the National Herbart Society, Frank McMurry, another leading Herbartian, replied to the argument that concentration caused individual subjects to lose their identities. Plainly, he said, it was a problem of self-interest. The specialists were fighting to preserve their own subjects as units in the child's mind, whereas the concentrationists were attempting to organize the curriculum as the child sees the world—as a concentrated whole.

McMurry said that there was only one important argument in the conflict: Related thinking is the highest level of thinking and, therefore, the most valuable. This meant that the specialists would have to give in. They would have to make sacrifices in order to gain this higher unity "just as the individual states yielded some of their peculiar rights for the sake of the higher unity, the central government."[26] McMurry's analogy is especially interesting. Its logical conclusion is that if the specialists did not yield, there would exist a state of educational anarchy.

To return briefly to the present day, certainly the primary problem in breaking down curriculum barriers when it has been attempted (particularly at the secondary school and university levels) has been getting specialists to sit down together. Such efforts have tended to be unsuccessful because each specialist believes that his or her field should constitute the organizing center. Whether a state of educational anarchy exists in the curriculum is, of course, a matter of conjecture. Nevertheless, to this day the curriculum remains largely an arena of separate subject matters, with subject specialists often competing for priority for their own subjects in the curriculum.

Another important point made by McMurry was that common school subjects were not sciences. They were not even well-systematized bodies of knowledge. Therefore, the objection that they would lose their structures or their unity was simply not applicable. Furthermore, even if they were highly developed sciences, their logical order of development was not in accord with the principles of learning and could not, therefore, determine sequence. After his reply to arguments against concentration or synthesis, McMurry offered his own choices for the central studies in the curriculum—literature in the early grades and history from the fifth through the eighth grades.

Literature, History, and National Goals

In the discussion that followed the reading of De Garmo's and McMurry's papers, Parker said that literature and history were a "powerful means of adjusting the child to the exact state of society in which he finds himself."[27] That was why they had been selected in Germany as the central subjects: "to make the German child feel that the Fatherland is the only land."[28] On the other hand, he said, the Germans had kept the study of science out of the elementary school for many years because they were afraid that the study of science would lead children to search for truth, to understand and doubt the infallibility of the present social structure and government. Yet Parker denied that science was the center of his curriculum organization. The only center was the child. But science must have a place in the curriculum that would make it a powerful means for human development. In his concluding remarks, Parker called attention to the tremendous opposition by church and state to Darwinian theory. "The study of nature has been the spectre, the horrible spectre," he said, "of those who would hold the human mind in subjection both in church and state."[29]

Herbartian Charles Van Liew, who had studied in Germany, was in general agreement with Parker's diagnosis of the reason why science had been kept out of German schools. The government, he said, dictated the subjects in the curriculum, and this was done for its own purposes.[30]

But Charles McMurry, who edited the Herbart Society's first yearbook, believed that fear of natural science as a revolutionary study was *not* the chief reason why it had been kept out of the schools. The primary reason was educational conservatism: The old classical studies were still considered of most value. This was just as true in America as it was in Germany. A second reason was even more significant from the standpoint of the educator, as it put the onus on the educator. It was simply that the problem of how to teach natural science in the elementary school had yet to be solved. No one had developed a course of study in science for the elementary school. Yet even in the high schools the natural sciences were struggling for a place in the curriculum on a par with the classical studies.

The Culture-Epoch Theory

Darwinian theory came to be interpreted in still another way. According to Darwin's evolutionary hypothesis, the embryos of most species from conception to birth recapitulated or passed through the various evolutionary stages of the species. It was not long before this finding of the biological sciences began to affect the fields of philosophy and psychology. An ancient theory dating back to Aristotelian philosophy—the idea that the child in his or her development must recapitulate the intellectual and moral development of humanity epoch by epoch—was given new credence. The idea was seized upon by the Herbartians as a principle for selecting content and material according to the child's stage of development.

Limiting Factors. It is clear that when carried over to the curriculum, the principle that ontogenetic or individual development recapitulates phylogenetic or race development ignored the external influences on the child—his or her environment. This was very different than the environment of the human race during its various epochs. The child, after all, was born into the highest or latest stage of development. A second limiting factor was that different individuals were born with different capacities for learning. This, combined with the environmental factor, meant that if the theory were valid one child would recapitulate the development of the race more rapidly than another and educators would still be faced with conflict between the individual and the curriculum.

Despite these limiting factors, the Herbartians eagerly adopted the culture-epoch theory. They did so for three reasons: (1) It was a theory of history, and history was considered the subject with greatest potential for character building; (2) culture epochs made curriculum integration easier—they could serve as "concentration centers" in the curriculum; and (3) neither the principle of the logical order of subject matter nor the principle of the psychological order of subject matter seemed adequate for the formation of a curriculum. The analogy between the development of the individual and the race appeared to be the best principle for connecting subject matter with the child.

The fact that the theory of the parallel development of the individual and the race had not been proven did not deter curriculum developers, especially since even psychologist G. Stanley Hall endorsed the view. He said that as children studied each epoch they would be purged of objectionable, obsolete kinds of racial behavior that otherwise might cause them trouble later in life.

Dewey on Culture Epochs.   Dewey, on the other hand, took a dim view of the culture-epoch theory and abhorred its educational interpretation. He pointed out that many of the phases in the embryonic period were very transitory and of little importance except to a biologist. It was also quite possible that the child completed the process of cultural recapitulation during the first two or three years of its life. Even if the hunting or nomadic impulse were present in the school-age child, it was only one impulse out of many, and there was absolutely no justification for spending a year of the child's school life on the hunting or the nomadic epoch.

Dewey's main objection was that the theory was focused on human cultural development but inferences were being made about child development, inferences that had no basis in fact. The conclusion that the epochs of the race were repeated in the child was unjustifiable.[31] More recently, Phillips and Kelly have pointed out that the tendency in the study of child development to adhere to recapitulationism reflects a continuing conceptual confusion in the field.[32] They find Piaget comparable to Hall in assuming that the stages of ontogenesis are related to those of phylogenesis. And they point out that there is no basis for assuming such a relationship since the "processes of development of the individual child and of evolutionary development are quite distinguishable."[33] This is of striking interest since Dewey made the same observation and warned about the conceptual confusion in 1896.

Be that as it may, the culture-epoch theory rapidly took hold in the curriculum. Teachers began to arrange material according to socioeconomic epochs, beginning with nomadic peoples in the primary grades and ending with a study of the industrial epoch in upper elementary grades.

The Influence of the Herbartians

Although the Herbartians never evolved a singular agreed-upon plan for unifying the curriculum and were unable to convince the Committee of

Fifteen (namely, William T. Harris) about the need for synthesis, they nevertheless gave the curriculum a new importance. This came about through their efforts to resolve the two leading curriculum problems of their day, an overcrowded curriculum and the exponential increase in knowledge. It was also the result of their emphasizing the value of various studies in the curriculum.

By 1906, the Herbartian movement was all but dead. Historians give different reasons for its sharp decline. Some, like Dunkel, say that Herbartians were never really linked with the thought of Herbart; he was simply a philosophical ghost in attendance at a society of educational theorists. And they paid him little heed.[34] But another, more fundamental reason was that Americans had begun to produce their own pedagogy and had no further need for European imports.

CHILD STUDY AND EDUCATIONAL THEORY

In the 1890s the movement that rivaled Herbartianism for pedagogical popularity was child study. Although labeled a fad by some and steeped in sentimentality by others, the child-study movement gained academic respectability after 1900, when it became associated with experimental psychology. But even in its early stages, child study had an impact on curriculum and method, particularly in the kindergarten. Early studies conducted by Hall, Bryan, and Hancock, for example, revealed that movement involving the large muscles should be free in young children. For this reason, and because of possible danger to the children's eyesight also revealed by child study, the handwork in kindergarten that required delicate coordination and precision was dropped from the curriculum.

It is important to note that leaders in the child-study movement saw it as an instrument for educational reform as well as a means for gaining new knowledge about children. As G. Stanley Hall, who started the movement, said, the method and curriculum of the school would have to change if practice was to be in accord with the new knowledge.

In its infancy, child study was closely tied to the school. Not only did teachers gather the data for those engaged in research, but teachers themselves became deeply involved in the process of child watching. What they themselves learned as they observed the children, questioned them, collected and compiled miscellaneous facts about them, wrote their biographies, checked their sight and hearing, and weighed and measured them for science was that each child was indeed unique. Whether this new insight was translated into action in the form of new ways of working with children was another question.

Classroom Application. Child study was both systematic and unsystematic, and much worthless as well as worthwhile information was accumulated. Quality of research, however, was not the primary problem for those trying to reform the schools. There was, after all, plenty of good research on which there was a consensus. The question was how could the findings be applied in the classroom? Their concern was well borne out by what happened (or failed to happen) to the findings of child study. An excellent illustration is the method of freely chosen activities that was confirmed by child study in the early years of the movement. The idea that the child should choose his or her own activities in an enriched learning environment had been promoted by Parker, and he was delighted when it was sanctioned by research. But it was not until well into the second decade of the twentieth century that the idea worked its way into the elementary classroom (via, of course, the kindergarten).

As child study gained academic status in the university, it lost its identification with educational concerns. The questions being asked by researchers were less often the questions asked by educators. When they happened to be the same, by coincidence, the answers took longer to have an impact on school practice because child study and education had become parallel developments. This continues to pose problems for today's teachers and children. Nearly all teacher education programs, at least at the elementary-school level, require courses in child development. But knowing the principles of child development does not automatically result in the selection of instructional methods most likely to have a positive effect on learning. Knowledge of the principles of child development has had no significant effect on methods of teaching.

Child study, or child development as it is now generally known, has continued to influence educational practice, but the delay in implementing findings continues to be a matter for genuine concern. The findings of child study do not, of course, answer the paramount curriculum question; although researchers have, on the whole, determined what children are able to learn at various ages, they cannot provide answers to what children should learn. The fact that it can be demonstrated that children can learn certain things or that their learning of certain things can be accelerated appreciably does not solve the problem of curriculum choices and priorities.

THE NEW EDUCATION—CONTRAPOSITIVE FORCES

Progressive education was inaugurated in Quincy, Massachusetts, in the late 1870s. By 1885, the "new education" was being discussed by everyone in educational circles, from kindergarten teachers to college presidents. Admittedly, they may not have been discussing the same things; to the faculty of Harvard College, the "new education" was the elective system that in the 1884–85 academic year had been adopted for freshmen. To the kindergarten teacher, it meant child development through nature's method of play and self-activity.

Other progressive ideas were being circulated well before 1890. Some superintendents were urging teachers to "individualize" their teaching. Object teaching, based on learning through "sense perceptions," was a Pestalozzian idea that had been around before midcentury, as indicated in the previous chapter, and was far from revolutionary after 1880. The idea of learning through practical operation, or *doing,* later conceptualized into a theory of education by Dewey, was advanced by speakers at NEA conventions as early as 1877 as a solution for the problem of teaching the book instead of the subject.

Well before the end of the nineteenth century, Parker and the Herbartians had developed curriculum schemes based on the organic unity of knowledge. Such prestigious educators as Nicholas Murray Butler of Columbia and Charles De Garmo of Swarthmore argued for curriculum reforms that would make apparent to the child the unity underlying the various studies in the curriculum. The school door had been opened to science, the social sciences, the arts, manual training, and home economics. Dewey and the Herbartians had attached high value to interest as opposed to will in the learning process (although they differed radically in their conceptions of interest, the Herbartians seeing it as something external that the teacher adds to subject matter to make it palatable and Dewey as something inherently present when the goals seem important to the child). G. Stanley Hall had opened a new field of study and proposed that it be the basis for curriculum development. In so doing, he put the child on center stage and gave sanction to the principle of learning through self-activity.

Thus the stage was set by 1895 for a progressive movement in education. But the movement lagged. The new ideas had no impact on the outcome of the deliberations of the Committee of Ten on Secondary School Studies or the Committee of Fifteen on Elementary Education. Yet those committees had been created in response to agitation for curriculum reform.

Social Philosophies and the Curriculum

Despite the popularity of the new educational ideas with many teachers and their endorsement by renowned educators, the traditional views of education, including a profound faith in mental discipline, maintained their grip on the vast majority of people, including superintendents of schools and school boards. But it was not just the iron grip of the educational doctrines of a dying world that checked the progress of progressive education; it was an amalgam of educational, social, and economic notions that protected the inertia of existing institutions. Nor was it simply the public at large and those who dominated the schools whose ideas retarded the progress of educational reform. Interestingly enough, it was the social philosophy of some reformers and educational leaders that proved to be a deterrent to change. As will be seen, their ideas served to reinforce dominant social and educational beliefs.

The Doctrines of* Laissez-Faire *and Individualism.   Faith in the individual and the power to get ahead were (and still are) familiar American doctrines. The idea implicit in laissez-faire is that nothing should limit or impede the free action of the individual; success or failure depends on self-effort. As applied to education, this means that self-effort rather than the methods of teaching or the educational offerings of the school is the controlling factor in the success of the individual. Hence, there is no reason to change the prevailing curriculum or system of instruction to meet individual needs. The educational cream will rise to the top, and the dregs will sink to the bottom. Helping the unfit to become fit by curriculum adaptation is out of the question; it would only defeat the purpose of the system, which is to weed out those unable to profit from a curriculum aimed at developing intellectual power.

The Social Ideas of William T. Harris.   Regarded as the intellectual leader of the education profession from the late 1860s until 1910, William T. Harris subscribed to laissez-faire and the cult of the individual. According to Curti, Harris firmly believed that individuals were obliged to subordinate themselves to the needs of existing social and economic institutions.[35] There were obvious conflicting elements in this philosophy. These he resolved to his own satisfaction by use of the dialectic (Hegelian) method of resolving antitheses into higher syntheses.

The educational result of this attempt to meet two conflicting philosophical goals—laissez-faire and social obligation—was a crystallization of the status quo. It was the purpose of education to serve the existing social and economic order. Yet educational goals could not be reformulated so that the curriculum could more adequately prepare the individual for such service. To do so would deprive the individual of his or her right to the culture of the race. The traditional curriculum had to remain intact. Thus, Harris took a dim view of manual training and vocational education. The individual was "free" to get ahead by his or her own efforts, although he or she might not profit from the traditional curriculum.

As indicated in the previous chapter, Harris insisted on an elementary-school curriculum consisting of grammar, literature and art, geography, mathematics, and history—the "five windows of the soul," which would pave the way to the cultural treasures of the past, even if one's formal education terminated with elementary school.[36] He frowned upon Pestalozzian ideas for two reasons: First, he believed that the philosophy of sense-perception detracted from the intellectual purpose of the school, which was to develop the power to fix attention on ideas, not feelings; and second, that the Pestalozzian concept of pupil self-government was antithetical to the social purpose of the school, which was to train the child to accept authority. For Harris, the school was a force for stability.[37]

Harris was a defender of the status quo and a successful one at that; he was a leading social philosopher and his ideas carried weight with educators.

But equally important, they confirmed what Americans already believed in: self-help and laissez-faire.

Social Darwinian G. Stanley Hall. Harris was a conservative rather than a reformer, so his defense of existing institutions and a traditional curriculum is hardly a surprise. What is surprising (at least in the "strange bedfellows" sense) is that reformer G. Stanley Hall also was a defender of the exist-. ing social order. A social Darwinian, Hall believed that social change was to come via the slow-paced process of evolutionary development. He did not believe that education was a remedy for societal ills because, given the process of evolution, education could not reverse or speed up the changes in human nature. What education could do was to identify the gifted, the "best blood," and give them better educational opportunities.[38] In this connection, Hall believed that heredity, not environment, was the governing factor in producing the fit and the unfit.

Hall advanced the radical thesis that the curriculum and methods of teaching be determined by the needs of the child as revealed through child study; the content of the curriculum was to be based on data from child development as determined by questionnaire and inventory. Hall wanted the curriculum to be individualized from the moment the child entered the school. To this end, he stressed the importance of ascertaining what children actually knew upon entering school and developing the child's program in accord with this knowledge[39]

In a very real sense, Hall's work provided the capstone for the works of Rousseau, Pestalozzi, and, to some extent, Parker because it supplied a "scientific" basis for child-centeredness. Unlike Hall, however, Parker saw the public school as a great force for the improvement of society.

Insofar as Hall's theory of curriculum development had authoritative underpinnings (experimental psychology), it was a radical-progressive idea. Oddly, however, his rationale for the individualization of education was conservative: It supported the doctrine of laissez-faire, for the purpose of individualization was to identify the gifted child, give him or her encouragement, and expend less energy on the dull child. Curti wrote about Hall's influence:

> Although Hall opened up new fields and emphasized new aspects of human life his influence was largely directed to the support of individualism and laissez-faire. This was the effect of the cult of child study, which tended to make the curriculum child-centered, and to single out for particular attention the gifted child.[40]

Child-Centeredness and Laissez-Faire. The point of importance in this quotation is that a child-centered curriculum is a laissez-faire curriculum; it does not direct itself to social needs and concerns. This was actually a contrapositive force in the progressive movement, both in the very early stages of the movement and in the 1920s. As Dewey stressed, educational reform cannot be conceived apart from social reform; the two are deeply interwoven.

When carried to its ultimate extreme, a child-centered laissez-faire curriculum is no organized curriculum at all. In the 1920s the child-centered curriculum was built, in some places, entirely on the momentary interests of children. By stressing individual values at the expense of social values, and by discounting the role of the school in social change, Hall cast the die for the progressive education of the 1920s, a mold that some progressive educators regarded as disastrous and tried their utmost to break.

In summary, the social philosophies of both Harris and Hall were contrapositive forces in the new education. The fear by the Herbartians, mentioned earlier, that Harris' report on the correlation of studies would convey the impression that educational reform was a fait accompli or not needed was certainly justifiable; that is what happened.

In developing his own curriculum theory based on laissez-faire, Hall literally turned his back on the mounting and often frightening problems being faced by a rapidly changing society. When the progressive movement in education finally gathered momentum it did so, in the words of Cremin, "as part of a vast humanitarian effort to apply the promise of American life—the ideal of government by, of, and for the people—to the puzzling new urban-industrial civilization that came into being during the latter half of the nineteenth century."[41]

THE DECLINE OF LAISSEZ-FAIRE—ENVIRONMENTALISM AND THE IDEA OF PROGRESS

"The recognition of the shortcomings of our individualistic social philosophy has made many people look at our schools from an entirely new point of view," wrote William D. Lewis, principal of Philadelphia's William Penn High School, in 1914.[42] During their school years students' attitudes toward society are shaped, warned Lewis. "If they emerge from the high school with an indifferent, selfish, laissez-faire philosophy, they will become either the unthinking victims or the plunderers of our devil-take-the-hindmost social order.[43]

American progressivists attributed many of the pervading social ills to a long-standing condition of "rugged individualism" or laissez-faire, and sought to attack these social ills through enlightened social action. The new progressive social philosophy was to generate a veritable revolution in the role and function of the high school.

The Concept of Planned Change

The outlook of the educational progressivists toward evolutionary improvement was that progress is possible but certainly not inevitable. Progress is most likely to occur when man *plans* for what he considers to be a better human condition and focuses his energies on achieving these goals. In other words, progress is not controlled by the laws of evolution but, rather, by man's control of nature. Education, of course, has an enormous role in making a better life.

The Ideas of Lester Ward. The new point of view had been in the making since 1883, when Lester F. Ward, in his now classic *Dynamic Sociology,* attacked the weaknesses of laissez-faire and proposed instead a planned society. Man had the obligation to sit in the driver's seat of life and *make* a better society, argued Ward. The only safe foundation for a progressive social order was the systematic education of the young. But universal education was not enough; a particular kind of education was needed that must provide the student with an understanding of his or her relation to society. Traditional education that stressed knowledge of literary abstractions rather than knowledge of objective realities was a "perverted system which, at best, only leaves the world where it finds it."[44]

Lester Frank Ward (1841–1913) was a giant on whose shoulders we stand where ideas about the curriculum are concerned. Ward was the architect of environmentalism in American education.[45] An authority in several fields of science, Ward was able to apply biological principles to humankind and society and formulate this great idea: The human, unlike all other creatures, has mastery over the impersonal forces of nature, and progress is achieved through applied human intelligence rather than by letting nature take its course. The means is education—the long-range instrument of progress. In order for individuals to develop their potential, they must be placed in a specially designed and stimulating environment (the school). This is the process of education—no different, argued Ward, than providing fruit trees or a field of wheat with a designed environment favorable to their higher development. Ward stated repeatedly that human intelligence was (and always had been) adequate for all practical purposes. There was no shortage of ability, only of opportunity.

Throughout his life, Ward attacked the eugenics movement and championed the cause of educational opportunity as the key to human progress. But the point of importance is that Ward did not make the case for educational opportunity merely on political grounds. He viewed education as a quality of the environment that is essential for human progress. In contrast to the chance process of biological evolution ("genesis"), Ward viewed education as the intelligent shaping of the environment ("telesis"). Ward provided a scientific base for Dewey's experimentalist philosophy.[46]

Ward's ideas have become so ingrained in the conventional wisdom that they are no longer regarded as revolutionary, and Ward is all but forgotten. "The present enormous chasm between the ignorant and intelligent, caused by the unequal distribution of knowledge, is the worst evil under which our society labours," wrote Ward in 1883.[47] More than a century later, Ward's words remain a challenge to democratic nations.

Curriculum Implications. Realization of the new ideal of social service was dependent on an understanding of the major social issues of the time—"interests" such as capital and labor and their influence on legislation, the trusts, the effects of child labor, corruption in government, and the social forces that bore upon these questions. The implications of social education for the content of the curriculum and methods of teaching were striking. For, as Charles W. Eliot had put it as early as 1892:

> No amount of *memoriter* study of languages or of the natural sciences and no attainments in arithmetic . . . will protect a man or woman from succumbing to the first plausible deduction or sophism he or she may encounter. No amount of such studies will protect one from believing in astrology, or theosophy, or free silver, or strikes, or boycotts, or in the persecution of Jews or of Mormons, or in the violent exclusion of non-union men from employment. One is fortified against the acceptance of unreasonable propositions only by skill in determining facts through observation and experience, by practice in composing facts or groups of facts, and by the unvarying habit of questioning and verifying allegations and of distinguishing between facts and inferences from facts, and between a true cause and an antecedent event. One must have training and practice in logical speech and writing before he can be quite safe against specious rhetoric and imaginative oratory.[48]

Popular education could only succeed, said Eliot, through instruction in reasoning. This would require direct practice. Reliance on the traditional studies to produce thinking not only was risky but it also was foolhardy, because it was based on the old theory of general (mental) discipline—that mental powers generated through the study of languages, for example, can be switched on to the problem of earning a living wage.

This theory was fast being abandoned in favor of direct and useful action. It had originally evolved to serve an aristocratic society and, in addition to being absolutely unfounded from a scientific standpoint, it did not meet the new social and industrial demands of a democratic society. These demands, rather than the findings of experimental psychology, proved to be the most powerful argument against mental discipline in the closing years of the nineteenth century and the first two decades of the twentieth. As noted by Kandel in his history of secondary education, the results of Thorndike's studies discrediting general (mental) discipline "fitted in admirably with the temper of the country which was ready to enter upon an expanded program of secondary education for all."[49] (Thorndike's studies on transfer are discussed in Chapter 4.)

Social Betterment and the Social Sciences

The citizen's ability to grapple effectively with the larger problems of society would require practice in doing so. To this end, the student's actual participation in the government of the school as a social system was being sought as well as training in judgment and sound reasoning. But civic intelligence also required the study of the social sciences. Ward's idea that man could, indeed *had* to, control the forces that shaped his welfare gave new prominence to the social sciences in the curriculum.

It was not that the social sciences were not already being taught. They were being taught, but mostly as memoriter studies. For instance, instead of studying the political functioning of the Eighteenth Ward, students were memorizing the dates of the various battles of the Revolution and Preamble to the Constitution of the United States. When civics was taught it was usually done through the history course. But the new social science instruction called for the study of "live" issues such as housing conditions in the poorer parts of the city.

By 1910, as a result of the new social and educational outlook and because teachers seemed neither willing nor able to apply historical facts to contemporary conditions, there was consensus among educators that civics should not be taught through history but as a separate course. There was also a demand that teachers colleges prepare teachers who could help students understand the facts of contemporary life and stimulate the desire for public service. The problem was that when civics finally became a part of the curriculum, as it did in most large school systems by 1920, many teachers taught about community welfare and political bossism the way they taught about the causes of the Punic Wars—by having students memorize the textbook.

DEMOCRACY AND EDUCATION

It was Ward's book that dealt the death blow to laissez-faire as a social system, provided the theoretical underpinnings for American Progressivism, and effected a revolution in the secondary curriculum. In establishing a new relationship between school and society he also irrevocably linked democracy and education, for at the heart of dynamic democracy lay the ability to make intelligent decisions, and this required training in citizenship as well as a certain atmosphere in the school itself. It was unrealistic, for instance, to suppose that pupils could learn to think independently in a situation that required unthinking obedience. Thus, it was quite naturally concluded that in order to produce good citizenship, the schools themselves would have to become laboratories for citizenship where school problems were solved.

Parker on Democracy and Education

As early as 1894, Francis Parker pointed to the common school as the key to human progress and fused the philosophies and fortunes of democracy and education. In a chapter in *Talks on Pedagogics* entitled "Democracy and Education," Parker wrote that the most important factor in learning is the social factor—that which children from all social classes and backgrounds learn from each other. "This mingling, fusing, and blending," wrote Parker, "give personal power, and make the public school a tremendous force for the upbuilding of democracy."[50]

Parker lay the foundation for the progressivist view that the democratic principle of mutual responsibility—the idea that each member of society contributes to the good of all—must be translated into educational goals that reflect the enormous responsibility of citizenship. But more important even than the formalized curriculum was the social power of the school to break down the clannishness and prejudices of people from all parts of the world who were learning together in the school. "The common school," wrote Parker, "is the embryonic democracy."[51]

Dewey Forges the Link

In 1916, Dewey's *Democracy and Education* was published. This remarkable work forged the definitive link between democracy as a social process for achieving man's highest goals and education as the democratic way of preparing people to make intelligent decisions about social change. Like Parker, Dewey saw the school as a democracy in microcosm. And like Parker, Dewey viewed education as a social process and a social function. But, cautioned Dewey, the "conception of education as a social process and function has no definite meaning until we define the kind of society we have in mind."[52] Thus, unless our ideal of society is clear, the definition of education as a social function would fit as appropriately in a dictatorship as in a democracy. And even in a democracy, the "social aim" of education could become perverted into a narrow national aim. This actually happened in the late 1950s and early 1960s, when the science and mathematics curricula were revised to meet the national goal of supremacy in space.

To Dewey, the democratic ideal of education was a "freeing of individual capacity in a progressive growth directed to social aims."[53] Education was growth, but it had a distinctly social as well as individual purpose.

Could not the desire for social change produced by education result in civil disorder, if not revolution? It could not, according to Dewey's definition of democracy. Dewey anticipated that question (which he must have felt would trouble educators as well as the lay public.) He answered it this way:

> A society which makes provision for participation in its good of all its members on equal terms and which secures flexible readjustments of its institutions through interaction of the different forms of associated life is in so far democratic. *Such a society must have a type of education which gives individuals a personal interest in social relationships and control, and the habits of mind which secure social changes without introducing disorder.*[54]

Perhaps the most important point to be made about the connection made by Dewey between the democratic ideal and his philosophy of education was that they were mutually reinforcing; indeed, democracy provided the conceptual framework for Dewey's idea of education. No less important is Dewey's definition of democracy as a social process, as an *experience* rather than simply as a form of government. In a very real sense, democracy and education were part of the same process of growth. That is why education could not be genuinely democratic unless democratic values pervaded the entire school.

Although Dewey made the definitive statement on democracy and education that formed the bedrock of progressive educational theory, the connection between an enlightened citizenry, social change, and the school was being made by educational practitioners and theorists well in advance of 1916. Indeed, Dewey himself advanced the educational goal of the development of social consciousness and conceptualized the school as an "embryonic society" (using almost the same words as Parker) in 1899 in three lectures that he delivered before parents and patrons of the Laboratory School he and his wife had founded at the University of Chicago. These lectures were published as *The School and Society.*[55] The lectures were given in the living room of Anita McCormick Blaine, heiress to the McCormick reaper fortune and benefactor of a number of reform causes, ranging from world peace to progressive education. She published the lectures at her own expense, and Dewey dedicated the book to her.[56] The book remains in print to this day.

In 1909 historian Ellwood P. Cubberley pointed out that well before 1900 the school had experienced a shift in purpose and direction. Said Cubberley: "The task is thrown more and more upon the school of instilling into all a social and political consciousness that will lead to unity amid diversity, and to united action for the preservation and betterment of our democratic institutions."[57] As Tyack has noted, around 1890 the concept of the state as an agency of social reform took hold in the United States.[58] The school was viewed by the society as the instrument of reform, and educators tried to give form to their new national mission.

THE REVOLUTION IN SECONDARY EDUCATION

No less important than the responsibility of the individual for progressive social change was the new relationship between the individual and the school. The democratic high school had a service to perform for each student entering its doors. It had to reveal to each person his or her dominant powers and develop them to the highest degree possible within the limits of time. It had to do this for an increasingly diversified population of boys and girls who heretofore would not have had the opportunity of gaining entrance to high school. It had to give truth to the democratic promise of opportunity for all. At the turn of the century, immigrants were arriving at a rate of about one million a year, and the major cities were populated by a majority of persons of foreign birth or foreign parentage.

Equal opportunity did not mean an identical curriculum for all; this would limit each student to the subjects accepted for college entrance regardless of their ability or interest in a purely academic curriculum. What it did mean was a flexible curriculum adapted to the real needs of individuals, while, at the same time, strengthening the ties which unite all citizens of a democracy. For this kind of program, the high school would have to break away from college domination. This was no easy task. The colleges, with the blessings of the Committee of Ten on Secondary School Studies, prescribed not only the subjects for college entrance but also their scope and treatment. The treatment was the same for the 90 percent who did not go to college as for the 10 percent who did. Until the high school was able to make its own curriculum, it would not be able to provide equal opportunity for all.

An American Invention

For several years after the investigations of the Committee of Ten, the high school continued to offer the traditional curriculum—English, mathematics, science, foreign languages (ancient as well as modern), history, and geography. Most school systems also adopted commercial or clerical curricula, but generally these courses did not enjoy the same status as the academic curriculum and were taught in separate schools in a number of cities, particularly along the Eastern seaboard. (In New York City, for example, as late as 1914, general high schools did not offer manual training, although this course was prescribed for graduates in most cities. The aim of manual training was appreciation of the significance of productive activities in modern life.)

Studies soon showed, however, that the American public was not receiving an adequate return for the increasing expenditures in education, mainly at the high-school level. Only a small percentage of pupils leaving the elementary school went on to high school, and of those only about one-third stayed on to graduate. Investigations into the career choices of youth, analyses of their social backgrounds, and the growing body of research on individ-

ual differences documented the heterogeneity of the high-school-age population. It was abundantly clear that if the high school was to do its best for each
pupil in accord with our democratic ideal, the high school would have to
become truly comprehensive in function. The education profession was
charged with this responsibility. The result was a peculiarly American invention: the comprehensive high school.

Educational Theory and the Adolescent

The theoretical basis for curriculum change was twofold. The main thesis of new educational theory held that the purpose of the school was to
foster growth by taking the pupils' present interests as points of departure
rather than to impart content that might be of use to them later in life.

The second stream of educational theory stemmed from new psychological knowledge about the adolescent. In this regard, G. Stanley Hall's work
Adolescence, which appeared in 1904, was a milestone.[59] It put the pedagogical spotlight on adolescence as a period of mental and physical development
and stimulated inquiries into the psychological significance of adolescence.
These studies had a profound effect on school organization, educational
aims, subject matter, and methods in secondary education.

Operationally, under the principles of the new educational theory subjects should be included in the curriculum only if they have immediate value
for the present needs and growth of the student. To build the curriculum on
the basis of mere tradition or deferred values was to invite the failure of the
student and the failure of the school. These principles also provided a basis
for revising or dropping existing subjects. In connection with the latter, the
new societal emphasis on efficiency and economy had a buttressing effect.
Those subjects that were dropped usually were the least popular and therefore the most expensive to offer. Greek was dropped from the curriculum
in many high schools for this reason.

Flexner's Modern School

According to at least one educational theorist, however, progressive
schools were "altogether too timid" in their elimination of "useless" subjects
from the curriculum.[60] In a brilliant and monumental essay entitled "The
Modern School," Abraham Flexner wrote that the purpose of education was
to develop in children the "power to handle themselves in our own world."[61]
This power was dependent on an understanding of the physical and social
world. The former required the ability to observe and interpret phenomena;
the latter, an understanding of contemporary industry, science, and politics.

Claims of traditional subjects for a place in the curriculum because of
historical or cultural value alone were not sufficiently compelling for their
inclusion; Flexner was inflexible about the criterion of utilitarianism. The

curriculum should include only that which had a purpose and the *"burden of proof would be on the subject, not on those who stand ready to eliminate it."*[62] Tradition alone was an inadequate criterion for justifying the inclusion of a subject in the curriculum. The objective of the Modern School was intellectual power, which, Flexner believed, would most likely be developed by realistic education.

The curriculum of the Modern School would be organized around activities in four basic fields: science, industry, aesthetics, and civics. But science would be the central field. Flexner also stressed the importance of making cross-connections between the four fundamental fields. The idea was not new, he said. What was new and needed was the courage to carry it out. Since a case could be made for neither, Latin and Greek would both be dropped in favor of modern foreign languages. Conventional mathematics and formal grammar also would be discarded.

Flexner saw the modern school as a center for scientific curriculum making, a laboratory school. The teachers would develop and test educational materials and methods as they proceeded with curriculum reconstruction in accord with Flexner's principles. They would be testing the validity of the principles. Their findings would serve as guidelines for curriculum development in other schools.

Flexner got his Modern School. In 1917 it opened as the Lincoln School of Teachers College, Columbia University. The Lincoln School was a cooperative venture of the General Education Board (which had been created by John D. Rockefeller in 1902 as an instrument for educational philanthropy) and Teachers College. The program of the Lincoln School is discussed in Chapter 4.

The three salient points made by Flexner were, first, that traditional education still permeated the school—educators were *not* bringing about the changes in the curriculum commensurate with new educational theory and the demands of society; second, that an affirmative case would have to be made for each subject in the curriculum based on its present-day utility; and third, that new educational ideas should be tested in a laboratory setting and the results disseminated to the educational world.

The Junior High School

The junior high school was foreshadowed by the recommendations of the Committee of Ten to introduce secondary-school subjects in the seventh and eighth grades. It was also a response to a substantially different problem: Compulsory education laws generally prescribed school attendance only until the child was fourteen years of age. With the 8-4 plan of school organization, the break between elementary and high school came at the wrong time. It was easier for many pupils, particularly those of uncertain purpose, to terminate their education with graduation from elementary school than to enter a distant and unfamiliar building and take new and strange subjects under several new and strange teachers. A three-year junior high school extending from the twelfth to the fifteenth year, particularly if the program provided the opportunity for election of courses in accord with pupils' interests and aptitudes, would retain many pupils through the period when most dropping out took place.

It was also argued by its proponents that the junior high school was supported by the findings of G. Stanley Hall and others that early adolescence is a period of changing and developing interests. A varied curriculum was needed that was exploratory in purpose. Those who objected to the junior high school argued that curriculum reform could be accomplished within the present organizational framework. Although administrative changes, per se, are no guarantee of an improved program, it can be said with certainty that junior high schools showed more activity in curriculum reform than did conventional schools. Junior high schools *could* be more experimental because they were not a part of the high school (which had its requirements dictated by the colleges).

In addition to beginning secondary education earlier, and starting each pupil on studies leading to a suitable goal, junior high schools were to provide training for those who would soon enter the world of work. The first junior high schools (originally called intermediate schools) were established in Berkeley, California, and Columbus, Ohio, in 1909, and in Los Angeles in 1910. The fact that by 1930 there were approximately four thousand junior high schools attests to the remarkable popularity of the new school. The 6-3-3 plan was well on its way toward replacing the old 8-4 system.[63]

The Curriculum. The curriculum principle of variety characterized junior high schools. In the more progressive schools pupils changed curricula and dropped courses freely. This created a concern on the part of many teachers and principals that the curriculum for some, at least, was composed of mere fragments. A related question was how long a course was to run to be profitable. The curriculum was frankly exploratory, but it was uncertain if the material could be reorganized into courses as short as two months or even two weeks with promise of satisfactory results. The values of some subjects could be realized only if courses continued longer than most students were likely to remain in school. Yet continuity was needed if education was to have an integrating rather than a disintegrating effect. Thus, curriculum development was also based on a second principle, that of continuity in learning.

Most educators subscribed to the principle that the junior high school program should become increasingly differentiated as the pupil continued in school. At the beginning there would be common or general education consisting of what all citizens should know. This would gradually decrease as pupils were spun off into differentiated curricula in accord with their different aims.

This reopened the question of what is a common, integrating education. It also posed the question of whether it was not undemocratic to segre-
gate pupils on the basis of future vocations at the age of twelve or thirteen.
It was also feared that those pupils who should have extended education
would be attracted to trade courses by short-term goals. According to Briggs,
who was instrumental in the development of the junior high school, there
was small chance that irrevocable errors of choice would be made at this
early stage, as long as mistakes were rectified when pupils changed their life
aims.[64]

Still, it was difficult in some schools to transfer into a new program
under the practice of curriculum tracking. And democracy demanded an
open-ended educational system that permitted all individuals to proceed with
their education as far as their capabilities, interests, and ambitions carried
them. This was most likely to happen when education was of a broad nature
for as long as possible. Even when "academic," "industrial," and "commercial" curricula were housed in the same junior high school, education very
often consisted of narrow training; pupils were not likely to be exposed in
any significant degree to knowledge that ought to be common to all.

Exploratory Courses. Although there was astonishing variation in
practice, many junior high schools offered general exploratory courses in
major fields of learning. The basic idea behind courses in general science,
general mathematics, general history, general social sciences, and general
language was to reveal to each pupil the possibilities of a general field of
knowledge and aid in the intelligent election of those subjects attracting his
or her interest. In line with educational theory, exploratory courses were to
be life-related through the elimination of artificial barriers between the various specializations within each field and through the application of its principles to everyday experience. Briggs explained the function of the exploratory
courses as follows:

> How will the exploratory course differ from those offered at present? In the
> first place, every detail will in itself be a fact worth knowing; nothing, abso-
> lutely nothing, as this period of a child's training will depend for its justifica-
> tion wholly or even largely on its deferred values. While thus being of worth,
> the facts presented will reveal the possibilities in the general field of learning.
> This means, of course, that they will cover a larger part of each field than
> now, that the work will for the most part be extensive rather than intensive.[65]

General learnings were also regarded as an essential part of a liberal
education. But the unique feature of exploratory courses was their "guidance" function; this was a way of discovering each pupil's interests and aptitudes so that he or she could be given intelligent guidance.

In practice, however, the general courses proved, on the whole, to be
disappointing and invited much criticism. In retrospect, this appears to be a
consequence of the failure to translate general aims into specific teaching

practices rather than a failure of the concept of exploratory learning, per se, to stand up under testing. Put another way, the idea of revealing to pupils the basic principles of the major fields of learning through unified courses had never been tested.

The Problems of Secondary Education

The first two decades of the twentieth century were given over by secondary educators to the urgent business of reshaping the curriculum along the lines of a new and utterly different educational and social philosophy. In so doing they were faced with enormous problems, both theoretical and practical—some seeming to defy solution.

In pushing secondary education down to the seventh grade, the school had put twelve-year-olds in a forked-road situation: They would have to choose a specialization. This was an absurdly early age to make a lifetime decision. Yet for many there would be no chance to try something else. Those separated by program tracks in junior high schools were unlikely to change their programs; they were cut off from associations with pupils pursuing different aims and life goals. In a very real sense this was predestination—the antithesis of the educational opportunity that educators had been trying to improve by increasing the holding power of the school. (As mentioned, the latter was the raison d'être of the junior high school.)

A similar problem existed in the high school. Curriculum tracking had led, in many cases, to social isolation, even where the various curricula were offered under the same roof. In such instances, students were unlikely to be aroused by new interests and unlikely to revise their ambitions. Equally important was the loss of opportunity to identify and acquire common interests and common ideals.

Theoretical Issues. The basic problem with which educators wrestled was how to provide a distinct curriculum for each individual that would meet personal goals while also meeting broad social needs. This raised several theoretical issues: Which were the courses that were most likely to meet social objectives or should all courses be revised to this end? Which courses should be required of all students? How should the problem of what appeared to be an innate dualism between vocational and so-called cultural courses, with its unfortunate social concomitants, be resolved? Even within the same subject there were various, apparently opposing, aspects. Science, for example, had applied and theoretical sides.

Related to the foregoing, should subjects be taught differently according to pupils' needs? The Committee of Ten had answered this question with a resounding "no." The committee had viewed preparation for college as the best preparation for life. Thinking on this question had undergone radical change. Indeed, many had swung to the opposite extreme, holding that preparation for "life"—for industrial efficiency and public service—was the best preparation for college.[66] Some educators believed that this was equally epigrammatic but just as baseless as the dictum of the Committee of Ten.

Dewey Points the Way.   In 1901, Dewey addressed a conference of secondary educators in Chicago on these same problems. It was time, he said, for separate vocational high schools to become integral parts of the city high school. As for the conflict in studies, this could be approached in two ways: (1) by viewing the curriculum in the context of the needs of the individual and (2) by viewing what appear to be opposing elements as complementary and essential parts of a whole. Training in a vocation, unless that training were moored in its cultural context, was narrowing. "Just as in life the technological pursuits reach out and affect society on all sides, so in the school corresponding studies need to be imbedded in a broad and deep matrix," said Dewey. The converse was also true: Those studies regarded as preparing for college were "relatively dead and meaningless unless surrounded with a context of obvious meanings"—such as studies in industrial arts, for instance.[67] In other words, their applications to human activities should be made apparent.

Dewey also spoke of another concern of secondary educators—fragmentation in the curriculum because of increasing specialization. Isolation was needed for the unhindered development of a specialization, he said. But the time came when it was necessary to pull the connecting elements of the various specializations together into a meaningful whole. That time had come. "The sole object of the separation is to serve as a means to the end of more effective interaction," he pointed out.[68] What subjects should be required of all students? Here Dewey stressed the importance of those subjects that "deal directly with problems of health, citizenship, and the means of communication through the vernacular."[69] The principle to follow in curriculum reorganization, Dewey said, was to view all the school studies in light of their place in human activities. Expansion of the curriculum should also follow this principle.

Dewey's criteria for curriculum development provided a theoretical vehicle for educators to use in their attempted escape from college domination. Educational theorists also followed Dewey's lead in developing specific principles for reorganizing the secondary-school curriculum. The influence of Dewey on Flexner's ideas is, of course, obvious. No less evident was his influence on Albert Yocum, professor of education at the University of Pennsylvania. According to Yocum, preparation for a vocation was being confused with preparation for life. This had produced "two almost equally unhappy extremes: a professional specialization which ignores general training and culture and an academic specialization which refuses to relate itself to life."[70] This, he said, was a crisis that could only be resolved by the "paralleling of general education and specialization, and the relating of each as fully as possible to life."[71]

Yocum pointed out that in their anxiety to individualize education, school people were inadvertently encouraging premature specialization. They were also excluding from the curriculum "much that all students should possess in common, whether as part of a common culture or as a means to the direct preparation for a common life from which a common culture can result."[72]

The Commission on the Reorganization of Secondary Education

These ideas had gained currency in 1913, when the National Education Association appointed a committee to develop fundamental principles for the reorganization of secondary education. The report of the Commission on the Reorganization of Secondary Education was five years in the making. Its impact on educational policy has yet to be equaled. As Cremin put it, "most of the important and influential movements in the field since 1918 have simply been footnotes to the classic itself."[73]

Bases for Curriculum Development. "Secondary education should be determined by the needs of the society to be served, the character of the individuals to be educated, and the knowledge of educational theory and practice available," wrote the commission, thereby indicating the bases for curriculum development.[74] All three—the society, the nature of the secondary-school population, and educational theory—had undergone changes requiring "extensive modification of secondary education."

But the overriding objective of the secondary school was to give flesh and blood reality to the ideal of democracy, declared the commission. Democratic education "should develop in each individual the knowledge, interests, ideals, habits, and powers whereby he will find his place and use that place to shape both himself and society toward ever nobler ends."[75] This was the dominant theme of the report and, by no mere coincidence, the theme of Dewey's *Democracy and Education,* published two years earlier.[76]

Cardinal Principles of Secondary Education. The commission named seven principal objectives "Cardinal Principles" of education: health, command of fundamental processes (reading, writing, arithmetic, and oral and written expression), worthy home membership, vocation, citizenship, worthy use of leisure, and ethical character. These objectives could best be met in a unified organization embracing all curricula—the comprehensive high school, a school with no counterpart anywhere in the world.

Far from being isolated, the objectives were actually closely interrelated; their interrelation must be reflected in the curriculum throughout the period of secondary education if the student was to be prepared for effective functioning in a democratic society. An illustration was the relation between vocational and citizenship education (social studies). Favored in the report was the "infusion of vocation with the spirit of service" and the "vitalization of culture by the world's work."[77]

The report addressed itself squarely to the formidable problems of secondary education, finding every subject in need of reorganization so that it could contribute more effectively to the seven cardinal principles. Indeed, the place of each subject in the curriculum was dependent on the value of its contribution.

Specialization and Unification. "With increasing specialization in any society comes a corresponding necessity for unification. So in the secondary school, increased attention to specialization calls for more purposeful plans for unification," stated the report, paraphrasing Dewey's words of nearly two decades earlier.[78] Unification would be accomplished mainly through *constants,* those courses required of all students. These were to be determined by the objectives of health, command of fundamental processes, worthy home membership, citizenship, and ethical character.

Unification was, of course, a fundamental purpose of education in a democracy. In addition to the comprehensive organization of the school itself and the curriculum in general education, unification could be attained through the mingling of students from all walks of life as they participated in social activities, school government, and athletics.

In addition to constants, the secondary school should provide *curriculum variables* (specialized courses determined by the student's goals) and *free electives* to be taken in accord with interests, generally to meet the objective of the worthy use of leisure (although electives could also be taken in accord with vocational needs or interests other than avocational).

The commission advanced two important principles in connection with specialization and unification: (1) The more the time for curriculum variables, the more purposefully should be the time spent on constants as a vehicle for unification and (2) the more differentiated the curriculum, the more important is the students' social mingling.

Continuous Progress. The idea that individual development is a continuous process was being emphasized in educational theory. An abrupt break between elementary and secondary education was therefore undesirable. On this basis, the commission endorsed the division of secondary education into junior and senior periods, each ordinarily three years in length and each with discrete purposes. The junior high school should offer the pupil an opportunity to follow his or her interests, to explore his or her abilities and aptitudes. Seventh-graders should not be required to select a specialization but, rather, should have some experience with a variety of vocations—agricultural, commercial, and industrial—plus homemaking for girls and, for some pupils, some work in a foreign language. The foregoing should be organized into short units so that every pupil could take several units. The commission stressed, however, that the work "should be of real educational value, in addition to its exploratory value."[79]

Both junior and senior high schools should be of the comprehensive type to provide students with a sound basis for a wise curriculum choice in addition to serving as organs of unification.

Curriculum Differentiation and Course Content. The commission endorsed the idea of teaching subjects differently in accord with the needs and interests of pupils. On the other hand, curriculum differentiation did not mean that the content of every course should be determined by the dominant element in the curriculum. Such a practice, warned the report, "would ignore other objectives of education just as important as that of vocational efficiency."[80]

Immediate Versus Deferred Values. As a reaction against formalism, some educators were advocating that pupils study only that which was of immediate interest or value to them. Here the commission drew the line: "This extreme," they declared, "is neither necessary nor desirable. They [pupils] should be helped to acquire the habits, insights, and ideals that will enable them to meet the duties and responsibilities of later life."[81] On the other hand, they should be encouraged to respond to present duties and responsibilities as well, as a foundation for future behavior.

Overage Elementary Pupils. In a section of the report dealing with the articulation of secondary education with elementary education, it was recommended that overage pupils who are retained in the elementary school when they can no longer benefit from it be admitted to the secondary school. "Experience has shown," argued the commission, "that the secondary school can provide special instruction for overage pupils more successfully than the elementary school can."[82] Judging by the policies of many contemporary school systems, this recommendation is as radical today as it was in 1918. In these systems, overage pupils are retained in the elementary school with a curriculum unsuited to their social and psychological development.

A Vision of Days to Come. It can be said in retrospect that the authors of the cardinal principles had not only an accurate grasp of the pedagogic present but also a remarkable sense of days to come. They, in no small way, determined the shape of the secondary school. They had a vision of secondary education for *all* youth. That vision was fulfilled in their century.

"The conception that higher education should be limited to the few is destined to disappear in the interests of democracy," points out the report prophetically.[83] Just as secondary schools should admit those who can no longer be served adequately by the elementary school, so should institutions of higher learning admit those whose needs are no longer met by the secondary school, maintained the commission.

The cardinal principles were more than a declaration of independence by the high school from college domination. As Arthur Wirth has suggested, the central point of the report was that the high school should meet the needs of all youth, "rather than cater to the minority that was college bound."[84] The authors had in mind a design to adjust the curriculum to changing times and a movement toward social democracy. But probably even they failed to realize the magnitude of their contribution to the field of curriculum development. Since its publication, the report has provided the framework for the development of the secondary-school curriculum.

The commission approached the problem of the curriculum through a study of adolescent and societal needs rather than the analysis of adult activities. Yet determining curriculum objectives through activity or "job analysis," a mechanistic approach to curriculum development, was at that time enjoying wide popularity. Job analysis was the mode for curriculum making of the Committee on Economy of Time of NEA's Department of Superintendence. The work of this committee is discussed in the following chapter.

Criticism of the Commission. The idea of the high school as a place for educating all of the children of all of the people—whether they were to go right into jobs or on to college—became part of the conventional wisdom during the early decades of the twentieth century. What is all too easily forgotten is that this view was revolutionary and, as Butts and Cremin pointed out, the

> change was signalized in the aims of secondary education as expressed by the Commission on Reorganization of Secondary Education in its famous *Seven Cardinal Principles of Secondary Education* in 1918. . . . Here was notice that American high schools would increasingly become concerned with education for all American youth rather than simply with the few who could profit from a traditional form of secondary education in the European sense of preparation for higher education.

And they went on to add that, clearly, the "problems connected with such a change of clientele were enormous."[85]

The point of importance is that over the years the American high school changed its direction from the Latin grammar school, brought over from England, to the academy and eventually to a uniquely American institution—the comprehensive high school. Early in this century, when strong pressures were exerted in certain quarters to adopt the dual European system of secondary education, with separate academic and vocational schools, the progressivists prevailed in creating a unitary system because it fitted the sentiments of the American people. To this day the report of the Commission on the Reorganization of Secondary Education has continued to provide the theoretical framework for the aims, form, and program of the high school. The reason is simply that the American people have never ceased to regard the high school as a place for educating all adolescents.

This is not to say that the commission's report has been without criticism. In 1985, for example, Ravitch faulted the commission for failing to include as aims of the high school "to transmit the accumulated wisdom of the past" and "to empower young people to make their own decisions about how to be socially useful."[86] What she does not point out is that today the high school still embraces the traditional subject matter curriculum, with its emphasis on separate academic areas. What progressive educators wanted to do was to enable students to perceive relationships among areas of knowledge, but the separate academic fields, with the main objective of the acquisition of "accumulated wisdom," won out. Moreover, the commission *did* state as an objective that education in a democratic society should develop in each individual the ideals and powers to become socially useful in his or her own way. And the report did give prominence to the democratic heritage and the teaching of history so as to reveal how the growth of our institutions relate to our present lives. To criticize the report of 1918 for failing to include in the curriculum the wisdom of the past and the empowerment of the rising generation to make their own decisions and to be socially useful is an unfortunate misreading of the historical record.

SOCIAL REFORM AND THE CURRICULUM

It has already been pointed out that progressive education was inaugurated in Quincy in the 1870s but gained little momentum until the decline of laissez-faire and the birth of interest in social and political reform. Known as American Progressivism, this interest grew to the proportions of a powerful movement in the years prior to World War I. American Progressivism provided the political vehicle for a uniquely American rationale for educational theory and practice.

The ultimate goal of American Progressivism was the improvement of the quality of life, particularly for the "submerged tenth" of society, the hidden poor who had been "discovered" by the more privileged classes. Although the movement was highly pluralistic, involving farmers, wage earners, laborers, businessmen, and humanitarians, all shared this goal in common. They shared another conviction as well: that education is the key to social betterment.

American Progressivism supplied the social interest, humanitarian spirit, faith in our institutions, and needed momentum to change the purpose of the school. As the purpose changed, so changed the curriculum. Education for social betterment required contact with reality. As indicated earlier, Ward and others who saw the school as a lever for social change faced the problem of the curriculum squarely; the artificial and ornamental would have to give way to the real and useful. The boundaries of the curriculum would be the boundaries of life.

It is highly significant that progressive education had its greatest vitality when it was fed by popular interest in transforming social and political institutions. Education, after all, was one of these institutions. It was also in the unique position of being both an instrument of reform and a focus for reform. When American Progressivism faded as a movement after World War I, the character of progressive education changed. It had lost its social focus. This caused serious philosophical and operational problems because the very definition of education was in terms of social reform. Dewey himself had couched his pedagogic creed in these terms, stating that "education is the fundamental method of social progress and reform."[87] Yet many progressive reforms were yet to come—compulsory education, child-labor legislation, woman's suffrage, establishment of the comprehensive high school, and the universalization of secondary education.

Education and the Immigrant

Not until the report of the Commission on the Reorganization of Secondary Education in 1918 did the education profession officially recognize the existence of different kinds of pupils with different kinds of needs. Yet as early as 1882, immigration from southern and eastern Europe began and soon developed into a veritable flood. Cubberley was probably articulating the view of most educators when he wrote in 1909 that the task of the school was to "amalgamate these people as a part of our American race . . . and to awaken in them a reverence for our democratic institutions."[88]

Philosophically speaking, "amalgamation" or Americanization required the child of the immigrant to adjust to the existing curriculum and existing methods of instruction rather than the reverse; this was considered an essential part of the assimilation process. It soon became apparent, however, that this was not to be, given the special needs of the pupils. Instruction in the rudiments of hygiene, for instance, was necessary for mere survival in the classroom. As such, it immediately assumed the highest priority. Likewise, the need for basic education in nutrition and homemaking forced these studies into the curriculum, even though they were not included in any syllabi. Eventually they were recognized as legitimate areas of study and included in the official curriculum of most schools. Thus, it might be said that changes in the nature of the school population had a direct impact on the curriculum, regardless of anyone's wishes to the contrary. Much more than this was involved, however; the school was rapidly assuming new responsibilities, formerly regarded as being indisputedly in the province of the home, church, or factory.

The Settlement View of Education

The settlement movement was a humanitarian response to the wretched lot of the urban poor, most of whom were newly arrived immigrants. Its purpose was synonymous with the purpose of the school in a democratic society: to make the democratic ideal a living reality. Indeed, the settlement was an educational institution in every sense of the word. But, unlike the school, its program was developed entirely from social needs and problems. Nor was education by the social settlement identified with scholarship: Knowledge was used to improve peoples' lives. The settlement took over where the public school left off (or never even started) in meeting the educational and social needs of people—adults as well as children—but in a segregated social setting.

John Dewey and Jane Addams.   Dewey was on the board of directors of Hull House in Chicago and was a close friend of Jane Addams, its founder. Watching the settlement house in action and being involved in its activities buttressed his conviction that education is the key to social unification. He also became convinced that the success of the settlement in providing adults with opportunities to discover and develop their talents was a viable reason for the schools to do much of the same kind of work with adults.[89]

The educational ideas of Jane Addams supported the educational theories of John Dewey. Both believed that learning is a continuous process and education is life. It was Jane Addams' conviction that the school was a sterile place for learning because it was disconnected from life. The real problem for educators, she concluded, was how to establish that connection. Yet Jane Addams' view of education was not narrowly utilitarian. In addition to vocational education, she wanted the factory-destined child to understand the social value and historical significance of the work he or she would soon be doing. "We have," she said, "a curious notion that it is not possible for the mass of mankind to have interests and experiences of themselves which are worth anything."[90]

The Settlement and Educational Reform.   The settlement view of education was a program that would serve all needs of children. Lillian Wald of New York's Henry Street Settlement, Jane Addams of Hull House, and their cohorts campaigned indefatigably for a broadened, individualized curriculum and legislation that would keep children in school longer. An experimental class for mentally retarded children in the Henry Street Settlement led to the creation of a special education program in the New York City public schools in 1908. Jane Addams saw the expansive program of the settlement as the protest against the limited program of the school.[91]

Rural Education

It must not be assumed that the movement to "socialize" education—to give the child's school experience a social value—was confined to the cities. If anything, the fervor for educational reform was even more pronounced in rural America. There were two reasons for this. First, farmers were directly dependent on education to reform outmoded farming practices; second, there was a movement afoot to stem the flow of farm youth to the cities by improving the standard of living in the country. The two were, of course, parts of the same problem.

Organizations such as the Farmer's Union and the American Society of Equity, both formed in 1902, focused their attention on the need for practical education in rural schools. The curriculum, they maintained, was just too book-oriented to solve the real-life problems of unscientific agricultural methods and resultant poverty. Declared one speaker at a farmers' institute in Wisconsin in 1901:

> Rotation of crops is as inspiring as the position of the preposition; the fertilization of apples and corn as interesting as the location of cities and the course of rivers; the economy of the horse and cow and sheep as close to life as the duties of the President and the causes of the Revolutionary War.[92]

It was plain that the future of farming lay in scientific agricultural education.

What should take the place of "useless knowledge" in the reorganized rural school curriculum? Demonstrations of better ways of doing things and making the widest possible use of one's environment starting with the school itself; school gardens to serve as laboratories for teaching agricultural principles; classroom discussion and investigation of new agricultural ideas; clubs with a real purpose such as a Livestock Club to determine which method of feeding will result in the greatest gains in weight.

That the regenerated rural schools really could and did transform farm life is the point of a fascinating book by Evelyn Dewey (Dr. Dewey's daughter) entitled *New Schools for Old.*[93] However, their real power to do so came with the passage of the Smith-Hughes Act in 1917, which provided federal aid for public vocational secondary education in home economics, agricultural, trade, and industrial subjects. The act provided that federal funds support in part the salaries of teachers and supervisors in the foregoing subjects and assist in their training.

THE NEW EDUCATION IN ACTION—EARLY EXAMPLES

Beginning with Parker's Quincy methods, there was a succession of pioneering efforts to put the new education into practice in private schools and public schools (sometimes entire school systems), schools struggling on the proverbial shoestring and schools heavily endowed, schools with a curriculum and schools with no curriculum, schools affiliated with universities and schools with no affiliation, urban schools and rural schools. The programs of these schools were as diverse as their founders' interpretations of pedagogical theory.

Even within the same category there were astonishing variations. To illustrate, there were schools with no firmly established curriculum because the goal was to develop curriculum, materials, and methods by testing certain theoretical principles; the curriculum of the Dewey School emerged in this way. On the other hand, there were schools with no curriculum because the goal was to eliminate "repressive influences" on children and develop a curriculum from their "spontaneous" interests. Often what emerged was a series of chaotic, fragmented activities or "happenings" (to use present-day parlance).

Of particular significance are the conflicting accounts of the success or failure of certain experimental schools. There was—and still is—much controversy over whether some schools really contributed anything of value to educational knowledge. About others, there can be no doubt as to the value of their contribution. In this category are the laboratory schools associated with teacher-education institutions. Here ideas were seen in action. These schools provided models of curriculum and teaching for an ever-widening circle of teachers from the time Parker assumed the principalship of the Cook County Normal School in 1883 until the post–World War II period. A trend away from using the laboratory school for preparing teachers began after World War II. Since then, many universities have closed their laboratory schools. It was believed that public schools would be better laboratories for teacher preparation and pedagogical experimentation because of their more heterogeneous populations. With the loss of the laboratory school, however, adequate controls for experimentation were lost.

The Dewey School

In 1896, two years after he came to the University of Chicago, Dr. Dewey, in collaboration with Mrs. Dewey, opened an experimental school. An integral part of the university, the school was to serve as a laboratory for testing John Dewey's educational theories. By the time Dewey resigned from the university in 1904, the Laboratory School was regarded by many as the most important educational venture in America.

Dewey said he hoped "to discover in administration, selection of subject matter, methods of learning, teaching, and discipline, how a school could become a cooperative community while developing in individuals their own capacities and satisfying their own needs."[94] Dewey's key hypothesis was that life itself, particularly those occupations that serve social needs, should be the focus of the curriculum. A second hypothesis was that freedom of expression was a necessary condition for growth, but such expression must be guided by the teacher. Freedom and informality were means to intellectual development, not ends in themselves.

The Curriculum. As Wirth points out in his discussion of the Laboratory School, "there was a well-considered curriculum design and the unifying theme was the story of emerging civilized experience."[95] Beginning with activities familiar to four- and five-year-olds because they were activities of the home, the developing curriculum led to the related study of occupations in early civilizations. Following the way of social evolution, it traced man's progress through discovery and invention to the occupations and organization of contemporary society. Here children entered secondary education and the work became more specialized. As indicated by Laboratory School teachers Mayhew and Edwards in their detailed account of the work of the school, the theoretical plan for the curriculum was hampered at this point by college entrance requirements.[96]

Dewey emphasized that the purpose of having little children study familiar activities was not that they should study the same things in school as they had already learned at home. The goal was for children to have the same natural interest in school as they have in the home and neighborhood. In Dewey's words, the "same motives which keep the child at work and growing should by used in the school as in the home, so that he shall not feel that he has one set of reasons which belongs to the school and another which is used at home."[97]

The Herbartians' recapitulation theory, to which Dewey was so much opposed, was not entirely refuted by his own thematic approach. But unlike the Herbartians, Dewey's curriculum was orchestrated for a larger democratic social vision.

Activities and the Curriculum. Activities were not performed for their own sake; they were purposeful—needed to solve problems that aroused the child's curiosity and drew upon his or her own creativity for their solution. This was the way the child would learn the basic skills of reading, writing, arithmetic, and spelling, skills needed to get information and as a means of communication. This kind of learning required more time than drill and rote memorization, but because it was goal-directed learning it was fundamental learning. Subject matter was a resource for problem-solving.

This approach was endorsed by the findings of child study. It was also Dewey's way of dealing with the problem of the overcrowded curriculum.

The Teaching Task. Pupils would initiate activities; teacher and pupil would make selections from the infinite body of factual material accumulated by man, taking what knowledge was appropriate for solving the problem at hand. Obviously, the selection of worthwhile experiences and suitable subject matter in light of the twin aims of developing individual powers and responsible social relationships was a heavy teaching demand. Although the misinformed portrayed teachers in the Dewey school as being merely decorative, concentrating their efforts on staying out of children's way, the reverse was actually true. So weighty was the intellectual load on the teacher that Dewey dropped the idea of having one teacher teach the children in all subjects. Instead, the school assumed a kind of modified departmentalization. Dewey's reason is worth quoting.

> One of the reasons for this modification of the original plan was the difficulty of getting scientific facts presented that were facts and truths. It has been assumed that any phenomenon that interested a child was good enough, and that if he were aroused and made alert that was all that could be expected. It is, however, just as necessary that what he gets should be truth and should not be subordinated to anything else.... The difficulty of getting scientific work presented except by those who were specialists has led to the change in regard to other subjects as well.[98]

Although one person was responsible for coordinating each child's program, the children learned to take their questions to the teachers who were specialists in whatever area a problem belonged. Nevertheless, key emphasis was given to curriculum synthesis, as the specialists were required to relate their expertise to the problems being investigated by the pupils.

Dewey's Conclusions. That Dewey's hypotheses were confirmed by his Laboratory School is evident in his subsequent writings. The social purpose of education and the effect of community on individual development that Dewey advanced in *The School and Society* in 1899 were affirmed with confidence in *Democracy and Education* in 1916. Dewey believed that his curriculum innovations in the Laboratory School were only a harbinger of the scientifically developed curriculum to come. He was to be disappointed. Progressive educators were fairly successful at doing away with the old but much less successful at building something new to take its place.

According to Lazerson, the Laboratory School also left its lasting imprint on the concept of a good teacher. "The Dewey teacher," writes Lazerson, "was flexible, experimental, knowledgeable of child development and of subject-matter. But I believe this became more than the definition of a progressive teacher. It became the language which defined the best teachers, an ideal to aim for."[99]

The Gary Plan

"Those who follow Professor Dewey's philosophy find in the Gary schools—as Professor Dewey does himself—the most complete and admirable application yet attempted, a synthesis of the best aspects of the 'schools of tomorrow.' "[100] So wrote journalist Randolph Bourne in 1916. His subject was the Gary Plan, an approach to socializing education that focused national educational attention on the southern end of Lake Michigan.

The Gary Plan was a scheme for combining educational philosophy with educational economy. It aimed to provide a myriad of educational opportunities for adults as well as children through the multiple use of facilities. Each school was organized as an "embryonic community." Work and study were done in a setting that was practical as well as intellectual. Physics laboratories, for instance, adjoined machine shops where practical application of scientific principles could be learned.

The learning-by-doing and social objectives of education were combined in a very practical way: the children did the work of the school. They operated the lunchroom, ordered and distributed supplies, and did the accounting for the school administration. Younger children were assigned as assistants to older children. The purpose was, explained Superintendent Wirt, to make the school "as much as possible like a large family wherein the younger children are learning consciously and unconsciously from the older, and the latter from contact with the younger children are learning to assume responsibility and take the initiative."[101] Here again we find the concept of the pupil as teacher associated with educational economy. (This was discussed in Chapter 2 in connection with monitorial teaching.)

Curriculum Fragmentation: The Platoon System.   The use of classrooms and other facilities by alternate groups was called the "platoon" system; while one group was being instructed in the three R's (in a two-hour block of time daily) another group was attending classes in music, science, social studies, physical education, or "auditorium." A daily hour was set aside for auditorium programs developed by pupils, teachers, or outside visitors. Even the primary grades were departmentalized.

Curriculum synthesis is not an easy task, even under the most favorable of circumstances. Departmentalization erects a formidable barrier to synthesis. Nevertheless, the two-platoon system, mostly along the lines of the Gary organization, spread like wildfire, even after cold water had been thrown on the idea by Abraham Flexner and Frank Bachman in their survey of the Gary schools. Flexner and Bachman found that Gary teachers tended not to familiarize themselves with what their pupils were doing in other subjects.[102] Yet such familiarity was a prior condition for breaking down the barriers between subjects. In the platoon schools, learning was compartmentalized even for very little children.

Although Flexner and Bachman found much that was commendable in the Gary Plan itself, such as the goal of learning through life activities and the enrichment by the school of community life, their account of defects in the execution of the Gary Plan far outweighed their positive findings. As a result, pedagogical interest in Gary quickly faded.

Learning and "Doing." Flexner and Bachman reported that the "helper" system in shops and the cafeteria was not working according to theory. The teachers, therefore, had a triple task—to guide the older children, keep the helpers out of mischief, and operate the commercial enterprise. Children were performing concrete tasks, but they were not necessarily learning. "Doing" in and of itself was no guarantee of learning. There had to be definite educational ends, and these could not be determined solely by the work to be done. As for the record-keeping done by pupils, this was having a miseducative effect because they were doing a slipshod job.

All of the foregoing were problems of supervision and administration. They did not invalidate the psychological or social principles on which the plan was based. Although Flexner and Bachman stressed this point, the effect of the survey was to cast serious doubt on the validity of the new education. Was this Flexner's intention? This seems unlikely considering Flexner's ideas in *A Modern School,* published two years earlier. Flexner appears to have believed that the grandiose claims made for the Gary Plan were unwarranted. According to Cremin, Flexner may have "set out to puncture the Gary bubble in the survey."[103]

Other Schools

Other educational reformers were attempting to make the new educational views operative in the years prior to World War I. Particularly interesting are the programs of the Elementary School at the University of Missouri, where the curriculum was organized on the bases of observation, play, stories, and handwork, and the work of Marietta Johnson at Fairhope, Alabama. Like, Dewey, Johnson believed that the curriculum should grow from occupations and activities of interest to children.

Space does not permit analysis and discussion of the many efforts of progressive educators to bring together theory and practice. A number of these experiments are discussed in detail by John Dewey and his daughter Evelyn in *Schools of Tomorrow.* Published in 1915, the book portrays vividly the spirit of curriculum developers in the early years of the progressive movement.

EDUCATION AND SOCIETY: A RETROSPECTIVE OF EVENTS

At this juncture it is useful to seek a perspective on the major themes that have shaped the events and institutions of the American educational experience. As discussed in Chapter 1 and shown in Figure 3–1, the period

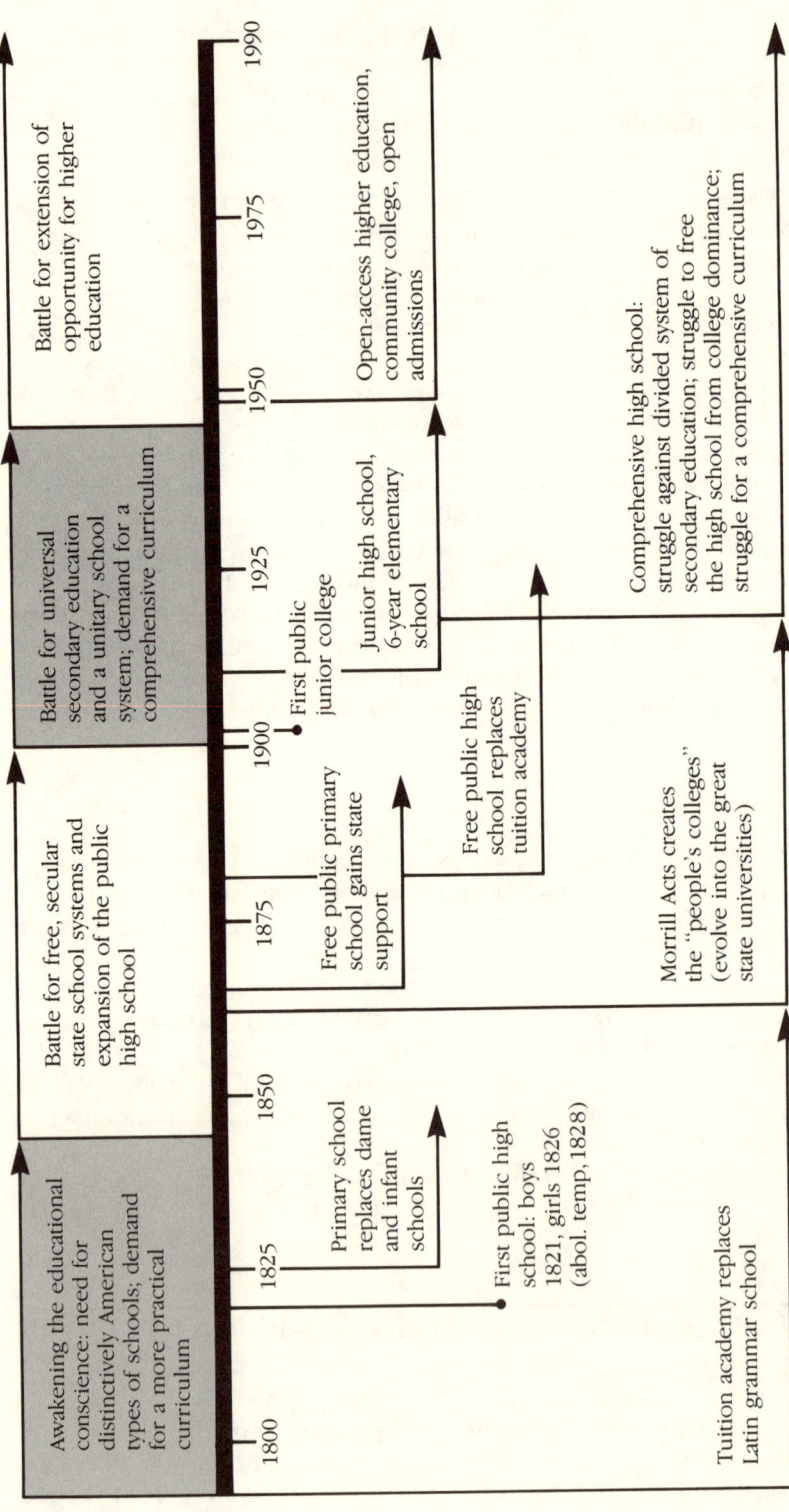

Figure *3-1.* Timeline: Major Periods and Institutions in the Struggle for American Educational Expansion, 1776 to the Present.

extending from the end of the American Revolution to the early decades of the nineteenth century was marked by the awakening of the American educational conscience and the recognition of the need to develop distinctively American types of schools, including a more practical curriculum to meet the needs of the new nation. Thus we find the academy replacing the Latin grammar school, the primary school replacing the dame and infant schools, and the appearance of the first public high schools along with the introduction of more practical studies. The period extending from the mid-nineteenth century to its closing years witnessed the battle for free secular public schools and the expansion of the public high schools. It was during this period that the free public high school replaced the tuition academy and federal support was provided through the Morrill Act of 1862 for the establishment of the "people's colleges," which were to emerge in the twentieth century as our great state universities. Coeducation in secondary and higher education also became established during the latter part of the nineteenth century.

The progressive educational reforms chronicled in the present chapter are portrayed in Figure 3–1 through the battle for universal secondary education and a unitary school system early in the twentieth century. Although this battle appeared to be won with the development of the comprehensive high school, as opposed to the dual system of secondary schooling prevalent in Europe, the forces for a divided system have continued to this day. In a similar vein, the struggle to free the high school from college dominance has continued throughout the twentieth century. Nevertheless, the secondary school curriculum grew in comprehensiveness. The laboratory sciences, vocational education, studio arts, and other modern studies gained a recognized place in the curriculum as the comprehensive high school emerged.

The years after World War II witnessed victory in the struggle for the extension of opportunity for higher education (almost a century after the passage of the Morrill Act). Yet as the twentieth century enters its closing decade, educators are still struggling with the problem of school dropouts and access to higher education for disadvantaged minorities. The curriculum problem concerning the needed core studies and their organization in the secondary school and college remains one of great debate, as discussed in the ensuing chapters.

The present chapter has been focused on the opening decades of the twentieth century. In this connection, a chronological perspective of events in education and society encompassing the first two decades of this century is presented in Table 3–1. As noted for Table 2–1 in the preceeding chapter, many of the events in society do not necessarily bear directly on the events in education, but these societal events are included to give the reader a flavor of the times. Nevertheless, it can be seen that the far-reaching progressive educational reforms undertaken during this time period were indeed a part of the vast social reforms taking place. The literary works of such American

TABLE *3-1* Timetable of Events in Education and Society: 1901–19

YEAR	EDUCATION	SOCIETY
1901	Research by Edward L. Thorndike and Robert S. Woodworth challenges the doctrines of learning transfer and mental discipline based upon the alleged superior qualities of traditional academic studies	President William McKinley assassinated, succeeded by Theodore Roosevelt; Panama Canal Treaty; Frank Norris: *The Octopus*
	Dewey makes the case for a unitary (comprehensive) high school as opposed to the dual European system with separate vocational schools	
1902	General Education Board created by John D. Rockefeller (later provides endowment for the establishment of the Lincoln School at Teachers College; funds the statewide curriculum development program, 1929–39)	Enrico Caruso makes his first phonograph recording; coal strike in U.S. (May–Oct.); *Times Literary Supplement* (London) first issued; Jacob A. Riis: *The Battle With The Slum;* Jane Addams: *Democracy and Social Ethics*
	John Dewey: *The Child and the Curriculum*	
1904	G. Stanley Hall: *Adolescence*	Theodore Roosevelt elected President; outbreak of Russo-Japanese War; work begins on Panama Canal; 10-hour workday in France; N.Y.C. policeman arrests woman for smoking in public; steerage rates for immigrants to U.S. cut to $10 by foreign lines
1906	Edward L. Thorndike (1874–1949); *Principles of Teaching*	Theodore Roosevelt makes first trip by a President outside the U.S. (visits Panama Canal Zone); Upton Sinclair: *The Jungle* leads to passage of U.S. Federal Food and Drug Act; first radio program of voice and music broadcast in U.S.; San Francisco earthquake kills 700
1907	William James (1842–1910): *Pragmatism*	Oklahoma becomes a state; financial panic; U.S. immigration restricted by law; S.S. *Lusitania* launched; breaks transatlantic record (5 days); second Sunday in May designated Mother's Day in Philadelphia

TABLE *3-1*   Timetable of Events in Education and Society: 1901–19

YEAR	EDUCATION	SOCIETY
1908	Gary Plan begins at Gary Public Schools (Indiana) Charles W. Eliot publishes *Harvard Classics*	William H. Taft elected President; Jack Johnson becomes first black world heavyweight boxing champion; General Motors established; Ford Motor Company produces the "Model T"; Wilbur Wright flies 30 miles in 40 minutes
1909	First junior high schools appear (Berkeley, California; Columbus, Ohio), leading to expanded curriculum for early adolescents (shift from 8-4 plan of school organization to the 6-3-3 plan)	Sigmund Freud lectures in U.S.; Frank Lloyd Wright: *Robie House* (Chicago); Picasso: *Harlequin;* first newsreels; Paul Ehrlich develops cure for syphilis; Robert E. Peary (U.S.) reaches North Pole; Rockefeller Sanitary Commission established (beginnings of Rockefeller Foundation); women admitted to German universities
1910	John Dewey: *How We Think* (rev. 1933) Beginning of the school survey (Boise, Idaho) First junior college (Fresno, California)	Mann Act passed; China abolishes slavery; Mark Twain dies (born 1835); Leo Tolstoy dies (born 1828); William James dies (born 1842); Jane Addams: *Twenty Years at Hull House*
1911	Committee on Economy of Time in Education (NEA). (Reports issued in the 14th, 16th, and 18th NSSE Yearbooks: 1915, 1917, 1918) American revision of Alfred Binet's IQ test (1905)	Ronald Amundsen (Norway) reaches South Pole; Marie Curie wins Nobel Prize (chemistry); Charles F. Kettering (U.S.) develops first practical automobile self-starter
1915	John Dewey and Evelyn Dewey: *Schools of Tomorrow*	World War I: first German submarine attack (Le Havre); German sub sinks *Lusitania;* first zeppelin attack on London; film: *Birth of a Nation* (D. W. Griffith); Albert Einstein: *General Theory of Relativity;* first transcontinental telephone call (N.Y. and San Francisco); Margaret Sanger jailed for writing *Family Limitation* (first book on birth control)

(cont.)

TABLE *3-1* Timetable of Events in Education and Society: 1901–19

YEAR	EDUCATION	SOCIETY
1916	John Dewey: *Democracy and Education*	World War I: Battle of Verdun; Woodrow Wilson reelected President; James Joyce: *Portrait of the Artist as a Young Man;* Theodore Dreiser: *The Genius* (censored in N.Y.); Carl Sandburg: *Chicago Poems;* national child-labor law enacted (voided by U.S. Supreme Court in 1918; subsequent law also voided in 1922)
1917	Abraham Flexner (1866–1959): *A Modern School* Smith-Hughes Act provides federal support for vocational education in the high school Lincoln School opens at Teachers College, Columbia University	World War I: U.S. declares war on Germany; John F. Kennedy born (assassinated 1963); Upton Sinclair: *King Coal;* George M. Cohan: *Over There;* Sigmund Freud: *Introduction to Psychoanalysis;* four women suffragettes arrested for picketing White House and sentenced to 6 months in jail; U.S. Senate rejects President Wilson's suffrage bill; Congress overrides Wilson's veto of literacy requirements for U.S. citizenship
1918	William H. Kilpatrick: "The Project Method" (popularized by Kilpatrick, projects had been used in the Dewey Laboratory School before the turn of the century) Commission on the Reorganization of Secondary Education (NEA, 1913–18): *The Cardinal Principles of Secondary Education,* makes definitive case for the comprehensive high school, comprehensive educational aims and functions, universal secondary education, and expanded opportunity for higher education Mississippi last state to ratify a compulsory school attendance law	Wilson's Fourteen Points for World Peace; Armistice signed; Willa Cather: *My Antonia;* U.S. Post Office burns magazine issues with installments of *Ulysses* (James Joyce); N.Y. Philharmonic Society bans works by living German composers; Mt. Wilson (Calif.) telescope completed; worldwide influenza epidemic (1 million dead in U.S., over 22 million dead worldwide by 1920); suffrage granted to women over 30 in Britain

TABLE *3-1*   Timetable of Events in Education and Society: 1901–19

YEAR	EDUCATION	SOCIETY
1919	Progressive Education Association (PEA) founded (disbanded, 1955) Winnetka Plan (Ill.) John B. Watson (1878–1958): *Psychology from the Standpoint of a Behaviorist* Ellwood P. Cubberley (1868–1941): *Public Education in the United States*	Prohibition Amendment (18th) to U.S. Constitution; President Wilson presides over first League of Nations meeting (Paris); race riots in Chicago; Wilson wins Nobel Peace Prize; H. L. Mencken: *The American Language;* Bauhaus founded (German school of modern architecture and design; closed by Hitler in 1933; key leaders move to Chicago)

Sources: *Annual Register of World Events* (London: Longman's, Green); Bernard Grun, *The Timetables of History*, rev. ed. (New York: Simon & Schuster, 1979); *The New York Times.*

writers as Frank Norris and Upton Sinclair, calling for industrial reforms and regulation to protect the public interest, were followed by corrective legislation.

This was also a time when new recognition was given to the authentic nature of the child and adolescent in human development and the need to forge the curriculum accordingly. Dewey's *The Child and the Curriculum* was published in 1902, G. Stanley Hall's *Adolescence* in 1904. Systematic research by Thorndike and Woodworth was challenging the doctrines holding that the traditional academic studies were superior to the modern studies in empowering the learner with mental discipline and learning transfer. Freud delivered his first lecture in the United States in 1909, and the first junior high schools appeared in that year to provide an expanded curriculum for early adolescents. William James' *Pragmatism* was published in 1907, when construction was begun on Frank Lloyd Wright's "Prairie House" in Chicago, integrating architecture and landscape and symbolizing the human oneness with nature. The Bauhaus school, founded in Germany in 1919, integrated the arts and crafts in industrial design and architecture. (But the Bauhaus later was to find Nazi Germany inhospitable as the Bauhaus faculty and students fled to Chicago, where their revolutionary ideas found a congenial home.)

Although coeducation in American colleges and universities had become well established during the last quarter of the nineteenth century, women were not admitted to German universities until 1909. Yet the battle for woman's suffrage in the United States was not to succeed until 1920, when the Nineteenth Amendment was passed. In 1915 Margaret Sanger was jailed for publishing the first book on birth control. The invention of the automobile self-starter in 1911 eventually served to make the automobile accessible to women drivers, who became freed from the confines of the home in ensuing decades. Child labor remained rampant, although legislation for compulsory school attendance had been enacted in all forty-eight states by 1918.

The battle for a unitary school system, led by Dewey from the beginning of the twentieth century, was to give rise to the comprehensive high school, a unique American invention, as called for in the report of the Commission on the Reorganization of Secondary Education, issued by the U.S. Bureau of Education at the end of World War I. Hence the provisions for federal support for vocational education enacted in 1917 were to be implemented for the most part in the comprehensive high school instead of in the separate vocational high school.

Dewey's *Democracy and Education,* published in 1916, was to gain universal interest and influence as it was translated into almost every language in the modern world. The publication of Einstein's *General Theory of Relativity* in 1915 provided a field approach or continuum of our knowledge of the universe in contrast to the then-prevalent discontinuity and atomism of physical science. Although not a necessarily connected development, but a parallel one, was the attack being leveled by experimentalist educators against the atomistic curriculum and their efforts to develop a sense of wholeness for the learner and the curriculum. In a similar vein, the mechanistic stimulus-response psychology was being challenged by gestalt psychology.

New laboratory schools were appearing in our colleges and universities, most notably the Lincoln School at Teachers College in 1917. The waves of immigrants to our major cities represented more diverse origins than in the nineteenth century, posing unprecedented challenges and responsibilities for the public school.

In examining the chronology of events in education and society as presented in Table 3–1, it can be seen that the events are not uniformly or sequentially developed. Historical events are not neatly sequential, though they are consequential. The forces for progress are always engaged in a constant struggle marked by temporary victories and repeated setbacks. Looking back, one cannot say "Those were simpler times."

PERSPECTIVE

In the last two decades of the nineteenth century, educational theorists shifted their focus from the methods of teaching and the atmosphere of the school to the curriculum itself. This was necessary because, as Dewey observed, reform was not a fait accompli with new methods and old subject matter. Furthermore, the problems of an overcrowded curriculum and the antipathy between traditional and new subjects literally cried out for resolution.

Theorists turned to unification as the solution for the overcrowded and fragmented curriculum because unification was a valid reflection of the nature of knowledge. Still to be determined, however, was which fields of knowledge should be the organizing centers for the curriculum. The Herbartians favored the traditional subjects of history and literature, whereas science, a newcomer in the curriculum, was the organizing center for Francis W. Parker's curriculum organization. Although Parker is remembered more as a champion of children than as a curriculum theorist, his ideas on the nature of knowledge were translated into curriculum principles that remain valid and unimplemented to this day. Parker was the first theorist to conceptualize the curriculum in light of democratic goals; clear thinking, he argued, was necessary in a democracy. Clear thinking meant related thinking, but this was not possible when each subject was isolated from all other subjects. The Herbartians also believed that related thinking was the best kind of thinking; it could be achieved only via a curriculum that reflected the basic unity underlying all knowledge. Thus, they attacked the problem of total curriculum synthesis. Never before or since has a body of educational theorists shown so much interest in total unification of the curriculum.

Ironically, although church and state alike looked askance at anyone's teaching *about* biological evolution, the work of Darwin affected the curriculum as it had never been affected before. The culture-epoch (recapitulation) theory, efforts to find a new curriculum synthesis that would accurately reflect the unity of man and nature, and the idea that education has an enormous role in the making of a better life—not to mention Dewey's definition of education as growth—all resulted from the influence of Darwin on social and educational thought.

Although the stage was set for a progressive movement in education long before it got under way, the social philosophy of laissez-faire was a strong contrapositive force; in education it meant that a pupil's success or failure depended on self-effort and that the curriculum should not be modified to meet individual needs; to do so would be tampering with a system containing a built-in mechanism for eliminating the unfit. For Hall, child development was curriculum development. The result: a child-centered school. But a child-centered curriculum is a laissez-faire curriculum; it does not direct itself to social needs and concerns. This was a contrapositive force in the progressive movement—a force that Dewey abhorred and opposed.

When progressive education gained momentum, it did so as part of the American Progressivist movement. The seeds of this movement were planted by Lester Ward with his concept of planned change. Unlike all other animals, the human could envision, chart, and work toward a social course, maintained Ward. Indeed, humans *had* to. But doing so greatly depended on education, not just education per se but realistic education. The implications of Ward's theory for the curriculum field were enormous. A realistic education meant a curriculum in accurate touch with life; ultimately this was to result in the extension of the bounds of the curriculum to the bounds of life itself.

In establishing a new relationship between school and society, Ward also irrevocably linked democracy and education. Parker and Dewey forged the link between democracy as a social process and education as the democratic way to prepare citizens to make intelligent decisions about social change. Dewey saw democracy and education as part of the same process of growth. He laid the groundwork for environmentalism, which came to undergird the modern social sciences.

The new responsibility of education for democracy fell heavily on the secondary school. The basic problem of secondary educators was how to provide a distinct curriculum for each individual that would meet both personal and social goals. According to educational theory, subjects should be included in the curriculum only if they had immediate value for the present needs and growth of the student. A veritable revolution had occurred in thinking about the curriculum since the report of the Committee of Ten in 1893.

Dewey's influence was maximal on the Commission on Reorganization of Secondary Education, which was appointed in 1913 to develop fundamental principles for the reorganization of secondary education. The dominant theme of the commission's report was the responsibility of the democratic high school to develop in each person the ability to shape himself or herself and society toward ever higher ends. The place of each subject in the curriculum was dependent on the value of its contribution to seven principal objectives of education that could best be met in a unified organization embracing all curricula—the comprehensive high school. The report determined the shape of the secondary school; subsequent reports have been but restatements of the original.

The Dewey School was a laboratory for the testing of Dewey's hypothesis that humanity's historic development, particularly those occupations that serve social needs, should be the focus of the curriculum. Dewey's hypothesis was confirmed by his Laboratory School. The Gary Plan was the first system-wide attempt to give the child's school experience a social value. The goal was learning through life activities in an "embryonic community," the school. Progressive education had its greatest vitality when fed by popular interest in transforming social and political institutions; the very definition of education was in terms of social reform.

NOTES

1. John Dewey, "The Situation as Regards the Course of Study," National Education Association *Proceedings* (Chicago: University of Chicago Press, 1902), p. 332.

2. Jerome Allen, "Have We a Science of Education?," *Education* 2 (January 1882): 287.

3. Dewey, op. cit., p. 333.

4. William T. Harris, "Textbooks and Their Uses," *Education* 1 (September 1880): 9.

5. Ibid., p. 9.

6. Lawrence A. Cremin, "Curriculum-Making in the United States," *Teachers College Record* 73 (December 1971): 209–10.

7. Francis W. Parker, *Talks on Pedagogics* (New York: E. L. Kellogg, 1894), p. 394.

8. Jack K. Campbell, *Colonel Parker: The Children's Crusader* (New York: Teachers College Press, 1967), p. 82.

9. B. G. Northrup, "The Quincy Methods," *Education* 1 (November 1880): 131.

10. Campbell, op. cit., p. 88.

11. Ibid.

12. Parker, op. cit., pp. 25–26.

13. Ibid., p. 408.

14. Ibid., p. 23.

15. Ibid., p. 377.

16. Ibid., p. 42.

17. Ibid., p. 62.

18. Harold B. Dunkel, "Voices from the Past," *The Elementary School Journal* 75 (Seventy-fifth Anniversary Issue, 1975): 4.

19. National Education Association, *Proceedings* (St. Paul, Minn.: Pioneer Press, 1895), p. 344.

20. Charles De Garmo, "Most Pressing Problems Concerning the Elementary Course of Study," *First Yearbook of the Herbart Society,* Charles A. McMurry, ed. (Normal, Ill.: 1895), p. 19.

21. Ibid.

22. Ibid.

23. Parker, op. cit., p. 393.

24. De Garmo, op. cit., p. 26.

25. Harold B. Dunkel, *Herbart and Herbartianism: An Educational Ghost Story* (Chicago: University of Chicago Press, 1970), p. 257.

26. Frank McMurry, "Concentration," *First Yearbook of the Herbart Society,* Charles A. McMurry, ed. (Normal, Ill.: 1895), p. 55.

27. "Discussion," *First Yearbook of the Herbart Society,* Charles A. McMurry, ed. (Normal, Ill.: 1895), p. 156.

28. Ibid.

29. Ibid., p. 157.

30. Ibid., pp. 182–83.

31. John Dewey, "Interpretation of the Culture Epoch Theory," *Second Yearbook of the Herbart Society* (Normal, Ill.: 1896), p. 93.

32. D. C. Phillips and Mavis E. Kelly, "Hierarchical Theories of Development in Education and Psychology," *Harvard Educational Review* 45 (August 1, 1975): 352–53.

33. Ibid., p. 354.

34. Dunkel, op. cit.

35. Merle Curti, *The Social Ideas of American Educators* (New York: Scribner, 1935), pp. 310–47.

36. William T. Harris, "What Shall We Study?," *Journal of Education* 2 (September 1869): 1–3.

37. Lawrence A. Cremin, *The Transformation of the School* (New York: Knopf, 1961), p. 20.

38. G. Stanley Hall, "Education: A Life-Long Development," *Chautauquan* 47 (July 1907): 155.

39. G. Stanley Hall, "The Contents of Children's Minds on Entering School," *Pedagogical Seminary* 1 (1891): 139–73.

40. Curti, op. cit., pp. 426–27.

41. Cremin, *The Transformation of the School,* op. cit., p. viii.

42. William D. Lewis, *Democracy's High School* (Boston: Houghton Mifflin, 1914), p. 4.

43. Ibid., p. 6.

44. Lester F. Ward, *Dynamic Sociology,* vol. 1 (New York: Appleton, 1883), pp. 70–71.

45. Laurel N. Tanner and Daniel Tanner, "Environmentalism in American Pedagogy: The Legacy of Lester Ward," *Teachers College Record* 88 (Summer 1987): 537–47.

46. Ibid.

47. Ward, op. cit., p. 602.

48. Charles W. Eliot, "Wherein Popular Education Has Failed," *The Forum* 14 (December 1892): 423–24.

49. Isaac L. Kandel, *History of Secondary Education* (Boston: Houghton Mifflin, 1930), p. 482.

50. Parker. op. cit., p. 421.

51. Ibid., p. 423.

52. John Dewey, *Democracy and Education* (New York: Macmillan, 1916), p. 112.

53. Ibid., p. 115.

54. Ibid.

55. John Dewey, *The School and Society* (Chicago: University of Chicago Press, rev. ed., 1915), pp. 16–18. (First published 1899.)

56. Gilbert Harrison, *A Timeless Affair: The Life of Anita McCormick Blaine* (Chicago: University of Chicago Press, 1979).

57. Ellwood P. Cubberley, *Changing Conceptions of Education* (Boston: Houghton Mifflin, 1909), p. 55.

58. David B. Tyack, "Ways of Seeing: An Essay on the History of Compulsory Schooling," *Harvard Educational Review* 46 (August 1976): 368–69.

59. G. Stanley Hall, *Adolescence* (New York: Arno Press and The New York Times, 1969; originally published by Appleton in 1904).

60. Abraham Flexner, *A Modern College and a Modern School* (New York: Doubleday, 1923), p. 98. (Originally published in 1916 in *American Review of Reviews,* 8: 465–74.)

61. Ibid.

62. Ibid., p. 99.

63. Ellwood P. Cubberley, *Public Education in the United States,* rev. ed. (Boston: Houghton Mifflin, 1947), pp. 554–55.

64. Thomas H. Briggs, *The Junior High School* (Boston: Houghton Mifflin, 1920), p. 39.

65. Ibid., p. 169.

66. Albert D. Yocum, *Culture, Discipline and Democracy* (Philadelphia: Christopher Sower Company, 1913), p. 19.

67. John Dewey, "Current Problems in Secondary Education," *The School Review* 10 (January 1902): 21, 25.

68. Ibid., p. 16.

69. Ibid., p. 8.

70. Yocum, op. cit., p. 25.

71. Ibid., p. 296.

72. Ibid., p. 28.

73. Lawrence A. Cremin, "The Revolution in American Secondary Education, 1893–1918," *Teachers College Record* 56 (March 1955): 307.

74. Commission on Reorganization of Secondary Education, *Cardinal Principles of Secondary Education* (Washington, D.C.: U.S. Bureau of Education, 1918), p. 7.

75. Ibid., p. 9.

76. See R. Freeman Butts, *Public Education in the United States: From Revolution to Reform* (New York: Holt, Rinehart and Winston, 1978), p. 20.

77. Commission on Reorganization of Secondary Education, op. cit., p. 16.

78. Ibid., p. 23.

79. Ibid., p. 24

80. Ibid., p. 22.

81. Ibid., p. 17.

82. Ibid., p. 19.

83. Ibid., p. 20.

84. Arthur G. Wirth, *Education in the Technological Society* (Scranton, Pa.: Intext, 1972), p. 125.

85. R. Freeman Butts and Lawrence A. Cremin, *A History of Education in American Culture* (New York: Holt, Rinehart and Winston, 1953), p. 592.

86. Diane Ravitch, "Curriculum in Crisis: Connections Between Past and Present," in John H. Bunzel (ed.), *Challenge to American Schools: The Case for Standards and Values* (New York: Oxford, 1985), p. 75.

87. John Dewey, "My Pedagogic Creed," *Dewey on Education,* Martin S. Dworkin, ed. (New York: Teachers College Press, 1959), p. 30. Originally published in *The School Journal* 54 (January 16, 1897): 77–80.

88. Cubberley, *Changing Conceptions of Curriculum,* op. cit., p. 15.

89. John Dewey, "The School as a Social Center," National Education Association *Proceedings* (Chicago: University of Chicago Press, 1902), pp. 382–83.

90. Jane Addams, "Foreign Born Children in the Primary Grades," National Education Association *Proceedings* (University of Chicago Press, 1897), p. 109.

91. Jane Addams, "The Subjective Necessity for Social Settlements," in Jane Addams et al., *Philanthropy and Social Progress* (New York: Thomas Y. Crowell, 1893), p. 10.

92. Cremin, *The Transformation of the School,* op. cit., p. 48.

93. Evelyn Dewey, *New Schools for Old* (New York: Dutton, 1919).

94. Katherine Camp Mayhew and Anna Camp Edwards, *The Dewey School* (New York: Atherton Press, 1936), p. xv.

95. Arthur G. Wirth, *John Dewey as Educator: His Design for Work in Education 1894–1904* (New York: Wiley, 1966), p. 198.

96. Mayhew and Edwards, op. cit., p. 237.

97. Ibid., p. 25.

98. Ibid., pp. 35–36.

99. Marvin Lazerson, "If All the World Were Chicago: American Education in the Twentieth Century," *History of Education Quarterly* 24 (Summer 1984): 176.

100. Randolph S. Bourne, *The Gary Schools* (Boston: Houghton Mifflin, 1916), p. 144.

101. Ibid., p. 101.

102. Abraham Flexner and Frank Bachman, *The Gary Schools* (New York: General Education Board, 1918), p. 77.

103. Cremin, *The Transformation of the School,* op. cit., p. 160.

SELECTED REFERENCES

Association for Supervision and Curriculum Development. *Perspectives on Curriculum Development 1776–1976,* 1976 Yearbook. Washington, D.C.: The Association, 1976.

Bourne, Randolph S. *The Gary Schools.* Boston: Houghton Mifflin, 1916.

Butts, R. Freeman. *Public Education in the United States From Revolution to Reform.* New York: Holt, Rinehart and Winston, 1978.

Cremin, Lawrence A. "The Revolution in American Secondary Education," *Teachers College Record* 56 (March 1955): 295–307.

———. *The Transformation of the School.* New York: 1961.

———. *Traditions of American Education.* New York: Basic Books, 1977.

———. *American Education: The Metropolitan Experience 1876–1980.* New York: Harper & Row, 1988.

DePencier, Ida B. *The History of the Laboratory Schools of The University of Chicago, 1896–1965.* Chicago: Quadrangle Books, 1967.

Dewey, Evelyn. *New Schools for Old.* New York: Dutton, 1919.

Dewey, John. *The School and Society.* Chicago: University of Chicago Press, 1899.

———. *Democracy and Education.* New York: Macmillan, 1916.

————. *The Educational Situation*. New York: Arno Press and The New York Times, 1969. (Originally published in 1904 by the University of Chicago Press.)

————and Evelyn Dewey. *Schools of Tomorrow*. New York: Dutton, 1915.

Flexner, Abraham. *A Modern College and a Modern School*. New York: Doubleday, 1923.

———— and Frank Bachman. *The Gary Schools*. New York: General Education Board, 1918.

Lewis, William D. *Democracy's High School*. Boston: Houghton Mifflin, 1914.

Mayhew, Katherine Camp, and Edwards, Anna Camp. *The Dewey School*. New York: Atherton Press, 1936.

National Society for the Study of Education. *Curriculum-Making: Past and Present*. Twenty-sixth Yearbook, Part I. Bloomington, Ill.: Public School Publishing Company, 1926.

————. *Critical Issues in Curriculum*. Eighty-seventh Yearbook, Part I. Chicago: University of Chicago Press, 1988.

————. *The National Herbart Society Yearbooks 1–5*. New York: Arno Press and The New York Times, 1969. (Originally published by the University of Chicago Press, 1895–1899.)

Nearing, Scott. *The New Education*. New York: Arno Press and The New York Times, 1969. (Originally published by Row, Peterson, and Company in 1915.)

Parker, Francis W. *Talks on Pedagogics*. New York: E. L. Kellogg and Company, 1894.

Rice, Joseph M. *The Public-School System of the United States*. New York: Arno Press and The New York Times, 1969. (Originally published by the Century Company in 1893.)

Strickland, Charles E., and Burgess, Charles, eds. *Health, Growth, and Heredity: G. Stanley Hall on Natural Education*. New York: Teachers College Press, 1965.

Wirth, Arthur G. *Education in the Technological Society*. Scranton, Pa.: Intext Educational Publishers, 1972.

————. *John Dewey as Educator: His Design for Work in Education (1894–1904)*. New York: Wiley, 1966.

4

Conflicting Currents in Curriculum Thought and Practice

History consists of events that compel our attention and is, therefore, incomplete. Other events that have taken place at the same time may be ignored by the historian, who includes only the facts that are important from his or her viewpoint. The upshot, as Descartes observed more than three centuries ago, is "that what is retained is not portrayed as it really is."[1] If the historian chooses to study the influence of business procedures on education in the early twentieth century, the progressive education movement is portrayed mainly as being concerned with an excessive emphasis upon efficiency. If instead of the many-sidedness of the progressive education movement historians offer us the child-centered school as the dominant event, our understanding of the past will not be improved.

In the broad sweep of successful historical movements, there are always conflicting currents against the mainstream, and the progressive education movement is no exception. This chapter is concerned with the drama of the main currents and crosscurrents that characterized the progressive education movement.

World War I marked a turning point for the new education, a change in focus that would precipitate a curriculum crisis. For many, social purpose perished with the war. In the 1920s the philosophical gap was filled by rampant individualism, rationalized by the new Freudian psychology. Individualism in the 1920s was manifested by protest and a search for self. Both had an enormous impact on pedagogical philosophy, particularly at the elementary-school level. The result was the child-centered school.

It should be emphasized, however, that throughout the 1920s most children attended schools that could not by any stretch of the imagination be labeled child-centered. We are discussing a movement that found its locus in private and university laboratory schools. Few public schools became child-centered in the conventional meaning of the term. Throughout the 1920s and 1930s, public schools tended to adopt progressive pedagogical innovations on a makeshift basis, taking ideas that lent themselves to the local situation; there was great diversity in the amount and kind of progressive practice. After the Progressive Education Association was founded in 1919, some public schools went so far as to incorporate its pedagogical principles into their philosophies. Here, also, there was tremendous variation in interpretation, and in many cases implementation was on paper only.

What happened to "socialized" education? In the elementary school the goal of social reform through a curriculum designed to improve the quality of life was rapidly eclipsed by socialized education with quite a different meaning. Socialized education in the new sense was a method of conducting class work. In the 1920s one heard much about the "socialized recitation." This was the beginning of the group process approach to pedagogy, which reached its zenith in the early 1950s. Socialized education had become a process, and the process had become the goal.

THE CHILD-CENTERED SCHOOL

Creative self-expression was the primary goal of the child-centered school of the 1920s. This was a striking change from the academic goals of traditional education. Most of the child-centered schools, however, did not have to undergo the ordeal of transition from an old to a new curriculum; they were new schools—play schools, country day schools, and activity schools—which had been founded specifically as exponents of the new pedagogical freedom and could start with a new slate.

The Problem of Curriculum Development

This still left the problem of curriculum development. At the beginning, it all seemed so very simple: The child would be the source for curriculum reconstruction. As such, however, the child provided very little guidance for curriculum builders. Subject matter and social reform offered concrete leads for curriculum development, controversial though these might be. As discussed later, this was not so with the child. Such was the dilemma of proponents of the child-centered school, which worsened throughout the 1920s.

Educational Theory and Child Centeredness

The requisite for true growth, maintained the protagonists of child centeredness, is freedom to develop naturally. Some reformers tried to implement the philosophy of Rousseau in its pure, undiluted form—leaving the child alone to develop his or her capacity for individual self-expression.

The Conception of Freedom. In general, reformers did not conceptualize freedom in terms of the kinds of experiences children *should* have for "complete living." Rather, the approach was negative: freedom *from* teacher domination, freedom *from* the millstone of subject matter, freedom *from* adult-imposed curriculum goals.

Implied in all this was that, left to their own devices, children would develop into something better than previous generations; they would be distinct personalities able to cope in new ways with the problems of their social order. Furthermore, they would be happier personalities because they could communicate with others freely and without self-consciousness. Thus, the twin goals of freedom were health in terms of personality and hope in terms of the flowering of a brand new kind of human being who was better able to build the good life for others and live it himself or herself.

Interestingly enough, the conception of freedom as child liberation re-emerged full-sized in the open-education movement of the 1970s. But the concept was treated by reformers as brand new. (Cremin has remarked on the "notoriously atheoretical, ahistorical character" of the open-education movement.[2])

Freedom and Creativity. Not surprisingly, the curriculum of the child-centered school was weighted heavily toward the creative arts; these, after all, were human vehicles for self-expression. Furthermore, this was the side of individual development that was most neglected by the traditional school, with its single-minded interest in intellective discipline. But children were not to have their innate creativeness and individuality polluted by exposure to the creations of adults—particularly adults in their own culture. A precept of child centeredness was that this new kind of person could not be developed by exposure to old models. Materials for creativeness—pens, pencils, paint, brushes, clay—could be provided, but no direction or criticism would be given.

Creativity and Teacher Guidance. The new hands-off policy was a reaction to the somber, domineering teacher of the traditional school whose sole purpose seemed to be the squelching of the child's initiative. As such, it was quite understandable. But was the new policy any less excessive than the old? And, practically speaking, could children be expected to produce new models by spontaneous generation or did they need exposure to the work of others?

According to Dewey, the method of surrounding the pupil with materials but not suggesting an end result or a plan and simply letting pupils respond according to whim, was ridiculous. "Such a method is really stupid," said Dewey in 1929, "For it attempts the impossible which is always stupid. . .

There are a multitude of ways of reacting to surrounding conditions, and without some guidance from experience these reactions are almost sure to be casual, sporadic, and ultimately fatiguing."[3] In the late 1920s and the 1930s, Dewey made some trenchant criticisms about what he apparently felt to be distortions and misinterpretations of his own theories and the new direction of the new education.

Dewey explained that the child who was denied the guidance of the teacher was not having an enriching experience; on the contrary, he was being impoverished. "There is no spontaneous germination in the mental life," Dewey said.[4]

Looking at the problem from the standpoint of the anthropologist, Margaret Mead concurred with Dewey completely. She described an experiment in which she supplied children of the Manus of New Guinea with pencils, paper, and encouragement but no criticism. The children, who had seen neither paper nor pencil and very few pictures, did not tire of drawing. But, said Miss Mead, "they produced nothing which remotely resembled art."[5] She concluded:

> Quick, adaptable, interested, if instead of drawing at random, they had been taught some definite style, they would have been doing good work in no time. But it would have to be a style consciously developed by gifted adults. From the spontaneous activity of children no such rewards are expected.[6]

Many protagonists of the "unfolding-from-within" theory of child development attributed it to Dewey. This is indeed puzzling, for in 1902 Dewey warned: "Nothing can be developed from nothing; nothing but the crude can be developed out of the crude—and this is what surely happens when we throw the child back upon his achieved self as a finality, and invite him to spin new truths of nature or of conduct out of that."[7] We can only conclude that many of Dewey's disciples had not read Dewey!

THE DOCTRINE OF INTEREST

"We do not dare leave longer to chance—to spontaneous, overt symptoms of interest on the part of occasional pupils—the solution of this important and difficult problem of construction of a curriculum for maximum growth."[8] So wrote Harold Rugg and Ann Shumaker in 1928 in their classic book *The Child-Centered School.* But this came as no bombshell to Rugg's fellow curriculum theorists. They (including Rugg) had in 1926 written of the necessity for the teacher to have at hand an outline of the concepts and generalizations that were to come out of instruction. Put more bluntly, the curriculum should be planned by the teacher in advance.[9] Interestingly, the list of twelve theorists who signed the set of principles for curriculum development in which this statement appeared included William Kilpatrick, who, in his writings on activity and interest, vigorously opposed subject matter that was "fixed-in-advance."

The important point in the foregoing is that experience had made it abundantly clear to many educational theorists that a curriculum based solely on the spontaneous interests of childhood was an impossibility. Such a program could have no sequence and no predetermined outcomes, not even predetermined psychological outcomes. Even a play school had to have objectives and a program that was planned to meet those objectives. Otherwise, the child might as well stay home.

Interest Defined

As shown in Chapter 3, there were many pedagogical definitions of interest. For Dewey, interest was something that a child has when the goals of a project or an activity seem important to him. In other words, interest was inherent in the activity itself rather than an extrinsic element. On the other hand, interest for many other theorists, the Herbartians, for example, meant something the teacher did *to* subject matter to make it palatable.

Educational Machiavellianism. Unfortunately, much of the interest in child-centered schools was of the latter category. Teachers mapped out their classroom strategies with Machiavellian cunning with the objective of getting children to express interest in certain topics for study.

Children are notorious in their desire to please adults, particularly their teachers. In light of this, it probably was not terribly difficult in most cases to get pupils to express interest in topics that they knew interested their teacher. How children often came by their "expressed interests" must have been distressing for the educational theorist connected with a laboratory school. Teacher manipulation in the choice of a plan is revealed in the following statement made by a second-grade teacher at the Lincoln School of Teachers College, Columbia University: "Had a child not been the one to suggest making a play city, the suggestion would have come from the teacher in such a way as to make the city a spontaneous piece of work."[10]

Determining Pupil Interests. In 1934, Dewey expressed concern that "interests" had come to mean choices expressed orally by the child. It was the teacher's task to be aware, more than the children themselves, of what the children want and need. "Any other course," he warned, "transfers the responsibility of the teacher to those taught."[11] Children tended to snatch at transient or accidental interests rather than enduring interests when asked what they would like to do. There were many dawning interests and tendencies within the child. It was the responsibility of the teacher to identify and cultivate those interests that are prized by the community and lead in the direction that the demands of society would take, argued Dewey.[12]

Ephemeral Interests and Curriculum Disintegration

But operational difficulties were only a part of the problem; the kernel of the controversy was the validity of the theory itself. Were immediate interests a valid focus for the curriculum? As indicated, experience had led some theorists to take a dim view. By the mid-1920s, it was beginning to appear that the road from the child's spontaneous interests led nowhere. The curriculum pattern that had resulted from taking this route was a series of disconnected activities. The result was an education that was disintegrative rather than integrative, making what Dewey called the "reconstruction of experience" in the direction of a unified philosophy almost an impossibility.

As Bode pointed out, the problem lay in the misinterpretation of the doctrine of interest. It was being viewed as a "mystical driving force which only needs to be released in order to produce automatically fruits worthy of education."[13] But the real travesty was the interpretation that the entire curriculum must be based on immediate interests. If the idea behind this was to make education more lifelike, real life just was not like that, argued Bode. In addition to one's immediate interests, there were long-range interests that required a sense of responsibility and a continuity of effort.[14]

Like Dewey, Bode warned of the folly of trying to build the curriculum on the quicksand of ephemeral interests. Dewey had proposed a way of staying off that dead-end road: to follow those tendencies of the child that correspond with societal values and demands. But four years later, Bode saw the progressive education movement as disastrously far along that road, leaving its social ideas farther and farther behind. In 1938, in a book entitled *Progressive Education at the Crossroads,* he warned:

> **Progressive education stands at the parting of the ways. The issue of democracy is becoming more insistent in all the relations of life. It implies a social and an educational philosophy which needs to be formulated and applied. *If progressive education can succeed in translating its spirit into terms of democratic philosophy and procedure, the future of education in this country will be in its hands. On the other hand, if it persists in a one-sided absorption in the individual pupil, it will be circumnavigated and left behind.*[15]**

By the end of World War II, there was a consensus among curriculum theorists that the immediate interests of learners were not an adequate basis for curriculum development; interests were, rather, a single determinant of what should be included in the curriculum. On the other hand, the learner's interests, tastes, and needs influenced the beginning point of the study of everything in the curriculum; to ignore this was to ignore motivation for learning. But a further dimension of the problem, one that had been generally overlooked by the protagonists of the child-centered school, was the role of education in modifying, expanding, and enriching the interests of learners.

This required a planned learning environment and planned learning experience consonant with sound principles of child development.

Well before this time, however, child centeredness, which looked at the child in abstraction, that is, disconnected from his or her social milieu, had caused a pedagogical crisis. It had provided an impossible basis for curriculum development—causing a kind of paralysis in the curriculum field. It had also disengaged education from its social moorings; yet, as indicated earlier, the very definition of education was in terms of social reform. Progressive education was at sea.

Romantic-naturalistic educators cycled back to the child as curriculum maker in the 1960s and early 1970s. Enthusiastic reformers treated the idea as new rather than inquiring into its historical rootings. As a result, mistakes were repeated and there was a failure to build upon earlier theoretical knowledge. But the old theoretical issues still obtained, and "letting the child follow his interests" failed once again as a curriculum theory.[16]

THE ACTIVITY MOVEMENT

Closely associated with the child's interests, impulses, initiative, and freedom was the idea of the child's doing—learning through activity. By 1933, the terms *activity movement, activity program,* and *activity curriculum* had become commonplace in pedagogical parlance. Used freely and sometimes interchangeably with these terms were *units, unit of work, central theme,* and *center of interest.* The terms *problem* and *project* had gained currency in the first two decades of the twentieth century. It is of interest that projects were used in the Dewey School before the turn of the century and in the Francis W. Parker School as early as 1901—well before they were systematized into a method by Kilpatrick in 1918.

As might be expected, the activity movement was confined for the most part to the elementary school. Most efforts to build the curriculum entirely around child activity were to be found in the primary grades. In the Parker School, for example, there were no subjects in either the first or second grade; the curriculum at these levels was based on "centers of interest," which were never the same two years in a row.

Evaluation in Activity Programs

Where public school enthusiasts jumped abruptly from a subject-matter format to a total program of activities, they soon tended to resume the traditional pattern for teaching the three R's; activities generally were continued in social studies and the creative arts. Although a curriculum organized in toto on the basis of activities seemed well-suited to the gifted and the above-average, it did not appear (as revealed by achievement test scores) to provide sufficient opportunity for the mastery of "basic skills" for the less able. On this basis, the time allocated for activities was reduced, and reading, spelling, and arithmetic were taught again as separate subjects.[17]

What is particularly significant is that although the goals of activity programs were in terms of child interests and experiences, in most cases program outcomes were evaluated in terms of the informational knowledge and skills associated with the traditional school program. The evaluation simply did not fit the goals. This situation is endemic to the curriculum field. As long as it exists, departures from the traditional and conventional will be doomed to failure before they even get started.

Activity as Movement

The activity movement was a reaction to the formal school, in which all learning was conducted in utter silence and the learner was to remain motionless unless given permission to move. As such, it was understandable that activity was defined in terms of gross, overt movement. Overlooked, however, was the idea that learning is in itself an active process; it can (and often does) go on without overt signs. Two additional factors contributed to the definition of activity as movement: the focus of the new education on creative self-expression and the influence of psychoanalytic theory, particularly that of Sigmund Freud, on education. The Freudians saw as the primary pedagogical goal the freeing of the child from "fixations" caused by repressive authority figures rather than the mastery of subject matter. They held that freedom from fixations could be achieved only through activities that brought out into the open the submerged ideas in the child's subconscious—his or her emotional conflicts.

The "Activity Curriculum"

Activity programs were, on the whole, expressions of child centeredness. Although some programs did have as their main objective the mastery of the traditional curriculum, these were in the decided minority; most proponents of activity conceived of education as a process that transcended codified knowledge. The objective was child growth through experience, active experience that was visible to the naked eye. For many, however, activity was an end rather than a means. Indeed, some even ascribed magical properties to child activity. The question with which we must concern ourselves here is: Was the "activity curriculum" a curriculum, or was it a method?

A Methodological Concept. According to Kilpatrick, from the standpoint of theory the concept of activity was methodological. "The activity conception by itself," he said, "does not and cannot suffice for a complete curriculum theory."[18] Kilpatrick arrived at his conclusion by analyzing definitions of an "activity curriculum" by writers in the field. Although the activity movement grew out of concern for the individual, which, in itself, has social implications, it was not based on principles of social theory. For this reason, he said, it was not a complete theory.

It is important to note here that the definition of an "activity curriculum" varied widely, leading the members of the Thirty-third Yearbook Committee of the National Society for the Study of Education to conclude that the term *activity curriculum* was worse than useless; it was absolutely misleading. Some definitions were completely indistinguishable from the definition of curriculum per se. Often the terms *activity* and *unit* were used interchangeably. But probably the most significant conclusion of the committee was that the ideas and issues in the activity movement were not new. As one committee member observed, the "activity movement thus far makes few, if any, new contributions to educational theory and practice."[19]

The Pitfall of Planlessness. The point made or implied by many of those surveyed was that the pitfall of planlessness made the "activity curriculum" an unsafe bet for the development of skills needed to function in society. It was also the lack of planned objectives that caused the "activity curriculum" to fall outside the pale of the definition of curriculum. Indeed, from the standpoint of theory, planlessness was as serious a deficit as the lack of social theory mentioned by Kilpatrick.

In general, the problems of the activity movement were the problems of the child-centered school. But the problems of the latter were brought into bold relief by theoretical interest in activity as a basis for curriculum development.

Impact on the Curriculum. As for the lament of theorists that the activity movement produced nothing new, it must be remembered that they lacked the perspective of history. The activity movement had a very important and lasting effect on the elementary curriculum, particularly in the social studies. Content in these fields was no longer separated into narrow divisions but was integrated around problems or units of experience. The idea that the solution of a problem required using material from several subject fields was inherent in the activity movement. This became the organizing principle for the social studies.

Nevertheless, it is regrettable that the concept of activity in the child-centered school was too often activity for its own sake rather than activity with a definite outcome in view. In such instances the child was literally left to make his or her own curriculum, and the results can most kindly be described as disappointing. In their attempt to humanize the school, reformers tried to humanize the curriculum. This took the negative form, in most instances, of a total rejection of any form of curriculum organization and a campaign to stamp out organized subject matter. But probably the most serious error of those who sought to develop a curriculum strictly from child interests was the disclaiming of social ideals. In the words of Bode: "If the curriculum is to be genuinely humanized, it must be based on social vision."[20] In the 1960s and 1970s, many efforts to humanize the curriculum suffered such a lack of social outlook.

THE PROJECT METHOD

In 1918, Kilpatrick published a theoretical treatise in which he identified the "purposeful act" as the building block for the curriculum and "child purposing" as the key to learning. Entitled "The Project Method" and published in the *Teachers College Record,* the article created the biggest wave of pedagogical excitement since the Herbartians' five formal steps of instruction; more than sixty thousand reprints poured forth into the educational world in the next quarter century. "The Project Method" brought Kilpatrick, a professor at Columbia's Teachers College and a protégé of Dewey, immediate and enduring fame.

Theoretical Backgrounds

Before discussing Kilpatrick's concept of the educational project, it is important to note the original meaning of the term *project.* (As Kilpatrick was quick to point out, he did not invent the term; it already had currency in certain educational fields.[21]) Dewey, it will be recalled, attempted to reproduce in his experimental elementary school the actual conditions of social life. Children learned about the work of man—the industries of life—by working (doing) rather than being passive receptors of information. The curriculum took the form of projects rather than formal school subjects; the school program resembled a series of workshops. Arithmetic, reading, history, science, and other subjects were brought in as needed to work out a given project. The idea behind this approach was that children would learn to think if they worked on problems of genuine interest to them. Thinking, Dewey stressed, *is* problem-solving. To Dewey, thinking was the key to intelligent action, as opposed to impulsive or routine action.

Dewey's Complete Act of Thought. Dewey's definition of thinking was the scientific method applied to all human problems, ranging from the simple problems of daily living to complex social problems and abstract intellectual problems. According to Dewey, there were five phases in the complete act of thought. These phases were not steps in the sense that they were necessarily in sequence; rather, they were, as Dewey explained in his book *How We Think,* the "indispensable traits of reflective thinking."[22] The five phases or "indispensable traits" were (1) defining the problem; (2) noting the conditions surrounding the problem—that is, identifying all the significant factors (this is a phase in gathering data concerning the problem); (3) formulating hypotheses for the possible solution of the problem; (4) elaborating (reasoning out) the probable value of the various hypotheses for solving the problem; and (5) actively testing the hypotheses to see which ideas offer the best solution for the problem.

From the foregoing it seems obvious that an educational project requires thinking as well as doing. And it seems clear that doing, in and of itself, is not necessarily evidence of thinking; indeed, doing can be random and mindless. What Dewey was trying to do was to make action, insofar as possible, intelligent action; the outputs from the process of thinking were to serve as guides for future experience. Yet, as just mentioned, there was a tendency of proponents of "activity programs" to regard overt doing as an end rather than a means.

According to Dewey, a worthwhile activity gave the child a chance to formulate and test solutions to problems, to practice the thinking process. This kind of doing was the basis for the project idea as he conceived it and made it operational in the Dewey School.

Home Projects. It was in science and agricultural education, however, that the project method revolutionized instruction. In the sciences, the laboratory method of teaching began to gain acceptance in the last decades of the nineteenth century. Prior to that, the lecture method was used and students seldom observed the phenomena that their teacher described. Laboratory work in high-school agriculture courses took the form of home projects; those students who lived on farms learned various approved practices in agriculture by trying them out at home under actual farm conditions. To illustrate, a project might be to try out a disease-resistant variety of wheat (developed by the state university) in an area plagued by the disease; the student would try it out and compare it with other varieties he (or his father) had been using. The aim of the home project was actually twofold: to improve contemporary practice in agriculture, thus improving the quality of life, and to develop lifelong openness to change via the experimental method.

Projects were undertaken by the agriculture student in the setting where he would be (and undoubtedly already was) farming; thus education and life were continuous. This was not the case when instruction was by lecture and textbook analysis, and totally removed from the scene of action. Furthermore, lectures and textbooks often dealt only peripherally with the concerns of farmers. With the project method, on the other hand, a student also had to do a considerable amount of reading and study to work out a project, but the information acquired was targeted to a definite concern. An important educational principle was involved here: Whereas subject matter in texts was "logically" organized, it was "psychologically" organized with project teaching.

The project method also became central to the school shopwork in industrial arts and in the vocational education programs in trades and industries.

Kilpartrick's Project Method

Kilpatrick's aim was to develop a pedagogical theory that would wed the educational psychology and the educational philosophy of the day. The psychology was Thorndike's "connectionism," also known as "S-R bond psychology," particularly Thorndike's "law" of effect.[23] The philosophy was, of course, the Deweyan view of education, which ironically was antithetical to "S-R psychology." The result of Kilpatrick's effort to unify these ideas was a definition of project so broad that it all but obliterated the distinctive aspects of the project method as used in agricultural education. For Kilpatrick, a project was a "wholehearted purposeful activity proceeding in a social environment."[24] The project method was proposed as a complete theory for curriculum development as well as a method; the curriculum was to consist of a series of projects.

The Doctrine of Purposeful Activity. According to Kilpatrick, problem-solving was a project as long as the child purposed to solve the problem. But Kilpatrick went on to hold that making something such as a boat or a dress, writing a letter, enjoying an aesthetic experience, *and* even drill were also projects. There was only one criterion for a project: "the presence of a dominating purpose." It was the attitude of the learner toward his or her work that counted. This was what made the difference between "drill as a project and drill as a set task."[25]

Did a suggestion for a project have to originate with the child? In his book *Foundations of Method,* which is mainly an elaboration of the ideas in "The Project Method," Kilpatrick addressed this question. Suggestions could come from the teacher as long as the "child wholeheartedly accepts and adopts the teacher's suggestions."[26] As Bode observed, this apparent contradiction in a philosophy that says that the curriculum must stem from child purposes is indeed puzzling. "At first sight," pointed out Bode, "the doctrine of purposeful activity seems revolutionary in tone. Presently, however, it appears to mean only that activity should be purposeful *as far as it can be made so.* This borders on the commonplace."[27]

A Child-Centered Theory. Nevertheless, when pinned down to an actual choice between the child and teacher, as he is in his dialogue in the *Foundations of Method,* Kilpatrick chooses the child. According to Kilpatrick, although it was *acceptable* for the child to adopt the teacher's suggestion as his or her own, it was *preferable* for children to have practice in all four steps of any given project: purposing, planning, executing, and judging. Granted the teacher could come up with a better plan. But, said Kilpatrick, "if you want to educate the boy to think and plan for himself, then let him make his own plan."[28] This was Thorndike's law of exercise. Furthermore, when the boy made his own plan his wholeheartedness of purpose was increased, leading to satisfaction and more learning. This was the law of effect. Kilpatrick's choice of child over teacher tilted his philosophical position indisputedly into the child-centered camp. For all intents and purposes, Kilpatrick was saying that the child must make his own curriculum.

Kilpatrick's definition of project is so general that one would be hard pressed to find anything done in the classroom that did not qualify as a project as long as it was done "wholeheartedly." "Child purposing" appears to be nothing more or less than child interest under a different label.

Differences with Dewey

As for the social theory that Kilpatrick found lacking in the activity method, it was, regrettably, still missing in his project method and for much the same reason. Although both individual and group projects required a "social environment" and group projects required "shared purposes," these are insufficient grounds for promoting the project method as a social theory. Like the activity method, Kilpatrick's project method was solely a method. Like the activity method, it stopped short of linking education with social problem-solving and the progressive improvement of society. Here is a very definite and crucial difference with Dewey, whose "complete act of thought" was a tool for building social power and insight through social problem-solving. Despite a token mention of "social environment," Kilpatrick's "purposeful activity" remains a child-centered approach.

Kilpatrick's project method was an attempt to marry two opposing theories—behaviorism and Dewey's method of intelligence. Behaviorists (connectionists) reduce education to the formation of the proper responses; as Bode put it, behaviorism is a "psychology that explains intelligence by explaining it away."[29] Here again was a fundamental difference with Dewey, who saw as the primary goal of education the free operation of intelligence.

There is a third difference with Dewey. Whereas Dewey's goal at his laboratory school was to develop a totally new curriculum starting with the experience of the young child and culminating with organized subject matter, Kilpatrick, on the basis that the child's future needs are uncertain, waged a battle against subject matter that was "fixed in advance." Kilpatrick left it to the child to put the scattered little pieces he had learned as needed into meaningful wholes.[30] (Apparently, the child not so inclined was simply to be let alone.) As Cremin explains, Kilpatrick's attack on subject matter "shifts the balance of Dewey's pedagogical paradigm to the child. The resultant child-centered emphasis calls to mind the very position Dewey himself rejected, first in *The Child and the Curriculum* (1902) and later in *Experience and Education* (1938)."[31]

Application

For some years, Kilpatrick's project method found its application almost entirely in the elementary school, where it was often indistinguishable from the activity method and unit teaching. (Indeed, to one educational theorist, at least, projects were "central teaching units."[32]) There were circus projects, doll-house projects, Indian projects, sand table projects, school carnival projects, farm projects, boat projects, post office projects, Eskimo projects, newspaper projects, zoo projects, Dutch projects, Mexican projects, and projects in medieval life. As Hosiac noted in 1923, the "puzzle is not to find projects but to decide which ones are the most worthwhile."[33]

When the project method of teaching finally did find its way into the secondary-school social studies curriculum, it was by way of interest in problem-centered instruction as a means for integrating subject matter, teaching reflective thinking, and helping youth to solve their problems.

Theoretical Difficulties

Not surprisingly, some of the criticisms leveled against the "project curriculum" were those associated with the "activity curriculum"; theorists called attention to the fragmentary and haphazard nature of a curriculum comprised entirely of projects. Bereft of sequence and design, such a curriculum would be impossible to evaluate objectively.

Emphasis on "Instrumental" Learning. According to Bagley and Bode, however, there was a far deeper theoretical difficulty. The project method failed to address itself to education that was not closely associated with immediate practicality.[34] The emphasis of the project method was on "instrumental" learning, on skills and knowledge as instruments for addressing more immediate concerns. According to Bagley, this implied that knowledge was of value only to the extent that it enabled the learner to solve problems. But only a small portion of the race experience was of the sort that would help someone out of some difficulty. Was the bulk of knowledge, including skill development and those content areas that require continuity and systematic treatment, to be obliterated from the curriculum? This was dangerous, argued Bagley, unless there was some compensating gain. The project method, which focused on "purposeful activity" and ignored the organization of what was to be learned, took too narrow a view of knowledge to abandon all in favor of a singular and loosely conceived method for curriculum development.[35]

Other "Dangers and Difficulties." A symposium on the "dangers and difficulties" of the project method was held at Teachers College in the spring of 1921. Discussed, in addition to the narrowness of a curriculum based entirely on instrumental values, were (1) the danger that children would select only manipulative (making and building) activities, many of which tend to remain at a relatively low cognitive level (in contrast with higher-level purposeful intellectual inquiries), (2) the danger of overemphasis on individualism—selecting projects that are not related to a common purpose and ignore the socialization process, (3) the difficulty of obtaining materials that bear directly on a given problem, and (4) the danger of neglecting to extrapolate general ideas from project experiences—failing to develop the power of thinking.[36]

The breadth of Kilpatrick's definition of an educational project also generated a multitude of problems. An amazing variety of things (including units of study) that were not normally associated with the term *project* were labeled as projects. "A project is *not a topic*—large or small," protested Kilpatrick at the Teachers College symposium. "What sense there can be in introducing this kind of confusion is more than I can see," he said.[37]

Ultimately, however, the biggest danger to Kilpatrick's project method was its association with child centeredness. Although Kilpatrick also protested that to follow the project method was *not* "to turn children loose to make their own decisions, to decide their own course," that it was "purposeful activity proceeding under wise guidance," it was the child-centered image that prevailed.

The Project Method Today

Today, the project method is all but forgotten in the educational literature. It does not even appear in the index of the *Handbook of Research on Teaching,* published by the American Educational Research Association.[38] Yet the project method continues to be a viable method of instruction in science, industrial arts, and various vocational subjects such as vocational agriculture.

CONFLICTING INFLUENCES ON CHILD-CENTERED SCHOOLS

In addition to the twin principles of child interest and activity, there were other pervasive influences on the child-centered school. It will be noted that these influences are philosophically incongruent. This same phenomenon is apparent in recent curriculum influences; witness the back-to-basics movement and efforts to add higher-order thinking skills in subject areas during the 1980s. From the historic experience, educators should have learned that basic skills cannot be developed effectively when severed from ideas and meaningful applications. And higher-order thinking skills cannot be developed when injected as a special or segmental emphasis into an inadequate curriculum. Thinking must be infused throughout a well-articulated curriculum.

Efficiency and Activity Analysis

Curriculum making in some child-centered schools was influenced by the obsessive interest in efficiency that swept the nation like a fever just before World War I and led to the appointment by the NEA in 1911 of a Committee on Economy of Time in Education. The committee's charge was to eliminate waste in the curriculum. The work of this committee is discussed in detail later in this chapter. It is sufficient to say here that the committee approached its charge by attempting to find out what knowledge children need to have in life by determining what knowledge adults actually use.

It will be recalled that the "modern school" described by Flexner in his essay was to be dedicated to the purpose of evolving a utilitarian curriculum. Flexner did not suggest that the curriculum be based on the activities conducted by adults in everyday living. Nevertheless, this was an approach used by curriculum makers in science and social studies at the Lincoln School of Teachers College (Flexner's "modern school").

Integration for Meaning

A second but far less conservative influence on the curriculum was a movement toward reordering and resynthesizing knowledge so that it was no longer broken up into meaningless fragments. As historian James Harvey Robinson, who provided the theoretical underpinnings for the movement, wrote in 1924: "Specialization, so essential in research, is putting us on the wrong track in education."[39] Robinson called for the *rehumanization* of knowledge. By this he meant the development of new integrations of subject matter to make it the least abstract possible. Said Robinson: "Our knowledge of man and his world must be reordered and restated; it must be put together with full regard to the ways in which the average person accumulates knowledge. It must be re-synthesized."[40]

Robinson's book, which was an expansion of an address given before the American Association for the Advancement of Science in 1922, provided a new and highly attractive theoretical base for curriculum synthesis. Its fundamental idea, that the importance of the various fields of knowledge "lies in their relation to ourselves and our fellow men," was instrumental in the development of proposals for integrated-experience curricula in progressive schools.[41]

Thus, in addition to the objective of creative self-expression, the child-centered school was influenced by the "scientific" curriculum movement and a radical new idea of curriculum synthesis for meaning. Unfortunately, however, the use of scientific measurement in curriculum making rarely went beyond activity analysis and the analysts tended to view the child as a miniature adult. Few attempts were made to evaluate new curriculum materials and experiences by controlled experiments. At the Lincoln School, regarded as one of the best and most influential progressive experimental schools, only a few comparative studies were conducted, and such experiments never involved the total curriculum. (A possible exception was the Eight-Year Study, which was not a Lincoln study per se. The Progressive Education Association's famous experiment in secondary education, the Eight-Year Study, is discussed in Chapter 5.)

EXEMPLARS OF THE NEW EDUCATION—WINNETKA AND THE LINCOLN SCHOOL

According to Rugg and Shumaker, who in 1928 examined the programs of more than one hundred so-called progressive schools, not many had abolished school subjects and not a single one had abandoned the subject organization in the upper elementary grades and the high school.[42] Even at the Lincoln School, categorized by Rugg and Shumaker as a child-centered institution, the elementary curriculum was based on units that recognized the various subject fields.

Generally speaking, the objective of curriculum makers in the 1920s was to reorganize subject matter in accord with the findings of child development. There was little questioning of the conventional school subjects by educational leaders; rather the emphasis was on curriculum adaptation, that is, using the principles of child development as a guide for the organization and placement of subject matter.

In Winnetka, Illinois, Superintendent Carleton Washburne and his staff conducted grade-placement investigations to determine when children could most effectively learn to read. They conducted similar studies on arithmetical operations, spelling words, and basic facts in history and geography. Following this approach to its logical conclusion, the Winnetka system attempted to adapt its curriculum to the needs of individual children. The method used—the forerunner of programmed instruction and mastery learning—is examined in the paragraphs that follow.

At the Lincoln School, emphasis was also on individual development but focused particularly on such educational ends as insights, appreciations, and creative power. At Lincoln, as in other laboratory schools, educational researchers made little progress in finding ways to measure such outcomes. Winnetka and the Lincoln School were very different models of curriculum development. Winnetka was committed to a subject organization, and Lincoln's was an "experimental" curriculum. But both were prototypes of the new education.

Winnetka

"Our observation has been that schools which attempt to develop all their knowledge-and-skill subjects from childlike activities often do a 'sloppy' job in giving the children mastery of the tool subjects and sometimes distort the so-called 'childlike' activities in an attempt to bring in knowledge and skills."[43] So wrote Carleton Washburne in 1926. Thus, the Winnetka curriculum was divided into two distinct parts: the "tool subjects," also called "common essentials," and activities. The "tool subjects," arithmetic, reading, the language arts, and, at first, the social studies, were subdivided into units of achievement. (Ultimately, the social studies were put in the activities curriculum.)

"Individual" Instruction. Children were allowed to work on a unit as long as needed for mastery. They worked independently, using self-instructive, self-corrective materials developed by the Winnetka staff. After each self-test, the child was given a check test by his or her teacher. Class assignments and recitations were abolished. All elementary grades in Winnetka were organized on this basis.

What came to be known as the "Winnetka Plan" was the first systemwide attempt to "individualize' the subject curriculum. It was based on the idea that the best way to improve the curriculum was to reorganize it so that each child could master it at his or her own individual rate. Pupil assignments were based on curriculum studies conducted by Washburne and his staff. They wrote teaching materials for reading, arithmetic, spelling, history, geography, and science. The idea was based on a plan for "individual" instruction developed in 1913 by Frederic L. Burk at the San Francisco State Teachers College laboratory school.

Curriculum Investigations. A major point of interest is that when Washburne began his work at Winnetka in 1919, textbooks and school programs (which tended to follow textbooks) were arbitrarily graded. In arithmetic, for example, some schools in the United States taught long division in the third grade whereas others introduced it in the fourth or fifth grade. Washburne and his associates conducted investigations involving more than five hundred cities to determine at what mental age children could most effectively learn the various arithmetical operations. They found that the mental age necessary for each arithmetical operation was considerably higher than the age at which it was usually taught in school.

The findings from this study formed the basis for arithmetic assignments made to individual pupils in the Winnetka elementary schools and influenced the content of textbooks throughout the United States and Canada; there was, for the first time, an attempt to gear the order of arithmetic topics to the developmental abilities of the child. Ultimately, however, Washburne was to be disappointed in the application of research findings to the teaching of arithmetic. Textbooks, after all, were still written in terms of the mental age of the average child, although research indicated it was the mental age of the individual that was the key to his or her learning effectively. Wrote Washburne in 1963: "Tradition and inertia (and lack of knowledge as how to individualize instruction) have made practice lag behind scientific findings in this (as in all fields)."[44]

The Two-Part Curriculum and the Learner. Washburne maintained that the distinction between the two parts of the curriculum was not apparent to the learner because sharp lines were not drawn between group and creative work and individual mastery of "tool" subjects. There were no signs, he said, of the "divided self," which some educational theorists feared might result from "individual" instruction in subject matter and social education in groups.[45].

Kilpatrick on Winnetka. But Kilpatrick raised some significant questions. For one, had Washburne fallen into the trap of identifying those subjects that could be taught on a mechanical basis as "the common essentials?" Kilpatrick pointed out that there was no agreement among educators on what constituted "*the* common essentials." "Not 'the common essentials' but 'some common essentials' that lend themselves to self-teaching assignment—these constitute the content of the first part of the Winnetka scheme," he contended.[46]

This theoretical issue is as timely today as it was when Kilpatrick raised it in 1924. Often we hear the terms *individualized instruction* and *programmed instruction* used interchangeably, and many proponents of programmed instruction believe erroneously that to use programmed materials is automatically to "individualize" instruction. Furthermore, this approach to individualization is often held as the best means of teaching the "basic" or "tool" subjects when the converse is true; certain subjects lend themselves to mechanical teaching more than do other subjects. This alone, however, does not make these subjects "*the* common essentials" or "*the* basic subjects." What is often forgotten is that there are many desirable educational outcomes that do not lend themselves to a system of self-teaching (programmed instruction).

Winnetka sought to provide for the development of ideals, habits, interests, and appreciations through the second part of the curriculum: creative self-expression and group work. Here Kilpatrick raised another important issue, that of the values attached to various subject matters. The curriculum was broken into two disconnected *unequal* parts. When all was said and done, the indisputable fact remained that the "common essentials" were the essentials in Winnetka.[47]

Kilpatrick suggested a plan with the emphasis reversed. The heart of the curriculum would be a series of projects in which there would be need for the use of basic skills in meaningful situations. Self-instructive materials correlated with the project work would be available for children to use as they became conscious of the need.

Curriculum Adaptation. The Winnetka Plan was a notable example of curriculum adaptation, the idea that the school could best be improved by rearranging the existing curriculum in accord with findings of child development. In this connection, nothing conveys the interest of educators in curriculum adaptation more clearly than the title of the Twenty-fourth Yearbook of the National Society for the Study of Education, published in 1925: *Adapting the Schools to Individual Differences.*

Forms of "individual" instruction such as the Dalton Plan, in which the student was assigned "jobs" in various curriculum areas, had access to as many "subject laboratories," and was given worksheets to complete, were popular because they did not call for any changes in the curriculum or textbooks. The learning centers found in many schools today are strongly reminiscent of the subject laboratories in the Dalton Plan.

The Lincoln School

The founding of the Lincoln School of Teachers College has already been described. In his essay *A Modern School,* Abraham Flexner stated the case for an experimental school that would develop and test curriculum principles and materials. Attention was to be directed particularly to the problem of curriculum synthesis within and between the major fields of knowledge. The old doctrine of discipline for discipline's sake was to be replaced by the criterion of utility.

Units of Work.   Unlike the Winnetka Plan, the curriculum of the elementary division of the Lincoln School was organized around the "unit of work." Operationally, however, the separate subject was still omnipotent. This was evident in the evaluation process; the final step of the unit was a summary of subject areas covered, and reporting to parents was by subjects.

Hypothetically, at least, the idea for a unit originated with the children; the child-centered school of thought held that nothing should be learned that does not arise from the child's interests or "felt needs." But as previously mentioned, units often were teacher-initiated or chosen "cooperatively" by teacher and class. When pupils showed little inclination to hunt for a worthwhile problem, the teacher had to compensate and assign one (theory notwithstanding). Details for the units—even teacher-assigned ones—were generally not planned in advance.

The new education held that subject matter and skills were most effectively learned when there was a real need for them. Theoretically, there was no place in the new curriculum for isolated subject matter and drill. Did Lincoln teachers dispense with subject matter and skill development except as the need arose? Put another way, were all skills—reading, for instance—taught via the unit of work? This decision, like all curriculum decisions at Lincoln, was individual. Some teachers relied completely on the unit as both the vehicle and the criterion for worthwhile learning. Thus, which arithmetical operations they taught depended on the children's need to use these processes to solve a problem about which they had become curious. Other teachers scheduled separate periods for instruction and practice in skill development. Second-grade teachers Katharine Keelor and Pauline Miner, for example, set aside thirty-five minutes per day for formal reading instruction (including an "individualized" silent reading program for able readers).[48]

Upon completion, units of work were broken down into subject-matter components to determine what kinds of content had grown out of the various activities. This was an essential part of summarizing and assessing the educational effectiveness of the unit. As an example, one teacher's summary of a fourth-grade unit on foods indicated that the pupils had done work in the following subjects of study: reading, composition, geography, history, science and household arts, fine arts, and arithmetic. The specific topics covered were listed under each subject; in history, for example, students had studied primitive ways of getting food. In composition, they had written original poems on orchards, farms, and gardens and a book on the jelly business. In geography, they had studied the effects of climate, altitude, and latitude on fruit growing.[49]

Significantly, reporting to parents was based on pupil progress in the traditional subjects, although the report card also had a section dealing with habits and attitudes. The latter included specific behaviors under the headings of appreciations, initiative, cooperation, responsibility, work habits, consideration of others, honesty and trustworthiness, personal habits, and health habits.

Curriculum Integration in the High School.   One of the purposes for establishing Lincoln School was to develop models for curriculum intergration. The Rugg social studies materials, developed in the 1920s at the junior-high-school level, helped to realize this promise. Curriculum synthesis was achieved through problem-focused study of American social, political, and economic institutions. The impact of Rugg's social studies (he was the first to integrate the social sciences into the social studies) was national; the materials were the first curriculum series in social studies. But more importantly, it was the very breadth of Rugg's conception of the social studies that provided the foundation for curriculum reorganization at Lincoln. As Nelson writes, "Not only the social sciences, but English, the physical and biological sciences, even mathematics, would be restructured under the broad umbrella of social studies, the central vehicle of curriculum essentials."[50] In 1927, plans were made to develop integrated courses at the secondary-school level.

The General Course.   The model for curriculum synthesis that evolved was the core, or "general course," an effort to integrate social studies, English, and the fine arts (except in the ninth grade, where the core was social studies and science). By 1935, about half of student time was spent in the core course, the balance being allocated to required and elective courses in mathematics, science, modern foreign languages, music, physical education, home economics, and the fine and industrial arts. Ultimately, the core courses that developed were

1. Seventh grade—Man and His Environment
2. Eighth grade—Early American Life
3. Ninth grade—Living in a Machine Age
4. Tenth and eleventh grade—Ancient and Modern Cultures (a two-year sequence)
5. Twelfth grade—Youth in America Today (vocations, the individual, family, citizen)

The integrated program had two major objectives: the development of the individual to full capacity and participation of the school in the progressive improvement of an industrial democracy. Here the influence of Harold Rugg and George Counts is evident: The secondary school was to participate in the process of social reconstruction.

Socioeconomic Realities   Problems and projects served as organizing centers for the curriculum in the general courses. The high-school staff at Lincoln attempted to include socioeconomic realities in the curriculum, particularly during the Great Depression of the 1930s. It was felt that firsthand experience with the problems of our society would be the best way to generate interest and concern on the part of youth and, not incidentally, to lay the groundwork for imaginative solutions when youth reached adulthood.

It was further believed that an intimate acquaintance with the problems of democracy was essential for personal development. Youth would find a purpose in life. Moreover, youth would discover that personal satisfactions harmonize with societal needs. Without purpose an "integrated" personality was an impossibility. A major goal of child-centered schools was "personality integration"; the term *integration* as used by educational philosophers during the 1920s and 1930s referred to personality. It was contended that a curriculum integrated through units or projects was the best, indeed, the *only* path to the larger goal of personality integration.

Field-Study Experiences.   It is every social studies teacher's dream to provide his or her students with extensive travel-study opportunities. At the Lincoln School the dream became a reality in 1937. A sizable grant from the Alfred P. Sloan Foundation made it possible to take large groups of students on trips to study the socioeconomic realities of American life as part of the core curriculum. As preparation for "Living in a Machine Age," 50 ninth-graders lived for 8 days in the homes of rural New England farmers to study a less-mechanized society than their own. As part of their study of "economic and social planning in a democracy," 50 twelfth-graders toured the Tennessee Valley Authority and various other cooperative enterprises in Georgia and Maryland. Fifteen eleventh-graders were selected to go to Pennsylvania and West Virginia to do a field study about communities that were then being affected by technological unemployment in the coal and steel industries.

An attempt was made to evaluate the educational outcomes of the eleventh-grade field-study experience. The investigation, conducted with the assistance of the Progressive Education Association's evaluation staff, found "evidence of an astounding development on the part of fifteen boys and girls in a relatively short time."[51] The group that went on the trip achieved more than the group that remained at home and, not surprisingly, they revealed greater sensitivity toward the social issues involved.[52]

Curriculum Research. Development of the core concept in a laboratory school was an unparalleled opportunity to gain theoretical knowledge in the curriculum field. Although it was believed that the core course was a more effective approach to learning than were the traditional subject courses, no one was really certain of this. Comparative studies would have afforded objective bases for assessment, but such studies never materialized at the Lincoln School.

Mention should be made here of the kinds of curriculum studies conducted at Lincoln. In 1926, Otis W. Caldwell, director of the school, described three types of curriculum studies in progress: a retrospective-descriptive study of a third-grade unit on boats, a study to determine what map facts were used by adults as a basis for curriculum construction in the social studies, and a similar study in biology.[53]

Obviously, these investigations were not part of a systematic attempt to test the theoretical bases of the new education. Nor were they efforts to test the effectiveness of the unit of work as a model for curriculum integration. Typically, curriculum making in the units of work (and later the core courses) was based on a combination of intuition, educational philosophy, and chance occurrences (spontaneous events). This process was labeled "experimentation." Yet those so engaged tended to shun the idea of putting on paper a curriculum that could be tested.

One must not get the idea that the Lincoln staff and its mother institution were unmindful of the need of studies that would produce an objective account of results. Although there was not a consensus that such studies were needed or even possible (the Teachers College faculty, labeled by some as "one big unhappy family," represented widely divergent outlooks), curriculum evaluation was a persistent area of concern for Rugg, Shumaker, Bonser, and undoubtedly other members of the Teachers College faculty.[54]

The Problem of Curriculum Evaluation. In 1934, in an appraisal of student achievement, L. Thomas Hopkins, Lincoln's curriculum specialist, and James E. Mendenhall, whose field was social studies, reported that there was a need for a new type of achievement test to determine the results of the new curriculum of the school.[55] Like most laboratory schools, Lincoln had demonstrated that clearly its students did not suffer in terms of achievement, as measured by standardized tests. But studies were needed to measure the additional kinds of learnings and benefits purportedly afforded students by the new curriculum.

One major point of interest is the long-abiding faith on the part of Teachers College that evidence supporting the school's program would ultimately be produced. This confidence persisted for more than two decades, despite the lack of systematic ongoing experimental research.

But in 1940, Lincoln, as one of the thirty secondary schools participating in the Eight-Year Study, submitted its final report on curriculum experimentation to the Commission on the Relation of School and College of the Progressive Education Association. Deep concern about the problem of curriculum evaluation was evident:

> We still face the problem of building evaluation instruments appropriate to our changing curriculum. Classroom teachers, who are themselves most largely responsible for creating learning opportunities, will have the largest share in developing the new evaluation techniques. They may require the services of specialists to insure that the new techniques have adequate objectivity, reliability, and validity, and that, so far as possible, the data derived from their use can be conveniently summarized and comparisons among students made possible.[56]

Mission Unaccomplished. The year 1941 marked the beginning of the end for the Lincoln School. Teachers College decided to merge it with the Horace Mann School, a subject-centered demonstration school also connected with the college. In 1947 a New York State Supreme Court decision dealt the final blow to the Lincoln School, upholding a decision by Teachers College to close the school and transfer the funds from the sale of land and buildings to the Horace Mann–Lincoln Institute. The decision of college trustees to close the Lincoln School was based on what had by then become only too obvious: it "had not functioned to the fullest extent of its potentialities for experimentation."[57] The credibility gap had become too wide for even the most faithful. Nevertheless, the Lincoln School might have survived if its endowment had not been depleted by Teachers College under the financial strains of the college during the crisis years of the Great Depression.

Curriculum Theory and Design. Why did the Lincoln School produce few objective accounts of results? From the outset, the inability of the staff to agree on the need for a curriculum design was a hindrance to productive experimentation. There was no paper curriculum to test. This is indeed regrettable, especially in view of the observation of Hollis L. Caswell that the Lincoln School curriculum "possessed substantial unity and rested upon a reasonably easily perceived theoretical base." (Caswell was the first head of the Department of Curriculum and Teaching, established at Teachers College in 1938.) Moreover, in the words of Caswell, "Rugg's search for a 'new synthesis of knowledge' was a definite, clear-cut approach to curriculum reorganization based on a well defined theory."[58]

But if the staff met the prior condition for a curriculum design, a curriculum theory, they were nevertheless unable to formulate and test an overall design based on that theory. According to Rugg and Shumaker, the staffs of the child-centered schools "displayed relatively little interest in either of these two matters (theory or design)."[59] Although they made this observation in 1926, this was to be the pattern of the school in the years to come.

Freedom and the Curriculum Planned in Advance. Throughout the 1930s there was an aversion by many on the Lincoln staff to any plan that would state in advance the concepts and generalizations to be taught or attitudes and appreciations to be developed: the ends of instruction. It was believed that any plan would hamper, indeed stultify, curriculum building by teacher and student. As Lester Dix, the principal of the Lincoln School, put it: "No plan or curriculum which removes that freedom can be defended."[60]

Little wonder, then, that there was no agreement on the need for a curriculum design. A curriculum planned in advance was simply contrary to the philosophy of many progressivists, not to mention the holder of the chair of philosophy at Teachers College, William Kilpatrick.

In his criticism of child-centered schools, Rugg observed that the individualistic, laissez-faire approach to program building had produced chaotic, disjointed, and unarticulated programs. "Rarely," he said, "are they designed in the light of a review of a careful record of the program of earlier years and of the most probably effective year-programs to follow it in the school career of the child."[61]

Research and the Unplanned Curriculum—An Impossible Duo. There is another point to be made, however, with the added perspective of history. Clearly, emphasis on the undesirability of a curriculum that was planned in advance was a primary factor in the lack of data concerning the results of new programs. Without a curriculum design there could be no research design. In this connection, an important incremental function of a research design is that it makes mandatory a statement of the objectives and procedures of the curriculum to be tested.

As indicated, a laissez-faire approach to program building was to be the pattern for almost the entire life of the school. Romanticism was substituted for experimentalism. Furthermore, the goal to recruit unconventional individualistic teachers made impossible the consensus in educational outlook necessary for the development of an articulated program.

Epilogue. In October 1946 the Horace Mann–Lincoln School staff published an article in the *Teachers College Record.* The piece was a long-overdue definition of the role of experimentation in educational improvement and a plea for the continued existence of the experimental school. The writers argued that most experimental schools had been founded during an era when free enterprise, a laissez-faire concept of government, and a liberal-individualistic outlook prevailed in our society. These forces affected the goals and organization of the experimental school and mitigated against the fulfillment of its charge. But times had changed. The experimental school staff now sought a philosophical consensus so that its professional responsibility for experimentation could be fulfilled. In stating the case for special experimental schools, the Horace Mann–Lincoln staff set out to clarify any semantic misunderstandings about the word *experimentation*. An experiment should have a clearly stated hypothesis and must bear a recognizable relationship to a theory suggested by a previous basic investigation. In addition, *it should develop as part of a pattern of associated experiments*. Last, but not least, it should be planned as part of a school program.[62]

One immediately recognizes that here at long last was the scientific method being proposed as the only acceptable basis for curriculum appraisal in a laboratory school. Dewey's philosophy of experimentalism would replace romanticism. Curriculum evaluation would be objective rather than impressionistic. There was absolutely nothing wrong with the idea; Bonser and Rugg had insisted on it and argued for it almost from the beginning. There was nothing wrong with the idea except that it came too late. The final piece in the 1946–47 volume of the *Teachers College Record* (the same volume in which the Horace Mann–Lincoln staff stated their case) was the court report upholding the closing of the school. The problem of the Lincoln School was the problem of the new education in microcosm. In 1929, Bonser observed:

> In too many progressive schools there has been no record made of what was done, no attempt to evaluate results or establish alleged achievements of growth by evidence, and little effort to analyze purposes and methods in terms of basic principle.... No error could be more unfortunate or more costly to progressive education than that of assuming that it is in opposition to the use of the scientific method or to the findings of valid scientific investigation.[63]

By the time progressive educators came around to realizing that they would have to deliver on their promises to produce objective evidence of results, it was too late. First, faith in the new education had been irreparably damaged. Many who only yesterday had been committed to curriculum integration over the traditional curriculum now joined the conservative countermove that was in the making. Second, over the years, laboratory schools such as Lincoln had done such a good job of disseminating and demonstrating ideas that it was doubtful whether "uncontaminated" populations to serve as control groups in experiments could be found, that is, pupils who were totally unexposed to unit teaching, integrated subjects, problem-centered teaching, activity programs, and the like. Impressive examples of publications disseminating the ideas and practices of the staff of the Lincoln School are such books as *Curriculum Making in an Elementary School* (1927) and *Children and Architecture* (1932). Both are detailed chronicles of systematic and creative curriculum development. The latter book, co-authored by a teacher and a research assistant at the school, describes how the sixth-graders engaged in a wide variety of stimulating projects and activities in a unit on architecture encompassing the fine arts, history, industrial arts and technology, mathematics, science, and the urban environment.[64]

TRANSFER OF LEARNING

One of the most portentous pieces of research for the curriculum field was conducted by Edward L. Thorndike in the early 1920s. In a huge study involving some 8,564 pupils, Thorndike sought to measure the relative disciplinary value of various high-school subjects by assessing gains in "general intelligence" that could be attributed to the study of one subject or group of subjects instead of another. For instance, he compared the gains in intelligence test scores of pupils who studied English, history, geometry, and *Latin* with those who studied English, history, geometry, and *shopwork*. Thus, he was trying to measure the relative disciplinary value of Latin and shopwork. Thorndike found that no one study (be it Latin or anything else) is more likely than any other study to result in a general improvement of the mind. Thorndike concluded:

> By any reasonable interpretation of the results, the intellectual values of studies should be determined largely by the special information, habits, interests, attitudes, and ideals which they demonstrably produce. The expectation of any large difference in general improvement of the mind from one study rather than another seems doomed to disappointment. The chief reason why good thinkers seem superficially to have been made such by having taken certain school studies is that good thinkers have taken such studies, becoming better by the inherent tendency of the good to gain more than the poor from any study. When the good thinkers studied Greek and Latin, these studies seemed to make good thinking. Now that the good thinkers study Physics and Trigonometry, these seem to make good thinkers. If the abler pupils should all study Physical Education and Dramatic Art, these subjects would seem to make good thinkers. These were, indeed, a large fraction of the program of studies for the best thinkers the world has produced, the Athenian Greeks.[65]

What Thorndike was saying was that those who had the most to start with gained the most regardless of the particular studies they pursued, and that there is no hierarchy of subjects for mental discipline. He also argued that learning is specific rather than a matter of mental discipline.

The Demolition of Mental Discipline

Actually, Thorndike's research was part of a chain of events that demolished the theory of mental discipline as a basis for curriculum development. It will be recalled from our discussion in Chapter 2 that educational theorists enthusiastically picked up Herbartian educational psychology, which stressed that new subject matter must be related in the pupil's mind to his or her previous learning. Thus, the "psychology" of mental discipline was abandoned in favor of Herbartian psychology. This happened in the United States by 1885. (In Europe, Herbartian psychology had taken hold some twenty years earlier.) Another early link in the chain was William James of Harvard, who proposed in his book *Principles of Psychology,* published in 1890, that psychology is a natural science. This left many in the intellectual world thunderstruck, because the study of the mind had always been the domain of philosophers. James said that the study of the mind must be based on the study of behavior, that it was fallacious to conceive of the mind as composed of separate faculties as did the faculty psychologists.

James was the founder of the school of objective psychology. His ideas were pursued, developed, and applied by Edward Thorndike of Teachers College. Other erosive influences on the notion of the inherent disciplinary value of the classical studies were the application of the evolutionary idea to society, child interests, the need for practical knowledge, and the necessity of the secondary school to meet the needs of an increasingly heterogeneous population.

Research on Transfer

Thorndike began challenging transfer shortly after the turn of the century. His first frontal attack was a study conducted with Woodworth in 1901, which showed that improvement in one mental function seldom brings about commensurate improvement in another function, regardless of similarity.[66] Transfer could occur, but not because of the disciplinary value of any classical study; it would occur only if the old and new activities had common content or methods of study.[67]

Curriculum developers could (and did) conclude from Thorndike's research that the best way to prepare a student for a given activity or goal was to have the student take a direct route: the study of the subject or the practice of the activity itself.

A host of studies was conducted in the decades of the 1920s, 1930s, and 1940s confirming Thorndike's findings on the relative disciplinary value of school subjects. Thorndike's study was repeated in 1927. Broyler et al. reported that the findings of their study concurred with the earlier study; both studies "agree in disagreeing with the traditional doctrine that Latin, algebra and geometry are the prime disciplinary subjects of high school."[68] Thorndike's study was repeated again in 1945 by Wesman, whose investigation "failed to reveal superior transfer to intelligence for any one of the achievement areas measured (Latin, German, French, mathematics, natural science, social studies, contemporary affairs) and indicated the desirability of direct training in mental processes rather than dependence on transfer from school subjects."[69]

But probably the most stunning attack (aside from Thorndike's 1924 study) on the idea that certain subjects have superior transfer to intelligence was delivered by the Progressive Education Association's Eight-Year Study. As is shown in the study, success in college is not dependent on credits earned in high school in the traditionally prescribed subjects, and integrative approaches to the curriculum actually produced superior results.

The Continuing Restatement of Disciplinary Values

Despite the evidence against the disciplinary properties of certain subjects, such as mathematics and Latin, the idea is far from dead. For instance, the notion is still cherished in liberal arts colleges that mathematics strengthens the intellectual power of reasoning. The endurance of the belief that the study of certain subjects (but not others) develops intellectual powers is revealed in this statement of ridicule by Clifton Fadiman:

> It is useful to know how to cook. Yet we cannot be seduced by such "subjects." Hard though it may be we must jettison them in favor of the basic subject matters. And there is no time for an eclectic mixture: only a few years are available in which to educe, to educate the rational soul. We cannot afford bypaths. We cannot afford pleasure.[70]

More recently, Latimer, a professor of classics, reported a lack of agreement among classicists about the disciplinary value of Latin.[71] Hence, we may be sure that there is a continuing belief among some in the automatic transfer of a classical education to general intelligence.

Effects of Thorndike's Studies

Thorndike's findings on transfer had an enormous effect on education. The findings were cited as justification for eliminating classical studies such as Latin and ancient history from the curriculum. Thorndike's findings on transfer produced two other striking effects. First, since Spencerian questions could no longer be answered on the basis of the disciplinary value of given subjects, there had to be other means of determining the relative values of studies. Educators' concern over finding such means was an important factor in the appointment by the NEA in 1911 of a Committee on Economy of Time in Education, charged with identifying the "minimum essentials" of the curriculum. There can be little doubt that Thorndike's emphasis on teaching specific knowledge and skills influenced the committee's decision to pursue a mechanistic approach to curriculum development. Second, Thorndike's work lent justification to the inclusion of technical studies in the curriculum taught as nearly as possible in the context in which they were to be used. Moreover, it could now be argued that these subjects were equal with the traditional classics and humanities. It is interesting to note, however, that such subjects lost their equality (if, indeed, they ever really had it) during the curriculum reform movement of the 1950s and 1960s. In the early 1970s, some educational policymakers, most notably the U.S. commissioner of education, deemed it necessary to reassert the "equal status" of vocational and academic subjects.[72]

Contemporary Thought on Transfer

During the curriculum reform movement of the 1950s and 1960s, there was renewed interest in general transfer. Although educational theorists looked again to wide transfer, their theoretical basis was *not* that of mental discipline. It was, rather, that inquiry-discovery and "learning how to learn" (ways of learning) as taught via the disciplines could be applied by students in new situations. According to Bruner, it was "indeed a fact that massive general transfer can be achieved by appropriate learning, even to the degree that learning properly under optimum conditions leads one to 'learn how to learn.' "[73] Bruner was clearly not calling for a return to the doctrine of mental discipline. Nevertheless, educational critics such as Hofstadter cited Bruner's statement in stating the case for mental discipline.[74]

Bruner and Dewey. Educational theorists in the 1960s were struck by apparent similarities between Bruner's ideas and those of Dewey. "Learning how to learn" and "inquiry-discovery" stem in no small way from Dewey's "reflective thinking." Yet there are important differences. Bruner was addressing himself to ways of learning *within individual disciplines* such as science and mathematics. He insisted that these would transfer to other kinds of problems faced by the student. Dewey, on the other hand, was referring to social problem solving as a task for which the school must prepare the rising generation. Here Dewey's idea was similar to that of Thorndike, who suggested that the best way to learn something was by the most direct route possible: to practice the process itself. Yet, unlike Thorndike, Dewey held that learning be generalized for transfer. Interestingly enough, Bruner did a complete about-face on his idea eleven years later. In 1971 he wrote:

> We shall kill ourselves, as a society and as human beings, unless we address our efforts to redressing the deep, deep wounds that we inflict on the poor, the outcast, those who somehow do not fit within our caste system—be they black or dispossessed in any way....

I would be quite satisfied to declare, if not a moratorium, then something of a de-emphasis on matters that have to do with the structure of history, the structure of physics, the nature of mathematical consistency, and deal with it rather in the context of the problems that face us.[75]

Structure and Transfer. During the 1950s and 1960s, educators enthusiastically picked up on the idea of the "structure of the disciplines" as a means for maximizing transfer. Bruner argued that understanding structures and fundamental principles "appears to be the main road to adequate 'transfer of training.' "[76] The emphasis during this period was on improving learning efficiency—but again within individual disciplines. The idea of the structure of knowledge failed to be a boon to transfer. First, most subjects had nothing resembling a single structure or organizing principle. Even in fields such as physics and mathematics, there was little if any agreement among university scholars on a single structure. Organizing principles change in accord with one's purpose in studying a given subject. Thus, the idea of structure was a fiction.

Another problem was that the "principles" and "concepts" of a discipline, even should there be agreement on which ones to include in a course of study, were studied within the confines of that discipline. Therefore, the most that could be hoped for was good future academic performance in that discipline. This, not incidentally, was the primary objective of teaching via "structure." Learning was to serve as a means for further specialized learning. The long-range purpose, however, was neither personal development nor social reform but national power: We were a warfare state seeking international supremacy in military-related scholarship. Paradoxically, the disciplinary doctrine was focused on abstract-puristic knowledge to the neglect of applied knowledge. Without practical application the possibilities for transfer were limited.

Shifting Tides. In the late 1960s what seemed to be a new progressive education movement began to develop. New child-centered schools and classrooms within schools that were part of the public school system began to emerge, and these were variously labeled open schools, alternative schools, or community schools. There were striking differences with the movement of John Dewey's time. For example, despite their humane aspirations, many advocates of these schools were uninterested in assessing the outcomes of their methods, whereas in the progressive education movement Ralph Tyler and his associates set about systematically to apply scientific principles to the experimental methods of instruction and curriculum development. These attempts culminated in the Eight-Year Study (described in detail in Chapter 5).

As Cremin points out, progressive education was the "educational phase of American Progressivism writ large . . . a many-sided effort to use the schools to improve the lives of individuals."[77] Thus progressive educators were profoundly and directly concerned with the transfer of learning, and their concern was manifested in a variety of approaches to relating schools to life.

What had appeared to be a new progressive education movement in the 1960s and early 1970s was short-lived. For one thing, the movement had its conservative side, such as schools growing out of programs of black self-determination that further segregated black students; and many Americans had an ingrained distrust of schools that remove youngsters from the main-stream school. For another, the countercultural part of the movement loudly rejected middle-class values, and it seems clear that this attack on the values of many (if not most) Americans had an economic impact. By the late 1970s a counterreaction against "humanizing" the schools set in, and the new theme was "back to basics." Many Americans (including educators) bought the idea that the best way of dealing with the widespread problems of youth disaffection, drug addiction, and unemployment was adolescents' mastery of basic skills. A "basic" curriculum was also a cheap curriculum, and the mastery of basic skills served, as it had many times before, as a convenient rationale for educational retrenchment.

It was soon found, however, that an emphasis on basic skills was unlikely to help children develop the competencies they need "to manage an increasingly complex adult life."[78] In the 1980s there was a growing awareness that "many problems of our youth originate in concrete decision-making situations that usually occur in the absence of an adult."[79] Students would have to learn problem-solving strategies that could serve them in everyday situations if they were to deal with their own social problems: drug addiction, health, sex, career, and dropping out of school are examples and, hopefully, the strategies would serve them well as adults. This was transfer of learning in the sense that progressive educators used the term in John Dewey's time.

Nevertheless, this was just a curriculum trickle: The raging curriculum current in the late 1980s was not transfer for social problem-solving—far from it—but raising academic requirements, with a special emphasis on science and mathematics in reaction to the growing alarm over the decline of American supremacy in the global marketplace. As in the era of the cold war and the space race, the school curriculum was to be turned to the academically talented and to serving narrow nationalistic needs while giving lip service to the wider social interest.

Enhancing Transfer

Teaching for transfer is a concern of all educators for the very obvious reason that we want school learning to be of use to the individual in later life. As Taba emphasized, "Since no program, no matter how thorough, can teach everything, the task of all education is to cause a maximum amount of transfer."[80] In view of this, it is interesting, as Ausubel points out, that "in most instances of non-vocational classroom learning, the goal of transfer is considered accomplished if prior learning experience facilitates the training of subsequent classroom learning tasks—even if the knowledge so acquired is neither applicable nor even applied to problems outside the classroom."[81]

Unfortunately, Thorndike chose to interpret his findings to buttress the theory of S-R psychology rather than seeing it as evidence of the need for subject matter that is designed to be highly generalized for applicability or transfer to a wide range of situations. The consequence was a doctrine of narrow specificity that has its legacy in modern-day behavioristic objectives. According to Cronbach, developmental objectives, where the teacher states how he or she would like the learner to function after instruction, are broader, more generalized, and more concerned with transfer than are narrow behavioristic objectives.[82] Thus, the curriculum in many schools includes environmental education, organized and taught so as to maximize the possibility that students will be able to deal with such problems as adult citizens. Developing social problem-solving skills has a similar transfer objective. There is no way to list all the occasions for transfer. Social problems are emergent situations. Nevertheless, suitable levels of accomplishment can be specified, as Tyler and his staff did in the Eight-Year Study.

Attitudes are one kind of learning that transfers widely. Negative attitudes transfer as well as positive attitudes, and the former can interfere with and even permanently damage a child's ability to learn. Here we are referring to attitudes toward one's self, one's teacher, adult authority, the school, the society, and the curriculum. Obviously, also, transfer of content and ways of learning is more assured when learning is stimulating and meaningful to the individual.

Transfer is never automatic. It requires that the organization of the curriculum and methods of teaching be directed to transfer as a goal. One theory of transfer is that broad generalizations, or "big ideas," increase the possibility of transfer as opposed to unrelated fragments of content. This means that a curriculum based on thousands of "behavioristic" objectives is not addressed to transfer. Transfer is also enhanced when pupils understand why they are engaging in a given activity or learning task. In this regard, research shows that transfer increases when pupils are deliberately made aware that what they are learning might be useful in another situation.[83]

SCIENTISM IN CURRICULUM MAKING

"Work up the raw material into that finished product for which it is best adapted," wrote Franklin Bobbitt in 1912.[84] Although Bobbitt was discussing a principle of industrial management, he was not addressing his remarks to captains of industry but to elementary teachers. The "finished product" to which he referred was not shoes or steel rails but children. In his article in

The Elementary School Teacher, Bobbitt, a member of the faculty in educational administration at the University of Chicago, attempted to show how one school system, the Gary system, was being operated at "100 per cent efficiency." Bobbitt argued that "waste" had been eliminated in the Gary schools by introducing the principles of "scientific management" used in the steel industry. (The Gary Plan was discussed in Chapter 3.) Other school systems could savor the economy and efficiency being savored by Gary.

"Scientific Management" and Education

Because of mounting national excitement over the new system of industrial management known as "scientific management" and the fact that the nation's schools in 1912 were being characterized by the press as grossly mismanaged, Bobbitt's prescription that education borrow the new technology fell on sympathetic (if not desperate) ears. He was invited by the National Society for the Study of Education to expand his ideas on scientific management as author of the society's Twelfth Yearbook. In the yearbook, Bobbitt made his point somewhat more trenchantly. The principles of management being applied in business and industry were particularly applicable to a "backward" institution such as education. The analogy between the two institutions, education and industry, was obvious; "education is a shaping process as much as the manufacture of steel rails," said Bobbitt.[85] Bobbitt's theme was that education must follow the example of industry and focus on the product. Standards for that product must be established and scales of measurement utilized to see "whether the product rises to standard." Educators now realized that "it is possible to set up definite standards for the various educational products. The ability to add at a speed of 65 combinations per minute, with an accuracy of 94 per cent is as definite a specification as can be set up for any aspect of the work of the steel plant," argued Bobbitt.[86]

Educators as Mechanics, Not Philosophers

It is highly unlikely that Bobbitt's argument for the need for educational standards met with objections from the nation's educational leaders. But his proposal for establishing these standards probably did: Standards for educational products were to be set by the business and industrial world. It was the role of men of practical affairs to decide what they wanted and the role of educators to determine how it could be produced and to produce it without question. Thus, educators would no longer be concerned with "what" of the curriculum but only the "how." As Callahan commented in his classic book on the influence of industry on public-school administration: "Doubtless many educators who had devoted years of study and thought to the aims and purposes of education were surprised to learn that they had misunderstood their function. They were to be mechanics, not philosophers."[87]

How would the needs and desires of practical men become known? The kinds of educational products they needed would be determined via the survey method. But the surveys would not be conducted by school people; scientific educational management as efficient as that found in the business world required that the surveys be conducted by those in business. In this way, education would be turned to the needs of business. With scientifically determined "job specifications," scales of measurement, and standards of attainment, said Bobbitt, "we shall have for the first time a scientific curriculum for education worthy of our age of science."[88] A few years later when his attention turned from school administration to curriculum making, Bobbitt himself used the survey for defining curricular aims and content.

Social Forces

It was Dewey's thesis that educational movements are but reflections of larger social movements. The efficiency movement in education was no exception. In the second decade of this century, a veritable mania for efficiency swept the country. No institution—the home, the church, or the school—escaped uncomfortable scrutiny and unfavorable comparison with that epitome of efficiency and economy, American business and industry.

Business Leadership. There is further support for Dewey's thesis. At the time Bobbitt published his ideas on the role of businessmen in determining educational objectives, men of influence were advancing a theory of business leadership for the society as a whole. Among them was Arthur Twining Hadley, president of Yale University, who, in his book *Standards of Morality* (1907), proposed that businessmen assume a larger role in the solution of contemporary social problems in return for protection of their vested interests.[89] Thus, Bobbitt's argument that businessmen should set educational standards was a not unexpected outcome of the theory of business leadership. (Actually, interest in efficiency in education began as early as 1815 with the monitorial instruction movement, although this was armylike efficiency in contrast to businesslike efficiency, which came to dominate the thinking of many school administrators in the twentieth century.)

Although easily explainable, the importance of Bobbitt's advocacy of a business-led educational system should not be underestimated. Two policies were set that appear to stem directly from this advocacy and continue to operate to this day: first, business values and procedures are the model for educational administration, with the result that educational decisions tend to be made on economic rather than educational grounds; and second, education (and government) has turned to business and industry for the solution of pedagogical problems. An illustration of the 1960s is "performance contracting," in which school systems turned to industry for learning systems to improve pupil performance in reading and arithmetic as measured by standardized achievement tests. Performance contracting failed to produce the results that were promised. This was disappointing yet hardly unexpected.[90]

While some educators continue to believe that business can do everything better—including education—others do not, particularly those who are concerned with improving teacher preparation. At least this seems to have been the case historically. In her study of the influence of business management principles on educators, Berman made the following intriguing observation.

> [W]hen one juxtaposes the twentieth century leaders of the efficiency movement cited by Callahan—Frank Ellsworth Spaulding, George Drayton Strayer, John Franklin Bobbitt, Ellwood Patterson Cubberley—against its opponents—William Henry Maxwell, James M. Greenwood, Burke A. Hinsdale, William Paxton Burris, Nicholas Murray Butler, Margaret Haley, Ella Flagg Young, Jesse H. Newlon, and eventually John Dewey—the most outstanding feature of the pro-efficiency group is their virtual lack of training or interest in teacher education. The most outstanding feature of those opposing an excessive emphasis upon efficiency is their overwhelming contact with either normal schools or teacher-training departments within other institutions.[91]

Drift and Mastery.   Closely related to the theory of business leadership was the idea that we must effectively direct and master our institutions, waging a never-ending battle against the all-too-human tendency to drift. It will be recalled that Lester Ward had argued that man can control and direct the process of human evolution through the use of his intellect. But there was an important difference between Ward's thesis and the prevailing doctrine of scientific management. Whereas Ward envisioned higher levels of human welfare being attained through intelligence and education, many analysts of political, economic, and social institutions between 1910 and 1929 saw managerial efficiency as the key to social betterment. By managerial efficiency man would control and change his social institutions; efficiency would produce the change from drift to mastery.

Walter Lippmann's *Drift and Mastery* (1914) popularized the idea that man must deal with life deliberately. Lippmann said that liberalism had created a period of drift. There was only one escape from drift: the application of the scientific method to contemporary institutions. "The scientific spirit is the spirit of democracy, the escape from drift, the outlook of a free man," wrote Lippman.[92] His commitment to science had the effect of raising public interest in efficiency, already at fever pitch, to an even higher level. For many Americans, efficiency was synonymous with science.

In education, mastery (as opposed to drift) was equated with efficiency. In a speech before the annual NEA conference in 1916, Lotus Coffman, dean of the University of Minnesota's school of education, said: "Purpose must take the place of destiny and there must be a change from drift to mastery. Our domestic and public affairs and our educational program must all be more efficiently organized."[93]

The Inefficient Curriculum.   Not the least of the effects of the national infatuation with efficiency was a barrage of criticism directed at the public-school curriculum. The curriculum was characterized by some critics as "impractical" and "ineffective" (failing to prepare for a living) and therefore a waste of the taxpayers' money. It was characterized by others as failing to prepare pupils in academic work and moral training. Still a third group criticized the school for its failure to hold pupils; this problem was regarded as a direct reflection of the curriculum and a source of educational waste. A fourth criticism was more of an ultimatum: Some reform economists demanded that either the schools show measured results of their outcomes in terms of social betterment or have their budgets reduced. In short, what was being called for by the critics was a more "efficient" curriculum, although what this meant certainly varied with the interests of the critics. Nevertheless, the critics, almost to a man (or woman), agreed about one thing: The schools were extravagant with public funds. Curriculum efficiency hence meant economy. This could be achieved by having pupils study *only* what they needed, nothing more. This way of thinking formed the backdrop for the operations of the Committee on Economy of Time, created in 1911 by the NEA's Department of Superintendence.

The Committee on Economy of Time

The demand that time in school be better spent was not new. As shown in Chapter 2, public concern about the number of times pupils went over the same work was voiced before 1830. And in 1888, Charles Eliot delivered an address before the Department of Superintendence in which he proposed that school programs be "shortened and enriched." But times had changed. "Better" was now equated with "economical" and "efficient."

However, there were three additional reasons for the committee's charge to define the "minimum essentials" of the curriculum. First, research had exploded the myth that certain subjects had value for mental discipline so there was urgent need for a new answer to Spencer's question "What knowledge is of most worth?" This would require new approaches to curriculum development. Second, friends of education as well as enemies were demanding that the selection of curriculum content be based on quantitative evidence instead of opinion. The quantitative method was being applied to the solution of all educational problems, including the definition of the "standard units" in a course of study. Last but not least was a growing body of research that seemed to show that the amount of time spent on a given subject had little influence on the results. The pioneering study (which was ignored by educators when first reported) had been conducted in 1897 by Rice, who concluded that more than fifteen minutes per day for spelling was utterly wasteful.[94]

The temper of the times was clear, as expressed in a speech by Leonard

Ayres of the Russell Sage Foundation to the Harvard Teachers Association. " 'How much?' and 'how many?' and 'with what result?' are going to displace guess-work, imagination, and oratory as criteria for shaping educational policies," said Ayres.[95]

A Critical Decision. Although it was also concerned with problems related to teaching and school organization, the Committee on Economy of Time spent the greater part of its energies on the problem of eliminating nonessentials from the curriculum. Determining the relative educational values of items of knowledge posed formidable problems, the answers to which were not to be found in educational theory. Up against the proverbial brick wall, the committee made a portentous decision for the curriculum field:

> If it is impossible to discover from educational theory fundamental tests for exclusion or inclusion, we are driven to the method of determining minimum essentials on the basis of the best current practices and experimentation which gives satisfactory results. Those results are satisfactory which meet adequately the common needs of life in society.[96]

Each assuming responsibility for a given curriculum area, committee members followed their own individual paths, searching for ideal educational practices. They did so without having first defined the terms *best, satisfactory,* and *adequately.* But this was only a minor theoretical difficulty in comparison with that posed by the committee's premise that present practice is desirable. For as Bode observed, "if we start with a wrong assumption no amount of energy and ingenuity in the manipulation of scientific technique will convert this initial error into a sound principle."[97]

Curriculum Making by Common Denominator. The first phase of the committee's work was to find out what was being taught (and where achievement data were available, what was being learned) in representative school districts and make recommendations based on the findings. The result was curriculum making by common denominator. To illustrate, in his report on arithmetic, Walter Jessup of Iowa State University noted that there was wide variation among the cities in the amount of time given to arithmetic. He recommended that the time devoted to arithmetic in the various grades not exceed the median time expenditure throughout the country. The first grade, for example, should not exceed seventy-five minutes per week as that was the median time expended in first grades.[98]

There was absolutely no theoretical basis for the idea that the median time spent on a given subject should become the standard. Yet this was what the committee found desirable for spelling, arithmetic, and handwriting.

This is not to imply that the committee's four major reports (published as the Fourteenth, Sixteenth, Seventeenth, and Eighteenth yearbooks of the National Society for the Study of Education) contributed nothing of value to educators. This would be manifestly unfair and misleading. What was being taught in other school systems was of intense interest to superintendents, and the surveys reported in the Fourteenth and Sixteenth NSSE yearbooks were widely circulated and discussed. However, prevailing practice was hardly a sound basis for curriculum improvement.

Determining Curriculum Content.   The second phase of the committee's work was to make recommendations concerning the content of the curriculum. All of the recommendations were based on the principle of social utility. The approach used for determining what should be taught was to find out what people who are living and working "successfully" need to be able to do and just what information and skills they need in order to live and work successfully. For example, Walter S. Monroe of the Kansas State Normal School at Emporia based his report on arithmetic

> upon the assumption that the primary purpose of teaching arithmetic in the elementary school is to equip the pupil (1) with the knowledge of facts, principles, and relationships existing between quantities, etc., which is needed to decide what arithmetical operations are to be performed in solving valuable practical problems and (2) with the skills which are necessary to perform these operations.[99]

Monroe defined a practical problem as "one that occurs in some human activity." Monroe approached his task by making a survey of the occupational, domestic, and personal activities in which an adult might be engaged. He used the lengthy and somewhat haphazard list of activities that resulted as an instrument for evaluating textbooks. The idea was to determine which arithmetic problems were useful enough to be included as minimum essentials. This same general approach for identifying the common essentials was used by other committee members in history, geography, civics, English, literature, and physical education. The committee relied heavily on the method of collective judgment, or consensus. Library books, for instance, were recommended on the basis of the number of times each book appeared on supplementary reading lists in fifty American cities. History content was selected by analyzing books, encyclopedias, newspapers, and periodicals to see which persons, places, and dates were most frequently mentioned. This calls to mind the kinds of curriculum research conducted at the Lincoln School in the mid-1920s, as discussed earlier.

Maxims for Teachers.   The most popular of the committee's reports was its fourth, published as Part II of NSSE's Eighteenth Yearbook. This report dealt with teaching methodology. Its popularity was undoubtedly a result of the fact that it offered specific rules for teaching the three R's. At first blush, here the committee appeared to be on more solid theoretical ground because it attempted to formulate the rules from experimental evidence. But again the results were for the most part unscientific as the evidence from which rules were derived was, in most cases, simply not conclusive. The following maxim for teaching arithmetic provides an interesting illustration: *"In borrowing it is better to increase the subtrahend by one than to decrease the minuend."*[100] This rule was based on only one study—with a population of *four adults.*

A Conservative Response. Nevertheless, it was the committee's initial decision to derive a curriculum from current practice, rather than the Committee's inadequate methodology, which was to plague the curriculum maker in succeeding years. For as Cremin put it,

> the Committee had ended by defining the goals of education in terms of life as it was, and hence by proposing a curriculum that would accommodate youngsters to existing conditions with little emphasis on improving them. This was hardly the progressive or Deweyan ideal, however much it was construed as such in some circles.[101]

A Reformist Concept with a Conservative Outcome

Paradoxically, the concept of a utilitarian curriculum was reformist. (As will be recalled from our discussion in Chapter 3, a utilitarian curriculum was the ideal envisioned by Flexner in his "modern school.") Utilitarianism, like child centeredness, was a reaction to the distance of the curriculum from life. But in a conservative, business-oriented society, the idea that nothing should be included in the curriculum that is not of use was given an economic rather than an educational interpretation: Teaching what is not reflected in adult activity is uneconomical.

Thus, although the concept of a useful curriculum was reformist in spirit, the committee's response was conservative—a static subject-matter curriculum, unconcerned with individual differences. It should also be noted that the committee's approach to curriculum making was contrary to the doctrine of interest. Pupil interest was insufficient justification for the inclusion of subject matter in the curriculum. Rather, it had to meet the criterion of usefulness in adulthood, in which case it would be the task of the teacher to *make* it interesting. Finally, although the child-centered school and conservative utilitarianism were conflicting currents, they both divorced education from the ideal of social reform.

The Doctrine of Specific Objectives

The committee's method for curriculum construction had the appearance of being scientific, and educators were striving for the academic respectability associated with science. Therefore, one would expect that this method would attract adherents. This is exactly what happened. Franklin Bobbitt, W. W. Charters, Charles C. Peters, and David Snedden, all professors of education, trod in the steps of the committee.

The Method of Job Analysis. "Let us discover what the activities are which make up man's life and we have the objectives of education," wrote Bobbitt in *The Elementary School Journal* in 1924.[102] It was Bobbitt's theory that the curriculum that prepared the learner for these specific activities was the curriculum that prepared the learner for "life." Since educational objectives were activities and activities were learned through performance, activity analysis discovered both the objectives of the curriculum and the curriculum itself. The method of activity analysis is also known as job analysis. As implied by the name, the method concerns the analysis of the specific activities in the performance of a given job, such as operating a machine. Bobbitt and Charters applied this method to curriculum construction, the implication being that whatever the schools taught could be reduced to twenty or thirty thousand specific mechanical skills or behaviors.

Job Analysis and Behaviorism. In addition to appearing businesslike and efficient, the new method was also highly compatible with the mechanistic psychology, behaviorism, which described human behavior in terms of S-R bonds. Habit formation and uniformity of response are the predominant concepts in both doctrines. Significantly, Charters wrote of the desirability of automatic responses on the part of the learner "when given situations recur frequently."[103] Indeed, behaviorism provided a theoretical basis for job analysis as a curriculum-making technique. Many educators (even Kilpatrick, as mentioned earlier) began describing education in connectionist terms. Peters, for example, actually defined education as the "acquisition of a large aggregate of 'hair-trigger sets' for responding to the particular problems that will confront the educand in the future."[104]

Needless to say, the ideal of humans behaving like automatons was the exact antithesis of the Deweyan ideal. Dewey, like Ward, saw the improvement of individual and social welfare through the expanding power of human intelligence. But, as shown earlier, behaviorism explains away the existence of intelligence. Like the child-centered school and the doctrine of specific objectives, behaviorism also contributed to the divorce of educational theory from the goal of social reform.

A Dangerous Deficiency. Obviously, not all educational objectives concern repetitive tasks. Far from it. In our society, many of the most important objectives, such as the ability to make adequate decisions in public policy matters, involve varying and unforeseeable conditions. Curriculum objectives such as these involve the transfer of learning rather than the repetition of identical operations. This points to a dangerous deficiency in activity or job analysis as a means for curriculum development; it is fixed on the lowest level of objectives—those requiring mechanical responses. Objectives that require higher-level thinking processes are avoided because they do not fit in a theory that trains people to act mechanically. Activity or job analysis simply cannot be made to cover the entire gamut of curriculum objectives.

"Educational Engineering." In his book *How to Make a Curriculum,* published in 1924, Bobbitt developed the committee's basic premise and methodology into a well-organized curriculum theory. Bobbitt compared the curriculum maker to an engineer. It was the task of the "educational engineer" to use his or her "educational surveying instruments" to locate the specific objectives in the various subject fields.[105] Education, said Bobbitt, should "prepare for the fifty years of adulthood, not for the twenty years of childhood and youth."[106] It was the task of the curriculum maker to define the major fields of adult experience and analyze them into smaller and smaller units until he or she found the specific activities to be performed. The specific activities, similar to job specifications in industry, comprised the content of the various subjects.

It is important to note that curriculum making by activity or job analysis in no way conflicted with the traditional subject organization of the curriculum. The "scientific" curriculum was the old subject curriculum with a new authority.

Obtaining Curriculum Objectives. Although Bobbitt and Charters were of one mind concerning the nature of subject matter, their ideas on the source for curriculum objectives differed. Whereas Bobbitt's scheme was to "discover" curriculum objectives by scientific analysis, Charters held that the philosopher sets up the aim and the analyst provides only the technique for working the aim down "into the terms of a curriculum."[107]

This difference is very significant. Bobbitt maintained that we can determine what people *should* do by identifying the things they do. Charters warned against this and saw activity analysis as a means for implementing previously selected objectives. It was Bobbitt's scheme that prevailed. The idea that curriculum objectives can be discovered by scientific means, much as one discovers oil, was basic to the new notion of curriculum making.

Peters and Snedden were educational sociologists who walked in Bobbitt's footsteps, endorsing the idea without question that the curriculum should consist of thousands of minute objectives to be obtained by consensus of opinion. Snedden's "sociological determination of objectives in education" divided educational objectives into two categories, production and consumption (the ability to do and the ability to appreciate). The result was to further compartmentalize vocation and culture.[108] This again was the antithesis of the Deweyan goal, which was to demolish the barriers between the social classes and between vocational education and education for leisure.

Clearly, the effect of job analysis was to atomize subject matter in the mind of both teacher and learner. This doctrine was diametrically opposed to the movement to humanize subject matter through curricular synthesis. Here again were conflicting currents in curriculum development.

Behavioral Objectives Revisited. In the late 1960s interest in specific ("behavioral") objectives was revived. A similar approach—analyzing subject matter into atomistic performance objectives—was used in the movement of two decades ago. Ironically, both movements were reactions against the discipline-centered curriculum that was patterned on the demands of the academic specialist rather than needed human abilities. But where the approaches taken by Bobbitt were designed to fashion objectives in line with specific lifelike adult tasks, the approaches taken during the late 1960s were behavioristic rather than behavioral. In effect, the model of the learner as conceived by the behaviorists was mechanical and not really life-related behavior. Nevertheless, present at the time of Bobbitt and Charters, and also during the late 1960s, was a countervening movement toward curriculum synthesis. However, in both instances, behaviorism was the educational psychology of the day. Finally, there was at both times a dominant faith among educators that technology would solve all educational problems, including those in the realm of curriculum and method. This faith was intensified in the late 1970s, when the popular press reduced the outcomes of education to the mechanics of basic skills.

Nevertheless, there is an important difference between these two movements that occurred a half century apart. Bobbitt's doctrine was reformist in spirit; it was based on the theory of utilitarianism. Although the curriculum produced by Bobbitt's method turned out to be the traditional curriculum with a new authority (that of "science"), his objective, nonetheless, was to make a curriculum that would prepare the learner to perform real-life activities. The contemporary "behavioral" objectives movement, on the other hand, has not subjected the curriculum to a reappraisal. The assumption is that content will not be changed, only divided into minute "behaviors." These are, in most instances, not behaviors at all in the sense of changes in relation to one's environment but verbalisms at a mechanical level. The following "behavioral" objective is illustrative:

> Given a diagram of the human body illustrating one or more human body systems (including skeletal, muscular, digestive, circulatory, and respiratory systems), [the student will] be able to name the body systems shown.[109]

The more explicitly defined the objective, the more it is likely to be confined to the lower cognitive process of simple recall. Yet ultraspecificity in objectives is called for in guides to writing objectives.

A Narrow-Minded Curriculum Without Coherence. Our discussion concerning the dangers and limitations of activity or job analysis as a method for curriculum making is equally applicable to the "behavioral" objectives approach. The result in both instances was a narrow-minded curriculum focused on lower cognitive processes. Both movements were static as far as the curriculum was concerned in that they viewed the curriculum as the means for adapting the learner to existing conditions.

It should also be emphasized that there is no end to the number of objectives that can be produced by dividing the curriculum into minute steps.

In more than one school system, where the curriculum has been atomized into thousands of "behavioral" objectives, teachers and students are subjected to preposterous burdens. But perhaps the most damaging result of breaking down the curriculum into minute particles is that it must, of necessity, lead away from an understanding of the unity of all knowledge. Obviously also, a disintegrated curriculum is not likely to help the student develop an integrated outlook or philosophy or lead to transfer of learning.

Science and Scientism

The theory of curriculum making that we have just examined was labeled "scientific" by its developers. This group, however, were more like true believers in an "ism" than scientists. Rather than testing their theory experimentally, they espoused it as an absolute truth. This is hardly the essential nature of science, for science requires the continual testing and correcting of its theories.

Furthermore, man had moved from a mechanistic to a holistic view of the world. The new world view was produced by Darwin's theory of evolution and investigation in the physical sciences. According to the theory of evolution, the species of life had common roots and had gradually changed into more complex forms over eons of time through a process of interaction between the organisms and their environments. The theory that nature is organically related ("organismic" theory in biology) and the theory that all groups of physical phenomena are connected ("field theory" in physics) were reflected in the field of philosophy, for the way man views the world affects his view of himself. Holism in philosophy and the sciences was reflected in the field of psychology with the development of gestalt psychology. Gestaltists argued that the mind reacted not to bits and pieces of a situation but to the total situation, the entire "field."

An Outmoded World View

The point is that mechanical analysis in curriculum making was based on an outmoded view of the world. As Dewey and Childs observed in 1933:

> The assumption implicit in the method of much of the work referred to is that processes and functions with which education deals are isolable, because they are independent of one another. This involves the philosophical notion that character, mental life, experience, and the methods of dealing with them, are composed of separable parts and that there is no whole, no integralness in them, that what seems to be a unity is in reality nothing but an aggregate of parts. This philosophy once dominated physical science. In physics and biology its inadequacy from a scientific point of view is now realized. Yet it has been taken over by that school of educational "science" which denies the importance of a philosophy in conducting education.[110]

According to the holistic view, a unity—be it a curriculum or the universe—is more than an assemblage of parts, for the parts are relating, interacting, and changing. Needless to say, if the mechanistic approach was based on an outmoded world view in 1920, it is infinitely more outmoded today. Yet mechanism reappears at periodic intervals in response to the demand for educational economy and efficiency: the behavioristic-objectives movement of the 1960s, the competency-based education movement of the 1970s, and "curriculum alignment" (teaching-to-the test) of the 1980s. The behavioristic-objectives movement led into (paved the way for) statewide programs of minimum-competency testing and reducing the curriculum to the lowest common denominators of basic skills.

Scientism, Technology, and the Curriculum

The scientism of Bobbitt and Charters was essentially rooted in technology. (It will be recalled that Bobbitt compared the curriculum maker to an engineer.) As has been shown, efficiency, an aim in industry where the process is mechanical, was adopted as a goal for all aspects of education including curriculum making. The job analysis approach to curriculum development was the factory system imposed on the curriculum. Bobbitt and Charters were technicians. They were nonphilosophical, placing their entire confidence in technology. The difference between this group, who labeled its curriculum theories "scientific," and those who argued that educational decisions should be based on carefully tested hypotheses, open to continuous verification and correction, is fundamental. Included in the latter group were Dewey, Bode, and Rugg.

CURRICULUM MAKING IN PUBLIC SCHOOL SYSTEMS

The work of the Committee on Economy of Time was given top billing at the annual meeting of NEA's powerful Department of Superintendence and published in yearbooks of the National Society for the Study of Education for four successive years (1916–19). One might imagine that the prominence given the new approach to curriculum construction would affect the public-school curriculum. This is exactly what happened. Reaction to the committee's effort to identify the "minimum essentials" was clearly evident in similar activity at the grass roots (school system level).

This activity assumed the proportions of a major curriculum reform movement in the 1920s. (By 1932 the library at Columbia's Teachers College had a collection of thirty thousand curricula.) In addition to the spate of course outlines, instructional materials, activities, articles, surveys, and yearbooks, there were two significant outcomes for the curriculum field: Curriculum development emerged as a field of specialization, and the teacher became a participant in curriculum development.

Despite the growing popularity of the idea of a utilitarian curriculum built by analyzing the "life situations" of adults, it cannot be assumed that this was the sole force behind the movement. There were other reasons why school people in the 1920s concluded that their curricula were sadly out-of-date. The impact of child-centered rhetoric, the project method, and new knowledge from the field of child development all contributed to a greater or lesser degree (depending on the school system) to the desire for reform and the ultimate result. As shown earlier, a dominant motive for curriculum research and the development of new materials was to adapt the curriculum to the individual child. Winnetka was the quintessential example. Nevertheless, the methods used were, in many instances, patterned directly after the methods of the committee.

Curriculum Development and the Superintendency

In 1922 the Department of Superintendence turned its attention officially to curriculum making at the school district level by announcing that its second and third yearbooks would be devoted to the discussion of existing elementary curricula and techniques for curriculum revision. (The topic for the first yearbook was the superintendency itself.[111]) The department also announced the establishment of a central bureau of curriculum research that would serve as a clearing house for ideas on improving the public-school curriculum. By 1926, a cooperative plan was organized among school systems for curriculum revision. A school system could belong to the plan if at least one administrator contributed part of his or her time to work on the problem of curriculum development in his or her own district. More than three hundred school systems were able to meet this criterion.

Turning again to the impetus for the movement, NEA's central bureau of research, mentioned earlier, published information concerning available research studies, descriptions of existing curricula, and discussions on the methods of curriculum construction in several yearbooks of the Department of Superintendence.[112] The yearbooks and the various bulletins published by the Department of Superintendence both encouraged school systems to revise their curricula and profoundly influenced how they went about it.

The Denver Plan

Known as the "Denver Plan," the Denver program for curriculum development became the prototype for curriculum revision in urban school systems. This plan, which involved teachers in curriculum making, was the brainchild of superintendent Jesse Newlon. Significantly, Newlon's plan was initiated in 1922 and in 1925 he was elected president of the National Education Association.

The Denver Plan was based on the organization of two types of committees, subject-matter committees and central organization committees. There were three sets of subject-matter committees, one for the elementary schools, one for the junior high schools, and one for the senior high schools. Subject-matter committees were comprised of classroom teachers only. Central organization committees were comprised of administrators and were concerned with such problems as graduation requirements, organization of curricula into majors and minors, experimentation, and innovation.

Experimentation. Curriculum experimentation was an important part of the Denver curriculum program. Proposed courses of study were tested experimentally, and one elementary school was designated "the curriculum school." This was consistent with Newlon's conviction that there should be centers of experimentation in every school system.

The Teacher. Newlon had a deep and abiding faith in the teacher as a professional. Because of this confidence and because he believed that the study of curriculum problems was the best possible kind of in-service training, Newlon put teachers at the heart of the curriculum-making process. This was indeed revolutionary at a time when teachers generally were not looked upon as being well versed in the classroom art, not to mention the writing of courses of study. In most city systems prior to 1920, the in-service education program consisted largely of demonstrations of teaching methods conducted by supervisors. Teachers were expected to follow the course of study to the letter, not to write it. Newlon's high regard for teachers, as revealed by the professional responsibilities he delegated to them, did much to improve the image of the teacher in school systems throughout the nation.

Newlon's curriculum program was well funded by his board, and teachers working on curriculum committees were freed from their classroom duties, sometimes for days at a time while they were so engaged. Other school systems, caught by the contagion of Newlon's enthusiasm about the program, tried curriculum revision by teacher committees. Often the results were disappointing. Puzzled and disappointed, the other superintendents failed to realize that there was at least one very significant difference between their program and Newlon's: They expected teachers to do the work after school (or were able to free only one committee member, and only then for writing the course of study).

The Method. Typically, Denver teachers determined the objectives and activities for a given course of study by analyzing the "life situations" facing the pupil. Thus, course content in junior high school home economics was determined by a survey of girls' home activities. In junior- and senior-high-school commercial courses, content was determined by an investigation of commercial practices in local business and industry. The words to be taught in spelling were determined by recent research on spelling.[113] A real coup for Denver, however, was the design of a unified junior-high-school social studies program organized around civic and social problems.

The subject-matter committees developed not only courses of study but also tests to measure student progress. The course guides were published as part of the Denver Research Monograph Series. Not suprisingly, thousands of these course guides were sold to school systems throughout the nation. (This also happened to the teacher-developed syllabi published by the Winnetka Public Schools in the 1920s; they were snapped up as soon as they were available.)

The Scope.   It is all too easy to overstate the extent of teacher involvement in curriculum making in Denver. In instances where experimentally developed textbooks and syllabi already were available, teachers did not write another course of study. (However, in a number of cities teachers wrote courses of study that did not even begin to measure up to existing textbooks and syllabi.) Having teachers write a course of study for every subject was as senseless as keeping them totally out of the process of course construction. The problem was summed up by Newlon and Threlkeld in these words:

> The policy of delegating entirely to teachers the making of curricula would be as fallacious as was the policy of leaving the teachers entirely out of this process, and would likewise fail to take account of the indispensable contribution that must be made by research and by specialists who, by devoting their lives to the study of teaching in particular subjects, become authorities in their fields.[114]

The Outcomes.   Interestingly, Newlon believed that the least important outcome of the Denver curriculum program was the courses produced by teachers. Far more important were better teaching, teachers' increasing interest in current educational thought, and the fact that teachers were actually requesting supervision.[115]

In 1927, Newlon left Denver for New York to become director of the Lincoln School. Ironically, Newlon was able to do more in the field of curriculum experimentation in the public-school setting than in an experimental school connected with a university. Only a few years after Newlon had left Denver, the Denver schools joined the Eight-Year Study.

Middletown

The vitally important question with which we must concern ourselves here is how typical were the efforts of teachers in Denver and Winnetka to make the curriculum better serve the child? What about the average city in America? The Denver and Winnetka systems were not typical. They were supreme examples of public-school progressivism, and their programs were excitedly discussed, envied, and emulated—although the emulation was not often successful. Undoubtedly, the school system of Muncie, Indiana, described by Robert and Helen Lynd in their classic study *Middletown,* was far more typical. In 1925, although there were signs of a token attempt to make subject matter more useful, the main currents of progressivism seemed to have passed Muncie by. The Lynds described what they saw:

> Immovable seats in orderly rows fix the sphere of activity of each child. For all, from the timid six-year-old entering for the first time to the most assured high school senior, the general routine is much the same. Bells divide the day into periods. For the six-year-olds the periods are short (fifteen to twenty-five minutes) and varied; in some they leave their seats, play games, and act out make-believe stories, although in "recitation periods" all movement is prohibited. As they grow older the taboo upon physical activity becomes stricter, until by the third or fourth year practically all movement is forbidden except the marching from one set of seats to another between periods, a brief interval of prescribed exercise daily, and periods of manual training or home economics once or twice a week. There are "study periods" in which children learn "lessons" from "textbooks" prescribed by the state and "recitation periods" in which they tell an adult teacher what the book has said. . . .[116]

Absence of a Total Scheme

In assessing the impact of what William Bagley called the "curriculum revision jamboree" of the 1920s, it does indeed appear that the most positive outcomes were in terms of teacher growth. The effect on the curriculum itself was to perpetuate old problems and create some new ones. The fact that separate teacher committees were created for each subject (with the exception of the social studies) and each educational level merely deepened the problem of articulation and made curriculum synthesis less possible. The separate-subject approach was the piecemeal approach to curriculum revision; in few if any school systems did committees consider the entire school program. Thus, there was no vision of an entire scheme.

Because activity analysis was the dominant method for determining curriculum objectives and content, teacher committees tended to focus narrowly on skill development, ignoring the development of the powers of reflective thinking and generalization, attitudes, and appreciation. Finally, in many school systems, curriculum making by teacher committees degenerated into a process valued simply because it was "the thing to do." Put another way, the means became the end.

THE EMERGING FIELD OF CURRICULUM

More than thirty years separate the forums of the National Herbart Society and the round tables of the Committee on Curriculum-Making of the National Society for the Study of Education. One cannot peruse the yearbooks of the National Herbart Society and NSSE's Twenty-sixth Yearbook without sensing the extent to which contemporary theory has been influenced by the conferences and writing of these two rather widely separated curriculum groups. There are striking similarities between their concerns; both saw clearly that advances in school organization had been made at the expense of systematic attention to the curriculum (as Rugg put it, "administration is ousting synthesis"[117]) and both were explicitly committed to the development of theoretical foundations for curriculum making. Finally, both sought synthesis.

But there were differences as well. Herbartian interest in synthesis stemmed from the problem of an overcrowded curriculum (see Chapter 2). In the 1920s the problem of the synthesis of knowledge still remained, but the Committee on Curriculum-Making also sought to bring together opposing positions in curriculum making. This was a far more difficult kind of synthesis because philosophical differences were involved. Take, for example, child growth versus social needs as the starting point for curriculum construction. After much debate (over a period of two years) the group finally agreed that both views were important, and both were incorporated in the composite statement.[118] The committee, under the leadership of Harold Rugg, had made a clear beginning in the search for a curriculum paradigm, taking into account the need to develop the curriculum in consonance with the nature of the learner and the ideals of a free society.

The Curriculum Specialist

According to Cremin, if the curriculum field had a beginning it was at Denver. Cremin writes: "Once the Denver pattern caught on, it was obvious that specialists other than the superintendent would be needed to manage the process, and it was for the purpose of training such specialists that the curriculum field was created."[119] Yet according to Caswell, "The curriculum has been a subject of study and innovation since the beginning of organized education."[120] And Seguel points to the Herbartians as the "pioneers in the curriculum field."[121] Cremin is talking from another vantage point—the status of curriculum as an academic specialization. As he tells us, the study of curriculum began initially as a subfield of educational administration. When curriculum making emerged as a field of professional activity in the 1920s, curriculum began to come into its own as an independent specialization.[122] Thus the curriculum field as we now know it can be traced to the involvement of classroom teachers in system-wide curriculum reform. Curriculum specialists were needed as consultants in the preparation of new courses of study and to direct the process itself. Eventually the interrelationships of the various subjects and learning activities that comprise the total school curriculum demanded attention.

As in other professions, the services of the curriculum specialist must rest upon the mastery of a common body of knowledge and skills. Rugg saw this clearly, and it lay at the heart of his deep concern for the reconciliation of opposing viewpoints. Did the committee really arrive at unity? According to Seguel, although they signed a joint statement, "it was a cautious and limited statement, although issues were clarified as a result of the decisions."[123] In his study of the Twenty-sixth Yearbook, Walker also concludes that "the hoped-for consensus on the foundations of curriculum making failed to come about."[124] Yet although the statement was cautiously limited, it was progress; it brought sharply into focus the elements of a theory; it was a paradigm or model in the making.

The Tasks of Curriculum Making

"The curriculum-maker must become a student of both the child and of society and the accumulating experience of the race."[125] So wrote the Twenty-sixth Yearbook Committee in their composite statement. The committee stressed that the key to curriculum making lay in the application of scientific principles. Looking at the process itself, there were, essentially, three tasks: to determine the objectives of education, the modes and materials of instruction, and the organization (appropriate grade placement) of learning experiences. The goals of education and the content of the curriculum would emerge from studies of American society and individual development. But above all, "care should be exercised to validate proposal changes experimentally."[126]

As Walker has pointed out, the "Twenty-sixth Yearbook is an admirable piece of work, deserving of more attention and appreciation than it receives," and that, unlike much recent work, it "kept everyone's eye pretty much on the ball of curricula and curriculum-making"[127] It was indeed admirable; it focused on the problem, and it was more: It established the foundational principles of curriculum development.[128] Whether the committee was cautious or wholehearted in its agreement matters little. The point of importance is that curriculum as a field of professional work emerged from these principles.

The study of curriculum achieved independent status with the organization of the Society for Curriculum Study in 1932 and the establishment of the department of curriculum and teaching at Columbia's Teachers College in 1938.[129]

The guiding idea in the work of Jesse Newlon at Denver was built into the department of curriculum and teaching at Teachers College: Supervision and curriculum improvement are an interactive process. More importantly, perhaps, over a half century later the organization of the department still reflects the idea that the improvement of curriculum, teaching, and supervision are a set of interconnected problems.[130] The department has held onto the concept of curriculum from the macro-aspect because it reflects the way curriculum work is done. (In other universities, curriculum and supervision are most frequently—and unrealistically—located in different administrative units of colleges of education.)

EDUCATION AND SOCIETY: A RETROSPECTIVE OF EVENTS (1920–29)

Table 4-1 chronicles some of the major events in school and society during the decade of the twenties. The decade was marked by the emergence of the curriculum as a field for systematic study in the United States. The monumental two-volume Yearbook of the National Society for the Study of Education under the editorship of Harold Rugg—*Curriculum-Making: Past and Present* and *The Foundations of Curriculum-Making*—was published in 1927. Unit teaching was developed, followed by the core curriculum at the Lincoln School to provide for curriculum synthesis and to meet the function of general education for children and youth. Further research by Edward Thorndike refuted the long-standing doctrines of mental discipline and transfer of learning, strengthening the case for modernizing the curriculum. The Denver Plan provided teachers with professional responsibilities and opportunities in curriculum development.

The year 1925 was marked by what came to be called "the world's most famous court trial," as John T. Scopes, a Tennessee high-school teacher, was convicted of having violated a state statute prohibiting the teaching of evolution as presented in the textbook *Civic Biology* by George Hunter. In that same year, Tennessee enacted a law prohibiting sex education in the schools. Harold Rugg's first volume of his social studies series was published, later becoming the leading texts for the junior and senior high school and noted for their frank treatment of the problems of American democracy.

The advent of radio was heralded by many educators as a new breakthrough for education, followed by the promises heralded for the motion picture during the following decade (even greater claims were to be made for the promise of television and the teaching machine during the 1950s).

On the wider scene, the decade opened with prohibition, leading no less a figure than Albert Einstein to comment: "The prestige of government has undoubtedly been lowered considerably by the Prohibition law. For nothing is more destructive of respect for the government and the law of the land than passing laws which cannot be enforced." To which he added, "The public house is a place which gives people the opportunity to exchange views and ideas on public affairs."[131] Speakeasies and crime flourished as the era came to be known as the Roaring Twenties. The decade ended with the economic collapse in Germany and the stock market collapse in the United States, beginning a world economic crisis and laying the ground for the rise of fascism and Naziism in Europe. The challenge to American democracy of

TABLE *4-1*   Timetable of Events in Education and Society: 1920–29

YEAR	EDUCATION	SOCIETY
1920	Unit teaching ("units of work") developed at Lincoln School	Senate votes against U.S. membership in League of Nations; 18th Amendment to Constitution goes into effect: prohibition throughout U.S.; 19th Amendment grants suffrage to women; Warren G. Harding elected President; Sinclair Lewis: *Main Street;* Eugene O'Neill: *The Emperor Jones, Beyond the Horizon;* Herman Rorschach (Swiss) devises "inkblot" test; first radio station in U.S. (Pittsburgh)
1922	Denver Plan initiated by Jesse Newlon	Mussolini forms Fascist government; Soviet states form U.S.S.R.; James Joyce: *Ulysses* published in Paris, U.S. Post Office burns 500 imported copies; Sinclair Lewis: *Babbitt;* Anne Nichols: *Abie's Irish Rose* (closes in 1927 after 2,327 performances in N.Y.); *Reader's Digest* founded; Eugene O'Neill: *Anna Christie;* Emily Post: *Etiquette*
1924	Franklin Bobbitt (1875–1956): *How to Make a Curriculum* W. W. Charters (1875–1952): *Curriculum Construction* Further research by Edward L. Thorndike refutes doctrine of mental discipline and learning transfer	Britain recognizes U.S.S.R., Woodrow Wilson dies (born 1856); Lenin dies (born 1870); Calvin Coolidge elected President; J. Edgar Hoover appointed director of Federal Bureau of Investigation (to 1972); Thomas Mann: *The Magic Mountain;* Mark Twain: *Autobiography* (post.); 2.5 million radios in U.S.
1925	Trial of John T. Scopes for violating Tennessee law prohibiting teaching of theory of evolution Tennessee prohibits sex education in schools	First woman elected governor in U.S. (Wyoming); Adolph Hitler: *Mein Kampf,* vol. 1; Theodore Dreiser: *An American Tragedy;* F. Scott Fitzgerald: *The Great Gatsby;* Sinclair Lewis: *Arrowsmith;* Franz Kafka: *The Trial* (post.); Charlie Chaplin: *The Gold Rush;* first Leica camera; Chrysler Corporation founded
1927	Harold Rugg (ed.): *Curriculum-Making: Past and Present* and *The*	Economic collapse in Germany; Sinclair Lewis: *Elmer Gantry;* Upton

TABLE *4-1*   Timetable of Events in Education and Society: 1920–29

YEAR	EDUCATION	SOCIETY
	Foundations of Curriculum-Making, 26th NSSE Yearbook, Parts I, II Core curriculum developed for secondary-level students at Lincoln School	Sinclair: *Oil;* John Dewey: *The Public and Its Problems;* first talking motion picture *(The Jazz Singer);* Ivan P. Pavlov: *Conditioned Reflexes;* Charles A. Lindbergh flies first monoplane nonstop N.Y. to Paris; Sacco and Vanzetti executed; Jerome Kern and Oscar Hammerstein II: *Showboat* (N.Y.); motion pictures are fifth largest U.S. industry
1928	Harold Rugg and Ann Shumaker: *The Child-Centered School* Henry Harap (1893–1981): *The Techniques of Curriculum Making*	Women's suffrage reduced from age 30 to 21 in Britain; Herbert Hoover elected President; D. H. Lawrence: *Lady Chatterley's Lover;* Eugene O'Neill: *Strange Interlude;* Upton Sinclair: *Boston;* Vernon L. Parrington: *Main Currents in American Thought;* George Gershwin: *An American in Paris;* Franz Boas: *Anthropology and Modern Life* (refutes Fascist master race theory); Alexander Fleming discovers penicillin
1929	John Dewey: *The Sources of a Science of Education* Alfred N. Whitehead (1861–1947): *The Aims of Education and Other Essays; The Function of Reason* Harold Rugg: *Man and His Changing Society,* first volume of a textbook series in social studies (terminated after 1940 because of right-wing attacks) Statewide curriculum development programs conducted by Frank Bachman and Hollis L. Caswell (1929–39) National Survey of Secondary Education undertaken by U.S. Office of Education	Secretary of Interior under Coolidge convicted of accepting bribe in Teapot Dome scandal; John Dewey: *The Quest for Certainty;* Robert and Helen Lynd: *Middletown;* Erich Maria Remarque: *All Quiet on the Western Front;* Vicki Baum: *Grand Hotel;* Museum of Modern Art (N.Y.) opens; end of silent films; Einstein: unified field theory; construction begins on Empire State Building (to 1931); Kodak introduces color film; "Black Friday" in New York with stock-market collapse, beginning of world economic crisis

Sources: *Annual Register of World Events* (London: Longman's, Green); Bernard Grun, *The Timetables of History,* rev. ed. (New York: Simon & Schuster, 1979); *The New York Times.*

the Great Depression of the ensuing decade impelled progressive educators to reexamine the role of the school in society and to undertake unprecedented measures to reconstruct the curriculum to meet the needs of children and youth.

PERSPECTIVE

The new education was buffeted by conflicting currents: laissez-faire individualism, mechanistic psychology, managerial efficiency, and curriculum adaptation (reorganization in accord with the findings of child development) as opposed to reconstruction. Public schools, even the most progressive, tended to seek curriculum adaptation rather than reconstruction, leaving the curriculum in some kind of subject organization. Winnetka is an example. Progressive experimental schools looked for more far-reaching forms of curriculum reconstruction. Thus, at the Lincoln School of Teachers College, Columbia University, the elementary curriculum was organized around the unit of work and the secondary curriculum around the general or core course.

Freedom in many child-centered schools (private and country day schools) was interpreted as a maxim to let the child alone—giving no suggestions as to goals or learning experiences and providing no guidance or direction. The child was to make his or her own curriculum. Disciples of child centeredness maintained that children's immediate interests and urges were certain to generate valuable educational outcomes, although Dewey warned that such expectations were foredoomed to disappointment.

Generally, reformers did not conceive of freedom in terms of the kinds of experiences children should have. Dewey's experimentalist theory was subsumed by progressivists, whose undertakings were largely a reaction *against* a formal and lifeless curriculum, regimentation, and autocratic methods of teaching. Like many a political party, progressive education committed the gross error of clinging to a negative platform long after a new program should have been developed. Freedom as child liberation was to reemerge in the 1960s and to fail, once again, in the 1970s. The child as a source for making his or her own curriculum put educators on an infinite number of dead-end paths.

Kilpatrick proposed his project method as a complete curriculum theory; he conceived of the curriculum as a series of projects. Whereas Dewey in his laboratory school used projects for problem-solving, Kilpatrick defined a project as any activity at all as long as it was "purposed" by the child and done "wholeheartedly." Child purposing was simply the doctrine of immediate interests with a new name.

Theoretical difficulties of the project method as a curriculum theory were essentially the same as those associated with the doctrine of immediate interests: curriculum fragmentation, the neglect of systematic treatment of subject matter, lack of scope and sequence, and the underlying assumption that the urges of children will release high-level cognitive outcomes. A theoretical difficulty associated with the project method in particular was its total emphasis on instrumental learning (knowledge for an immediate purpose) and the implication that knowledge was of value only if it could contribute to the solution of an immediate problem.

Despite the fact that by the mid-1920s theorists were warning of the pitfalls of planlessness, educators in many progressive schools could not agree on the need for a curriculum design. Without a design indicating the end points of instruction, objective evaluation was, of course, impossible. Laissez-faire individualism, the fear of formalism, of slipping back into the old mold (or a new one), and the fundamental tenet of progressivism—freedom—all contributed to the failure of experimental schools to conduct systematic research that might have substantiated their claims to afford students with benefits unattainable in traditional schools. The Lincoln School was the quintessential example.

The decision of NEA's Committee on Economy of Time to answer Spencerian questions on the basis of the "best" present practices had formidable implications for the curriculum field. Bobbitt developed a well-organized theory from the committee's groundwork. To Bobbitt, life activities comprised both the objectives and the content of the curriculum. The activities were identified by consensus of opinion (questionnaire) and atomized into performance objectives by activity or job analysis (the process of dividing a given job into small steps). Bobbitt and Charters called their method "scientific," although they presented it as a valid principle rather than a hypothesis to be tested. Mechanistic curriculum making was a factory method superimposed on the school.

Although the conception of knowledge as thousands of tiny discrete parts rather than a unity is based on a long-outmoded world view, it was revived with the behavioral-objectives and back-to-basics movements. Atomism in curriculum making and behaviorism in psychology share the same fundamental concept of learning as operant conditioning. The result of Bobbitt's approach was a traditional, static subject-matter curriculum.

Although laissez-faire individualism and mechanism were conflicting currents, they both divorced education from the goal of social reform.

Out of the curriculum revision movement of the 1920s, curriculum development emerged as a field of specialization and with the teacher as a participant in course construction. Curriculum as a field of professional work is based on the principles developed by the Committee on Curriculum-Making, appointed by the National Society for the Study of Education in 1924. From these principles, it was stressed that any signal effort at educational reform would need to be validated experimentally—taking into account the selection, organization, and design of the curriculum in accord with the nature of the learner and the ideals of a free society. To this day, there is a persistent failure on the part of educational reformers to follow this guiding idea.

NOTES

1. René Descartes, "Discourse on the Method" (1637), in *Philosophical Works,* translated by E. S. Haldane and G. R. T. Ross, vol. 1 (New York: Cambridge University Press, 1911), pp. 84–85.

2. Lawrence A. Cremin, "The Free School Movement—A Perspective," *Today's Education* 63 (September–October 1974): 72.

3. John Dewey, "Individuality and Experience," in *Art and Education* by John Dewey et al. (Merion, Pa.: Barnes Foundation Press, 1929), p. 180.

4. Ibid., p. 181.

5. Margaret Mead, "The Meaning of Freedom in Education," *Progressive Education* 8 (February 1931): 110.

6. Ibid.

7. John Dewey, *The Child and the Curriculum* (Chicago: University of Chicago Press, 1902), p. 24.

8. Harold Rugg and Ann Shumaker, *The Child-Centered School* (New York: Arno Press and The New York Times 1969; first published by World Book in 1928), p. 118.

9. Harold Rugg et al., "The Foundations of Curriculum-Making," Chapter 1 in *The Foundations of Curriculum-Making,* Twenty-sixth Yearbook, Part II, National Society for the Study of Education (Bloomington, Ill.: Public School Publishing Company, 1927), p. 19.

10. Katharine L. Keelor, *Curriculum Studies in the Second Grade* (New York: Teachers College Press, 1925), p. 5.

11. John Dewey, "Comments and Criticisms by Some Educational Leaders in Our Universities," Chapter 5 in *The Activity Movement,* Thirty-third Yearbook, Part II, National Society for the Study of Education (Bloomington, Ill.: Public School Publishing Company, 1934), p. 85.

12. Ibid.

13. Boyd H. Bode, *Progressive Education at the Crossroads* (New York: Newson and Company, 1938), p. 54.

14. Ibid., pp. 52–55.

15. Ibid., p. 44.

16. William H. Engler, *Radical School Reformers of the 1960s* (unpublished doctoral dissertation, Rutgers University, 1973).

17. For some insightful comments by educational practitioners concerning their experience with activity programs, see "Comments and Criticisms by Some Educa-

tional Leaders in the Field," Chapter 6 in *The Activity Movement,* op. cit., pp. 105–43.

18. William H. Kilpatrick, "Definitions of the Activity Movement To-Day," Chapter 3 in *The Activity Movement,* op. cit., p. 64.

19. William S. Gray, "Statements by Members of the Committee," Chapter 9 in *The Activity Movement, op. cit., p. 192.*

20. Boyd H. Bode, *Modern Educational Theories* (New York: Macmillan, 1927), p. 40.

21. William H. Kilpatrick, "The Project Method," *Teachers College Record* 19 (September 1918): 320.

22. John Dewey, *How We Think,* rev. ed. (Lexington, Mass.: D. C. Heath, 1933; first published 1910), p. 116.

23. Based on his experiments with animals, Thorndike concluded that learning was simply a matter of connecting the right stimulus with the right response. Taking this idea further, Thorndike evolved his "laws" of learning—the "laws" of exercise and effect. The law of exercise held that when stimulus or response is exercised, the bond or connection becomes stronger. Conversely, when a bond is not exercised it becomes weaker. The law of effect held that an individual tends to strengthen bonds that result in satisfaction and weaken bonds that result in annoyance.

24. Kilpatrick, op. cit., p. 320.

25. Ibid., pp. 321, 334.

26. William H. Kilpatrick, *Foundations of Method* (New York: Macmillan, 1925), p. 207.

27. Bode, *Modern Educational Theories,* op. cit., pp. 161–62.

28. Kilpatrick, *Foundations of Method,* op. cit., p. 212.

29. Bode, *Modern Educational Theories,* op. cit., p. 191.

30. Kilpatrick, *Foundations of Method,* op. cit., p. 357.

31. Lawrence A. Cremin, *The Transformation of the School* (New York: Knopf, 1961), p. 220.

32. See Charles McMurry, *Teaching by Projects* (New York: Macmillan, 1920).

33. James Hosiac, "Types of Projects and Their Techniques," *The Journal of Educational Method* 3 (March 1923): 290.

34. William C. Bagley, "Dangers and Difficulties of the Project Method and How to Overcome Them," *Teachers College Record* 22 (September 1921): 290; Bode, *Modern Educational Theories,* op. cit., p. 151.

35. Bagley, op. cit., pp. 291–93.

36. William H. Kilpatrick, "Dangers and Difficulties of the Project Method and How to Overcome Them," *Teachers College Record* 22 (September 1921): 283–321.

37. Ibid., pp. 286–87.

38. Merlin C. Wittrock (ed.), *Handbook of Research on Teaching,* 3rd ed. (New York: Macmillan, 1986).

39. James Harvey Robinson, *The Humanizing of Knowledge* (New York: George Doran, 1924), p. 63.

40. Ibid., p. 70.

41. Ibid., p. 64.

42. Rugg and Shumaker, op. cit., pp. 86–87.

43. Carleton Washburne, "The Philosophy of the Winnetka Curriculum, Chapter 11 in *Curriculum-Making: Past and Present,* Twenty-sixth Yearbook, Part I, National Society for the Study of Education (Bloomington, Ill.: Public School Publishing Company, 1927), p. 227.

44. Carleton W. Washburne and Sidney P. Marland, Jr., *Winnetka: The History and Significance of an Educational Experiment* (Englewood Cliffs, N. J.: Prentice-Hall, 1963), p. 38.

45. Washburne, op. cit., p. 227.

46. William H. Kilpatrick, "An Effort at Appraisal," Chapter 6 in *Adapting the Schools to Individual Differences,* Twenty-fourth Yearbook, Part II, National Society for Education (Bloomington, Ill.: Public School Publishing Company, 1925), p. 281.

47. Ibid., pp. 284–85.

48. An experiment to determine the comparative effectiveness of formal reading instruction and "individualized" silent reading was conducted in the early 1920s by teachers Keelor and Miner with the assistance of Laura Zirbes. See Laura Zirbes, *Practice Exercises and Checks on Silent Reading in the Primary Grades* (New York: Lincoln School of Teachers College, 1925).

49. James S. Tippett et al., *Curriculum Making in an Elementary School* (Lexington, Mass.: Ginn, 1927), pp. 167–68.

50. Murry R. Nelson, "Rugg on Rugg: His Theories and His Curriculum," *Curriculum Inquiry* 8 (Summer 1978): 122.

51. G. Derwood Baker, "An Eleventh-Grade Field Study: The Coal Industry," *Educational Research Bulletin* 17 (October 19, 1938): 174.

52. Louis Raths, "Some Evaluations of the Trip," *Educational Research Bulletin* 17 (October 19, 1938): 207.

53. Otis W. Caldwell, "The Lincoln Experimental School," Chapter 16 in *Curriculum-Making: Past and Present,* op. cit., pp. 280–89; Rugg and Shumaker, op. cit., p. 126.

54. Frederick G. Bonser, "Curriculum-Making in Laboratory or Experimental Schools," Chapter 26 in *Curriculum-Making: Past and Present,* op. cit., pp. 353–62.

55. L. Thomas Hopkins and James E. Mendenhall, *Achievement at the Lincoln School* (New York: Teachers College Press, 1934).

56. Lincoln School of Teachers College, "Final Report to the Aikin Commission on Curriculum Changes and Experimentation in Lincoln School 1932–1940" (mimeographed report, Teachers College, Columbia University, 1940), p. 46.

57. "Court Upholds Closing of Horace Mann-Lincoln School," *Teachers College Record* 48 (May 1947): 533.

58. Hollis L. Caswell, in a letter to the authors of this text, May 29, 1976.

59. Rugg and Shumaker, op. cit., p. 115.

60. Lester Dix, *A Charter for Progressive Education* (New York: Teachers College, 1939), p. 67; see also L. Thomas Hopkins, "Curriculum Development," *Teachers*

College Record 37 (February 1936): 441–42 (the entire February 1936 issue of the *Teachers College Record* is devoted to the programs of the Lincoln School).

61. Harold Rugg, *Culture and Education in America* (New York: Harcourt Brace, 1931), pp. 302–3.

62. Staff of the Horace Mann-Lincoln School, Teachers College, "Charting a Course for Educational Progress," *Teachers College Record* 48 (October 1946): 53–56.

63. Frederick G. Bonser, "Ten Years of Progress in Elementary Education," *Progressive Education* 6 (January-February-March 1929): 15–16.

64. Staff of the Elementary Division of the Lincoln School, Teachers College, *Curriculum Making in An Elementary School* (Boston: Ginn, 1927); Emily Ann Barnes and Bess M. Young, *Children and Architecture* (New York; Bureau of Publications, Teachers College, 1932).

65. Edward L. Thorndike, "Mental Discipline in High School Studies," *Journal of Educational Psychology* 15 (January 1924): 1–22; (February 1924), p. 98.

66. Edward L. Thorndike and Robert S. Woodworth, "The Influence of Improvement in One Mental Function Upon Efficiency of Other Functions," *Psychological Review* 8 (May, July, November, 1901): 247–62, 384–95, 553–64.

67. Edward L. Thorndike, *The Principles of Teaching* (New York: A. G. Seiler, 1906), p. 244.

68. C. R. Broyler, Edward L. Thorndike, and Ella Woodward, "A Second Study of Mental Discipline in High School Studies," *Journal of Educational Psychology* 18 (September 1927): 382.

69. Alexander Wesman, "A Transfer of Training from High School Subjects to Intelligence," *Teachers College Record* 46 (March 1945): 391–93.

70. Clifton Fadiman, "The Case for Basic Education," in *The Case for Basic Education,* James D. Koerner (ed.) (Boston: Little, Brown, 1959), pp. 7–8.

71. John F. Latimer, *The New Case for Latin and the Classics* (Washington, D.C.: Council for Basic Education, January 1973), p. 15.

72. Sidney P. Marland, Jr., "Career Education Now," address delivered at the 1971 convention of the National Association of Secondary School Principals, Houston, Texas (January 23, 1971).

73. Jerome S. Bruner, *The Process of Education* (Cambridge: Harvard University Press, 1960), p. 6.

74. Richard Hofstadter, *Anti-intellectualism in American Life* (New York: Knopf, 1963), Chapter 13.

75. Jerome S. Bruner, "The Process of Education Revisited," *Phi Delta Kappan* 53 (September 1971): 21.

76. Bruner, *The Process of Education,* op. cit., p. 25.

77. Cremin, op. cit., p. viii.

78. Maurice J. Elias and John F. Clabby, "Teaching Social Decision Making," *Educational Leadership* 45 (March 1988): 52.

79. Ibid., p. 53.

80. Hilda Taba, *Curriculum Development: Theory and Practice* (New York: Harcourt Brace Jovanovich, 1962), p. 121.

81. David P. Ausubel, *Educational Psychology: A Cognitive View* (New York: Holt, Rinehart and Winston, 1968), p. 164.

82. Lee J. Cronbach, *Educational Psychology,* 3rd ed. (New York: Harcourt Brace Jovanovich, 1977), p. 65.

83. Ausubel, op. cit., p. 161.

84. Franklin Bobbitt, "Elimination of Waste in Education," *The Elementary School Teacher,* vol. 12 (February 1912), p. 269.

85. Franklin Bobbitt, *The Supervision of City Schools: Some General Principles of Management Applied to the Problems of City-School Systems,* Twelfth Yearbook, Part I, National Society for the Study of Education (Bloomington, Ill.: Public School Publishing Company, 1913), p. 11.

86. Ibid., p. 15.

87. Raymond E. Callahan, *Education and the Cult of Efficiency* (Chicago: University of Chicago Press, 1962), p. 84.

88. Bobbitt, *The Supervision of City Schools,* op. cit., p. 49.

89. Arthur T. Hadley, *Standards of Morality* (New York: Macmillan, 1907).

90. See Daniel Tanner, "Performance Contracting: Contrivance of the Industrial-Governmental-Educational Complex," *Intellect* 101 (March 1973): 361–65.

91. Barbara Berman, "Business Efficiency, American Schooling, and the Public School Superintendency: A Reconsideration of the Callahan Thesis," *History of Education Quarterly* 23 (Fall 1983): 308.

92. Walter Lippmann, *Drift and Mastery* (New York: Kennerly, 1914), p. 151.

93. Lotus D. Coffman, "The Minimum Essentials Versus the Differentiated Course of Study in the Seventh and Eighth Grades," National Education Association *Proceedings* (Chicago: University of Chicago Press, 1916), p. 957.

94. Joseph M. Rice, "Futility of the Spelling Grind," *The Forum* 23 (April 1897): 163–72.

95. Leonard P. Ayres, "Measuring Educational Processes Through Educational Results," *The School Review* 20 (May 1912): 309.

96. Harold B. Wilson, "Minimum Essentials in Elementary-School Subjects," Chapter 1 in *Minimum Essentials in Elementary-School Subjects—Standards and Current Practices,* Fourteenth Yearbook, Part I, National Society for the Study of Education (Chicago: University of Chicago Press, 1915), p. 16.

97. Bode, *Modern Educational Theories,* op. cit., p. 79.

98. Walter A. Jessup, "Current Practices and Standards in Arithmetic," Chapter 8 in *Minimum Essentials in Elementary-School Subjects—Standards and Current Practices,* National Society for the Study of Education, op. cit., p. 129.

99. Walter S. Monroe, "A Preliminary Report of an Investigation of the Economy of Time in Arithmetic," Chapter 7 in *Second Report of the Committee on Minimum Essentials in Elementary-School Subjects,* Sixteenth Yearbook, Part I, National Society for the Study of Education (Bloomington, Ill.: Public School Publishing Co., 1917), p. 111.

100. Walter S. Monroe, "Principles of Method in Teaching Arithmetic as Derived from Scientific Investigation, *Fourth Report of the Committee on Economy of Time in*

Education, Eighteenth Yearbook, Part II, National Society for the Study of Education (Bloomington, Ill.: Public School Publishing Co., 1919), p. 84.

101. Cremin, op. cit., p. 196

102. Franklin Bobbitt, "The New Technique of Curriculum Making," *The Elementary School Journal* 25 (September 1924): 49.

103. W. W. Charters, *Teaching of Ideals* (New York: Macmillan, 1927), p. 24.

104. Charles C. Peters, *Foundations of Educational Sociology* (New York: Macmillan, 1930), p. 38.

105. Franklin Bobbitt, *How to Make a Curriculum* (Boston: Houghton Mifflin, 1924), p. 4.

106. Ibid., p. 8.

107. W. W. Charters, "Functional Analysis as the Basis for Curriculum Construction," *Journal of Educational Research* 19 (October 1924): 214–21.

108. David Snedden, *Sociological Determination of Objectives in Education* (Philadelphia: Lippincott, 1921).

109. Caroline M. Dillman and Harold F. Rahmlow, *Writing Instructional Objectives* (Belmont, Calif.: Fearon, 1972), p. 51.

110. John Dewey and John L. Childs, "The Underlying Philosophy of Education," Chapter 9 in *The Educational Frontier,* William H. Kilpatrick (ed.) (New York: The Century Co., 1933), p. 289.

111. National Education Association, *The Status of the Superintendent,* First Yearbook of the Department of Superintendence, National Education Association (Washington, D.C.: The Association, 1923).

112. National Education Association, *The Elementary Curriculum,* Second Yearbook of the Department of Superintendence, National Education Association (Washington, D.C.: The Association, 1924); Third Yearbook, *Research in Constructing the Public School Curriculum* (1925); Fourth Yearbook, *The Nation at Work on the Public School Curriculum* (1926).

113. Jesse H. Newlon and A. L. Threlkeld, "The Denver Curriculum—Revision Program," Chapter 13 in *Curriculum-Making: Past and Present,* op. cit., pp. 229–48.

114. Ibid., p. 240.

115. Jesse Newlon, "Outcomes of Our Curriculum Program," National Education Association *Proceedings* (Washington, D.C.: The Association, 1925), p. 803.

116. Robert S. Lynd and Helen M. Lynd, *Middletown* (New York: Harcourt Brace, 1929), p. 188.

117. Harold Rugg, "Introduction," in *The Foundations of Curriculum-Making,* op. cit., p. 1.

118. Committee on Curriculum-Making, *The Foundations of Curriculum-Making,* op. cit., pp. 11–28.

119. Cremin, "Curriculum-Making in the United States," *Teachers College Record* 73 (December 1971): 213.

120. Hollis L. Caswell, "Emergence of the Curriculum as a Field of Professional Work and Study," in Helen F. Robison (ed.), *Precedents and Promise in the Curriculum Field* (New York: Teachers College Press, 1966), p. 1.

121. Mary Louise Seguel, *The Curriculum Field: Its Formative Years* (New York: Teachers College Press, 1966), p. 46.

122. Cremin, "Curriculum-Making in the United States," op. cit., p. 213.

123. Seguel, op. cit., p. 130.

124. Decker Walker, "The Curriculum Field in Formation," *Curriculum Theory Network* 45 (No. 4, 1975): p. 279.

125. Committee on Curriculum-Making, op. cit., p. 14.

126. Ibid., p. 23.

127. Walker, op. cit., p. 279.

128. Daniel Tanner and Laurel N. Tanner, "The Emergence of a Paradigm in the Curriculum Field," *Interchange* 19 (Summer, 1988), 50–67.

129. See Hollis L. Caswell, "Persistent Curriculum Problems," *The Educational Forum* 43 (November 1978): 99–110.

130. Laurel N. Tanner, "Being True to Our Traditions," in *The Department of Curriculum and Teaching: The Next Fifty Years* (New York: Teachers College Press, 1989), in press.

131. Albert Einstein, "My First Impressions of the U.S.A.," interview for *Niewe Rotterdamsche Courant,* 1921, republished in Albert Einstein, *Ideas and Opinions* (New York: Crown, 1954), p. 6.

SELECTED REFERENCES

Association for Supervision and Curriculum Development. *A New Look at Progressive Education.* 1972 Yearbook. Washington, D.C.: The Association, 1972.

———. *Perspectives on Curriculum Development 1776–1976.* 1976 Yearbook, Washington, D.C.: The Association, 1976.

Bobbitt, Franklin. *How to Make a Curriculum.* Boston: Houghton Mifflin, 1924.

Bode, Boyd H. *Modern Educational Theories.* New York: Macmillan, 1927.

———. *Progressive Education at the Crossroads.* New York: Newson and Company, 1938.

Callahan, Raymond E. *Education and the Cult of Efficiency.* Chicago: University of Chicago Press, 1962.

Charters, W. W. *Curriculum Construction.* New York: Macmillan, 1924.

Collings, Ellsworth. *An Experiment with a Project Curriculum.* New York: Macmillan, 1925.

Cremin, Lawrence A. *The Transformation of the School.* New York: Knopf, 1961.

———. "Curriculum-Making in the United States," *Teachers College Record* 73 (December 1971): 207–20.

———. *Traditions of American Education.* New York: Basic Books, 1977.

———. *American Education: The Metropolitan Experience 1876–1980.* New York: Harper & Row, 1988.

Dewey, Evelyn. *The Dalton Laboratory Plan.* New York: Dutton, 1922.

Dewey, John. *The Child and the Curriculum*. Chicago: University of Chicago Press, 1902.

———. *How We Think,* 2nd ed. Lexington, Mass.: D.C. Heath, 1933; originally published in 1910.

Dix, Lester. *A Charter for Progressive Education*. New York: Teachers College Press, 1939.

Drost, Walter H. *David Snedden and Education for Social Efficiency*. Madison: University of Wisconsin Press, 1967.

Hilgard, Ernest R., and Bower, Gordon H. *Theories of Learning*. New York: Appleton-Century-Crofts, 1966.

Kilpatrick, William H. *Foundations of Method*. New York: Macmillan, 1925.

Kliebard, Herbert M. *The Struggle for the American Curriculum 1893–1958*. Boston: Routledge & Kegan Paul, 1986.

National Society for the Study of Education. *Adapting the Schools to Individual Differences*. Twenty-fourth Yearbook, Part II. Bloomington, Ill.: Public School Publishing Co., 1925.

———. *Curriculum-Making: Past and Present*. Twenty-sixth Yearbook, Part I. Bloomington, Ill.: Public School Publishing Co., 1927.

———. *The Activity Movement*. Thirty-third Yearbook, Part II. Bloomington, Ill.: Public School Publishing Co., 1934.

———. *Critical Issues in Curriculum*. Eighty-seventh Yearbook, Part I. Chicago, Ill.: University of Chicago Press, 1988.

Parkhurst, Helen. *Education on the Dalton Plan*. New York: Dutton, 1922.

Rugg, Harold, and Shumaker, Ann. *The Child-Centered School*. New York: Arno Press and The New York Times, 1969 (originally published by World Book Company in 1928).

Seguel, Mary Louise. *The Curriculum Field: Its Formative Years*. New York: Teachers College Press, 1966.

Taba, Hilda. *Curriculum Development: Theory and Practice*. New York: Harcourt Brace Jovanovich, Inc., 1962.

Tippitt, James S., et al. *Curriculum Making in an Elementary School*. Lexington, Mass.: Ginn and Company, 1927.

Washburne, Carleton W., and Marland, Sidney P., Jr. *Winnetka: The History and Significance of an Educational Experiment*. Englewood Cliffs, N.J.: Prentice-Hall, 1963.

Part *III*

IDEAS AND IDEALS— CONFLICT AND CONSENSUS

Few, if any, of those who bemoan the evil influence of the progressive educators would send their children into the kind of schoolroom which was common sixty years ago.
—JAMES B. CONANT, 1961

5

The Crisis Years for the Curriculum

Child centeredness in the 1920s effectively detached education from the goal of social reconstruction. After the onset of the Great Depression of the 1930s, educators scurried back to the social definition of education. Indeed, interest in social reconstruction took the form of an educational revival. Educators were determined to achieve social reform through educational means. But the original power of the social definition of education, which peaked during the American Progressivist movement, was gone. It was dissipated in the child-centered school. Ultimately, it was the child-centered image of the new education that prevailed.

What social reconstruction meant in terms of the curriculum was a question of crisis proportions. Yet, as important as it was, this was far from being the only crisis for the new education in the 1930s and 1940s. Attempts to derive a curriculum from the immediate interests of children had, thus far, failed. Progressive education was still a negative movement in search of a program, or, more bluntly, in search of a subject matter (although the term *subject matter* still caused many educators to bristle during the 1930s and 1940s). A third crisis was the need for more objective evidence of the benefits of the new education, not the pious rhetoric of progressivists that they were "affiliated only with the good in education."[1] As progressive education entered the 1930s, it was more of a religion than a science. A fourth crisis was that the best-organized theory in the curriculum field was the "scientific" theory of Bobbitt and Charters based on a production model of man. In the conflict between atomism and holism as a basis for curriculum building, atomism had taken the lead in theory building. The fundamental issue here was whether behaviorism or gestalt theory would provide the theoretical basis for the curriculum. As indicated in Chapter 4, gestalt theory provided a welcome theoretical foundation for the Deweyan view of man as a thinking being rather than a cog in a machine.

SOCIAL RECONSTRUCTION

In times of crisis the schools are inevitably put in the position of being held responsible both for the crisis itself and for finding a solution. In the 1930s educators found themselves depicted by leftists as tools of capitalism and therefore responsible for existing conditions. From the right came the accusation that educational theorists were plotting to overthrow the government by pedagogical means—a curriculum calculated to make children enemies of the present social order. The New Deal program of the Roosevelt administration was evidence that the government looked to more education for less privileged Americans as a way out of the national emergency, although the educational programs of the New Deal were not part of the educational system. Educational theorists, however, regarded the curriculum as not only a way out of the Great Depression but as the means for preventing future social and economic crises.

As Emerson pointed out in his celebrated essay "Compensation," even the most tragic events have their positive outcomes.[2] For educators, a providential outcome of the Depression was that it provided a badly needed sense of direction for curriculum development.

Repudiation of the Machine Model of Man

In the depths of the Great Depression, leading educational theorists produced a philosophical statement that fortified the Deweyan view of education with the holistic theories of philosophy and gestalt psychology. In *The Educational Frontier,* which was the definitive philosophical statement of the 1930s, the position was that "organisms, selves, characters, minds are so intimately connected with their environments that they can be understood only in relation to them."[3] Dewey and Childs, who co-authored two of the chapters, sharply repudiated the work "done in the name of science" that was concerned largely "with the impersonal phase of education," which had "reduced personality as far as possible to impersonal terms."[4] These terms did "lend themselves most readily to factual and statistical treatment," but this was hardly a basis for building a curriculum.

The integrated-experience curricula that were developed by educators in the next two decades were based on two holistic concepts: the idea that the learner develops in interaction with his or her entire environment (the "whole child" idea) and the concept of the unity of knowledge. These concepts clashed head-on with the technological or corporate approach to determining curriculum content.

A final reason for the repudiation of mechanism by leading educational theorists was that it substituted the goal of efficiency for a social theory. As Cremin wrote about Bobbitt, "His results may well have sparkled with precision, but in the process he had given up the progressive quest for a better life through education."[5]

The Decline of Mechanism

Actually, two factors led to the decline of mechanism as a basis for curriculum development in the 1930s. First, it was being attacked, as Bode put it, "from every direction—as an explanation of purposive behavior, of the behavior of nonpurposive living organisms, and even of the facts that constitute the domain of physics."[6] Second, national emergencies, particularly those that involve social strife, tend to have a liberalizing effect on the curriculum. It is recognized in times of emergency that "emergent" situations (as opposed to "established" textbook situations) require inventive, creative solutions. As will be recalled from our discussion in Chapter 4, a curriculum built by job analysis is not concerned with emergent learnings such as social problem solving but focuses on learnings in which all factors are known and all outcomes are predictable. Because an atomized curriculum conceals rather than deals with social problems, it cannot be expected to prepare students to generate creative solutions. The challenge to progressive education during the Great Depression was to match the need for societal reconstruction with a curriculum in harmony with the wider democratic social conscience.

The Reconstructive Curriculum

In repudiating mechanism because it was based on the assumption that technology could substitute for a social program, educators came upon the horns of their dilemma: Progressive education had also failed to come to grips with the relation between school and society. Although many progressivists claimed that the cooperative attitudes developed in progressive schools would "carry over" into the out-of-school environment and result in social reconstruction, a growing number in the 1930s were, understandably, skeptical. Bode opined that the idea "that habits of cooperation, consideration of others, recognition of responsibility for group welfare, and the like . . . will automatically bear fruit in the form of insight into our economic . . . and other standards, involves a strain on our credulity."[7]

"Socialized Education." Unfortunately, the cooperative-attitude-group-process approach to a reconstructed society (no change in curriculum content needed) prevailed throughout the progressive era, particularly in the elementary school. This idea was popular in public schools as well as private schools because it reduced "socialized education" to a neat method. No messy controversial content had to be dealt with, yet educators could (and did) pat themselves on the back for doing their bit for a better society.

This kind of program was recommended by Carleton Washburne on the ground that it avoided the "evils of indoctrination." "Social thinking," said Washburne, "can be developed through socialized activities within the schools themselves, through group enterprises or projects where each individual is contributing his own special interest or ability to do something in which the whole group is interested."[8] Significantly, the idea that "social thinking" could be developed through an educational program designed to enable students to understand the forces at work on their society was not proposed by Washburne as an alternative to indoctrination. Perhaps he feared that such a program would be interpreted as indoctrination. More likely, as an administrator serving a priviliged clientele, he sought to justify a "progressive" curriculum devoid of social controversy. At any rate, the idea that cooperative group projects in the classroom will singlehandedly result in the reconstruction of society is so farfetched as to border on the absurd. Yet this very conservative view of the curriculum as an instrument for social change enjoyed enormous popularity during the progressive era and still remains popular.

Social Realities. *The Educational Frontier,* referred to earlier, was a restatement of Dewey's philosophy in a Depression setting. The aim of education was still to enable human beings to understand their environment so that they could control it rather than being controlled by it and, in their control, make a better world with each succeeding generation. Stated in the context of the evil days that had fallen on our society, it meant the understanding of the "transforming forces which came in with machine industrialization . . . the growth of cities and congestion of population in crowded quarters . . . the shift from small shops, where men worked together in close companionship, to huge factories with their impersonal character, . . ." all this while the "theories, the watchwords, and slogans of the earlier agrarian period have been maintained and cherished."[9] But opening up minds to social realities required the abolition of the "outworn and irrelevant ideas of competitive private individualism," substituting instead activities and materials that accurately reflected present societal conditions.[10]

This was no small order for the timid and weak at heart. Other than the risks involved in bringing students into contact with the realities of social, economic, and political institutions at a time of economic exigency, there was the question of how to do it. Hard-hitting though it was as an appeal to reform, *The Educational Frontier* was weak on specifics concerning curriculum, materials, and methods. In this connection, the unavailability (nonexistence) of teaching materials was the most serious problem for teachers who wanted to help students understand the social forces at work in their society. In the 1970s educators would be faced by a similar situation. Although one of our most critical national problems was depletion of natural resources, curriculum materials tended to promote a "fewer pitch level of consumerism."[11]

EXPERIMENTALISM VERSUS INDOCTRINATION

Should a socially reconstructive educational program be based on an a priori social program? This idea held great attraction for some because it was a way out of the fog and confusion surrounding the curriculum of the new education. Life for progressive educators groping for a subject matter would be immensely simplified; the goals of the program would be the goals of the curriculum. Furthermore, the fact that the goals for school and society were the same would be reflected in a blissfully simple concept of method. When progressive teachers no longer had to encourage the child to do his or her own thinking (conclusions were predetermined along with the social program), they could stop being absorbed with individuals in their classrooms and think only of the group. Participation also would have a new meaning: Instead of the identification of problems for study, it would mean working together on a program with all details prescribed and worked out in advance.

Despite the appeal of an a priori program as a refuge for harried educators, it was simply not in accord with the Deweyan goal of an education that would enable individuals to direct and progressively improve their own institutions. It was contrary to the democratic ideal, which is to have individuals do their own thinking. It was contrary to the gestaltist concept of man as an insightful being rather than a bundle of conditioned responses; education as conditioning was nothing more than indoctrination since it left out preferences and decision-making. It was contrary to the philosophy of experimentalism.

Experimentalism

"The ultimate aim of experimentalism is to develop individuals who can intelligently manage their own affairs, at times 'alone,' more usually in shared or joint enterprises."[12] So wrote progressivist John Childs in 1931. Man interacts with and studies his environment with the thought of making it better serve his needs. In a very real sense, experimentalism is the philosophy of the American frontier; man not only struggled with and adapted to his environment, he controlled it. According to Dewey, the orchestrator of experimentalist theory, man could also control the forces of urban and industrial civilization and use technology in the service of humanity.

Experimentalists see the school as the instrument for creating a society that will be guided by the experimental method in its continuous reconstruction. This means a society composed of individuals with experimental minds who realize that specific solutions will need to be discovered by experimental procedures for each of the social problems in our society.

Of fundamental importance in experimentalist philosophy is its method. This is the experimental method, the scientific method applied to social and moral problems. Experimentalists believe that this is the best way for man to solve the problems of life. This goal has tremendous implications for the curriculum. First, knowledge is valued as a means for improving experience, rather than an end in itself, and, similarly, theory is inseparable from the practical uses to which it is put. Second, the very idea of a self-directed, experimental-minded individual implies the existence of intelligence rather than an operant-conditioning model of man. Insight enables individuals to make choices that go beyond old experience.

Third, a dominant objective of experimentalism is to improve the control of the individual over events. Experimentalists have great faith in the experimental method in this regard, for it is through experimentation that man has learned the consequences of many of the happenings in which he participates. But in the classroom this means that the child must learn to make intelligent connections between his or her acts and their consequences. Without this, no sense of control is possible, and the individual grows up to believe and behave as though he or she is at the mercy of fate.

Fourth, to the experimentalist, mind does not exist apart from feeling. The two are inherently connected. In terms of teaching and learning, this means that the cognitive and the affective are inextricably interwoven.

Finally, it goes without saying that a curriculum based on this theory will continually relate the school to life outside of the school.

Experimentalism parallels and buttresses the democratic process. Democracy and experimentalism share the same key concept: an improved life and a better society through the reconstruction of shared experiences. It is hardly surprising, then, that experimentalism—which has as its method the testing of plans of possible action—became the dominant educational philosophy of the 1930s.

Pedagogical Demands.   Experimentalism is a demanding philosophy. Not only does it require the free and open examination of social and moral issues but also the conception of all knowledge as tentative and subject to correction. This required an open and critical-minded approach, which raised many problems for teachers, for all beliefs and prejudices—including those a teacher might happen to hold—are reduced to hypotheses. And, as shown earlier, teachers in the early 1930s had additional problems; statements of experimental philosophy spelled out few leads as to actual classroom procedures.

A House Divided—The Indoctrination Controversy

That the school can regenerate society along democratic lines by restructuring its own methods is an evolutionary rather than a revolutionary idea. Yet, to many progressivists the idea was indeed revolutionary. Instead, they opted for a child-centered pedagogy stripped of any wider social mission. To other progressivists, experimentalism did not go far enough. In the depths of the Great Depression, a stronger social-reform mission for education was needed. The educational task, they argued, was a fundamental recon-struction of the social order. The idea of a *planned* new social order (a con-crete program on which to base a curriculum) seemed to them a better and safer bet than the idea of a *planning* society at a time when intellectuals were speculating whether the nation would go Communist or Fascist.

Education or Indoctrination. To other progressives, the prescrip-tion of social beliefs was indoctrination, not education. The controversy over the social task of education caused a rift in the Progressive Education Associa-tion from which it never recovered.

"The remedy for shortcomings of the progressive education movement is not to prescribe beliefs but to specify the areas in which reconstruction or reinterpretation is an urgent need," wrote Bode in 1935.[13] Bode's viewpoint on the nature of the school's responsibility for social reconstruction was pub-lished in the first volume of *The Social Frontier,* a fascinating and dynamic journal that provided a forum for reformist progressive educators in the 1930s. To Bode, there was only one sense in which education in a democracy could facilitate change—by helping the student to understand the forces bearing on his or her society. When the school starts to give convictions about society, this is indoctrination. But, pointed out Bode, education "is in-doctrination in the belief that the individual has the right to a choice of be-liefs."[14]

The controversy over the school's social task raged on throughout the 1930s. Some were sure that the schools could and should remain enclaves of neutrality—leaving out of the curriculum any reference to surrounding conditions. Dewey saw this approach as inevitably resulting in the perpetua-tion of the forces of reaction: An educational stance of "neutrality" put the social philosophies of laissez-faire and individualism above criticism and kept students and teachers in ignorance of the issues they had to face. To Dewey, the "problem was not whether the schools *should* participate in the produc-tion of a future society (since they do so anyway) but whether they should do it blindly and irresponsibly or with the maximum possible of courageous intelligence and responsibility."[15]

On the other hand, Dewey pointed out, "it is unrealistic to suppose that the schools can be the *main* agency in producing the intellectual and moral changes, the changes in attitudes and disposition of thought and purpose, which are necessary for the creation of a new social order."[16] In comparison with other educational forces, the school was a minor force at best. Even so, Dewey emphasized, although it could not alone manage social change, the school was necessary for developing the attitudes and understandings re-quired for social improvement.

Throughout the 1930s, Dewey called upon teachers to understand the social forces at work in America. Those who had a grasp of which forces were outmoded and which held promise for a better future were in a better posi-tion to see what was needed in our society and make educational decisions based on their insights.[17]

The Curriculum and the Class Struggle. Also throughout the 1930s, some educators who had no patience with the experimentalist point of view urged that teachers use the concept of the class struggle in their teaching. According to the radical wing of the education profession, the only way to change education was by revolution; power would have to be transferred to a different social class and the needed changes in education would come about as a matter of course. Although it was unrealistic, to say the least, to suppose that the schools could, by themselves, foment a revolution, informing pupils about the class struggle (with vivid illustrations about the plight of the downtrodden class) would at least pave the way. Theodore Brameld, then a young instructor at Long Island University, called upon teachers to "influence their students, subtly if necessary, frankly if possible, toward acceptance of . . . the collectivist ideal."[18]

To Dewey, the class struggle as a framework for teaching was out-and-out indoctrination and hence inimical to the method of intelligence (experimentalism). Dewey proposed instead a study of the conflict between older and newer economic, cultural, scientific, political, philosophical, and religious forces in our society.[19] Indeed, quipped Dewey at an NEA conference, it would be almost a revolution if educators were to recognize social change and act upon that recognition in the schools.[20]

By the mid-1930s the idea of developing a curriculum for social reconstruction no longer occupied center stage in the drama of education in the Great Depression. The issue had not been resolved but had been superseded by a more urgent national educational concern—the "youth problem." The plight of millions of unemployed youth ill-prepared to do much of anything clearly pointed to a wide gap between the curriculum and the needs of youth. The new focus on needs did not mean that educators had abandoned the notion of education as an instrument for social reform; social reconstruction was approached through the goal of civic responsibility and competence, viewed by educators as an "imperative need of youth." This shift in focus is discussed later.

THE PROGRESSIVE EDUCATION ASSOCIATION AND SOCIAL REFORM

In 1947, Harold Rugg observed that the seven purposes of the Progressive Education Association (PEA) all referred to the child. None referred to society, "to man's crucial social conditions and problems."[21] The seven guiding principles were (1) Freedom to Develop Naturally, (2) Interest the Motive of All Work, (3) The Teacher a Guide, Not a Task-Master, (4) Scientific Study of Pupil Development, (5) Greater Attention to All That Affects the Child's Physical Development, (6) Co-operation Between School and Home to Meet the Needs of Child-Life, (7) The Progressive School a Leader in Educational Movements.[22]

Despite the pleas of a strong reformist group within the PEA, the board of directors and most of the membership remained encapsulated in child centeredness through the terrible 1930s and well into the 1940s. This gives one pause for thought, for it was this same association that one night in 1932 was burning with excitement after hearing a speech that dared the schools to build a new social order.

Counts' Challenge

The speech was entitled "Dare Progressive Education Be Progressive?" and the speaker was George S. Counts of Teachers College. The question was rhetorical. Progressive education would have to be progressive or evade its most important task. Counts told the association that their narrow child-centered conception of education was highly compatible with the life-style and goals of the upper middle class. Typically in the upper-middle-class family, life revolved around the child and his or her interests. Parents wanted their children insulated from the seamy side of life and the children of less fortunate races. In order to become truly progressive, the PEA would have to emancipate itself from this class, face social realities, and "fashion a compelling and challenging vision of human destiny."[23]

A Curriculum for Indoctrination.　The PEA would have to rid itself of foolish fears about indoctrination that were preventing the development of a dynamic and meaningful educational program that bound together school and society. It was incumbent upon the teachers in our society to take the mantle being extended them by destiny, develop a plan for the good (collectivist) society, and fashion a curriculum based on this plan that would shape the social convictions of the coming generation.

Although Counts' speech deeply stirred the PEA and led to the appointment of a Committee on Social and Economic Problems (with Counts as chairman) charged with promoting the study in schools of economic and social problems, the program outlined by the committee was never approved by PEA's board of directors. The committee's program was published independently in pamphlet form under the title *A Call to the Teachers of the Nation.*

The Call to Teachers.　The committee called upon teachers to develop educational programs that would cultivate social rather than egoistic impulses. Instructional materials

> should emphasize the history of human labor, the evolution of peaceful culture, the development of democracy, the rise of industrial civilization, the trend toward collectivism in economy, the emergence of a world order, the conflicts and contradictions in contemporary society, and the various theories, philosophies and plans of action designed to deal with the difficulties and problems of the age.[24]

Also, since the future would undoubtedly bring a reduction in the hours of labor and an increase in leisure time, the curriculum should give attention to the development of recreational interests. The committee entertained the hope that the proper utilization of leisure would create a cultural revolution among the masses.

Obviously, individual teachers could not make this kind of program operational. They would "fall before the onslaught of witch-hunters or some selfish interest." This meant that progressive teachers would have to band together in a strong organization "militantly devoted to the building of a better order...."[25]

According to Frederick Redefer, in a reminiscence years later, few teachers bothered to even read the report, much less band together to build a new society.[26] Thus, to Dewey's observation that the school cannot alone build a new social order must be added the factor of teacher indifference.

Two Camps

Redefer recalls that in 1932 the PEA's board was divided into two camps, one that believed that "social mindedness" required the direct and realistic study of social issues and the other that believed that "social mindedness" would result if schools emphasized cooperation instead of competition and group mindedness instead of individuality. As Redefer put it, "they had faith that if children could be made good at heart, then the social heart would become good."[27]

Those in the first group argued that cooperative classroom activity would not be enough to awaken the social conscience. Those holding this view were appalled by the board's own inability to agree to take a stand on crucial social issues. They observed that although the very board members who were committed to cooperation were warm, sympathetic human beings, they were oblivious to the street scene outside the hotel where the board was meeting: Men were fighting each other for scraps of food from garbage cans.

The failure to respond positively to the social situation cost the PEA its chance to assume a leading role in what was by 1932 becoming a powerful new movement. State and national planning boards were established in the Great Depression to determine what measures could be taken to avoid past errors and build a healthy and progressive society. As NEA's historian Edgar Wesley pointed out, educators entered enthusiastically into this movement. They tried new materials and methods with a vision of a new society evolving out of a new education.[28] This movement led to the identification of new educational aims that are examined later. Suffice it to say here that the PEA's anxiety to avoid the taint of radicalism and the split in its membership between those believing that education should focus merely on the child and those believing that it should involve the wider world of the child kept it on the sidelines during the period of reconstructive activity. Meanwhile NEA's Educational Policies Commission (established in 1935), the American Council on Education, the New Deal's National Youth Administration and Civilian Conservation Corps, and the American Federation of Teachers were all part of the vital new movement. It should be emphasized, however, that NEA's interest in vocational education, pupil welfare (health services, guidance and counseling), improved rural education (better facilities, expanding services, and a more functional curriculum), and Indian education was of long standing.

Again in 1938 and 1939, the PEA ducked the issue of educational and social choices. The split on the nature of effective social education even prevented the PEA from developing a statement of the philosophy of progressive education until 1944. By that time, membership had dwindled to the point where some were saying that it would be wisest to close shop. In 1944, in an effort to shake off its parochial image and develop a new image consonant with the broadening interests of educators (including the development of a world safe for democracy), the PEA changed its name to the American Education Fellowship. The AEF adopted a policy statement that defined good education as the "process of living and learning by which the child becomes an understanding adult citizen with strong concern for the development of a world in which free men can and will act together, even fight if necessary, for the common good."[29] Recognizing that good schools could only thrive in a good society, the AEF also committed itself to a program of social reform. Its social goals were "adequate health services, recreation, good housing, a chance for assured employment, and democratic civic practices which will do away with religious and racial intolerance."

But the policy came years too late. The vitality of the organization had diminished because of the debilitating split during the previous eleven years. After World War II, the AEF still failed to evolve a program based on its new philosophy. This was in no small way the result of a new fear—that of having any similarity whatsoever with the Communist Party line during an era of McCarthyism. On the other hand, the failure to develop an educational program also reflected the failure of curriculum developers generally to come up with much that was really new after World War II. In 1953 the AEF changed its name back to the Progressive Education Association, just in time for its demise (really a mercy killing) in 1955.

Postmortem

Cremin, in his postmortem of the Progressive Education Association, points out, "time and again after 1919 progressive causes arose that the Association simply refused to countenance."[30] In addition to shunning association with other progressive causes, the PEA failed to adapt its educational goals to changing times.

Dewey's Criticism. Although they called themselves followers of Dewey, association members stopped following Dewey after 1930. It was then that Dewey criticized progressive schools for centering curriculum making on the arts—music, drawing, dramatics, and literary composition. This was fine, Dewey said, for furthering the "private appreciations of, say, the upper section of the middle class."[31] But a curriculum with this focus failed to come to grips with the study of society. A truly progressive education required a "searching study of society and its moving forces."

In 1934, Dewey said that the entire curriculum should be organized around the study of society and directed toward social goals.[32] This would serve to unify a curriculum that was lacking in intellectual organization and educate the rising generation to deal with our social troubles. Both were urgently needed, said Dewey.

Rather than developing models for curricula with a social core, headmasters and teachers in the private and country day schools who controlled the policies of the Progressive Education Association continued, not too surprisingly, to cater to the educational demands of their clientele. A perusal of the association's journal, *Progressive Education,* reveals that the arts continued to be the focus for the curriculum of progressive schools through most of the association's lifetime.

Lynd's Criticism.   The association was also criticized by Robert Lynd in 1930 for failing to broaden the curriculum in progressive schools to include cultural realities and for behaving more like a religion than a science.[33] Interestingly enough, Stanwood Cobb, the PEA's founder, portrayed the progressive education movement as a religion. In a reminiscense in 1971, Cobb said the movement "had a spiritual vision of the child and a zeal and fervor almost religious in nature."[34] Science had yielded to sentiment.

Turning back to Lynd's criticism of the PEA in 1930, Lynd opined that the continuous reaffirmation of faith in PEA principles by its members was not helping progressive education to deal with its most urgent problem, that of building an adequate theoretical foundation. What was needed, said Lynd, was research into the problems facing progressive education. With the notable exception of the Eight-Year Study, which developed relatively late in the PEA's life, this did not happen. As shown in the previous chapter, the failure of experimental schools to conduct systematic, objective research was a failure of the new education generally.

It is also of great interest that in his reminiscence referred to previously, Cobb emphasized that the pioneers of the PEA did not want to be allied with social reform. Indeed the term *new education* was unacceptable to them because it "implied affiliation with Europe's New Educational Fellowship whose 'new schools' were closely allied with progressive political movements."[35]

Undoubtedly, the failure of the Progressive Education Association to align itself with other progressive movements was a grievous political error.

But this alone did not kill the association. The evidence is that a far more important factor in the demise of the association was its inability to adapt to, or even recognize, social change and resultant curriculum demands until it was too late. The McCarthyism of the cold war era dealt the final blow. During the years when the PEA was rendered impotent by the child-versus-society debate, the Educational Policies Commission became the voice of the education profession on curriculum matters.

THE EIGHT-YEAR STUDY

The most important and comprehensive curriculum experiment ever carried on in the United States was the Eight-Year Study, sponsored by the Progressive Education Association in the 1930s. The study grew out of the realization of secondary educators that they would never be able to establish an experimental basis for curriculum revision unless they were granted the freedom to do so by the colleges. College entrance requirements determined the major part of the secondary curriculum; these requirements had frozen the curriculum into sixteen Carnegie Units.

Thus, in 1930 the PEA took the first step by establishing a commission to deal with the problem of the relation between school and college. In 1931, after a year's study, the commission issued a report on the shortcomings of the secondary school. Most of these shortcomings could be attributed at least indirectly to the unsatisfactory relation between school and college that made fundamental reconstruction an impossibility. The curriculum was unrelated to the real concerns of youth. It had neither the purpose nor the direction needed for unity and continuity. Schools did not know their students and failed to be concerned about what happened to them after graduation (or dropping out). The content and organization of the curriculum prevented the student from developing his or her own educational power. Nearly always the curriculum was laid out in isolated fragments as work for the students to do. They passed through the curriculum with neither an awareness nor an understanding of the forces shaping human destiny and were left unprepared for community life. Anthropologically speaking, the schools were failing as inductors of the young into society.

The commission doubted whether success in college was dependent on the study of certain subjects for a prescribed length of time. The time had come to test this assumption and plan a better education for secondary schoolers.

The Experiment

The commission gained the cooperation of more than three hundred colleges and universities in 1932, and a plan was developed that released a small number of secondary schools (to be chosen by the commission's directing committee) from the restrictions of college entrance requirements. The waiver from the usual subject and unit requirements would be for a five-year period beginning with the class entering college in 1936. The colleges were assured by the commission that "only schools of the highest character and established reputation would be selected." This was not the primary concern of the commission, however, in selecting the schools. It was, rather, that the schools chosen had to be willing to experiment in a "progressive" direction.

Apparently, not all of the schools selected actually lived up to these expectations. Twenty-one years later, Wilford Aikin, director of the study, said that were he to do it again, any school "failing to carry on significant curriculum developments" would "be dropped early in the study."[36]

The Thirty Schools. Be that as it may, the committee chose thirty schools that seemed both willing and able to conduct exploratory studies and make creative changes in the secondary-school curriculum. Schools began to change their curriculums in the fall of 1933. The commission did not prescribe a curriculum to be tested. Each school determined what changes should be made in the curriculum in view of the special needs of its students and the community. The schools did different things (made different curriculum changes) in accord with local needs, and they received detailed reports of outcomes from the evaluation staff of the Eight-Year Study for local use. Since the schools had different problems, evaluations were also different. As Cronbach points out, the question of which school was doing the best job would have been a "false question."[37]

The key point, which has long been forgotten by educators and policy-makers, is: "Different curricula produce different profiles of outcomes."[38] The emphasis today is on public comparison of outcomes, although the schools, their needs, *and* the curricula being compared may be very different. We ask "false questions." Recently, Ralph W. Tyler, who worked with the Eight-Year Study, asserted that the "biggest error" in the wave of reform of the 1980s was the assumption that all schools are alike and have the same problems.[39]

The schools in the Eight-Year-Study were both public and private (approximately half were public), located from Los Angeles to Boston and Madison, Wisconsin, to Tulsa, Oklahoma. Students came from all walks of life. One city high school with 2,500 students was described by Aikin as having "several rather large minorities," drawing its enrollment from the lower-middle and lower classes, and sending only 10 percent of its graduates to college. At the opposite extreme was a private school with three hundred students, drawing its pupils from the highest socioeconomic levels and sending nearly all of its graduates to college.[40] The other schools were described by Aikin as falling somewhere between these extremes. Six of the participating schools were laboratory schools connected with universities. However, most of the participating students were in public schools.

Functions of Evaluation. Evaluation was an ongoing process from the beginning of the experiment. It had to be. To begin with, data concerning the progress of the college-bound students had to be obtained for the colleges. And then there were the new programs; the participating schools needed to be able to identify the strengths and weaknesses of the programs to make improvements on the basis of evidence. Last, but not least, the clarification of objectives demanded by a program of evaluation was needed to give direction to curriculum change. A number of the schools had vague and fuzzy objectives, which had to be clarified to serve as guides for curriculum development and the construction of evaluative instruments. (As pointed out in Chapter 4, objective evaluation is simply not possible without the definition of desired outcomes. Some progressive schools were unwilling to state the end points of instruction, as they feared that this would limit teachers' freedom to experiment.)

Undoubtedly, one of the most monumental tasks of the evaluation committee, headed by Ralph W. Tyler of the University of Chicago, was to help the participating schools develop instruments to evaluate student progress in terms of objectives that dealt with thinking processes. The only tests available were for measuring achievement in the traditional subject curriculum. Interschool evaluation committees were formed for the objectives that were most commonly stressed by the Thirty Schools, such as the development of effective ways of thinking, increased sensitivity to social problems, and effective work habits and skills. Each committee's task was to define an objective in terms of the behaviors sought and to identify ways of obtaining evidence about these kinds of behavior. These methods—tests, questionnaires, interviews, and the like—became the basis for evaluative instruments developed by Tyler's staff. The instruments were used in appraising student progress.

College Follow-up Study. The second phase of the evaluation program took place in the colleges. Each graduate of the Thirty Schools was matched with another student in the same college who had graduated from a school not in the Eight-Year Study and, thus, had met the usual college entrance requirements. The students were matched on the basis of age, sex, race, scholastic aptitude scores, home and community background, and interests. The matching was done by the colleges. Through personal interviews and information from college records and college personnel, the College Staff of the Eight-Year Study became well acquainted with each student. A total of 1,475 matched pairs of students were studied.

The Findings

Established beyond question by the study was the fact that the graduates of the Thirty Schools were not handicapped in college by their experimental high-school programs. Graduates of the Thirty Schools had higher grade point averages, received more academic honors, and were found to be more precise, systematic, and objective thinkers and more intellectually curious than their matchees. Furthermore, they were more actively concerned about what was happening in the world, earned more nonacademic honors each year in college, and were more resourceful in meeting new situations.

Interestingly enough, those students graduating from the six schools judged to be the most experimental (departed most from tradition) "were strikingly more successful than their matchees. Differences in their favor were much greater than the differences between the total Thirty Schools and their comparison group. Conversely, there were no large or consistent differences between the least experimental graduates and their comparison group."[41]

It was thus clear that, at least as far as the Thirty Schools were concerned, the more experimental the school, the greater was the success of students in college. It was also evident that success in college does not depend on the study of a prescribed sequence of "subjects" in high school.

Curriculum Development in the Thirty Schools

"My teachers and I do not know what to do with this freedom. It challenges and frightens us. I fear that we have come to *love our chains*."[42] This remark made by one principal a short time after the Thirty Schools were selected probably reflected the feelings of many in the experiment. Here, in a very real sense, was the predicament of progressivism in the 1930s. As Dewey had warned, it was time to stop being a movement of protest and to start the search for a new curriculum. Thus, it was one thing to sit back and blame the problems of the high-school curriculum on the "strangle hold of the colleges." It was quite another thing to build something better when that strangle hold was removed. This was progressivism's moment of truth.

Curriculum Consultants.   The Thirty Schools were guided in their efforts to make significant curriculum changes by specialists in the field of curriculum. As indicated earlier, the policy of the directing committee was to encourage and assist each school in developing its own plans rather than deciding what curriculum changes should be made.

As mentioned previously, the Commission on the Relation of School and College issued a report indicating areas needing improvement by secondary schools. These suggestions provided a starting point for many of the schools. But this was hardly enough to help the schools find a sense of direction. Those that asked for help were provided curriculum consultants. Years later, Aikin (who served as a curriculum consultant as well as director of the study) said that "many of the Thirty Schools were ready for such assistance long before it was available to them. Had that been done earlier and in greater abundance, the contribution of the Eight-Year Study to secondary education would have been greater than it was."[43]

The curriculum staff of the Eight-Year Study attempted to keep each school informed of developments in other schools, made class visits, taught demonstration lessons, and conducted workshops or "curriculum clinics." Each member of the staff visited each school once for the purpose of getting mutually acquainted. After that, visits were made only by invitation. Some schools made very little use of the staff, either because they were doing little curriculum revision or they felt able to bring about even thoroughgoing change without much help. Other schools that were attempting a total reconstruction of their curriculum asked for all the help they could get. Interestingly, the services of staff members were sought more by the public schools than by the private schools. According to Aikin, those schools that took the most advantage of staff assistance made the most significant curriculum changes.[44]

Curriculum Synthesis.   Although each school went its own way in making changes in the curriculum, there were three goals sought by all schools: (1) to identify ways of breaking down the barriers between subjects so that the real meaning of fields of knowledge could be made apparent to the student, (2) to encourage student self-direction, and (3) to provide individual guidance. Schools attempted to bring the curriculum closer to the real concerns of youth by designing fusion courses, core curricula, broad-fields courses, culture-epoch courses, and career-centered courses. (In some schools the problems of job training and employment were studied in core curricula based on adolescent needs.)

Giles, McCutchen, and Zechiel reported that schools experimenting with fusion courses such as mathematics-science found that the scope of a course was determined by the logical organization of one of the fields. This not only made one field the "handmaiden" of the other but resulted in irrelevant subject matter as far as the actual purposes of the unified course were concerned.[45] (It should be added, parenthetically, that in the early 1970s a similar problem was encountered by those attempting to develop unified science courses. Although one field of science did not become the organizing center, the result tended to be lamination rather than synthesis: a layer of physics, a layer of chemistry, and a layer of biology.[46])

Forced to find organizing centers other than systematized bodies of knowledge, teachers and curriculum consultants turned to a problem-centered core curriculum. Subject matter from various fields was brought in as needed for the understanding and solution of problems.

The culture-epoch approach, where content was controlled by broad themes, was used by the Horace Mann School of Teachers College, Columbia University, to unify the curriculum. It will be recalled from the discussion in Chapter 3 that this idea for curriculum integration was strongly supported by the Herbartians before the turn of the century. This was a very broad approach to unification, far broader than fused studies such as mathematics-science or English-social studies because a culture epoch could be dealt with in terms of its literature, science, art, music, economic system, social system, or political system. A criticism frequently associated with this approach to curriculum synthesis was that although the senior year was usually devoted to a study of contemporary American problems, the entire first three years (grades nine through eleven) were devoted to a study of the past.

In 1950, just eight years after the study, only one of the schools in the experiment had continued to develop a core curriculum.[47] One might well ponder the reasons why this was so when the results of the study so strikingly favored the continued development of this approach to curriculum reorganization. McCarthyism, which began in the late 1940s, led to the censorship of content. Problem-centered core curricula required the free and open examination of the issues that marked our economic and political life. This was not easy in an era of censorship of content and guilt by association. Even the NEA's Educational Policies Commission took the position in 1949 that members of the Communist Party should not be employed as teachers. Little wonder, then, that many teachers were unwilling to subject our economic system to scrutiny for fear of being labeled "Red." The social and political forces of the day exerted a far stronger influence on the curriculum than the findings of the Eight-Year Study.

Criticisms

There has been a host of criticisms of the Eight-Year Study. According to Kerlinger, a serious control weakness in the experiment was self-selection; children who go to progressive high schools, argues Kerlinger, may differ in attitudes toward learning from children who go to traditional high schools.[48] This criticism of the Eight-Year Study does not hold because approximately half of the Thirty Schools were public and there was no self-selection in these schools. There is no evidence to show that those students attending public schools did not do as well as other students.

An earlier criticism was made by Jensen, who questioned whether the in-service training given teachers in the Thirty Schools is indicative of a failure to control significant teacher factors.[49] In-service education for teachers was part of the experiment for obvious reasons. For example, it would not have been possible to supply the colleges with data on candidates who did not meet the traditional requirements unless the schools had been helped in finding objective measures of knowledge and power attained. The fact that special assistance for teachers was part of the experimental variable (the colleges undoubtedly would not have entered into the agreement if this guidance had not been assured) renders Jensen's criticism invalid.

Yet another criticism concerns the staff who conducted the evaluation of the Eight-Year Study. According to Lancelot, since those persons were nearly all educational liberals, their findings are suspect, despite the fact that the evaluators were, as put by Lancelot, "held in the highest esteem by others of their profession."[50] However, the matching of the comparison populations, and the assessment of their achievement, was done by the colleges. Moreover, there is no more severe test than the rating of one's fellows. This is so in any field—be it science, philosophy, literature, law, or education. Hence, Lancelot invalidates his own criticism; that the evaluators were held in the highest esteem by others in their field was the strongest possible affirmation of their objectivity. Lancelot's criticism is illustrative of the line of thinking of many critics of the Eight-Year Study.

Far more important, scientifically speaking, was the criticism that the per-pupil expenditure was appreciably greater in the experimental schools. Ralph W. Tyler, who directed the research, denied this, stating that the average costs in both groups were nearly the same.[51] Interestingly, no critic of the Eight-Year Study challenged the finding that there is no single pattern of high-school preparation for success in college.

Corroboration

A number of studies have been reported that buttress the findings of the Eight-Year Study. Young studied 130 matched pairs of college and university students who had taken business and industrial courses in high school in addition to their college preparation. The students were matched for age, sex, IQ, high-school grade point average, and socioeconomic status, with one of each pair having elected five or more business and industrial courses. Young found that the students who had elected freely in business and industrial courses achieved significantly higher grade point averages in college than did their matchees. This study, like the Eight-Year Study, shows that the college-preparatory pattern is not sacrosanct. Moreover,

> Not only does there seem to be a point of "no return on investment" in the college preparatory curriculum, but failure to recognize the value of so-called nonacademic programs may deprive many students of enriching experiences important to their success in college. . . .
>
> Art, music, homemaking, industrial, and business courses (have) come to be considered unimportant. At best they are indulged in only if time permits, and only as "fillers" here and there to relieve a stringent academic program. Students who otherwise might have concentrated in these subject areas feel the stigma attached to any preparation not considered academic. . . .
>
> It is an ironic paradox that the more capable students, whom the discouraged ones emulate and who gain entrance to the more exclusive universities and colleges, profit significantly in college from high school business and industrial experiences.[52]

A similar study by Whitener found that students who had taken a considerable number of courses in art and music in high school performed at least as well in college as those who had pursued additional academic course work in preparation for college. Initial differences in aptitude, high school achievement, and socioeconomic status were corrected by analysis of covariance, and both groups pursued similar majors in college.[53]

Impact of the Study

The Eight-Year Study was not a continuing force after the experiment. According to some, the study was a casualty of World War II: The findings were released in 1942, when war headlines blotted out matters such as national educational experimentation. After the war the criticism of progressive education that began in the late 1930s gained in intensity. This, combined with the cold war, strengthened educational conservatism. The international situation caused a return to more authoritarian and traditional programs. These came to be superseded by the discipline-centered reforms as the answer to the crisis in national security. Interdisciplinary curricula became a casualty of that crisis.[54]

Most of the criticisms of the secondary-school curriculum that were made in the early 1930s by the Commission on the Relation of School and College remain valid today. The curriculum still lacks direction and unity. College preparatory students still follow a rather traditional sequence. Since students cannot possibly take more than a small proportion of the curricular fare, they supplement their required courses with a conglomerate of unrelated electives, smorgasbord or warehouse style. It is still "customary for a pupil to patch together all sorts of pieces—two units here, one there, a half unit elsewhere."[55]

Although curriculum experimentation has not increased in the secondary school, the national passion for equality of educational opportunity is stronger than ever. As a result, the tendency in a growing number of states is to provide the opportunity for all high-school graduates to attend college, even those who do not follow a prescribed college preparatory course. In California, for example, every high-school graduate is guaranteed admission to a state-supported junior college. Thus, the national emphasis has been on open-access higher education rather than on a reconstruction of the secondary-school curriculum. Nevertheless, during the 1980s state mandates for more academic course work required for high school graduation served to impact the options for nonacademic enrichment electives and vocational studies. These mandates clearly served political purposes rather than educational purposes.[56]

Yet the Eight-Year Study is alive and well today in the educational literature for at least three reasons: (1) It is the only comprehensive longitudinal curriculum experiment in American education (as of this writing); (2) the problem that the study was concerned with—the development of a curriculum that is serviceable to youth and in meeting the function of general education—is still with us; and (3) its effects on education have become increasingly evident with the passing years—in the "cold light" of history. Its early critics could not have known, for example, that there would be widespread acceptance of the idea that schools could develop educational programs that would interest students, meet their needs, and at the same time provide them with the preparation they needed for success in college. Nor could they have known that the study would buttress the movement of the high schools away from the domination of college entrance requirements.

Whatever the importance of the results of the study in freeing the high schools for curriculum development, there was another lasting effect on education at all levels: evaluation as a means for improving teaching and the curriculum in the action place of the school, and making teachers more thoughtful about their work. This was an effect of the efforts of experimentalists generally, such as Ralph Tyler, and not just the Eight-Year Study. Lee Cronbach describes the implications in these words:

> Evaluation was a vehicle for missionary activity to encourage teachers to think about how they might do their job differently, to think about why they were teaching and what they were doing. That was more a product of Ralph Tyler's work than anything that came out of the measures themselves. This line of inquiry enabled Tyler's students to give direct service to front-line educators. It was the most powerful piece of training Tyler's students had, and it was a denial of cloistered academic research. Research was not to be above politics, not to be defined in pure answers, but to be a means of getting into the political arena, and understanding its tensions and its problems.[57]

Significantly, the in-service workshop was developed during the Eight-Year Study to provide time and assistance for teachers to develop instructional programs and materials and to gain new knowledge and skills for their work. "The workshop quickly became recognized as an effective instrument for the inservice education of professionals."[58]

Finally, as Mackenzie points out, the concepts of curriculum and evaluation used in the Eight-Year Study have been shown "again and again" to be useful for elementary, secondary and higher education.[59] There is a continuing need to draw upon and build on these conceptualizations, which has also kept the study alive.

STATEWIDE CURRICULUM DEVELOPMENT PROGRAMS

City school systems had inaugurated the curriculum revision movement in the 1920s. By 1930, state departments of education had become actively interested in comprehensive programs of curriculum development. The work of state curriculum programs during the 1930s was of enormous importance for two reasons: First, a vast number of school systems, teachers, and students were influenced by these programs. Second, development in curriculum theory and practice resulted from the stimulus of these programs. Michigan, Kansas, California, New Mexico, Maryland, and nearly all of the southern states had well-organized, long-range programs. In Virginia more than 18,000 teachers, all county supervisors, and many faculty members from state colleges and universities were involved.

From Curriculum Making to Curriculum Development

Up to 1930, curriculum development and instruction were conceived as two quite distinct although related functions. The common term was *curriculum making*. But in the 1930s and 1940s, as Caswell had pointed out, "State curriculum programs took the lead in making a highly important redefinition of the meaning of the curriculum. . . ." The transformation of the concept of curriculum is indeed fascinating. The first state programs, in the words of Caswell, "accepted the traditional concept of the curriculum as a course of study." But operationally, this was inadequate. "Courses of study gathered dust on shelves," recalls Caswell. "It became increasingly clear that revision of the curriculum should have as its central purpose the improvement of instruction, and that curriculum programs must utilize many means to achieve this end in addition to writing courses of study."[60]

Thus the state curriculum programs left their imprint on curriculum theory and practice. In the 1930s and 1940s the concept of curriculum development shifted from writing courses of study to the improvement of learning experiences for students.[61] A theoretical dualism between instruction and the course of study was untenable because it simply did not work out in practice. Yet in the 1960s and 1970s there was a swing to separate the two.

The state programs themselves provide an evolutionary account from classical curriculum making to curriculum development. Thus the product of the Alabama program in 1930 was *Course of Study for Elementary Schools*, developed through wide participation (including more than five thousand teachers), and referred to as "the total instructional program."[62] Although the recommendation was made that curriculum revision be continuous, when the course of study was finished the teacher's role in curriculum development was over (except for following the guide).

The Florida curriculum program melded the production of courses of study with the improvement of instruction. As Seguel points out, this made the need for continuous teacher growth and study seem more logical.[63] Yet teachers still tended to regard the curriculum as subject-matter objectives. Lessons learned from the Florida program about "how to set a whole state to work without intimidating the least prepossessing and most traditional of its teachers"[64] paved the way to the Virginia program in the fall of 1931. Teachers had to begin where they were on instructional improvement. It was hoped that, as they made a course of study, they would see the limits of its usefulness. And even if the course were followed slavishly by some teachers, if it was well-prepared some improvements in the child's experience were sure to ensue.

The Need for Teacher Involvement. Caswell reports that the Virginia program and those that followed "led to the general acceptance of the idea that classroom teachers generally must take a major part in curriculum programs since change in practice depends upon their ability and willingness to modify existing teaching procedures,"[65] The Virginia program widened the vision of teachers and improved their competence. Moreover, it enormously increased the use of modern instructional materials in the schools and the amount and quality of supervision. Curriculum development was now seen as incorporating the improvement of instruction with the development of courses of study.

Lay Participation

No insignificant factor in the success of state programs in the 1930s and 1940s was lay participation. In Virginia, after a professional committee had developed a tentative statement of the aims of education for Virginia's schools, one hundred lay persons, representing various groups, were asked to study the aims critically and make suggestions. The replies were used by the committee in making a revised report. The aims were also submitted to the editors of various newspapers in the state with a request for suggestions. This was most helpful when new programs with many departures from traditional practice were introduced in the schools. The support of parents and others had made it more possible to use the new courses of study effectively.[66]

There is a point to be made here in a time of public criticism of the schools, or any time. A curriculum reform program that fails to carry citizens with it will surely encounter opposition or halfhearted support. In discussing the Great Depression, the period when he achieved great success in Alabama, Florida, and Virginia, Caswell writes:

> We thought those years were hard, and indeed they did present many difficulties.... Yet when I compare the situation then with the situation now—contrasting the realities that confronted us with those that you face— the present situation seems more difficult. Constructive and needed curriculum change today will require all the vision, knowledge, competence, and persistence that curriculum leaders can muster.... During the worst of the depression years, public confidence in the fundamental importance of the schools was never undermined.[67]

Whatever the conflicts concerning education during the 1930s, the critics and reformers looked to the potentialities of public education. In contrast, the radical critics and reformers of the 1970s sought to undermine the public confidence in public education.

ELEMENTARY-SCHOOL CURRICULUM RESEARCH

As shown in the previous chapter, elementary-school curriculum research during the 1920s was slanted toward curriculum adaptation. In Winnetka, for example, studies were conducted to determine the optimum time for beginning instruction in skills such as reading and fundamental arithmetic processes. Improvement of instruction in the various subjects of the curriculum was thus bound up tightly with the principles of child growth and development. As stressed in Chapter 4, these investigations were concerned, in the main, with fitting the conventional subjects to the child rather than with evaluating new forms of curriculum organization. Undeniably, making the traditional curriculum serve the child better was a revolution in and of itself (and one that passed many schools by).

Be that as it may, the activity movement had reached the public schools by the 1920s. Kilpatrick's project method in particular stimulated great interest in programs in which the interests of the child provided the starting point for the selection and organization of curriculum content. Despite the tremendous theoretical problems of activity "curricula" (see Chapter 4), there was a need to test the relative worth of activity and subject-matter curriculum organization.

Research on the Activity Curriculum

The educational literature of the 1930s contains scores of studies designed to assess the relative value of activity and subject-matter curricula. The overwhelming majority of studies used standardized achievement tests that were developed in terms of subject-matter curricula. Some studies did attempt to evaluate gains in terms of both subject matter and activity goals. Unfortunately, these were in the decided minority. In most studies, however, investigators concluded that activity curriculums led to little or no loss in the mastery of basic skills and subject-matter knowledge, while producing substantial gains over a subject organization in goals involving thought processes and responsible independence.

The New York City Experiment. The most comprehensive and well-designed of these investigations was a New York City experiment involving some 75,000 children and 2,500 teachers over a six-year period. In 1935 the Board of Education of New York City launched an experimental program with "progressive" educational methods. Typical schools were designated as "activity schools." These schools were encouraged to develop curriculums based on units and projects originating from pupil interest rather than traditional textbook learning. Although 70 schools initiated experimental programs, it was not feasible to conduct a careful evaluation on such a large scale. Most of the research involved 8 activity schools, each matched with a control school. The schools were matched for neighborhood, average intelligence, and socioeconomic status of pupils.

The research program was aimed at measuring growth in a wide variety of educational outcomes, both tangible and intangible. Tests of study skills, social attitudes, "work spirit," and individual adjustment were developed by J. Wayne Wrightstone, then a research associate at Teachers College. Evaluation procedures included both tests and classroom observations.

Activity children surpassed control children in growth in critical thinking, initiative, leadership, and other objectives of activity curriculums. Control pupils gained somewhat more in some academic subjects (notably arithmetic), although the differences were small and statistically unreliable. Unquestionably, the objectives of the activity program had been achieved. In their final report on the experiment, Jersild, Thorndike, and Goldman concluded:

> While the control children seem to have a slight but statistically unreliable advantage as far as achievement in academic subject matter is concerned, the activity children surpass the controls in the frequency with which they exercise such presumably wholesome activities as leadership, experimentation, self-initiated enterprises, participation in oral discussion, and the like. The activity children have more experiences and show more tangible accomplishments in the field of arts and crafts. The activity children, as already noted, tend to be superior in tests that call for intellectual operations. (These were the Wrightstone tests of working skills, explaining facts, applying generalizations, critical thinking, and current events.)[68]

Discipline and Curriculum Organization.   Of great interest is the fact that children in the activity program also tended to surpass the control children in discipline. This is contrary to the opinion held by many teachers (and parents) that children in traditional programs show better discipline and "respect for school authority." In the first three of the five semesters in which the children were observed, the control children exhibited fewer behavioral problems, whereas the activity children showed better discipline in the last two semesters. As Jersild, Thorndike, and Goldman emphasized:

> The greater degree of freedom and self-direction afforded by the activity program has not been a signal for poor discipline and disorder on the part of the pupils. Rather, according to the findings in connection with the "work spirit" category, as well as according to the independent testimony of observers who have visited many classes and have gone into the same classes day after day, the pupils have risen to the occasion in a highly satisfactory way.[69]

Wrightstone's Study.   Wrightstone conducted an important study in which he focused on outcomes that were emphasized by progressive educators, such as being able to interpret facts, apply generalizations, work independently, and organize materials. Using matched pairs of elementary and secondary pupils from three pairs of public-school situations, he found that in no case (other than the quantity of recitation in classrooms) did the subject-centered schools show a statistically significant superiority over the experimental schools.[70] Schools with various kinds of reorganized curricula demonstrated a significant superiority in recall of physics and chemistry facts, literature acquaintance, and working-skills ability. In reporting the results of his study, Wrightstone concluded that his findings were "tentative proof of the validity of the educational theory and principles upon which the newer-type practices in the selected schools are established."[71]

Decline of Interest in Activity Organization.   Despite these encouraging findings, interest in the activity organization of the elementary curriculum, as revealed by the educational literature, had faded by the mid-1940s. This is a striking parallel with the core curriculum. In both cases, research findings were highly encouraging but the interest of educators dropped off nonetheless. Research findings were not used as a basis for curriculum decision-making.

Educational Objectives

By the mid-1940s, the idea that the curriculum should be derived directly from children's interests had been, by and large, superseded by the idea that it should be derived from adult claims of children's interests. The result was a set of a few broad goals such as the following:

1. For each child to develop self-confidence and self-respect
2. For each child to gain the respect of other children
3. For each child to become better able to attack and solve the problems that face him or her
4. For each child to discover and develop his or her talents
5. For each child to evaluate his or her own growth.

Social Goals.   As shown earlier, the elementary school never really developed curricular designs based on the goal of social reconstruction. The nearest thing to the core curriculum in the elementary school was the unit, which, in most instances, had as its primary aim developing democratic behaviors such as cooperative skills and social responsibility. True, the units often carried social themes. But as shown earlier, emphasis was on social skill development rather than on the selection of content intended to help children understand and cope with the social forces bearing upon their lives.

By the end of the 1940s, elementary schools attempting to derive a curriculum directly from the interests of children were as scarce as the proverbial hens' teeth. The trend was for those charged with curriculum development first to determine curricular objectives, then, as stated by Shores, to "make attempts to adjust these through consideration of grade placement, sequence, and method according to their best judgments of what the interests and needs of children are."[72]

Thus, curriculum adaptation, the approach to curriculum improvement favored by educators in the 1920s, had attained unquestionable supremacy over more radical revision. Well before 1950, this approach was evident in curriculum research that looked mainly to the solution of problems connected with the traditional curriculum rather than attempting to build new curriculum designs. Despite the fine rhetoric in the 1940s about the "whole child," curriculum research seldom was conducted in relation to an entire curriculum pattern appropriate for a whole individual. It dealt, rather, with segments of the curriculum.

NEEDS AND THE CURRICULUM

Although the objective of meeting children's needs never left the pedagogical literature, it nevertheless underwent a complete transformation. In the child-centered rhetoric of the 1920s, the terms *needs* and *interests* were often used interchangeably. Needs, like interests, could be made apparent to adults only through the overt actions and oral choices of children. By the 1950s, the magical properties associated with needs and interests had all but vanished. Adult claims of children's need were derived variously from the literature on child growth and development, the demands of a democratic society, and the group dynamics movement.

After World War I, the idea of the secondary school as a place for educating all youth, those going into jobs as well as college, received growing emphasis. The synthesis of democracy and education was a challenge to secondary educators to produce an education that would serve the needs of every adolescent. Secondary educators formally accepted the challenge in 1918. The new aims of the secondary school were stated by the Commission on Reorganization of Secondary Education in its *Seven Cardinal Principles of Secondary Education*. This statement and its significance are discussed in considerable detail in Chapter 3. The point to be emphasized here is that six of the seven aims were concerned with the personal and social needs of youth.

Youth and the Great Depression

Nevertheless, it was not until the 1930s that educators were confronted with shocking and incontrovertible evidence that the schools had failed to reach millions of youth. During the early years of the Roosevelt administration, thousands of illiterate enrollees in the Civilian Conservation Corps were taught to read and write by the CCC's educational program (which also awarded eighth-grade certificates, high-school diplomas, and even some college degrees). Yet education was only a minor concern of the CCC.

Curricular Implications of Emergency Programs. Other emergency programs also provided unemployed youth who were not in school with educational opportunities. The National Youth Administration (part of the Works Progress Administration) was established in 1935 to provide out-of-work youth with an opportunity "to work, to learn, and to assume their responsibilities in this civilization."[73] Two important curriculum innovations may be at least partly credited to the NYA: the idea of relating studies to actual work on a project (this was adjudged "an outstanding success") and the socialization and personal enrichment deriving from socially useful work.[74]

The WPA organized and ran thousands of nursery schools as well as educational programs for adults. Thus, the downward and upward extension of educational opportunity was another, although temporary, result of the Great Depression. Federally supported nursery schools (for children with mothers working in war-related industries) reappeared in World War II and again in the 1960s and 1970s as day care centers for less-privileged Americans.

Youth Surveys. It is not possible with the limitations of space to adequately describe the plight of youth during the early 1930s. Youth between the ages of sixteen and twenty-four accounted for one-third of all the unemployed. Thousands of young people had taken to the road. Those who found their way into transient camps were found to be pitifully unprepared for anything but the most simple kinds of work. As we have seen, what came to be known as the "youth problem" had profound implications for the school curriculum. The chief problem facing youth was unemployment. School programs had failed to change with changing vocational requirements. But there were other factors in successful living: health, citizenship, and recreation, to mention a few. Meeting the needs of youth hinged on adequate knowledge concerning these needs. Hence, hundreds of surveys were conducted in the 1930s by state and local committees to provide a basis for giving youth its chance and improving the work of the school.

American Youth Commission. Taking the lead in the study of youths' problems was the American Youth Commission, created by the American Council on Education in 1935. The commission embarked on an enormous task, conducting and publishing fact-finding studies and formulating policies and programs of action. Its goal was to develop a comprehensive program for the education of all youth. Interestingly, the educational objectives released by the commission in 1937 (based on a sampling of 250,000 adolescents and young adults) were very similar to the *Cardinal Principles.* There were two new aims, however: mental health and continued learning.[75]

The Educational Policies Commission. As was mentioned earlier, the Educational Policies Commission was created by the NEA in 1935 to deal with the crisis in education caused by the Great Depression. Deeply concerned about the educational needs of Depression children and youth, the commission evolved four comprehensive aims of education: (1) self-realization (inquiring mind, reading, writing, calculating, speech, health, recreation, aesthetics, character); (2) human relationship (respect for humanity, friendships, cooperation, courtesy, home membership); (3) economic efficiency (vocation, consumer economics); and (4) civic responsibility (social justice, social understanding and action, critical judgment, tolerance, democratic citizenship).[76]

The report evoked considerable discussion but not the heated controversy generated by the commission's proposals in a later policy statement, *Education for ALL American Youth,* which is discussed later.

It has already been pointed out that the New Deal turned to agencies other than the schools to achieve its educational ends. The schools were in desperate straits in the 1930s: Hundreds were closed, literally forced to neglect youth because of economic exigencies. It was understandable, therefore, that educators were very much distressed that the schools were bypassed by the federal government. In a 1938 report the Educational Policies Commission sharply criticized the New Deal educational policy. "Education, when organized as a part of the relief service, has often been weak and ineffective," said the commission.[77] "It must not be assumed that the agencies dealing with relief, with health, or with recreation can carry any significant part of the systematic program of education for which the schools are organized."

The commission saw real danger that because of the need for relief, two systems of education would develop, a state and local administration for those in school and a national system for youth and adults who were no longer in the public-school system. As a result, the commission recommended that new educational programs be consolidated with the existing school system. Prophetically, the commission warned that unless these educational programs were made integral to the schools, they would be abandoned once the emergency was over. Before the 1930s closed, the prestigious commission had become the responsible spokesman for the education profession.

The Regents' Inquiry in New York State. One of the most illuminating studies on the needs of youth was undertaken in the late 1930s by the Board of Regents of New York State. The study, which considered all pupils who leave school—dropouts as well as graduates—revealed a wide gap between the curriculum and the needs of youth.[78]

Among the findings of the study were a lack of guidance with regard to curricular choice, leading to poor choices by many students, a poor relationship between the school and local business and industry, and overwhelming evidence that the progressive aims of education, to which many educators gave lip service, generally were not being implemented. Despite the rhetoric about meeting the needs of students, there was a chasm between the aims and the actual program. There was an urgent need, said the report, for "experimentation with the school program in an attempt to come closer to the aims of education."[79]

Postwar Proposals of the Educational Policies Commission

It is little wonder, then, that the educational blueprint drawn up by the Educational Policies Commission after World War II was more explicit and detailed than any of its previous proposals. In the mid-1940s, this blueprint took shape in the form of three volumes describing the progressive educational programs in two mythical communities, American City and Farmville.[80]

Not surprisingly, after the events of the 1930s, the school system in American City served children and youth ages three to twenty. School was in session twelve months a year, with camping experiences constituting an integral part of the program. The facilities for promoting mental and physical health and helping children overcome learning disabilities were "among the best in the world." Needless to say, in the commission's model educational program, general aid to education from the federal government was a reality.

The Elementary Curriculum.   "It is never supposed that the curriculum is made when a book is published; rather it is made as children live."[81] So wrote the commission in *Education for ALL American Children*. Since this was a visualization of progressive theory put into practice, it is not surprising that goals were not in terms of subject-matter mastery but the child and his or her society; "the curriculum," argued the commission, "should be planned to insure both to pupils and society the benefits of valuable learnings."

Curriculum planning was visualized as being continuous, with the teacher at the heart of the process, although laymen also would be involved. The commission's position on the role of the elementary school in social reconstruction was basically the same as that of Carleton Washburne and many others in the early 1930s. The elementary school was not to be charged single-handedly with the job of saving the world from destruction, but the elementary school had to see to it that children's educational experiences made for "better living."[82]

The curriculum envisioned by the commission was planned, but the emphasis was on flexibility. Curriculum planning was based primarily on the principles of child development and the need for children to learn democratic ways (adult claims of children's needs). Significantly, after arguing that the curriculum is not divided into segments in real life, the commission then proceeded to discuss it in terms of communication skills, arithmetic, social studies, science, health, and art. Throughout the discussion of curriculum development, the point was stressed that teachers must be participants in the entire process. Also stressed was the fact that a progressive curriculum will differ from community to community, from school to school, and even from child to child in accord with local and individual needs and demands. Nevertheless, the report emphasized that all good schools help children to develop (1) skills in the "three R's," (2) the habits and skills of critical thinking, and (3) their individual talents.

The chapter on the elementary-school curriculum offered little or nothing that was really new and hence caused little debate. What was new and radical (and ammunition for conservative taxpayers groups) was the proposal that the school assume many of the functions that were previously assumed by the home (such as health care).

The Needs of Youth. The secondary-school curriculum was to grow out of the needs of youth. According to the commission, there were ten "imperative educational needs of youth":

1. All youth need to develop salable skills and those understandings and attitudes that make the worker an intelligent and productive participant in economic life. To this end, most youth need supervised work experience as well as education in the skills and knowledge of their occupations.
2. All youth need to develop and maintain good health and physical fitness.
3. All youth need to understand the rights and duties of the citizen of a democratic society, and to be diligent and competent in the performance of their obligations as members of the community and citizens of the state and nation.
4. All youth need to understand the significance of the family for the individual and society and the conditions conducive to successful family life.
5. All youth need to know how to purchase and use goods and services intelligently, understanding both the values received by the consumer and the economic consequences of their acts.
6. All youth need to understand the methods of science, the influence of science on human life, and the main scientific facts concerning the nature of the world and of man.
7. All youth need opportunities to develop their capacities to appreciate beauty in literature, art, music, and nature.
8. All youth need to be able to use their leisure time well and to budget it wisely, balancing activities that yield satisfactions to the individual with those that are socially useful.
9. All youth need to develop respect for other persons, to grow in their insight into ethical values and principles, and to be able to live and work cooperatively with others.
10. All youth need to grow in their ability to think rationally, to express their thoughts clearly, and to read and listen with understanding.[83]

This basis for the secondary-school curriculum was bitterly attacked by essentialist critics. These attacks are discussed shortly. Meanwhile, when the second edition of *Education for ALL American Youth* was published in 1951, James B. Conant, president of Harvard, was chairman of the Educational Policies Commission and Dwight D. Eisenhower, president of Columbia, was a member of the commission. Thus, the report carried the imprimatur of both institutions and both leaders.

The Secondary-School Curriculum. Secondary education in American City included grades seven through fourteen. The thirteenth and fourteenth grades were also part of the community college program. Included in the secondary-school curriculum were four divisions of learning: (1) vocational preparation, (2) individual interests, (3) common learnings, and (4) health and physical education. Common learnings were designed to deal with those needs that youth hold in common: civic competency, consumer economics, family life, and language communications skills.

Even after the well-publicized Eight-Year Study, this was a radical proposal. The conventional labels for some subjects had disappeared as they were synthesized as a core curriculum termed *common learnings*. Mathematics courses were offered, but they were designed to dovetail with the student's vocational or college preparatory interest. History was taught in the eleventh grade as the history of American civilization, which also included American literature and was designed to help students connect the past with the present.

The lessons learned by educators in the 1930s are strikingly evident in the commission's proposal for secondary education. Tenth-graders in Farmville, for instance, spent a major part of their time studying the world of work. Students were able to make college plans late because the community college was built into the secondary-school program. Guidance was central to the secondary-school program. Furthermore, guidance was available to students who left school, whether or not they remained in the district, as were all of the school's services.

Did the commission's visions for postwar education have a greater impact on the curriculum than earlier proposals for meeting the needs of youth? According to Cremin, "once they appeared they were quickly incorporated into education syllabi across the nation." "In retrospect," writes Cremin, "there is little doubt but that they summed up as well as any contemporary publications the best-laid plans of the teaching profession for American education in the postwar decades."[84] Meanwhile, however, the criticisms of progressive education were mounting; the new pressures on the schools were of quite a different nature. The critics' call for a return to the "fundamentals" soon drowned out the commission's call for a more functional curriculum.

Life-Adjustment Education

In the early years of the new education, progressive educators had centered their attention on the young child. It will be recalled that the child-study movement generated interest in curriculum change in the opening years of the twentieth century. Until the 1930s most curriculum innovations—Kilpatrick's project method, for instance—found their application in the elementary school. It was true that attempts at curriculum integration in the form of broad-fields courses such as general science and general language had filtered up to the junior high school well before this time. Nevertheless, the real reformist thrust did not find its way into the high school until the 1930s, when the "youth problem" was placed squarely at the educator's door. As shown earlier, educational reform was later given a setback by World War II.

After the war, with the findings of surveys such as the Regents' Inquiry still uncomfortably fresh in their memories, reformers turned again to the secondary school. One outcome was the Educational Policies Commission's "imperative needs of youth" statement. Another was what came to be known as "life adjustment."

Destined to become the most unfortunate label ever associated with the new education, the term *life-adjustment education* originated at a conference sponsored by the Vocational Education Division of the U.S. Office of Education in 1945. There was considerable discussion at the meeting about high-school students who were on the so-called general track—who were being served neither by the college-preparatory program nor by the vocational-education program.

It is of interest that in the 1970s and 1980s educators again focused attention on this population. In 1972 the New York State Commission on the Quality, Cost, and Financing of Elementary and Secondary Education recommended abolition of the general track.[85] But the unmistakable trend in the United States was a sharp rise in the percentage of students in the general track (not to be confused with general education). As so often happens, developments elsewhere—in this case, higher education—had added a new dimension to the problem. Entrance requirements had been lowered at many four-year colleges, and community colleges had hardly any requirements for admission. As Boyer points out, "students soon discovered that even with a 'general' course of study they could gain admission to all but the most highly selective higher-learning institutions."[86]

At the same time, with the establishment of separate area vocational schools following the Vocational Education Act of 1963, many students who might otherwise profit from vocational studies understandably refused to leave their home high school even on a shared-time basis to partake in such studies because it meant sacrificing their participation in student activities and in the life of their home high school. The establishment of separate specialized area vocational high schools also served to diminish the comprehensiveness of the curriculum of the comprehensive high school, with the result that it was giving priority to the college-preparatory curriculum while relegating other students to the general track. At the same time, the function of general education—the learnings that need to be shared by all enlightened members of a free society—was sadly neglected in favor of basic education for the noncollege-bound youth.

The period of educational retrenchment through "back to basics" (the latter part of the 1970s and early 1980s) was accompanied by a marked increase in school dropouts, who were mainly youngsters in the general track and were from disadvantaged home backgrounds.[87] Well-designed vocational education programs in the comprehensive high school, coupled with concerted employment placement efforts, had served over several decades to improve the holding power of the high school. But, as a study by the U.S. Department of Education found, the "access of students to good (vocational) programs is not ensured."[88] The problem of the general track—or more specifically, the problem of a good curriculum for every student—has not disappeared with changing entrance requirements at institutions of higher education.

Turning back to the 1945 meeting on life-adjustment education, Charles Prosser introduced a resolution calling for a program for the students in the educational no-man's land of the general track (60 percent of high-school youth), which would prepare them for satisfying lives and gainful employment. Prosser argued that this population, constituting the vast majority of high-school students, would not "receive the life adjustment training they need and to which they are entitled as American citizens" unless school administrators and vocational education leaders put their heads together and developed a program for them.[89]

Prosser's resolution was unanimously adopted and the Office of Education sponsored a series of regional meetings during 1946 that led to a consensus that (1) the life-adjustment needs of a majority of our youth were not being met by secondary schools; (2) the school curriculum must be revised to include functional experiences in the areas of practical arts, home and family living, civic competence, and health and physical fitness; and (3) the major proportion of our youth need a supervised program of work experience.[90] A Commission on Life Adjustment Education for Youth was established as an outcome of these conferences. Emphasized by the commission was that life-adjustment education was not to be interpreted as mere "adjustment to existing conditions"; it emphasized "active and creative achievements" and placed a "high premium upon learning to make wise choices, since the very concept of American democracy demands the appropriate revising of aims and the means of attaining them."[91]

There were only two commissions on life-adjustment education, each of which functioned for three years. No new commission was appointed in 1954 because the attack on progressive education was in full swing and every program that was not academic (including vocational education) was tagged derisively as life-adjustment education.

The so-called life-adjustment movement was an attempt of postwar educators to eliminate the gap between the secondary-school curriculum and the needs of youth. That many of our youth saw little if any value in the curriculum of the high school was apparent. In the early postwar period, approximately one out of every two who entered the ninth grade failed to graduate four years later.

The goal of life adjustment, according to its advocates, was not to produce conformity and adjustment but a more realistic program for high schoolers. The mistake of this group was not in their goals but in their choice of a label. "Adjustment" has decided overtones of passivity and acquiescence rather than the mastery of one's environment. Throughout the 1930s and 1940s the term *emotional adjustment* was used interchangeably by many progressivists with a *well-integrated personality*. This was anathema to the social reconstructionists.

Mental health was certainly an educational goal that was subscribed to by most progressivists, but the goal of adjustment clashed head-on with the Deweyan goal of environmental mastery. Thus, the concept of adjustment plagued progressivists long before the life-adjustment effort. Taba saw the problem clearly in 1934 when she wrote: "The mental hygiene program in progressive schools has wrestled with the formidable problem of adjusting the individual to a fundamentally maladjusted society, the standards and values of which are in conflict with those held by progressive education."[92]

Progressive education was in the untenable position of being unable either to resolve the issue of social reform or to attempt to fit the person to his or her society. Therefore, as Taba observed at the time, its programs represented a "halfway compromise between accepting and rejecting the dominant scheme of life."

The progressivists were never able to resolve this problem. It is indeed an irony that the critics of progressive education damned the entire movement as an effort toward conformity and complacency when growth, change, and environmental mastery were the goals of most progressivists.

The "Persistent Life Situation" Proposal

One of the most interesting developments in the curriculum field in the early postwar years was a design for a curriculum built on continuing life situations.[93] Developed by Florence Stratemeyer and her associates at Teachers College, the proposal was based on a principle derived from studies on transfer of learning: School learning is more likely to be carried over into life out of school if the problems studied in school are similar to those faced out of the school.

The goal of a curriculum based on recurring life situations is to help children and youth develop constantly broadening insights and deepening generalizations about problems of significance to them. Here was a response to the findings of studies such as the Regents' Inquiry that the schools had little influence on the lives of youth: Educational activities begun in school were usually dropped when students left school.

Although the aim of this curriculum is to meet the needs of children and youth throughout their entire lives, needs also determine the choices of problems to be studied. Teachers become aware of concerns "by noting the games learners play, what they stop to watch, how they work out problems of interest to them ... what they reveal about themselves by the voluntary choices they make and the experiences they seek."[94] Like Kilpatrick, Stratemeyer and her associates stressed that not all children's interests are equally valuable; good curriculum planning requires that teachers know the difference between superficial interests and those that will lead to the development of useful generalizations. But as in the case of Kilpatrick's project method, it is preferable for the problems studied to be based on the child's immediate concerns rather than on adult claims of children's needs. The focus on the child's immediate concerns makes the persistent life-situation proposal a child-centered proposal.

Examples of persistent problems in various developmental stages (early childhood, later childhood, youth, and adulthood) were suggested, but there was no preplanned design, for it was believed by the developers of the "persistent life situation" proposal "that the intrinsic motivation provided by specific concerns of individuals and groups will, in the long run, result in a more effective selection of learnings than will any preplanned structure."

THE CONSERVATIVE ASSAULT

By 1950 it was apparent in the curriculum field that the disciples of Dewey had gone their various ways; the curriculums they proposed had different centers of emphasis. As just indicated, Stratemeyer and her associates insisted that the curriculum should grow out of the concerns and interests of learners. Smith, Stanley, and Shores, on the other hand, argued that the curriculum should grow out of the needs of society.[95] Curriculum scholars, teachers educators, and professors of social and philosophical foundations endlessly debated the issues arising from these and other orientations for curriculum development.

While curriculum developers were engaged in controversies over curriculum goals, criticisms concerning the aims, methods, and content of the public-school curriculum were building up to a crescendo. The rallying cry of the critics was "back": back to the "fundamentals," back to "basic" education, back to the acquisition of logically organized bodies of knowledge, back to drill and memorization, back to learning tasks that require strict training and hard effort (so much the better if the learner was not interested in what he or she was doing). In short, the critics were calling for a return to education based on the mental discipline and faculty psychology theories of the previous century.

Although the evidence was that children learned as well or better with the new education, professional educators were never able to convince the public of this. The critics argued that "frills" (art, music, dramatics, industrial arts, physical education), a curriculum related to life out of school, and active learning experiences had led to neglect of the three R's, juvenile delinquency, and the undermining of our society.

Many of the critics sincerely believed that the schools were neglecting the development of skills. Others clamoring for a return to the fundamentals had purely economic motives: A narrower curriculum was a less-expensive curriculum. Still a third group of critics were academicians who argued for a return to the traditional values and intellectual discipline. They subjected the new education to a searching, if not always accurate, analysis.

The Pattern of Criticism

It will be recalled that before 1890, public education was pronounced a miserable failure by critics who carped that children were being "spoon-fed"; education had been made too easy, and music and art were stealing time that should be devoted to the fundamentals. The rumbling of the critics continued but was drowned out for many years by criticisms of traditional education.

The turning point came during the so-called life-adjustment proposal. Critics lumped all modern pedagogical ideas under the catchword "life-adjustment education." The more articulate critics wrote volumes to show how progressive education and life-adjustment education were one and the same. Professional educators were deeply concerned about "attacks on the public schools" but never offered an effective rebuttal or, indeed, much of a rebuttal at all. Magazines and newspapers were filled with criticisms of curriculum innovations, but only seldom could one find an educator's defense of these innovations in the popular press.

For the most part, educators remained silent. Was this because they had themselves lost faith in the new methods of teaching and changes in curriculum organization? Or did they count on public support which "was all too often nonexistent"?[96] No one ever really knew. Perhaps it was that in not knowing how to handle the criticism, educators did nothing. Perhaps the popular press was inhospitable to the defense of progressive education at a time of cold war and McCarthyism. Again it must be remembered that this was an era of fear. Defenders of the new education, particularly programs that explored controversial issues, could well be accused of subversion. Nevertheless, it is still remarkable that educators did so little to forestall the demise of a movement representing the main current of educational thought for over a half century. As Cremin put it: "The surprising thing about the progressive response to the assault of the fifties is not that the movement collapsed but that it collapsed so readily."[97]

Criticism from the University

The most powerful critics of the new education were university academicians, and the most effective and articulate of them all was Arthur Bestor, a historian at the University of Illinois. In tune with the other critics, Bestor called for a return to the pedagogical past, for the "restoration of learning."[98]

Criticism of Curriculum Synthesis.   Particularly important were Bestor's criticisms of efforts to break down the barriers between subjects. According to Bestor, synthesis of knowledge should be the last stage in education; it should follow years of systematic study of individual disciplines. "For students who must conclude their education with high school, an integrated course in the senior year is appropriate. For students who go on to more advanced study, however, the wisest plan is to wait until the college years."[99]

Bestor's recommendation totally ignored the findings of the Eight-Year Study. It will be recalled that all of the participating schools attempted to develop unified curriculums. It will also be recalled that the graduates of these schools exceeded their matchees in intellectual power. According to Bestor, the school could best help students acquire the ability for social problem-solving through study of history. The disciplined intellectual effort required would equip the youth with the maturity of judgment needed for the solution of social problems. Here Bestor ignored the findings of research on transfer: Learning is most apt to "carry over" when situations confronted out of school are similar to those studied in school.

Criticism of Educational Goals.   Much of Bestor's criticism was directed against the idea that it was the job of the school to meet the needs of youth. This was tantamount to saying that the school should take over the responsibilities of the home, and what was worse, according to Bestor, it caused the school to neglect its primary task, intellectual training.

Bestor slammed into the proposal of the Educational Policies Commission for defining education in terms of youths' imperative needs. While criticizing the school for lack of intellectual rigor, Bestor's own analysis contains serious distortions. "Why is there no reference to arithmetic" in *Education for ALL American Youth,* Bestor asks?[100] In fact, arithmetic (and mathematics) was discussed; it was provided for through college preparatory, vocational, and elective programs.[101] No matter what one's philosophical persuasion, misstatements such as this make Bestor's entire thesis suspect. Be that as it may, it was Bestor's opinion (he offered no supporting evidence) that it is the business of the school to meet only one need—intellectual training.

Criticism of Life-Adjustment Education.   Bestor's most vitriolic attack on the commission's proposal concerned life-adjustment education—although the term life adjustment was not used in connection with the proposed curriculum.

> "Life-adjustment" and similar programs are monstrosities in the literal sense of the word, for they consist in the abnormal development of certain features of the school's program and the withering of other and more important programs.
>
> ... A well-intentioned but incidental concern with the personal problems of adolescents has grown so excessive as to push into the background what should be the school's central concern, the intellectual development of the students. To such an extreme have many educationists gone that they seem anxious for the school to satisfy all imaginable needs except those of the mind.[102]

Reading Bestor's attack on life-adjustment education, one is struck over and over again with the improvident choice of the label "life adjustment." Bestor completely misconstrued the motives of educators. He wrote that a program that prepares neither for college nor a vocation can have but one purpose: to teach the student "to know his place, to keep it, and to be content with it—in short ... to provide him with 'life adjustment' "[103]

Even more vehement was the attack by Columbia's Richard Hofstadter. Also a historian, Hofstadter wrote that the "road to life adjustment" began when free secondary-school education became available to all youth.[104] A second unhappy milestone, according to Hofstadter, was reached when the *Cardinal Principles of Secondary Education* supplanted the ideas of the Committee of Ten and the aims of secondary education went beyond the objective of developing the mind. The goal of a truly democratic education ruined the secondary school. Wrote Hofstadter: "Paraphrasing Lincoln, the educator-for-democracy might have said that God must love the slow learners because he made so many of them. Elitists might coldly turn their backs on these large numbers, but democratic educators, embracing them as a fond mother embraces her handicapped child, would attempt to build the curriculum upon their supposed needs."[105] Educators had reached their destination, said Hofstadter, when pleasure in schooling became a primary goal and students were learning "not Shakespeare or Dickens but how to write a business letter." Needless to say, Hofstadter welcomed the changed pedagogical atmosphere after *Sputnik.*

In the 1980s the schools underwent a siege of criticism once again by essentialist, perennialist, and (religious) fundamentalist critics. Although the pejorative use of such labels as "progressive education" and "life adjustment" was replaced by "humanistic education" and "secular humanism," the accusations were virtually identical: "lack of academic standards" (especially in science and mathematics), "lack of intellectual training," lack of discipline," "neglect of basic subjects," and "need to stress facts and skills." "The reform movement of the 1980s," wrote two educators, "echoes the 1950s rather than calling for a new era of excellence."[106]

The Effects of Criticism

Returning to the 1940s and 1950s, the onslaught of the critics was the most serious crisis of the new education. Needless to say, it did not weather this criticism well. The effect of criticism on the secondary school was to bring to a halt what had hardly begun. On the other hand, the elementary school emerged from the attack much as it had been before the attack. Whereas attempts to integrate secondary-school subjects were dropped quickly, unit teaching was continued in the elementary school. Moreover, elementary teachers continued to be concerned with the emotional, physical, and social requirements of the developing child.

Although the new education collapsed as an organized movement, it left a curriculum legacy, which raises the question of what kind of victory the critics won. The curriculum legacy is the subject of Chapter 6.

THE SEARCH FOR A MIDDLE GROUND

Among the more important curriculum proposals in the decade of the 1940s was an attempt by a committee of Harvard University faculty in arts and sciences and education to synthesize the best elements of traditional education with the best elements of the new education. The famous Harvard Committee was appointed in 1943 by James B. Conant, then president of Harvard, to study the problem of general education in a free society. In the introduction to the "Report of the Harvard Committee," *General Education in a Free Society,* Conant pointed out that during the war there had been much thought about education, and he asked the reader to drop his educational biases and explore with the committee "ways and means by which the great instrument of American democracy can both shape the future and secure the foundations of our free society."[107]

It is important to note that Conant used the term *general education* rather than liberal education. Conant was well aware that the latter term had an elitist connotation, that of education for the privileged few, whereas he was attempting to realize the democratic commitment to universal education. As McClellan points out, a primary concern of the Harvard Committee "was to free the great tradition of liberal education from the snobbish, class-ridden caricature of itself."[108] This was absolutely essential if Harvard was to realize its mission as the guardian of the intellectual tradition in American education and become a major force in influencing secondary schools and institutions of higher education toward providing for every youth a cultural background equal to that of the favored few.

The Harvard Report focused on the objectives and means of general education for both school and college. The dominant aim of education was "to prepare an individual to become an expert both in some particular vocation or art and in the general art of the free man or citizen. Thus the two kinds of education once given separately to different social classes must be given together to all alike." The chief abilities to be developed through general education were "to think effectively, to communicate thought, to make relevant judgments, to discriminate among values."[109]

The Harvard Report recommended that the curriculum provide continuing contact with the fields of history, art, philosophy, and literature so that the student would "feel the impact of those general ideas and aspirations which have been a deep moving force in the lives of men."[110] Recognizing the need for a principle of unity ("without it the curriculum flies into pieces"), the Harvard Committee suggested that this principle might be developed in the comprehensive high school through recognition of the interdependence *and* equality of all courses and activities.[111] The committee did not suggest the breaking down of subject barriers through a new curriculum organization such as the core curriculum.

The Harvard Report was a plea for educators to reconcile their differences concerning traditional and experimental values in education by extrapolating and combining the best elements of each doctrine. Nevertheless, educators at midcentury remained sharply divided on the needed direction and shape of the curriculum.

There are striking differences between the Harvard Report and *Education for ALL American Youth*. The Harvard Report is an attempt to adapt liberal education to the needs of contemporary society. *Education for ALL American Youth,* on the other hand, is a progressive-experimentalist approach to curriculum development: Education is defined in terms of the needs of youth and society. Despite these differences, Conant in 1945 enthusiastically endorsed both documents, denying that there was a contradiction between them.[112] According to McClellan, this denial is revealing because by the late 1950s Conant's thoughts on education were very different from the spirit of either of these documents; Conant had become "the Cold War Warrior," contended McClellan.[113] But this is an unfair appraisal of Conant when it is recognized that his report on the American high school during the post–*Sputnik I* hysteria served to save the comprehensive high school at a time when there were enormous pressures to abandon it in favor of the European dual system of schooling. He was a champion of general education in school and college. He wrote powerfully, eloquently, and prophetically about the "social dynamite" festering in our central cities as a result of an inadequate curriculum, school dropouts, youth unemployment, and social disaffection. He recognized the necessary interdependence of general education and vocational education, and warned repeatedly of the dangers of abandoning the democratizing function of the comprehensive high school.[114] No college

president, indeed no individual since Conant has taken such an abiding interest in the comprehensive high school and its democratizing function in serving the common and special needs of all of our youth.[115]

EDUCATION AND SOCIETY: A RETROSPECTIVE OF EVENTS (1932–55)

The events in Table 5-1 span the eras of the Great Depression, World
War II, and the postwar reconstruction. The New Deal under Franklin D.
Roosevelt was accompanied by unprecedented studies of the problems of
children and youth, such as those conducted by the American Youth Commission of the American Council on Education and the NEA's Educational Policies Commission. The Great Depression also witnessed the establishment of
the first department of curriculum (Curriculum and Teaching at Teachers
College, Columbia), the formation of the Society for Curriculum Study
(which was to become the Association for Supervision and Curriculum Development), and the conducting of systematic research on the curriculum in
actual field settings—such as the studies by J. Wayne Wrightstone in New
York City on the effects of progressive approaches to the curriculum at the
elementary level and the monumental Eight-Year Study (1933–41), which revealed the advantages of integrated, problem-focused core designs for general education and provided compelling evidence challenging the traditional
college preparatory curriculum.

Synoptic textbooks treating curriculum as a systematic field of study
were appearing, along with Dewey's classic *Experience and Education*
(1938).

The host of social-reform programs of the New Deal included the establishment of several uncoordinated nonschool educative agencies to deal with
a range of needs—from nursery schooling to youth unemployment, leading
the Educational Policies Commission to call for the administration of these
programs through a bona fide educational agency working closely with the
schools. The consequence of failing to provide for such an arrangement was
that most of the programs were disbanded after the emergency. (Similar
problems were to arise during the War-on-Poverty program of the Johnson
Administration three decades later.) The crisis of the Great Depression witnessed the call for educational reconstruction, led by George Counts, but the
main reform currents were formed and guided by the experimentalists, who
viewed the reconstructionist prescriptions as educational indoctrination.

The oppression of Nazi Germany and Fascist Italy impelled many leading scientists and other intellectuals from those nations to emigrate to the
hospitable shores of the United States. With the advent of World War II, the
Eight-Year Study and other progressive curricular-reform efforts came to be
overshadowed. One of the most exciting and provocative educational jour-

TABLE *5-1* Timetable of Events in Education and Society: 1932–55

YEAR	EDUCATION	SOCIETY
1932	Establishment of the Department of Curriculum and Teaching, Teachers College, Columbia University by Dean James E. Russell (first department of its kind) with Hollis L. Caswell as chair Society for Curriculum Study established; merged in 1942 with the Department of Supervision and Directors of Instruction (NEA) to become the Association for Supervision and Curriculum Development George S. Counts (1889–1974): *Dare the School Build a New Social Order?*	Franklin D. Roosevelt elected President; U.S. troops under Gen. Douglas MacArthur drive out the "bonus army" of war veterans from Washington, D.C.; James T. Farrell: *Young Lonigan;* Aldous Huxley: *Brave New World;* popular song: *Brother, Can You Spare a Dime?*
1933	Eight-Year Study (1933–41) begins (sponsored by Progressive Education Association)	Franklin D. Roosevelt inaugurated as President, appoints first woman as Cabinet member (Frances Perkins, Secretary of Labor); U.S. "bank holiday"; Roosevelt's "New Deal" begins; TVA created; Prohibition repealed; U.S. recognizes USSR; Adolf Hitler appointed Chancellor of Germany, granted dictatorial powers; first concentration camps erected by Nazis; book burnings by Nazis; Chicago World's Fair opens; *Ulysses* allowed into U.S.; electronic TV developed; emigration of scientists, authors, artists, and political refugees from Germany (including the Bauhaus school of architecture and design) to the U.S.
1934	*The Social Frontier,* a progressive educational journal, begins publication; renamed *Frontiers of Democracy* in 1939; publication ended 1943 *The Activity Movement,* 33rd NSSE Yearbook, Part II	Roosevelt's "New Deal" gains momentum; Albert Einstein: *My Philosophy;* Ruth Benedict: *Patterns of Culture;* John Dewey: *Art as Experience;* James Hilton: *Good-Bye, Mr. Chips;* Nazi "blood baths"

(cont.)

TABLE *5-1*   Timetable of Events in Education and Society: 1932–55

YEAR	EDUCATION	SOCIETY
1935	American Youth Commission created by the American Council on Education (1937: *Secondary Education for Youth in Modern America;* 1942: *Youth and the Future)* Educational Policies Commission created by NEA (disbanded 1968) Hollis L. Caswell and Doak S. Campbell: *Curriculum Development* J. Wayne Wrightstone: *Appraisal of Newer Practices in Selected Public Schools* (experiment in New York City evaluating progressive curricular approaches over six-year period) John Dewey Society founded	President Roosevelt signs U.S. Social Security Act and Rural Electrification Act; Huey Long assassinated; James T. Farrell: *Studs Lonigan;* Sinclair Lewis: *It Can't Happen Here;* John Steinbeck: *Tortilla Flat;* George Gershwin: *Porgy and Bess* (N.Y.); CIO organized by John L. Lewis; Luftwaffe formed
1937	Society for Curriculum Study: *The Changing Curriculum* Boyd H. Bode (1873–1953): *Modern Educational Theories*	Spanish Civil War enters second year; Japanese seize Peking, Shanghai, Nanking, and Hangchow; John Dos Passos: *USA;* Picasso: *Guernica;* insulin used for diabetes; Roosevelt dedicates Bonneville Dam (Ore.); Amelia Earhart lost on Pacific flight; dirigible *Hindenburg* burns after transatlantic flight (Lakehurst, N.J.); Golden Gate Bridge opens; 40-hour workweek established in U.S.
1938	John Dewey: *Experience and Education* Boyd H. Bode: *Progressive Education at the Crossroads* Educational Policies Commission: *The Purpose of Education in American Democracy* Howard M. Bell (American Youth Commission of the American Council on Education): *Youth Tell Their Story*	Japan withdraws from League of Nations; Chamberlain meets with Hitler; Roosevelt recalls U.S. Ambassador to Germany; pogroms in Germany; House Un-American Activities Committee formed; John Steinbeck: *The Grapes of Wrath;* Carl Van Doren: *Benjamin Franklin;* Irving Berlin: *God Bless America;* Nobel Prize (physics): Ernest Lawrence (cyclotron); FM invented

TABLE *5-1* Timetable of Events in Education and Society: 1932–55

YEAR	EDUCATION	SOCIETY
	National Council of Teachers of English: *A Correlated Curriculum* William C. Bagley (1874–1946): "An Essentialist's Platform for the Advancement of American Education"	
1941	Lincoln School merged with Horace Mann School, resulting in the end of the Lincoln School, Teachers College (opened 1917)	World War II: Lend-Lease Bill signed; Japanese bomb Pearl Harbor; U.S. and Britain declare war on Japan; Germany and Italy declare war on U.S.; Manhattan Project (atomic bomb) begins; U.S. Supreme Court upholds Federal Wage and Hour Law restricting work of 16-year-olds and setting minimum wage for interstate businesses
1942	H. H. Giles, S. P. McCutchen, and A. N. Zechiel: *Exploring the Curriculum* (Eight-Year Study)	Internment of Japanese-Americans on West Coast to inland camp; Tokyo bombed by U.S.; U.S. defeats Japanese at Midway; Germans reach Stalingrad; Ghandi arrested by British; Irving Berlin: *White Christmas;* Enrico Fermi splits the atom; first automatic computer developed (U.S.)
1944	Education Act of 1944 (Britain) requires, for the first time, "secondary education for all" through public funding; establishes a Ministry of Education (renamed Department of Education and Science in 1964) to carry out the "national policy for providing a varied and comprehensive (educational) service in every area" Educational Policies Commission: *Education for ALL American Youth* (rev. 1952)	World War II: D-Day landings in Normandy; first flying bombs hit London; Warsaw uprising; Roosevelt elected for fourth term; Dumbarton Oaks conference in Washington, D.C., discussion on UN; Gunnar Myrdal: *An American Dilemma;* Tennessee Williams: *The Glass Menagerie*
1945	Report of the Harvard Committee: *General Education in a Free Society*	World War II: Yalta Conference with Roosevelt, Churchill, and Stalin; Roosevelt dies; Harry S.

(cont.)

TABLE *5-1*   Timetable of Events in Education and Society: 1932–55

YEAR	EDUCATION	SOCIETY
	Educational Policies Commission: *Education for ALL American Children* (rev. 1948) Prosser Resolution on life-adjustment education	Truman becomes President; Mussolini killed; Hitler suicide; Berlin surrenders to Russians; "V.E. Day" ends war in Europe; Labour Party defeats Churchill; U.S. drops atom bombs on Hiroshima and Nagasaki; Japan surrenders, marking end of World War II (35 million war dead plus 10 million killed in German concentration camps); Vietnam formed as independent republic under Ho Chi Minh; George Orwell: *Animal Farm;* woman's suffrage enacted in France
1947	Florence B. Stratemeyer et al., *Developing a Curriculum for Modern Living* (rev. 1957) Educational Testing Service founded Over 1 million war veterans enroll in colleges under U.S. "G.I. Bill of Rights"	Peace treaties signed in Paris; Tennessee Williams: *A Streetcar Named Desire; The Diary of Anne Frank* published; transistor invented (U.S.); first black signs major league baseball contract (Brooklyn); President Truman issues Loyalty Order for federal employees, eventuating in the proliferation of the loyalty oath in most states as contractual requirement for the employment of faculty in public schools and colleges
1949	Ralph W. Tyler: *Basic Principles of Curriculum and Instruction* Edward L. Thorndike dies (born 1874)	Harry S. Truman inaugurated President; People's Republic of China proclaimed under Mao Tse-tung; Nationalist Chinese forces move to Formosa; North Atlantic Treaty signed; Israel admitted to UN; German Federal Republic established; U.S.S.R. tests its first atom bomb; Arthur Miller: *Death of a Salesman;* George Orwell: *1984;* clothes rationing ends in Britain
1953	B.F. Skinner: *Science and Human Behavior*	Dwight D. Eisenhower elected President; U.S. Congress creates

TABLE *5-1*   Timetable of Events in Education and Society: 1932–55

YEAR	EDUCATION	SOCIETY
	Arthur Bestor: *Educational Wastelands* First black appointed to faculty of Ivy League college (visiting professor at Brown)	Dept. of Health, Education, and Welfare; Rosenbergs executed; Nobel Peace Prize: General George C. Marshall (Marshall Plan, 1947); Nobel Prize for Literature: Winston S. Churchill; U.S.S.R. explodes hydrogen bomb; Alfred C. Kinsey: *Sexual Behavior in the Human Female*
1955	American Education Fellowship (formerly the Progressive Education Association) disbanded Rudolf Flesch: *Why Johnny Can't Read* White House Conference on Education	Civil rights boycotts in Montgomery, Ala.; J. Lawrence and R. E. Lee: *Inherit the Wind;* Sloan Wilson: *The Man in the Gray Flannel Suit;* Albert Einstein dies (born 1879); atomically generated power first used in U.S. (Schenectady, N.Y.)

Sources: *Facts on File* (N.Y.: Facts on File, Inc.); *Annual Register of World Events* (London: Longman's, Green); Bernard Grun, *The Timetables of History,* rev. ed. (New York: Simon & Schuster, 1979); *The New York Times.*

nals, *The Social Frontier,* founded in 1934, ended publication in 1943. The Lincoln School closed with its merger with the Horace Mann School at Teachers College in 1941.

Despite these setbacks, the prospects for the end of World War II were met with optimism for progressive educational and social reforms. Gunnar Myrdal's *An American Dilemma* appeared in 1944, addressing the historic plight of blacks in America and pointing the way to fulfilling the "American Creed" through civil-rights reforms and extending educational opportunity to all regardless of color. The Education Act of 1944 in Britain required for the first time "secondary education for all" through public funding. (It will be recalled that public funding for secondary education in the United States was a nineteenth century development, and that the movement for universal secondary education gained full momentum with the *Cardinal Principles* report of the 1918 Commission on the Reorganization of Secondary Education.) Renewed efforts were made to reconstruct the curriculum in school and college to meet the function of general education, to strengthen the comprehensive high school as the prototypical educational institution of American democracy, and to extend educational opportunity upward through the community college and the state university.

A new era of standardized testing opened with the establishment of the Educational Testing Service in 1947, along with the uses and misuses of such tests for pupil sorting, tracking, and guidance. The cold war and McCarthyism took their toll with the rise of censorship of schoolbooks, notably the Rugg series in social studies, and the disbanding of the Progressive Education Association (American Education Fellowship) in 1955. The loyalty oath became a contractual condition for the employment of faculty in public schools and colleges. Tax conservatives and essentialists were calling for curriculum retrenchment through "back to basics." Progressive educational efforts were unfairly labeled "life-adjustment education."

Yet, with the growing extension of educational opportunity the American public would not turn back the clock on the progress that had been made. Civil rights boycotts were breaking out in the South. The U.S. Supreme Court in 1954 held that "separate educational facilities are inherently unequal," ushering in an era of school desegregation in the South and North. The White House Conference on Education in 1955 gave renewed optimism for the democratic prospect. The infamous Scopes Trial (1925) was successfully dramatized on Broadway in 1955 as *Inherit the Wind.*

On the global scene, the Marshall Plan was deemed a success in the reconstruction of Europe. The British Empire came to an end. The Atomic Age was being heralded as providing such a cheap source of energy that energy conservation would never again be a problem.

PERSPECTIVE

The Great Depression provided a badly needed sense of direction for curriculum development. It led to the decline of curriculum making by job analysis, since an atomized curriculum conceals rather than deals with social problems. Nevertheless, attempts to define the relation between school and society led to deep-seated clashes of opinion. Curriculum makers in the early 1930s were torn by the question as to whether the school should indoctrinate for social change. Experimentalism, which has as its method the testing of possible plans of action, is inimical to indoctrination contended Dewey.

The elementary school chose the cooperative-attitude-group-process approach to social reform. The secondary school experimented with problem-centered core curriculums that required students and teachers to examine the social forces bearing on society. McCarthyism, and its attendant censorship of content, along with cold war pressures, led to the decline of the core curriculum.

Fear of the taint of radicalism, the inability to recognize social change, and the devastating split created by the child-versus-society debate caused the Progressive Education Association to stand on the sidelines while the Educational Policies Commission became the spokesman on the curriculum. Yet the Eight-Year Study, which was sponsored by the association's Commission on the Relation of School and College, was the most important educational experiment ever conducted in this country. The thirty secondary schools in the experiment attempted to break down the barriers between subjects. The study proved beyond question that there is no single best pattern of preparation for college. "Thirty Schools" graduates earned higher grades in college and were found to be more systematic, precise, and objective thinkers than their counterparts at other schools.

Despite the encouraging findings, by 1950 only one of the Thirty Schools continued to experiment with the core curriculum. A striking parallel is drawn with the elementary school; despite favorable research findings, educators lost interest in activity programs. In neither case were the findings of research used in educational decision-making. But the Eight-Year Study stimulated curriculum revision. State curriculum programs in the 1930s resulted in a shift from curriculum making to curriculum development and energized the teacher's role.

By the mid-1930s the idea of developing a curriculum for social reconstruction no longer held center stage in the drama of education in the Great Depression. Although the issue had not been resolved, it was superseded by the problems of Depression youth that pointed to a gap between the curriculum and the needs of youth. In proposals of the Educational Policies Commission, social reconstruction was approached through the goals of civic responsibility and competence.

Despite shibboleths such as the "whole child," curriculum research in the decade of the 1940s seldom was conducted in relation to a total curriculum pattern. Well before midcentury, curriculum adaptation, the approach to curriculum improvement favored by educators in the 1920s, had attained supremacy over more radical revision in the elementary school.

The fatal mistake of the so-called life-adjustment effort was not its goals but its name. The critics had a field day. Strangely, educators offered little if any rebuttal to the barrage of criticism leveled at progressive education.

At midcentury the new education had all but yielded to the forces of conservatism, but not without leaving a legacy. With all its ambiguities, conflicting persuasions, and vulnerability to misapplication and misinterpretation, the new education somehow raised the expectations of the public in education as the means toward a better life for their children. Although conservatism may have had its victories, American education was not ready to return to the old education.

NOTES

1. Francis M. Froelicher, "A Liberality of Spirit," *Progressive Education* 4 (July–August–September 1927): 149.
2. Ralph Waldo Emerson, *Works of Ralph Waldo Emerson* (Boston: Houghton Mifflin, 1883), pp. 77–104.

3. John Dewey and John L. Childs, "The Underlying Philosophy of Education," Chapter 9 in *The Educational Frontier,* William Kilpatrick (ed.) (New York: The Century Company, 1933), p. 290.

4. Ibid.

5. Lawrence A. Cremin, *The Transformation of the School* (New York: Knopf, 1961), p. 200.

6. Boyd H. Bode, *How We Learn* (Lexington, Mass.: D. C. Heath, 1940), p. 214.

7. Boyd H. Bode, "The Confusion in Present-Day Education," Chapter 1 in *The Educational Frontier,* op. cit., pp. 20–21.

8. Carleton W. Washburne, "Indoctrination Versus Education," *The Social Frontier* 2 (April 1936): 213.

9. John Dewey and John L. Childs, "The Socio-Economic Situation and Education," Chapter 2 in *The Educational Frontier,* op. cit., pp. 46–49.

10. Ibid., p. 71.

11. C. A. Bowers, "Curriculum and Our Technocracy Culture: The Problem of Reform," *Teachers College Record* 78 (September 1976): 54.

12. John L. Childs, *Education and the Philosophy of Experimentalism* (New York: Appleton-Century-Crofts, 1931), p. 93.

13. Boyd H. Bode, "Education and Social Reconstruction," *The Social Frontier* 1 (January 1935): 22.

14. Ibid.

15. John Dewey, "Education and Social Change," *The Social Frontier* 3 (May 1937): 235.

16. Ibid., p. 237.

17. John Dewey, "The Teacher and His World," *The Social Frontier* 1 (January 1935): 7.

18. Theodore Brameld, "Karl Marx and the American Teacher," *The Social Frontier* 2 (November 1935): 55.

19. Dewey, "Education and Social Change," op. cit., p. 237.

20. John Dewey, "Education for a Changing Social Order," National Education Association *Proceedings* (Washington, D.C.: The Association, 1934), p. 745.

21. Harold Rugg, *Foundations for American Education* (New York: Harcourt Brace, 1947), p. 563.

22. As quoted in Cremin, op. cit., pp. 243–45.

23. George S. Counts, "Dare Progressive Education Be Progressive?," *Progressive Education* 9 (April 1932): 259.

24. The Committee of the Progressive Education Association on Social and Economic Problems, *A Call to the Teachers of the Nation* (New York: John Day, 1933), p. 22.

25. Ibid., p. 26.

26. Frederick L. Redefer, "Resolution, Reactions, and Reminiscences," *Progressive Education* 26 (April 1949): 189.

27. Ibid., p. 188.

28. Edgar B. Wesley, *NEA: The First Hundred Years* (New York: Harper & Row, 1957), p. 308.

29. American Education Fellowship, "Objectives and Program of the American Education Fellowship," *Progressive Education* 22 (October 1944): 9.

30. Cremin, op. cit., p. 272.

31. John Dewey, "How Much Freedom in the New Schools?," *The New Republic* 63 (July 9, 1930): 206.

32. Dewey, "Education for a Changing Social Order," op. cit., p. 752.

33. Robert Lynd, "Education and Some Realities of American Life," *Progressive Education* 7 (May 1930): 170–79.

34. Walter H. Drost, "A Visit with Stanwood Cobb," *The Educational Forum* 35 (March 1971): 288.

35. Ibid.

36. Wilford M. Aikin, "The Eight Year Study: If We Were to Do It Again," *Progressive Education* 31 (October 1953): 11.

37. Lee J. Cronbach, "Tyler's Contribution to Measurement and Evaluation," *Journal of Thought* 21 (Spring 1986): p. 51.

38. Ibid.

39. Jean Evangelauf, "At 86, a Minister's Son Still Spreads the Gospel of Educational Reform," *The Chronicle of Higher Education,* July 20, 1988, p. A.3.

40. Wilford M. Aikin, *The Story of the Eight-Year Study* (New York: Harper & Row, 1942), p. 28.

41. Dean Chamberlain et al., *Did They Succeed in College?* (New York: Harper & Row, 1942), p. 209.

42. Aikin, *The Story of the Eight-Year Study,* op. cit., p. 16.

43. Aikin, "The Eight Year Study: If We Were to Do It Again," op. cit., p. 14.

44. Ibid., p. 12.

45. H. H. Giles, S. P. McCutchen, and A. N. Zechiel, *Exploring the Curriculum* (New York: Harper & Row, 1942), p. 35.

46. Laurel N. Tanner, "The Swing Away from Science," *The Educational Forum* 36 (January 1972): 235.

47. Frederick L. Redefer, "The Eight-Year Study . . . After Eight Years," *Progressive Education* 28 (November 1950): 34.

48. Fred N. Kerlinger, *Foundations of Behavioral Research,* 2nd ed. (New York: Holt, Rinehart and Winston, 1973), p. 365.

49. Gale E. Jensen, "Basic Questions for an Evaluation of the Eight-Year Study," *School and Society* 64 (November 16, 1946): 348–49.

50. W. H. Lancelot, "The Eight-Year Study Still Awaits Fair Appraisal," *School and Society* 62 (November 3, 1945): 282.

51. Ralph W. Tyler, "A Comment on Professor Lancelot's Criticism of the Eight-Year Study," *School and Society* 59 (June 3, 1944): 396.

52. Robert W. Young, "The Irrational Curriculum," *National Association of Secondary School Principals Bulletin* 51 (September 1967), p. 47.

53. Scott Whitener, *Patterns of High School Studies and College Achievement* (unpublished doctoral dissertation, Rutgers University, 1974).

54. Jerome S. Bruner, *The Process of Education* (Cambridge: Harvard University Press, 1960).

55. Aikin, *The Study of the Eight-Year Study,* op. cit., p. 8.

56. William H. Clune et al., *The Implementation and Effects of High School Gradua-tion Requirements* (New Brunswick: Center for Policy Research in Education, Rutgers University 1989).

57. Cronbach, op. cit., p. 51.

58. Laurel N. Tanner, "Contributions of the Eight-Year Study," *Journal of Thought* 21 (Spring 1986): p. 34.

59. Gordon N. Mackenzie, "Ralph W. Tyler in Retrospect: Contributions to the Cur-riculum Field," *Journal of Thought* 21 (Spring 1986): 53.

60. Hollis L. Caswell, "Emergence of the Curriculum as a Field of Professional Work and Study," in Helen F. Robison (ed.), *Precedents and Promises in the Curricu-lum Field* (New York: Teachers College Press, 1966), pp. 2–3.

61. Ibid., pp. 1–11.

62. Mary Louise Seguel, *The Curriculum Field: Its Formative Years* (New York: Teachers College Press, 1966), p. 143.

63. Ibid., p. 144.

64. Ibid., p. 147.

65. Caswell, op. cit., p. 10.

66. Hollis L. Caswell and Doak S. Campbell, *Curriculum Development* (New York: American Book, 1935), pp. 473–80.

67. Hollis L. Caswell, "Realities of Curriculum Change," *Educational Leadership* 36 (October 1978): 27–28.

68. Arthur T. Jersild, Robert L. Thorndike, and Bernard Goldman, "A Further Com-parison of Pupils in 'Activity' and 'Non-Activity' Schools," *Journal of Experimen-tal Education* 9 (June 1941): 308.

69. Arthur T. Jersild, Robert L. Thorndike, and Bernard Goldman, "An Evaluation of Aspects of the Activity Program in the New York City Elementary Schools," *Jour-nal of Experimental Education* 8 (December 1939): 206.

70. J. Wayne Wrightstone, *Appraisal of Newer Practices in Selected Public Schools* (New York: Teachers College Press, 1935).

71. Ibid., p. 116.

72. J. Harlan Shores, "A Critical Review of the Research in Elementary Curriculum Organization 1890–1949," *University of Illinois Bulletin* 47 (September 1949).

73. Betty Lindley and Ernest K. Lindley, *A New Deal for Youth* (New York: Viking, 1938), p. 218.

74. Ibid., p. xiii.

75. American Youth Commission, *Secondary Education for Youth in Modern America* (Washington, D.C.: American Council on Education, 1937).

76. Educational Policies Commission, *The Purpose of Education in American De-mocracy* (Washington, D.C.: National Education Association, 1938).

77. Educational Policies Commission, *The Structure and Administration of Educa-tion in an American Democracy* (Washington, D.C.: National Education Associa-tion, 1938), p. 30.

78. Ruth E. Eckert and Thomas O. Marshall, *When Youth Leave School: The Regents' Inquiry* (New York: McGraw-Hill, 1938).

79. Ibid., p. 310.

80. Educational Policies Commission, *Education for ALL American Youth* (Washington, D.C.: National Education Association, 1944); Educational Policies Commission, *Educational Services for Young Children* (Washington, D.C.: National Education Association, 1945); Educational Policies Commission, *Education for ALL American Children* (Washington, D.C.: 1948).

81. Ibid., p. 100.

82. Ibid., p. 115.

83. Educational Policies Commission, *Education for ALL American Youth,* op. cit., pp. 225–26.

84. Cremin, op. cit., p. 332.

85. Manly Fleischmann, *Report of the New York State Commission on the Quality, Cost and Financing of Elementary and Secondary Education* (New York State: The Commission, 1972), Chap. 7, p. 6.

86. Ernest L. Boyer, *High School: A Report on Secondary Education in America* (New York: Harper & Row, 1983), p. 79.

87. Murry R. Nelson, "Issues of Access to Knowledge: Dropping Out of School," Chapter 10 in *Critical Issues in Curriculum,* Eighty-seventh Yearbook, National Society for the Study of Education, (Chicago: University of Chicago Press, 1988), pp. 226–43.

88. Charles S. Farrell, "Quality of Teaching in Vocational Education Needs Improvement, U.S. Science Panel Says," *The Chronicle of Higher Education,* September 28, 1983, p. 14.

89. U.S. Office of Education, *Life Adjustment Education for Every Youth,* Bulletin No. 22 (Washington, D.C.: U.S. Government Printing Office, 1951), pp. 15–16.

90. Ibid., p. 17.

91. U.S. Office of Education, *Vitalizing Secondary Education: Report of the First Commission on Life Adjustment Education for Youth* (Washington, D.C.: U.S. Government Printing Office, 1951), pp. 32–33.

92. Hilda Taba, "Progressive Education—What Now?," *Progressive Education* 11 (March 1934): 166.

93. Florence B. Stratemeyer et al., *Developing a Curriculum for Modern Living* (New York: Teachers College Press, 1947).

94. Ibid., p. 337.

95. B. Othanel Smith, William O. Stanley, and J. Harlan Shores, *Fundamentals of Curriculum Development* (New York: Harcourt Brace, 1950).

96. See Robert C. Morris, "The Right-Wing Critics of Education: Yesterday and Today," *Educational Leadership* 35 (May 1978): 628.

97. Cremin, op. cit., p. 347.

98. Arthur Bestor, *The Restoration of Learning* (New York: Knopf, 1956).

99. Ibid., p. 63.

100. Ibid., p. 118.

101. Educational Policies Commission, *Education for ALL American Youth,* op. cit., p. 233.

102. Bestor, op. cit., p. 120.

103. Ibid., p. 117.

104. Richard Hofstadter, *Anti-intellectualism in American Life* (New York: Knopf, 1963), Chapter 13.

105. Ibid.

106. Ronald Podeschi and David Hackbarth, "The Cries for Excellence: Echoes from the Past," *The Educational Forum* 50 (Summer 1986): 430.

107. Report of the Harvard Committee, *General Education in a Free Society* (Cambridge, Mass.: Harvard University Press, 1945), pp. ix–x. Used by permission of Harvard Committee on General Education.

108. James E. McClellan, *Toward an Effective Critique of American Education* (Philadelphia: Lippincott, 1968), p. 99.

109. Report of the Harvard Committee, op. cit., pp. 54, 55.

110. Ibid., pp. viii–ix.

111. Ibid., p. 29.

112. James B. Conant, *Public Education and the Structure of American Society* (New York: Teachers College Press, 1945), p. 33.

113. McClellan, op. cit., p. 114.

114. James B. Conant, *The American High School Today* (New York: McGraw-Hill, 1959); *Slums and Suburbs* (New York: McGraw-Hill, 1961); *My Several Lives* (New York: Harper & Row, 1970).

115. Daniel Tanner, "Splitting Up the School System," *Phi Delta Kappan* 61 (Oct. 1979): 92–97.

SELECTED REFERENCES

Aikin, Wilford M. *The Story of the Eight-Year Study.* New York: Harper & Row, Publishers, 1942.

———. *Thirty Schools Tell Their Story.* New York: Harper & Row, 1942.

Association for Supervision and Curriculum Development. *A New Look at Progressive Education.* 1972 Yearbook. Washington, D.C.: National Education Association, 1972.

———. *Perspectives on Curriculum Development: 1776–1976.* 1976 Yearbook. Washington, D.C.: The Association, 1976.

Bestor, Arthur. *The Restoration of Learning.* New York: Knopf, 1956.

Bowers, C. A. *The Progressive Educator and the Depression: The Radical Years.* New York: Random House, 1969.

Butts, R. Freeman. *Public Education in the United States: From Revolution to Reform.* New York: Holt, Rinehart and Winston, 1978.

Chamberlain, Dean, et al. *Did They Succeed in College?* New York: Harper & Row, Publishers, 1942.

Childs, John L. *Education and the Philosophy of Experimentalism.* New York: Appleton-Century-Crofts, 1931.

Counts, George S. *Dare the School Build a New Social Order?* New York: John Day Co., 1932.

Cremin, Lawrence A. *The Transformation of the School.* New York: Knopf, 1961.

————. *American Education: The Metropolitan Experience 1876–1980.* New York: Harper & Row, 1988.

Educational Policies Commission. *Education for ALL American Children.* Washington, D.C.: National Education Association, 1948.

————. *Education for ALL American Youth—A Further Look.* Washington, D.C.: National Education Association, 1952.

Giles, H. H.; McCutchen, S. P.; and Zechiel, A. N. *Exploring the Curriculum.* New York: Harper & Row, 1942.

Graham, Patricia A. *Progressive Education: From Arcady to Academe: A History of the Progressive Education Association.* New York: Teachers College Press, 1967.

Hofstadter, Richard. *Anti-intellectualism in American Life.* New York: Knopf, 1962.

Kilpatrick, William, ed. *The Educational Frontier.* New York: Appleton-Century-Crofts, 1933.

Kirst, Michael. *Who Controls Our Schools?* New York: Freeman, 1985.

Lazerson, Marvin. *American Education in the Twentieth Century: A Documentary History.* New York: Teachers College Press, 1987.

Lazerson, Marvin; McLaughlin, Judith Block; McPherson, Bruce; and Bailey, Stephen K. *An Education of Values: The Purposes and Practices of Schools.* New York: Cambridge University Press, 1985.

National Society for the Study of Education. *Child Development and the Curriculum.* Thirty-eighth Yearbook, Part I. Chicago: University of Chicago Press, 1939.

————. *American Education in the Postwar Period: Curriculum Reconstruction.* Forty-fourth Yearbook, Part I. Chicago: University of Chicago Press, 1945.

————. *The Curriculum: Retrospect and Prospect.* Seventieth Yearbook, Part I. Chicago: University of Chicago Press, 1971.

————. *Critical Issues in Curriculum.* Eighty-seventh Yearbook, Part I. Chicago: University of Chicago Press, 1988.

Report of the Harvard Committee. *General Education in a Free Society.* Cambridge, Mass.: Harvard University Press, 1945.

Seguel, Mary Louise. *The Curriculum Field: Its Formative Years.* New York: Teachers College Press, 1966.

Smith, B. Othanel; Stanley, William O.; and Shores, J. Harlan. *Fundamentals of Curriculum Development.* New York: Harcourt Brace Jovanovich, 1950.

Smith, Eugene, and Tyler, Ralph W. *Appraising and Recording Student Progress.* New York: Harper & Row, 1942.

Stratemeyer, Florence, et al. *Developing a Curriculum for Modern Living.* New York: Teachers College Press, 1947.

Tanner, Daniel. *Secondary Curriculum: Theory and Development.* New York: Macmillan, 1971.

————. *Secondary Education: Perspectives and Prospects.* New York: Macmillan, 1972.

6

The Curriculum Legacy

According to Cremin, the progressive education movement "became a victim of its own success. Much of what it preached was simply incorporated into the schools at large."[1] Thus, as indicated in the previous chapter, although progressive education collapsed as an organized movement, it left a curriculum legacy. Which ideas of reformers still live in the curriculum? What curriculum questions wrestled with by reformers for more than a century still remain unanswered? (For this, too, is part of the legacy.) The progressive education movement is now—and has been—undergoing a searching reappraisal, one which will surely continue over the final years of the twentieth century. What is the significance of this reappraisal for the school curriculum? These questions form the basis for discussion in this chapter on the curriculum legacy.

LEARNING AS INQUIRY

It will be recalled from the discussion in Chapter 2 that the intellectual revolution of the seventeenth and eighteenth centuries, from which the inductive method of science emerged, generated a new conception of educational method. This was the theory that one learns best from direct observation and experience. Object teaching was a nineteenth-century educational reform based on this idea. Although proponents of object teaching tended to view it as a kind of reading readiness exercise for young children (improving observation and expression), the method contained some of the elements of inductive science: careful observation, the collection of data based on observation, and generalization based on observed relationships among cases. Wesley observed that whether or not nineteenth-century American scientists knew anything about Pestalozzi and his object teaching, their method was indeed similar.[2]

As shown in Chapter 3, Parker's Quincy system, a program that in the 1870s generated much pedagogical excitement, stressed observation, description, and generalization. Geography, nature study, and arithmetic were taught inductively. In their laboratory school at the University of Chicago, the Deweys sought to develop in children a "habit of considering problems."[3] In discussing the rationale for curriculum development for the school, Dewey emphasized the difference between the superficial attention paid by a child to subject matter when he or she is told to attend in order to learn, and *reflective* attention—judging, considering, and deliberating. The latter was possible only when the child had a question of his or her own; self-directing curiosity was a necessary condition for developing intellectual methods of inquiry. Dewey believed that the process goal of problem-solving was better suited to individual and societal needs than the traditional goal of acquiring knowledge through memorization. For Dewey, the main objective of education was social power and insight. A truly educated individual had the ability to meet social problems with considered (as opposed to impulsive) action. Thus, the ultimate goal of developing the child's natural desire to understand into disciplined methods of inquiry was social progress. Dewey's ideas on reflective thinking were systematized into a method in 1910.[4] Grounded in a social framework, Dewey's conception of educational method was based on the idea that thinking is problem-solving.

The point is that whatever the prevailing fashion, the idea of learning as inquiry still lives in the curriculum.

Reasonable Learning

The deceptively simple idea that learning must be reasonable was one of the tenets of experimentalist curriculum reform. Dewey saw a pedagogical defect in object teaching missed by other critics of this method. (See the discussion in Chapter 2.) In *Democracy and Education,* Dewey argued that object teaching was based on the fallacious premise that the properties of an object had to be known before it could be intelligently used; thus object teaching always began with the elements of an object and proceeded to the whole.[5] This was a misapplication of the principle that learning must begin with the simple and proceed to the complex. The *use* of the object was the simple thing, said Dewey, and he gave an illustration—a kite. Certainly the properties of a kite involved size, proportion of parts, and angles, but so what? The important thing was the individual's purpose—the use one intended to make of the object. "*After* one has gone through the process, the constituent qualities and relations are *elements,* each possessed with a definite meaning of its own. The false notion referred to takes the standpoint of the expert, the one for whom elements exist; isolates them from purposeful action, and presents them to beginners as the 'simple' thing."[6] What Dewey was saying was that one does not always learn best by starting with component parts. Learning must, above all, be reasonable. Beginning with the kite and what is done with it is, to say the least, more reasonable and natural than starting with wood, string, and angles. Dewey's point was destined to become part of the curriculum legacy. In traditional education, learning was seldom natural or reasonable. What Dewey was also saying was that the inductive method is not always the best approach to learning.

The method of beginning with the whole and proceeding to the component parts is upheld by gestalt theory. Whole-part teaching is generally supported by the findings of research. Nevertheless, as noted by Foshay, the whole-part-part-whole controversy still rages on as if there were no generalization to follow.[7] As an example, Foshay points to the tendency of elementary schools to consider subject areas as sets of skills to be mastered—as parts, not wholes. History becomes dates, reading becomes phonics, writing becomes spelling and grammar. Parts are easy to evaluate, but there is a price to be paid for the fragmentation: The learner is denied a vision of the whole, and learning becomes less than reasonable. Foshay recommends that children be given frequent overviews of schooling, so they know what they should be able to do when they complete it and so that a view of the whole is always before them.[8]

For learning to be reasonable, it must appear to the student to have a purpose: It must make sense. Not surprisingly, some educational critics remain uncommitted to this principle. For example, Hirsch argues that to insist that learning materials make sense undermines the teaching of traditional knowledge to children. In Hirsch's words, "children take great joy in learning vaguely understood information that will only later be fully meaningful to them."[9] This was the very idea that Dewey pilloried in *Democracy and Education*. "Since life means growth," he wrote, a *"living creature lives just as truly and positively at one stage as at another, with the same intrinsic fullness and the same absolute claims."*[10] Recent research bears Dewey out: Children often are caused debilitating distress, not joy, by the failure to understand.[11]

Related to the foregoing, Goodlad found in his study of American education that a substantial proportion of students did not know what they were supposed to be doing in class (did not understand the bases for errors in their work or the teacher's instructions).[12] Clearly, although the principle that learning must be reasonable is part of the curriculum legacy, unreasonable learning is still part of the curriculum.

The Progressivists and Problem-Solving

The close association of experimentalism with social evolution was discussed in Chapter 5. For Dewey, the experimental method applied to social problems was the only guarantee of social evolution—of a society that was both humane and harmonious.

In the elementary school, progressivists attempted to implement the Deweyan ideal of active inquiry through units, activities, and projects. Field trips, excursions, observation, and discussion were absorbed into the school.

Because the progressivists saw education as inquiry, the scope of the school broadened immeasurably. Unit teaching in the elementary school weathered a storm of essentialist criticism that lasted for nearly two decades. No matter how thunderous the critics' demands for a return to mental discipline, elementary pedagogical theory continued to stress the conception of learning as investigation. However, in the social studies, as group inquiry became formalized into a method, the goal of learning to solve problems through reflective thinking tended to become subservient to the goal of developing social skills. In no small way, the stream of influence from the group process movement all but drowned out the original objective. Moreover, the elementary school never really saw itself as an instrument for social reform. How the elementary school saw its mission in this regard was discussed in some detail in the previous chapter.

In the 1930s, the secondary school became concerned with helping students to think intelligently about social problems. Although educational theory had long stressed that the ability to solve social problems was absolutely necessary in a democracy, it was not until the onset of the Great Depression that this objective was considered with any urgency. Since social problems rarely fall within one subject field, teaching problem-solving led quite naturally to the development of the problem-focused core curriculum.

Of profound importance is the fact that schools participating in the Progressive Education Association's famous Eight-Year Study viewed problem-solving as a total process beginning with the definition of the problem and ending with action, that is, implementing the decision. More is said about this shortly, when we examine contemporary approaches to teaching social problem-solving.

The thinking process was labeled variously as *problem-solving, critical thinking, reflective thinking, intelligent thinking, functional thinking,* and *scientific thinking* by teachers in the Eight-Year Study.[13] It was demonstrated by the study that in teaching problem-solving the best results were obtained when all teachers in the school agreed on the approaches involved and the language used in defining the process. It was believed that Dewey's complete act of thought was a paradigm for thinking in all subject domains when knowledge is addressed to social problems.

In recent years we have come to realize that each discipline has its own modes of inquiry and system of thought (although many processes of inquiry are not the unique function of a given discipline). When teaching social problem-solving, however, we are concerned with the application of knowledge, not the conceptual scheme that determines the process of investigation in a given discipline. Theoretical concepts from mathematics, science, political science, and the like are connected in application. Moreover, social problem-solving is approached on an interdisciplinary basis; hence Dewey's paradigm for reflective thinking (which he intended for social problem-solving) is appropriate. In a problem-centered interdisciplinary course, teachers from the disciplines involved must agree on the operational procedures in problem-solving as well as the semantics used in describing the process.

As indicated in Chapter 5, widespread criticism, McCarthyism, and an emphasis on the discrete disciplines during the late 1950s and early 1960s effectively dispatched progressive educators' efforts to teach social problem-solving. Nevertheless, the idea that the school has a responsibility for teaching pupils to deal with social problems remained as part of the curriculum legacy. During the late 1980s, new science curricula were being introduced, revealing the interfaces of science and society.

Before leaving this section on the progressivists and problem-solving, it is important to emphasize that many teachers followed the Deweyan ideal of encouraging children to identify problems of interest to them and of importance to their community. Along the lines of experimentalism, the children planned, executed, and evaluated solutions. The damning by the critics and the failure of teachers to write about these undertakings have obscured the fact that many projects were of great value—both as learning experiences and as contributions to society.

As La Brant observed, it is paradoxical that the new education became associated with a lack of responsibility when developing social responsibility was an important progressivist goal.[14] In one project mentioned by La Brant, junior-high-school students were able to persuade the city fathers in their town to extend the sewage system to a disadvantaged area. Commenting on the learning outcomes of such projects, La Brant said:

> The formulation of questions came directly from the students, and the resulting work offered them not only development of specific skills in reading, writing, numbers, and social responsibility, but gave them the additional highly important experience of thinking critically (on their mental level) about what they had accomplished and how one goes about learning anything.[15]

Developing social responsibility continues to be a fundamental curricular goal. Although it is rooted in the position taken by Rugg, Counts, and other theoreticians in the 1920s that the curriculum must reflect the needs of society, it is also traceable to personality theory. (According to the latter, desirable self-development requires participation with others in the realization of social goals.)

Discovery Learning

During the late 1950s and the early 1960s, "how scientists work" again provided a model for curriculum developers; but this time the model was discipline-focused, not social problem–focused. Discovery teaching (which has many enthusiastic adherents) was a disciplinary effort to teach children to think like scientists instead of children. It was thought that the thrill of discovering a scientific concept autonomously would not only result in more

effective learning but also instill in children the desire for further, more significant discoveries. (The main goal of learning during this period in our
educational history was national supremacy in scientific fields rather than
personal-social development.)

Most inquiry-discovery courses follow the "inductive approach," in
which the student induces abstractions or generalizations from specific cases.
Thus, inquiry is equated with induction. The implication is that discovery
cannot occur deductively, that is, when the teacher or student begins with a
generalization and inquires into the specific cases, applications, and interpretations for which the generalization is valid—possibly even arriving at new
generalizations. In the literature on discovery, deductive strategies have been
equated with didactic or receptive teaching, in which the rule or generalization is presented by the teacher, who also gives an example followed by
problems for students to solve mechanically by the rule. As indicated previously, this is one way to teach deductively but not the only way. The deductive method can involve inquiry and discovery.

A Disciplinary Approach.   Unlike the advocates of teaching problem-
solving during the 1930s, proponents of learning as inquiry in the 1960s emphasized that the inquiry process differs from subject to subject.[16]

This idea clashed head-on with strong claims that learning the heuristics of discovery results in general problem-solving ability. Bruner, for example, maintained that learning the "fundamental structure" of a discipline (all
the better if learned through discovery) enables the individual to solve all
sorts of problems.[17] Yet, as discussed in Chapter 4, the research on transfer
did not support Bruner's contention. According to this research, if we expect
students to be able to solve social problems, we should provide them with
direct experience in solving social problems. It should also be noted that
Bruner's claim was never substantiated by the research on discovery.

Theoretical Issues.   Bruner stated the foregoing claim for transfer as
a contention. In an article published a year later he was more cautious, hy-
pothesizing that four benefits derive from discovery learning: intellectual
power, intrinsic motivation, the learning of heuristics to solve problems, and
memory processing.[18] He suggested that this hypothesis be tested in the
schools. It never was.

According to Kagan, the discovery approach requires more involvement by the learner and results, therefore, in his or her giving maximal attention to a task.[19] This argument is similar to Dewey's preference for "reflective" attention over externally imposed attention. Additional advantages cited
by Kagan for discovery learning are that the task becomes more valuable to
the learner because of the intellectual effort expended, a growing expectancy
by the learner that he or she can solve intellectual problems autonomously,
and freedom from depending on the teacher.

Nevertheless, pointed out Kagan, there were some compelling arguments against the discovery method. Impulsive children are at a disadvantage: They make more errors in the inferential method than reflective children. Less-motivated children are also at a disadvantage: They are apt to lose interest in the task if they are not immediately successful. Last, but not least, are the developmental factors. We must ask ourselves what a child is capable of learning at a given stage of development because intellectual growth is a developmental process. Hence seven-year-olds may not have learned the meaning of a problem. Eight-year-olds do not, as a rule, stay within the constraints of a problem. Dewey (and later Piaget) had pointed out that the heuristic style of the child is qualitatively different from that of the mature scholar. Yet such findings were ignored during the era of disciplinary curriculum reform.

The classic argument against the discovery method was by Wittrock: Discovery takes time.[20] The remarkable thing about race experience, said Wittrock, is that everyone need not discover everything anew; it is all recorded in language, and one can (and should) profit from these records of the experiences of others. This argument is strikingly similar to one made in 1880 by William T. Harris against laboratory teaching. (See Chapter 3.) A most important conceptual issue discussed by Wittrock was the equating of discovery learning with induction. Said Wittrock:

> It is just as plausible to assume that the learner begins with a higher order generalization, from which he derives specific conclusions and thus discovers answers and even generalizations. That is, there are probably several different processes involved in discovery. Induction has no exclusive identity with discovery learning.[21]

Oddly, educational theorists have continued to identify discovery learning exclusively with induction. Deduction is identified with verbalism and rote learning. Be that as it may, as Cronbach points out, "In any course, induction can develop only a fraction of what is to be taught."[22]

The excitement about discipline-centered discovery methods soon faded from the educational literature, along with interest in the idea of "structure of a discipline." A modicum of attention is given to discovery learning in the *Handbook of Research on Teaching,* and there is no hint of the fascination that once surrounded "learning by discovery."[23] Unfortunately that belongs to history and history alone, for as Cronbach observed in the late 1970s, "The research has not come to grips with the problem of combining inductive and expository modes in a curriculum sequence."[24] Such research is still badly needed. We need to know more about the great range of approaches to the curriculum and how these approaches interact and become transformed into the working power of intelligence.

Discovery Learning and Operant Conditioning. It is of considerable interest that discovery learning is incompatible with operant conditioning. Proponents of conditioning-extinction theories view learning as a matter of the reinforcement of correct responses, the minimizing of errors, and the extinction of incorrect responses. On the other hand, if the learner is allowed to engage in finding things out for himself or herself, he or she will inevitably make mistakes.[25] Although mistakes can be fruitful in learning, behaviorists contend that to allow the learner to make mistakes may serve to "reinforce" errors. Hence, proponents of conditioning-extinction theories are at theoretical loggerheads with those who believe that learners can profit from their mistakes.

The incompatibility between self-discovery and conditioning theories is important because it once again demonstrates the futility of discussing means without objectives. If the educator is more concerned with the student's long-range development of insight than the mastery of a single mechanical skill, the incompatibility between self-discovery and operant conditioning will not be an issue.

Teachers as Inquirers. As Victor E. Weisskopf, a physicist, tells science and mathematics teachers, science is not a collection of facts and correct answers. It is curiosity, discovering things, and asking why is it so. The teacher's curiosity must stay alive if the student's excitement is to stay alive.[26] And as Henrietta Schwartz observes, the "same may be said about any domain of knowledge, not just science."[27]

The teacher's curiosity could not be expected to stay alive if teachers were regarded as technicians—deliverers of a tamper-proof curriculum—yet this was exactly what happened. A striking contradiction of the discipline-centered curriculum reform movement of the 1950s and 1960s was that the curriculum packages were to be teacher-proof while teachers were to use discovery methods in the classroom. Teachers were left out of the process of developing and implementing the curriculum, yet they were expected to use the inquiry method in their teaching. They were not expected (or even permitted) to be curious or modify their teaching to suit particular conditions. As the present authors had noted, "How the learner was to become an inquirer when the teacher was to be regarded as a mere technician simply defied common sense."[28] In the perspective of history, it seems odd that the scholar specialists did not recognize the obvious—if we expect students to become inquirers, teachers must also be inquirers. These specialists only needed (like Weisskopf) to look at their own experience; they all had teacher-models who were inquirers, and they themselves, as teachers, had communicated the excitement of their own discoveries to their students.

Two Modes of Thought

As noted, proponents of discovery learning equated inquiry with induction. They cast aside admonitions such as this one by Shulman and Keislar: "justification of curriculum development which stresses inductive teaching on the ground that induction is the *sine qua non* of scientific behavior is a half-truth at best."[29] Scientists deduct as well as induct, and even engage in didactic and receptive activities. What they do depends on their objectives in a particular situation. Therefore, the induction model of scientific behavior, so popular in the 1960s, was based on a romantic fiction. But the larger, more important question still lay in the realm of objectives and priorities. Even granted the validity of Bruner's assertion that the "schoolboy learning physics *is* a physicist,"[30] although this certainly is not borne out by the research in child development (Piagetian theory, for instance), this does not answer the question of what the schoolboy *should* be taught.

Returning to the question of inductive and deductive teaching, it is of importance and interest that the philosophy of learning based on induction began to develop in the seventeenth and eighteenth centuries with the inductive method of science. The latter was indeed a revolution in the way of acquiring knowledge. Traditionally, the intellectual method of the Western world had been to begin with a generalization or major premise from accepted (religious) authorities, and then deduce a logical conclusion. This was the deductive method of Aristotle adopted by Scholasticism. In the seventeenth century, Francis Bacon attacked this method of arriving at truth as having no relation whatsoever to real experience and being a mere linguistic exercise.

The new philosophy of learning that took form with the inductive method of science associated the deductive method with playing around with words and regarded it as a closed system of thought. For inductive science was nothing less than a revolution, a breaking away from a system of thought—Aristotelian and Scholastic deductive methods—that had shackled men's minds for centuries. The distrust of deduction has persisted to this day, despite the fact that we think both deductively and inductively. The situation is analogous to the public distrust of a strong central government that dates back to colonial times. We no longer fear the tyranny of the British crown, but the suspicion of a powerful central government persists nonetheless.

Conant pointed out that the so-called scientific method is a misnomer. Scientific knowledge has not advanced from a single method. "One can safely say," wrote Conant, "that the natural sciences as they stand today are the result of the careful use of the *empirical-inductive* method of inquiry together with the imaginative use of the *theoretical-deductive*."[31] The creator of a theory, a broad conceptual scheme (which began, of course, as a hypothesis), is following the theoretical-deductive mode of inquiry. Most of the striking advances in science have been generated by the theoretical-deductive method of inquiry. According to Conant, "The greatest scientists can and have used both modes of thought; the empirical-inductive is by itself insufficient to generate advances in scientific theory."[32]

Two points made by Conant have important implications for the curriculum. First, both modes of thought are valid and both are needed in problem-solving. "Just as a man needs two legs to walk on, the social sciences need two types of thinkers, if the advance is, as it should be, to meet the needs of a free and highly industrialized society."[33] The second point is that the notion that scientific knowledge today is the result of the interconnection of generalizations arrived at by the empirical-inductive method is false. In general, curriculum developers of the 1960s labored under the misconception that there exists a single scientific method known as the "inductive approach." Nor is there evidence to indicate that the curriculum field is moving toward a recognition of the validity of theoretical-deductive thinking. With a few exceptions, most curriculum textbooks continue to equate discovery learning with the inductive method.

New Theoretical Bases

Deeply rooted in the philosophy of John Dewey, the idea of learning as inquiry has never left the educational literature. A corollary of this idea is that learning must be self-directed. In recent years, educators have found three new theoretical bases to support these ideas: (1) the work of Piaget and his associates, which makes it clear that the child plays an active role in his or her own intellectual development and that direct experience is essential for the development of intelligence, (2) research on the education of the disadvantaged that points to the importance for school achievement of an environment fostering self-impelled inquiry, and (3) the work of Bloom and his collaborators, which defined higher-level cognitive objectives as those involving the development of thinking processes rather than simple recall.[34]

These theoretical ideas have resulted in new thinking about curriculum and teaching. Taba, for example, focused attention on the development of teaching strategies for fostering skills of autonomous thinking. She found that teacher behavior has an enormous influence on the development of pupils' thought patterns. Taba developed an in-service teacher education program based on the idea that an individual's thinking effectiveness depends greatly on the nature of the thinking experiences he or she has had. The goal of the program is to train teachers to gear their behavior and specific curriculum content to the development of productive and autonomous thinking. Although the program focuses on the inductive discovery of generalizations, the application of generalizations to new phenomena is also emphasized.[35]

Principle Versus Practice in Inquiry Teaching

In the 1970s and 1980s, despite powerful pressures loosed on the schools to return to "the basics," many educators continued to believe that inquiry learning is at the heart of education. In the social studies and history, for example, these educators rejected unequivocally any demand that there be a return to traditional approaches and the memorization of events, facts, and dates.[36] Nevertheless, although teachers believe in inquiry in principle, practice is another matter entirely. As Morrissett reports about the history classroom, teachers typically rely on classroom lectures coupled with regurgitative reading assignments from the textbook.[37] The history of inquiry methods in history classrooms is a sad but familiar tale: "Although popular during the 1960s, the (inquiry) approach appears to have lost momentum during the past two decades."[38]

Science teachers also continue to emphasize the importance of an inquiry-based approach. Yet, as in the social studies, the development of inquiry skills in students has fallen far short of expectation. As four scholars noted in the 1980s, "For many years, the science education community has advocated the development of inquiry skills as an essential outcome of science instruction and for an equal number of years science educators have met with frustration and disappointment."[39] It is not that science teachers believe less in inquiry teaching. Indeed, in his longitudinal study of biology teachers' attitudes toward inquiry, Tamir found that over a ten-year period their attitude toward learning by inquiry had been strengthened.[40]

Yet there is, willy-nilly, a discrepancy between belief and practice. According to Welch and his colleagues, the reasons appear to reside in the pressure felt by teachers to teach facts—"things which show up in tests"—and in the nature of the teacher education and supervision that they receive. "Many teachers are ill-prepared, in their eyes and in the eyes of others, to guide students in inquiry learning, and over one-third feel they receive inadequate support for such teaching."[41]

In the late 1980s there was much interest in "teaching thinking" (in no small way stemming from the recommendations of a rash of national reports on education). However, the approach taken in most "thinking skills programs" was generally not the inquiry process, in which students begin by identifying a problem, but skills taught in isolation. For example, students are asked a question which they must answer, substantiating their conclusion. The ability to identify conclusions and supporting statements is an important higher-order educational objective, but it in no way should be confused with knowing how to use the inquiry process.

As Paul Hurd and his colleagues observe, "what a given teacher, believes, knows and does will determine the form science education will take for a given student."[42] The same may be said about all curriculum areas. A teacher knows and often does what is deemed important by teacher educators and supervisors. The problem of implementing the idea of learning as inquiry is multifaceted, yet there are classrooms in which the idea has leaped from the literature into real practice.

Scientific inquiry is the method of gaining knowledge and transforming it into working power. Inquiry as a mode of instruction —especially inquiry that is concerned with problems of significance to the life of the learner and to the wider society—can never become out of date. As noted earlier, the inquiry approach taken in the national curriculum-reform projects of the late 1950s and the 1960s neglected the nature of the learner and instead fashioned the curriculum in line with the narrow concerns of university scholar specialists in the separate disciplines. General education and interdisciplinary studies were neglected. The Deweyan problem method or method of intelligence, engaging the learner in problem-solving of personal and social significance, was never implemented during the era of discipline-centered curriculum reform (the 1950s and 1960s). In contrast, the leading experimental schools in the Eight-Year Study, such as the laboratory school at Ohio State University and the Lincoln School, utilized the Deweyan problem method in addressing the concerns of youth and the problems of society to meet the function of general education. But during the 1950s and 1960s, the application of knowledge was neglected in favor of specialized theoretical knowledge.

Finally, not only did the teacher-proof curricula of the national discipline-centered projects of the 1950s and 1960s mitigate against inquiry learning, but virtually every project claimed that it was inquiry-based regardless of orientation and implementation. Inquiry-discovery learning became a cliché for selling curriculum packages and, with few exceptions, systematic and independent research and evaluation were avoided as the projects were promoted through the authoritative testimonials of university scholar-specialists who developed the disciplinary curriculum packages.

Social Forces and Problem-Solving

In the late 1960s the public-school curriculum came under fire for lack of "relevance." The disciplinary reforms of the late 1950s and 1960s had removed the curriculum in the sciences and mathematics far from human problems and concerns and into the realm of the research scholar. "Disciplinarity" was the password in curriculum reform. A reaction was not long in coming. Throughout the 1960s enrollments in physics plummeted. Many young people turned to the social sciences and humanities, searching for educational experiences that would bring them into touch with the "real world."

There was no doubt that the demand for relevance in the curriculum was a result of social forces. The society itself was rife with protest, demonstrations, and demands. A closer look showed that there were symptoms of what some called a "sick society." Almost overnight people who had been bypassed by our society, those whom Michael Harrington called the "invisible" poor, shot into visibility. These were the people of Appalachia, the migrant worker, the urban poor. Poverty, racial discrimination, and the spoiling of our environment reemerged as popular issues. Idealistic youth demanded not only a more "relevant" curriculum but also means by which they could become involved in combating social ills and making a better world.

For the second time in a half century, liberal educators wrestled with the ideal of making the bounds of life the bounds of the curriculum. The new curriculum password was "relevance."

Road to "Relevance." Means adopted by the public schools and colleges to make the curriculum more relevant were legion: special projects, mini-courses, alternative schools, external programs, contracts, individualized curricula, the revision of existing courses and the development of new ones. Some of the major curriculum reform projects in undergoing revision added topics that were related to social problems. But these changes were nothing comparable to the post-*Sputnik* reforms. When the relevance crisis happened, the era of massive federal funding was over.

In general, there was a threefold approach to a more relevant curriculum: (1) adding to existing courses topics of concern to children and youth (such as environmental protection, drug addiction, and the meaning of the law); (2) providing educational "alternatives" as a response to the demand for freedom of choice (ranging from the choice of a school with a given curricular focus to a smorgasbord of electives at the secondary-school level to allowing elementary-school pupils to study what interests them); and (3) including in the curriculum out-of-school activities of a social-service nature.

The curriculum itself never underwent any coherent reconstruction. Efforts to relate subject matter to student interests were largely of an ad hoc nature, leaving the individual disciplines and subjects intact. Many of the ad hoc changes had a fragmentary and temporal quality that was disturbing to educators who sought substantive reconstruction of the curriculum in the light of pervading social problems. Mini-courses and other peripheral innovations could be wiped out at a moment's notice—and were, with the shift to a skills model of education in the late 1970s.

The idea that education must be related to real life, which received its most influential formulation from Dewey, is part of the curriculum legacy. Nevertheless, as Foshay has observed, the question of how this should be done is one of the persistent problems of the curriculum field.[43]

Although fundamental curriculum change requires that the curriculum be examined as a whole, educators have approached the job of relating knowledge to life on a piecemeal basis. The piecemeal approach to curriculum development is one of the critical issues in curriculum and also part of the legacy.

Activism Versus Considered Action. In the late 1960s educators were criticized for failing to gear their curricula to social problems. Despite surface similarities, their response to such criticisms was very different from the response of educators in the 1930s. As a result of the emphasis on disciplinarity, inquiry had been divorced from action. In the educational literature the term *inquiry* had come to be associated with theoretical constructs in science or mathematics rather than social problem-solving. This kind of thinking all but obliterated the concept of inquiry as a necessary concomitant of social problem-solving.

Activism replaced problem-solving based on reflective thinking. It is not difficult to see how this came about. For one thing, as just mentioned, inquiry under the disciplinary principle became linked with the production of theoretical knowledge rather than social problem-solving. A second reason was that activism was the approach to alleviating peoples' problems in the larger society. Another stream of influence that was central was the affective-existential stream, which values "acting on feeling" rather than "acting on thinking."

Dewey repeatedly warned that action without thinking is as bad as thinking without action. In problem-solving, action must be directed by a leading idea. Otherwise, "intellectually it leads nowhere," said Dewey. "It does not provide knowledge about the situations in which action occurs nor does it lead to clarification and expansion of ideas."[44] When students are stirred by a social problem and want to be involved in its correction, they have the self-directing interest that can lead into action of value to the community and themselves. The next steps, which involve the gathering of relevant facts, the formulation of a plan of action, execution of the plan, and evaluation, are crucial if action is to be intelligent action. When schools encourage children and youth to "be involved" but do not teach problem-solving as a total process, they are missing out on the supreme challenge to education in a free society.

In the late 1970s activism in the larger society subsided into a do-your-own-thing situation ethic. Some scholars believe that Watergate and other events in recent years disillusioned many activists of the 1960s, leading them to give up on societal improvement and focus on self-improvement. The trend in the larger society toward looking inward was reflected in the curriculum; self-gratification was the theme of "values clarification," a widely used method of moral education in the schools.[45] Meanwhile, not surprisingly, interest in teaching social problem-solving declined.

A counterswing of the pendulum was inevitable. The result was a wave of school reform focused on tests and numbers. As in the 1960s, the slogans for reform were nationalistic: Schools were urged to raise test scores so that bright students could guard us from the twin threats of Japanese economic competition and Soviet missiles.

Without fundamental reconstruction the curriculum will, just as inevitably, remain vulnerable to succeeding fads and fashions.[46] The legacy showed educators that they needed to build on previous knowledge with an ever-increasing effectiveness, not follow fads. Yet they have not learned this.

INTEREST AND MOTIVATION

Basic to the idea that learning should be self-directed is the theory of interest in education. The Deweyan concept that the learner must be interested in the learning task if he or she is to learn remains vital in educational theory. Viewed broadly, the concept itself has survived, indeed flourished. There are, however, any number of interpretations. To many educators, interest is something added to subject matter; one can, for example, introduce an elementary social studies unit on Hawaii by bringing in a hula skirt to show the class—thereby "interesting" potentially uninterested children. (This is referred to in the literature as the "motivation" for a lesson.)

Dewey had nothing good to say about efforts to "attach some form of seductiveness to material otherwise indifferent." This, he said, was "soft" pedagogy.[47] As discussed in previous chapters, Dewey's conception of interest was materials and methods that were vitally connected with the learner's purposes and present powers. If material had to be made interesting, it meant one of two things: Either it was unrelated to the learner's present life or the relationship was there but the teacher had not seen it. Dewey took an uncordial view of rewards, punishments, and artificial inducements as motivational devices. Being a pragmatist, he thought it just good sense to make the connection between the pupil's present interests and abilities and the teacher's goals. If this worked, there was no need for coercion or artificial inducements. If it did not work, the child's powers should be explored for clues to other approaches that would work.

According to Taba, a "more reasonable" approach than Dewey's to following the criterion of interests is to take advantage of students' interests in what is taught. Not to do so "means overlooking potent motivation and courting the possibility of ineffective learning."[48] It is difficult to see how this is more reasonable or different from Dewey's approach. At bottom, both said that it is foolish not to make a connection that exists between the interests and goals of the learner and the educational goal. As good teachers know from experience, Dewey and Taba are right. Nevertheless, the teacher must also plan for the building of new interests. Theoretical discussions about interests somehow seem to center on the use of existing interests in meeting educational objectives rather than the goal of stimulating and developing new interests.

In accord with the findings of the experimentalists during the early decades of the twentieth century, recent research supports intrinsic motivation over extrinsic motivation or positive reinforcement through external rewards as advocated by the behaviorists. Students working for external rewards (positive reinforcement) are found to be more concerned with getting the right answers quickly, whereas students intrinsically motivated tend to engage in deeper, more meaningful approaches and to be more independent in their learning.[49]

Although educational theory favors intrinsic motivation (the student's present purposes and goals) over extrinsic motivation (artificial inducements and, to use Dewey's words, "bribes of pleasure"), practice generally follows the latter. One might well ponder why. First, taking advantage of the learner's interests requires knowing what they are and where they are. This is, of course, a prior condition for individualizing instruction. Many teachers take the path of least resistance, which is to add something of interest (the same something for everyone) to subject matter in order to make it palatable.

A second reason is that increasingly educational materials come in complete packages. Everything is included, including the motivation. Packaged learning materials make it difficult to follow Dewey's maxim of connecting materials with pupils' purposes and present powers.

Finally, there is the problem of teacher education. Although the idea of "personalizing" education is exalted in many educational methods courses, when it comes down to tactics, prospective teachers are given very little help or experience in how to get learners self-motivated.

Generally, there is little or no theoretical disagreement about the value of interest in learning. Research shows that learning is more efficient when learners are intrinsically interested. It also shows that many students have poor attitudes toward their classwork; in a word, they find it "boring." For example, in noting that national assessments of science education have shown that nearly one-third of high-school students find science class "often" or "always" boring, and teachers report that developing students' interest in science is a serious problem, Hamrick and Hardy found that by improving the curriculum, a school faculty can increase student interest and achievement. In an experimental study conducted by Hamrick and Harty involving sixth-grade general science students, the sequence of textbook chapters in the course was changed in order to establish interrelationships among major concepts for experimental students, who "exhibited significantly higher science achievement, significantly more positive attitudes toward science, and significantly greater interest in science" than the group for whom content was not resequenced.[50]

Learners as Choosers

Dewey continually stressed the link between doing and thinking. In the 1920s the advocates of the expression of immediate interests and impulses parted company with Dewey over this issue. They tended to believe that what the child learned was insignificant. What mattered was his or her interest in it. Their approach was emotional, whereas Dewey's was intellectual.

"Affective Education." In the early 1970s there was a resurgence of the idea that cognitive goals matter little; what really matters is the learner's feelings and emotions. Pupils' own feelings and emotions were exalted, if

not deified. It was said that learners cannot, and indeed, should not learn what others select for them as this is an imposition of the values and purposes of others on the individual. Thus, once again, to one group of theorists at least, the primary goals of learning were affective.

The emphasis in both the 1920s movement and the movement a half century later was emotional, and both stressed the idea that the most important learning has to do with the learner's felt problems. But where the progressivist believed that the individual's problems could be identified on the basis of his or her interests, the advocate of affective education takes a more direct route: getting children to express their feelings and talk about their problems. A final difference is that child centeredness in the 1920s was powerfully influenced by Freud's thinking, which stressed the danger of repression. The most profound influence on the affective-education movement, on the other hand, has been the philosophy of existentialism. Although there are many diverse threads in existentialist educational theory, they coalesce on one point: preoccupation with self.

The fundamental objectives in most schools today are cognitive, although nearly all good teachers try to make their pupils feel good about their efforts to learn and their successes in learning. Similarly, good teachers try to convey to a learner that despite a low evaluation of his or her academic achievement, they value him or her as a person. Nevertheless, the primary goal of good teachers is to help children learn, not to make them feel good. Interestingly enough, most schools that attempted to gear their educational programs primarily to affective goals were urban schools that had not learned to help educationally disadvantaged children develop cognitive skills.

The Selection of Learning Tasks.   An idea with deep roots in progressivist educational theory is that youngsters must be permitted to work on problems and tasks of interest to them. The principle of self-selection springs in no small measure from the democratic ideal that individuals shall be allowed to discover and develop their interests through responsible self-direction. Thus the school must provide opportunities for learners to explore possibilities.

The legacy holds that curriculum developers must not be torn by the child-versus-society orientations. The curriculum must embody both individual and societal goals. Hence some goals are chosen by learners and others are imposed by the adult society. If the school is to succeed, these two sets of goals must be formulated as complementary rather than conflicting.

Motivation: Conflicting Currents

As we have seen, the followers of Dewey eschewed artificial motivations. They believed that a learner is best motivated when material bears a close relationship with his or her experiences. This idea was in accord with the views of gestalt psychology.

The intense controversy over the behaviorist and gestaltist psychological outlooks was in full swing in the 1920s and 1930s. Central to the behaviorists' conception of learning was the process of conditioning: systematically changing the learner's environment to obtain desired responses. Because behaviorists believed that human behavior is not determined by purpose, they were not concerned with the learner's ideas, feelings, past experiences, or present interests. Clearly, the two streams of psychological thought that most influenced progressive pedagogy were gestalt or field theory and Freudianism. The latter stressed meeting pupils' basic needs and the careful diagnosis of the causes of learning and behavior problems.

Field Theory Versus Behaviorism.   Today there are two major positions in learning theory: reinforcement theory (operant conditioning) and cognitive-field theory. Reinforcement theory looks upon the learner as a detached intellect. Affective and social processes have no place in learning.[51] As indicated in previous chapters, the designer of an operant-conditioning curriculum is not concerned with the learner's interests or purpose. Because the theory is completely mechanical, learning objectives are a number of small tasks. Reinforcement theory avoids traffic with such objectives as creativity, problem solving, self-direction in learning, and personal autonomy.

Interestingly, cognitive-field theory has roots in gestalt theory, which was concerned with problem-solving processes. Although cognitive field theory focuses on intellective processes, it does emphasize affective goals and processes. Indeed, the key difference that emerged between gestalt and reinforcement theories is that purposes and motivations were viewed as important to learning by gestalt theorists because they believed the learner responds as a whole person, not automatically like a vending machine. Cognitive-field theory embraces this holistic conception of the learner.

Although the controversy over behaviorist and cognitive learning theories subsided during the 1940s and 1950s, it picked up momentum in the late 1960s and is today more bitter than ever. Some have suggested taking the best values of both theories and combining them. The question of "best values," however, remains at the heart of the conflict. Indeed, the two theories are so antithetical as to defy conciliation.

Contemporary studies on intellectual development support the progressivist view that motivation is in no small way a product of the learner's past experience. Bloom, for instance, stresses the importance for cognitive and affective functioning of environmental encounters in the early years.[52]

According to Atkinson's and Featherstone's theoretical construct, *approach-avoidance* motivation, a child's experiences will determine whether his or her school behavior is generally dominated by the motive to achieve or the motive to avoid failure.[53] Piagetian theory suggests the importance for intrinsic motivation of the infant's interaction with his or her environment—both inanimate objects and human beings. Infants must have human models to emulate for socialization and intellectual development.[54] A rich body of literature on the learning problems of disadvantaged children and youth points to the importance of experiential background for interest, purpose, and motivation.

The field theory view of the learner as a whole organism who responds as a whole to a whole situation received a boost by the War on Poverty of the 1960s. Poverty, incompetence, and lack of motivation for schooling were seen as interrelated. Moreover, Piagetian theory is at one with the field theorists, who define learning as a process by which the learner reorganizes his or her "field," his or her perceptual and psychological world. It is an accepted principle in medicine that one does not simply deal with an organ (the heart or lungs, for example) as though it is independent of the whole body. This buttresses the progressivist principle that one cannot deal with the child's mind in abstraction, as an entity apart from his or her body and his or her environment. The "whole child" is one of the most significant conceptions in the curriculum legacy.

Contemporary Practice.   One would imagine that the weight of the evidence is such that schools would follow a field approach to motivation, viewing the learner as a total organism in the context of his or her environment. In general, this has not happened, although the field approach is used, to a greater or lesser degree, as an educational model in some nursery schools and kindergartens.

There are at least three reasons why schools have not attempted to gear their programs to cognitive-field theories of learning. First, if followed to its logical conclusion, this approach requires resources that many schools do not command. One thing progressive educators learned was that it is not enough for teachers to "consider" the whole child: The teacher must have on hand a variety of specialists and resources. Although some school systems have diagnostic centers to investigate the whole child to discover why he or she has a particular problem, these are in the distinct minority. Moreover, those schools that do have diagnostic centers cannot meet the demand. The ability of schools to meet the needs of the whole learner will require a reordering of societal priorities.

Second, many educators adhere to the belief in a mind-body dualism that is implicit in the doctrine of mental discipline. For such individuals the whole person is a myth; the school need only concern itself with the training of the mind.

Finally, but not last in importance, is the ever-sharper controversy over conditioning-extinction and gestalt-field theories. Many proponents of more humane education recoil from the operant-conditioning view of the learner. Such persons are convinced that affect (feelings, emotions, values, and the like) is central to intrinsic motivation. On the other hand, there are those who see the use of behavior modification procedures as a viable substitute for intrinsic motivation. The latter often argue that "educational engineering" is a much less expensive procedure than finding out why a person behaves as he or she does. But here again we are forcibly brought back to the question of goals. If the primary goal of education is a person who is nonpurposive and conforming, and programmed only for "approved responses," then operant conditioning may indeed be less expensive. But if the primary goal is a creative person able to deal with the problems we have been unable to solve, as well as future problems that we cannot begin to envisage, then "educational engineering" could well be the more expensive approach.

It is obvious that a given learning theory entails far more than just a set of learning principles; it is also a view of humankind. Curriculum workers and teachers must recognize this fact, even though it complicates life for them enormously as they go about the business of educational planning. One cannot simply take the learning principles and leave the philosophy; the two are inseparable.

INDIVIDUAL DIFFERENCES

Another fundamental principle in the curriculum legacy is that the curriculum must be geared to the needs of individuals. Implied in this principle is that individuals are different in the ways they learn as well as in their abilities, interests, and tastes. As an illustration, some children may understand an explanation from their peers that they could not understand from an adult. It is often forgotten that tastes attach to ways of learning as well as to the selection of content. As Taba so wisely observed, teachers must provide individuals with a variety of modes of learning—reading, research, writing, discussing, experimenting, observing, analyzing, manipulating, and constructing—if they are to have equality of opportunity to learn.[55] Taba made this point in 1962. In the 1970s and 1980s providing equal opportunity to learn grew in importance as a social goal, and the need to better understand the nature of individual differences in classroom performance intensified with the realization that basic education was insufficient to the task. During the 1980s, research on differences in learning led to this conclusion: "different learning processes need to be engaged in different students in order to best help them learn the desired material."[56] For example, the performance of weaker students has been improved "by encouraging them to search for relationships and organization present in the material being learned."[57]

The point of importance is that research on individual differences corresponds to conceptions about the nature of individual differences, which in turn have their roots in a social philosophy. Thomas Shuell has noted that the early work on individual differences that started with Galton and Binet viewed individual differences in an elitist fashion: Some children are endowed with a great capacity to learn, while others are not. Their research on individual differences was largely descriptive and predictive.[58] But in the 1960s an egalitarian social philosophy gained great vigor in America. As President Lyndon Johnson pointed out at the National Education Association convention in 1965, it had been there all the time: "No strain in our national life," he said, "is more deeply rooted or more enduring than (our) faith in learning. It is the pathway to opportunity and the good life."[59]

The "immense question," as Johnson put it, was not to determine who was talented enough to receive quality education but: "How can a growing nation in an increasingly complex world provide education of the highest quality for all of its people?"[60] The search for the answer involved problems of educational opportunity in the classroom. But it must also "look beyond the classroom to the family and to the surroundings and environment of the student. The process of learning is not a carefully defined and isolated segment of a person's life. It is part of an organic whole, embracing all the forces which shape the person."[61]

As Shuell points out, the egalitarian philosophy was soon reflected in a changed conception of individual differences.

> Thus there was a growing feeling that individual differences in performance were largely, if not exclusively, the result of differences in the learning experiences that individuals have and not the result of "talent," "ability," and other difficult-to-modify factors, emphasized by traditional, "elite"-oriented conceptions of individual differences.[62]

The work of Bloom on mastery learning is egalitarian, despite the tendency to implement such learning in mechanistic ways. Bloom is an environmentalist whose researches have led him to conclude that individual differences in school learning are human made rather than determined in the individual at the time of conception. Bloom contends that "almost all the students can learn to a relatively high level anything the schools have to teach."[63] This strengthens the need for curriculum improvement and recognizes the responsibility and capacity of educators to determine the curriculum and the modes of learning. And it increases their responsibility to provide a curriculum that is in the best interests of the student and our society.[64]

Environmentalism had had other influences on research on individual differences. As Shuell indicates, individual differences are conceptualized not in terms of inherent ability but in terms of differences in knowledge and the ability to use appropriate learning processes. The same idea was advanced a century earlier by Lester Ward, who argued that the gulf between the ignorant and the intelligent was "caused by the unequal distribution of knowledge" rather than by differences in brain power.[65]

Environmentalism in pedagogy has a long history; the social philosophy that all are entitled to an equal opportunity to learn was instrumental in the American Revolution. Since the onset of the child-study movement, the literature has stressed that teachers should be aware of differences in learners and teach them accordingly. The principle is, nonetheless, vulnerable to sociopolitical forces. The post-*Sputnik* curriculum hierarchy and emphasis on academic excellence blurred the diversity of human beings and pushed the non-academically inclined adolescent into a dark corner (if not out the school door). A similar situation prevailed in the 1980s, when many states mandated increases in the academic subjects required for high-school graduation. These changes were regulatory and tended to avoid grappling with the problem of curriculum improvement. The schools complied by simply offering students more of the same while failing to develop a coherent curriculum to meet the function of general education. Moreover, the opportunities for students to pursue exploratory, enrichment, and vocational studies were curtailed, along with their participation in student activity programs.

When curriculum reforms are narrowly directed, or when they are undertaken for the benefit of one population at the expense of others, such reforms run counter to the wider social interest. This has been a persistent problem in the curriculum field throughout the twentieth century.

Approaches to Individualizing Instruction

Recent years have witnessed a shift in the way educators approach the problem of individualizing instruction. In the 1950s and 1960s many schools attempted to base their instructional pattern in reading on the principle that children of the same chronological age differ widely. The individualized reading approach begins with children selecting their own reading material; there must be many books available that span wide differences in ability. The idea of this reading program is to develop literacy through the literary experience. This way of teaching reading involves a specific set of procedures. As one reading expert notes, "it is not a laissez faire practice."[66]

The "back-to-basics" retrenchment extending into the 1980s found the basal reading system as the dominant approach in teaching reading. In many schools the programs were mandated: Teachers had no choice of a reading program, and the instructional system was based largely on principles of operant conditioning. The programmed reading materials were identical (although students worked at a different pace), yet the approach carried the label of "individualized learning." Nor was this concept of "individualization" confined to the elementary school: It was not uncommon to teach grammar, world geography, and U.S. history by packet reading in many high schools, especially in the inner cities. Students were assigned workbook pages that were photocopied and categorized into packets. Discussion and interaction were at a minimum. Teachers were committed to the concept of an individualized program, but there was confusion about the educational approaches most appropriately followed in order to meet this principle in the legacy. Hence the principle of individualization was reduced to a mere label as the approach taken was a convergent lockstep one in which the only variation was the rate of speed in completing the assigned worksheets.

The Organizational Approach. Schools have most often approached the problem of meeting individual needs through administrative means—by the way schools are organized and students are grouped. In recent decades, nongraded schools, middle schools, "open" schools, "alternative" schools, flexible scheduling, and multiage grouping were all intended to solve the problem of individualizing instruction. Obviously, simply to package something differently does not change the contents. In the perspective of history, it seems clear that with the exception of isolated instances, the reforms were not accompanied by curriculum reconstruction (although, often intended) but served as mere administrative schemes for standardization and efficiency.

Grouping and Tracking. No approaches to individualizing instruction are as controversial as ability grouping and tracking. Ability grouping and tracking have a long history. Passow points out that "With the advent of group intelligence tests and standardized achievement tests around World War I, ability grouping became a commonplace practice by which schools attempted to cope with student diversity and provide for individual differences."[67]

Enormous changes had taken place in American society in the twenty-five years between the reports of the Committee of Ten (1893) and the Commission on the Reorganization of Secondary Education (1918). A new educational philosophy, which was guided by societal as well as individual needs in a democracy and stemmed from the work of John Dewey, had come to have a great influence on educators. Whereas the Committee of Ten oriented its report toward college-bound students, proposing a fairly rigid curriculum, the 1918 commission's report reflected responsibility for those youngsters whose education would end with high school, recommending that high schools offer curriculums that would meet the need for specialization (vocational and other human endeavors) as well as unification (the attainment of common ideals and social cohesion). Now the high school was to offer both a unified curriculum for all and a diversified curriculum to meet the different needs of a polyglot pupil population.

Interestingly, although the commission's report was not issued until 1918, the comprehensive high school (a public high school offering college preparatory and vocational programs) was the most popular kind of secondary school in the United States after the turn of the century.[68] Schoolmen had become increasingly interested in adapting the curriculum to the talents and abilities of individual students. As Passow observes, "curricula involving grouping and tracking increasingly became one of the most popular means of choice."[69]

Oakes argues that the real motive behind the comprehensive high school was to prevent social mobility, "to socialize newcomers to their appropriate places in society."[70] The only way that one can test the validity of her assertion is by examining primary sources, namely the commission's report itself. There is no evidence from the report to support Oakes' claim. The report of 1918 clearly and repeatedly called for curriculum unification to meet the common needs of youth in a democracy and diversified studies to meet their different needs without tracking them for social predestination. As Cremin has noted in comparing the report of 1918 against the report of 1893:

> Now, (1918) the "given" of the equation was no longer the school with its content and purposes, but the children with their backgrounds and needs. Equal opportunity now meant simply the right of all who came to be offered something of value, and it was the school's obligation to offer it. The magnitude of this shift cannot be overestimated; it was truly Copernican in character.[71]

It is important to distinguish grouping from tracking. Students may be grouped in the same classroom for a variety of learning activities or they may be grouped, subject by subject, according to ability. However, the common practice has been to group students by ability in virtually all subjects with the exception of electives, often using standardized test results as a major criterion for such grouping. When grouping is implemented "across the board," it becomes tracking, such as when vocational students in high school are tracked together in history, social studies, literature, and so on. Administrative scheduling considerations often become a vehicle for such tracking. The *Cardinal Principles* report of 1918, and the progressivists during the ensuing decades, pointed to the need for heterogeneous grouping for general education or common learnings, while providing for diversified programs to meet the specialized needs of a polyglot pupil population.

Aside from the lack of validity in using standardized tests for determining pupil grouping and tracking, the practices of ability grouping and tracking have failed to produce higher achievement. In fact, there are deleterious effects of social segregation through tracking. An enormously important principle in the legacy is equal access to the curriculum. There is evidence that tracking restricts access to knowledge. In Goodlad's study on the state of American education, he found profound differences in curriculum content from track to track. In English, for example, high-track classes were more oriented toward reading literary works and expository writing, whereas low-track classes were more likely to be taught basic skills and listening, and to engage in rote learning. High-track classes gave more time to higher-order cognitive processes—making inferences, for example. Teachers of upper-track classes were viewed by their students as more enthusiastic in their instruction, having higher expectations, and more concerned about them than students in low-track classes. Teachers in upper-track classes were also perceived as explaining the work more clearly.[72] Goodlad concludes that students in low-track classes are "instructionally disadvantaged."[73] In high schools where equal access to the curriculum is valued, students are not segregated into program tracks.

This is not to say that schools should not fulfill their specialization function, which requires that students have access to different programs. As Passow points out, the old curriculum questions still obtain: *"What kinds of grouping* are needed—together with other elements of curriculum and instruction—to facilitate and enhance learning and teaching? What common knowledge and what different knowledge is needed and what processes contribute to making such knowledge accessible to learners with diverse needs and cognitive and affective characteristics?"[74]

The *Cardinal Principles* report of 1918 clearly addressed these problems and endorsed a unified or comprehensive secondary school with a curriculum to fulfill a unifying function through general education and a diversified function for specialized (college preparatory, vocational), exploratory, and enrichment education.

Individualized Instruction as Skill Development. The swing to a skills model of learning in the mid-1970s caused a similar change in the conception of individualization. In many schools, individualizing instruction became equated with the reduction of the curriculum to subskills. Individualized instruction involving filling in blanks, circling answers, and listing information became a total program, encompassing language arts, social studies, and science. The science curriculum in many elementary schools consisted entirely of ditto sheets designed for self-paced learning. Social studies was also taught as sets of skills, via the workbook or kit. Reading became word-attack skills divorced from the literary experience. In these schools mechanics passed for education; the growth objectives of the curriculum were largely eclipsed.

The late 1980s brought the discovery that in "countless" New York City elementary and junior high school classrooms there were some children who had never read an entire book. As the eighties closed, a drive was launched by Teachers College, Columbia University, to put "real books" in classrooms.[75]

Of course, using real books in classrooms instead of segmental exercises in workbooks is hardly a new idea: It permeated the progressive educational literature before the turn of the century. During the 1970s, the focus in many schools was on segmental skills to match the items on state minimum-competency tests, ignoring what had been learned many decades earlier, and denying many children the opportunity to enrich their lives through the enjoyment of literature. At the same time, because the state tests failed to include writing, children and youth were provided little opportunity to express their ideas in writing. The "antidote" of the late 1980s was a program of "writing across the curriculum." But more than a separate program or antidote is needed. Reading and writing are more than skill subjects: They are modes of communication of ideas. As the progressivists found during the early decades of the twentieth century, reading and writing for the communication of ideas must permeate the entire curriculum.

Mastery and Individualized Learning

The idea of "individualizing" instruction by allowing each child to master the curriculum at his or her own speed is not new. It will be recalled that Carleton Washburne followed this principle in Winnetka. In the 1920s pedagogical attention was centered on Winnetka, where children worked as long on a learning task as was necessary to master it.

Mastery Learning. When an entire class proceeds at the same rate, there are variations in quality of learning. Washburne dealt with this problem by varying time instead of quality. Some forty years later, Carroll identified the amount of learning time allowed as an element in his Model of School Learning.[76] Building on Carroll's model, Bloom theorizes that learning time and quality of instruction are "alterable conditions" which, if adjusted to the needs of individual learners, can result in most students learning what only some now learn. Bloom states that "most students can attain a high level of learning capacity if instruction is approached sensitively and systematically, if students are helped when and where they have learning difficulty, if they are given time to achieve mastery, and if there is some clear criterion of what constitutes mastery."[77]

Bloom's theory is both radical and optimistic, for it assumes that any student can learn anything in the curriculum, given the proper conditions. In fact, schools tend to be nervous places where students are hurried through the curriculum without enough time and help to learn. As a result, many are "derailed" early in their school careers. Bloom is emphatic about the need to provide special help for all children with learning problems, and at the earliest possible time.

Bloom's theory that most student failure can be overcome by adjusting the learning conditions in school is essentially contiguous with progressivist theory. But under the mastery learning model, education is conceived as finite rather than a developmental process. As Cronbach states, "Mastery seems to imply that at some point we get to the end of what is to be taught.[78] The authors of this text believe that education should be thought of as turning points, not terminal points.

Bloom's mastery plan is primarily appropriate for hierarchical or sequential subject matter. Mastery of one unit is the basis for later ones. (Algebra is sequential in this sense, but literature is not.) Moreover, under such a mastery schema the subject matter to be learned tends to be "closed"; there is one right answer to each question. Mastery procedures are inappropriate for higher levels of reading, organizing and communicating ideas, scientific inquiry, divergent thinking, creativity, and developmental objectives such as self-expression, sensitivity to social problems, and appreciation of literature, art, and music.

Mastery learning has been coupled with the movement toward behavioristic objectives and accountability. This is indeed regrettable, since the principles underlying Bloom's theory are sound: giving students enough time and the help they need to achieve. Developmental psychology provides the basis for Bloom's theory, but mastery learning becomes behavioristic in application. Bloom leaves the question of what should be taught open, as well he should; his is a theory of learning, not of curriculum.[79] But mastery learning favors sequential subject matter and the kind of content that can be broken down into subskills. Thus the technique itself dictates what is most worth learning: basic skills. Bloom is, willy-nilly, shaping the curriculum.

Washburne was faced with the same problem but divided the curriculum into two separate realms: the "common essentials" and activities. (As discussed previously, even this was theoretically indefensible.) Mastery learning is viewed as a total educational program; those objectives that do not fit the system are simply omitted.

A problem with mastery learning cited by Bloom himself is that the better students do less well under that approach. "I readily admit that the top 10 percent of the students in a class are likely to get less out of these procedures than the remaining 90 percent of the students in the same class," Bloom writes. His justification for the use of mastery learning is "that the schools need to improve the life chances for most of the students—even if the teachers are not as even-handed as some of the critics would desire." Bloom argues that mastery learning "is likely, in the long run, to bring more schoolchildren to a high level of school achievement than will a policy that gives much more to the top than the bottom children."[80]

Clearly a democracy needs schools in which all children have the opportunity to develop optimally. Policies that favor some children at the expense of others—no matter who or how many—are contrary to our ideal of equal opportunity.

In sum, Bloom's theory that schools must serve developmental purposes is contiguous with the curriculum legacy, but translation of the theory into practice remains to be achieved. When so-called "mastery learning" is translated into a behavioristic drill-skill repertoire, it works against the developmental process. Narrow skill-performance measures do not translate into generalized learning and the ability of the learner to apply skills in new situations, nor to increase the learner's understanding and control of new situations in school and society.

CURRICULUM SYNTHESIS

Recognition of the need to "rehumanize" and "resynthesize" knowledge is part of our curriculum inheritance. On the debit side of the ledger, however, not much progress has been made in recent years toward this goal. "A new integration, novel and ingenious," as James Harvey Robinson put it in 1924, is no more of a reality now than it was then.

Still, although the concept of the interdisciplinary curriculum emerged bruised and battered from the disciplinary reforms of the 1950s and 1960s, there is no doubting its survival. As noted at several points in this text, during the period when the national emphasis was on the disciplines, many educators continued to believe that an interdisciplinary format is better for the elementary grades in social studies. Curriculum planners still do not generally favor a discipline-centered approach in elementary social studies or science, for example. Curriculum coherence was a victim of the austerity (minimum competency) curriculum of the late 1970s and early 1980s and the nationalistic wave of reform in the mid- and late 1980s. State legislatures and schools paid attention to *A Nation at Risk* (1983), the report of the National Commission on Excellence in Education, appointed by the U.S. Secretary of Education.[81] The commission had criticized secondary schools for providing a "curricular smorgasbord" and recommended a "core" of studies, which were labeled the "Five New Basics." (The report is discussed in detail in Chapter 7.) The point of importance here is that in the late 1980s many states required more courses in English, history, and mathematics for high-school graduation and imposed tests for graduation from high school. Regulatory changes were confused with curriculum development by many teachers and administrators. The problem of curriculum content and articulation was not often dealt with.[82] The conception of general education in *A Nation at Risk* was essentialist; the common core was not a coherent core but the traditional system toughened up. Nevertheless, the concept of curriculum synthesis itself is still very much alive.

As the 1980s closed, most of the interest and effort to integrate the curriculum for general education were in higher education, not in the schools. For example, a report by the Association of American Colleges concluded that engineering undergraduates receive an incoherent education in the liberal arts and called for curriculum integration.[83] The report was based on a review of transcripts of engineering graduates and questionnaires completed by university administrators. Engineering professors tend to agree about the need for curriculum synthesis but see a problem with implementation: Most liberal arts professors have shown little interest in integrating their disciplines. Several other reports issued during the 1980s reiterated this problem and the need to develop a coherent curriculum to meet the function of general education in the college.[84] The concern for general education in the college curriculum that was so paramount during the 1940s and 1950s was revivified during the 1980s.

At the secondary-school level, educators were still struggling with the aftermath of curriculum retrenchment through "back to basics" and state-mandated subject requirements. Although the need for a coherent curriculum for general education in the secondary school was reappearing in the literature after decades of neglect, the knowledge gained from the Eight-Year Study was all but forgotten. The practice has been to tack onto the curriculum special courses in reaction to special interests and external demands. Rather than incorporating legitimate social concerns into the curriculum in social studies, health and science, for example, new studies are added, ranging from alcohol and drug abuse to suicide and AIDS, from nuclear war to women's studies, and so on.[85] Instead of life education, we have death education. (Although there is a journal called *Death Education,* there is no journal of life education.) The problem-focused core curriculum developed in the Eight-Year Study provides an invaluable model for addressing the concerns of youth and the problems of society within a coherent framework for general education. The alternative is a segmental, fragmented curriculum with subjects treated in isolation.

The Broad-Fields Approach

A step toward curriculum synthesis favored by many high schools and colleges is the broad-fields approach. Broad-fields courses were first organized in the colleges as an attempt to introduce students to the methods of inquiry and generalizations applying to broad fields of knowledge rather than single disciplines. Students were thus enabled to conceptualize a whole field rather than narrow, unrelated parts. Interdisciplinary courses in the humanities, including history, literature, music, and art, are a relatively recent innovation in the secondary school, as are interdisciplinary courses interfacing science and society.

The call for broad-fields courses, along with problem-focused studies, can be found in the reports of the 1918 Commission on the Reorganization of Secondary Education. For example, the commission held that the broad field of social studies would provide for greater curriculum unity, and would be more appropriate for adolescents in developing an understanding of society, than the study of the separate social sciences. The commission also proposed that the social studies be capped by a senior course in the Problems of American Democracy. Over the ensuing decades, not only did the social studies gain universal recognition, but many high schools proceeded to offer the problems course at the senior level. Over the years, the social studies became less of a broad-fields approach and served more as a rubric for a variety of courses ranging from government and economics to psychology and sociology. By the late 1960s the social studies were losing ground to the discipline-centered curriculum while the senior problems course was disappearing.

Nevertheless, the need for curriculum unity and interdisciplinary approaches to knowledge remains persistent. The goal of interdisciplinary studies is understanding—getting a grasp of a total field and bridging the gaps among the parts. Synthesis does not mean putting the parts together as one would the ingredients for a cake but applying relationships among the parts and subjecting them to generalization. This is easier said than done, particularly since fragmentation has become firmly entrenched in the secondary school curriculum.

As a part of the curriculum in general education, some colleges offer an interdisciplinary course in the natural sciences (biology and the physical sciences). Such courses are designed to acquaint students with the methodology of the broad field rather than specialized knowledge. This bears out what was said earlier about processes of inquiry not being the unique function of a given discipline. In a natural science course, one can, for example, deal with the questions of how hypotheses are formed in natural science, the major criteria of an acceptable hypothesis, how hypotheses are verified, and what is established by the verification of a hypothesis in natural science.

Limitations. Typically, with the broad-fields approach, knowledge is still separated from real life. Most humanities courses are approached chronologically; history dominates the study of "great issues" or broad themes. Moreover, students rarely are provided with the opportunity to engage in the performing arts; knowledge finds no expression in action; the emphasis is on information and connoisseurship in the arts, to the neglect of studio work. In accord with the essentialist reaction, developments in art education, as Jackson points out, have further emphasized the "intellectual dimensions of art instruction." Indeed, a buzzword in the late 1980s was "discipline-based" art education—instruction in visual art that "draws upon aesthetics, art criticism, art history, and art production, which are said to constitute the four foundational disciplines of art."[86]

Another limitation is that a broad-fields curriculum (with courses in natural science, social studies, and humanities) still does not reflect the interrelations between and among the broad fields.

Clearly, the need for curriculum synthesis remains an enduring and signal element of the progressivist-experimentalist legacy. As the 1980s were drawing to a close, there were indications that the need for such synthesis was being recognized so as to reveal the interrelationships of science, technology, and society. For example, in 1989 the American Association for the Advancement of Science issued a series of reports in launching "Project 2061." The reports provided a rationale for recommending that the elementary and secondary school curriculum be reconstructed "to reduce the sheer amount of material to be covered; to weaken or eliminate rigid disciplinary boundaries" and "to present the scientific endeavor as a social enterprise that influences—and is influenced by—human thought and action; and to foster scientific ways of thinking." The reports went on to stress the need to reveal the interfaces of science and society through connecting ideas rather than isolated facts. Perhaps most significantly, it was held that, "Educational reform must be comprehensive, focusing on the learning needs of all children."[87] It was announced that Phase II of the project will include the development of alternative curriculum models, materials, and research.

The Personal-Social Problems Approach

For Dewey, the function of knowledge was "to minister to better living." Dewey called for a curriculum organized around social problems. The progressivists responded and in so doing found a way to synthesize the curriculum: the core curriculum based on pressing social problems and issues. Today a number of colleges and universities offer interdisciplinary courses with a core approach. Ethnic studies, ecology, social planning, urban studies, and women's studies are illustrations of the problems approach to curriculum synthesis. It is of interest and importance that the courses are aimed at problems, not at synthesizing the curriculum. Synthesis is natural and essential.

An illustration of the personal-social problems approach at the middle-school level is the BSCS Human Sciences Program, which is "designed to support the students as they pass through the often difficult transition period between childhood and adolescence."[88] The program takes into account not only the learner but the problems of society and knowledge extended beyond the purview of the specialized disciplines. Examples of problem areas are "Where Do I Fit as a Person?," "How Does My Community Protect My Health?," and "Moving Ideas and Images." The Human Sciences Program is activity-centered. Such curricular approaches were a marked departure from the approaches taken by BSCS during the late 1950s and the 1960s when the discipline-centered doctrine prevailed.

As discussed earlier, the late 1980s witnessed a renewed recognition by certain leading professional associations, such as the American Association for the Advancement of Science (AAAS), of the need for curriculum synthesis. In launching "Project 2061," the AAAS recommended that new models of curriculum be developed (extending through the elementary and Secondary school) to reveal the interrelationships of science, mathematics, technology, and society in order to address common problems in such areas as human population, world food supply, energy, the living environment, physical and mental health, social change and conflict, and so on—through teaching methods consistent with the nature of scientific inquiry. Again, this call for curriculum synthesis to meet the function of general education contrasted sharply against the discipline-centered curriculum of the cold-war years, and against the old subject curriculum as exemplified by the essentialist state-mandated requirements and the essentialist proposals for the "new basics" during the 1980s.

PSYCHOLOGY AND THE CURRICULUM

Another problem that continues to plague curriculum scholars is that psychology has become the basic educational science. Most educational controversies rage around theories of learning rather than the content of the curriculum. This is a reflection of the domination of the curriculum field by psychological thought. As a result of this domination, the educational problem has been recast in terms of method. The underlying assumption of this point of view is that there is an agreed-upon body of knowledge called the curriculum. Educators need only concern themselves with how it can be mastered. (The mastery theories of Washburne and Bloom are exemplars of this orientation.)

Undoubtedly the reason why psychology has become the science of education is that, although it is not as fully developed as the natural sciences and although it is comprised of warring sects, psychology is amenable to quantitative treatment. The result is that educators' questions tend to revolve around the placement of content and methods of teaching while fundamental philosophical questions go unasked. There are mounds of psychological data, and its availability has determined the curriculum questions asked.

The problem was sharply delineated by Melby in 1939 in the final pages of the NSSE yearbook, *Child Development and the Curriculum*. Melby questioned the assumption upon which the yearbook was based: that the task of curriculum developers is to rearrange content in accord with the principles of child development. Wrote Melby:

> If the present writer understands the point of view of the Yearbook, it assumes that there is in existence a body of subject matter, the learning of which constitutes an education. The immediate educational problem, therefore, is that of determining when or at what stage of development such material can best be taught. If one accepts this basic point of view, he will no doubt feel that the present volume is a significant contribution.
>
> [The writer] wishes to challenge the major assumptions upon which the project is based. From his point of view there is no existing body of subject matter, the mastery of which constitutes an education.... Since all children are unique and dynamic organisms, it does not seem appropriate to speak of the relation of the curriculum to child development as if the curriculum were something already in existence and something the child must somehow master. We should rather ask what experiences would contribute most to the development of an individual child, of a given personality in process of growth.
>
> Let us add, also, that the point of view taken by the writer recognizes fully the place of subject matter in education. It regards subject matter, however, as a means and not as an end in itself.[89]

Nearly thirty years later, in a piece entitled "Implications of Psychological Thought for the Curriculum," Huebner declared that the curriculum field "has been led astray by an overdependency upon the category 'learning.'" "Clearly," said Huebner, "this category must be one of the tools of the curriculum person. It is not, however, the major category."[90] Huebner also emphasized that psychology is in search of its own theoretical knowledge; it does not set out to answer curriculum questions.

As noted earlier, the existence of theoretical knowledge in psychology has, to a great degree, actually governed the curriculum questions asked. More recently, Macdonald noted, "This is probably a fair indictment of education in that the major impetus for curriculum development growing from the foundation areas seems to have found its point of entry through psychologically shaped applications."[91]

In the 1970s some educators used stage theories in child development as curriculum theories. Hierarchical stage theories are nothing more or less than an attempt to explain the course of human development from infancy to adolescence. As Cremin has pointed out in citing Dewey, at best developmental psychology, like any individual science, can offer only partial insights into educational problems.[92]

The problem is further complicated by the fact that there are warring factions with psychology. The behaviorist outlook currently attracts adherents in academic circles in psychology and educational psychology. Adherents have been attracted from the curriculum field as well. Hence many curricularists have become enamored of an atomistic approach to curriculum development (behavioristic objectives). The resultant focus on those skills that can be most easily measured has led to further confusion between training and education. (Operant conditioning is training. Behaviorism refuses to consider such concepts as insight or intelligence that are associated with education.)

Higher-Order Thinking

In the aftermath of the curriculum retrenchment of back-to-basics, by the late 1980s researchers turned once again to higher-order thinking. The reductionist curriculum of basic education had resulted in teaching segmental and isolated facts and skills and surface memorizing for the test. Researchers were rediscovering that such learning is readily forgotten, as contrasted with learning that occurs within a broad framework of meaningful interrelationships. It was also being rediscovered that the mere accumulation of material for recall on a test mitigates against the kind of learning that enables the student to generate motivation and power for continued learning in new situations. A recent review of the research on these concerns reveals that contemporary researchers were rediscovering what the experimentalists had revealed decades earlier:

> All too often, classroom evaluation places heavy emphasis on the recall or recognition of comparatively isolated pieces of information to which the students have earlier been exposed. This encourages surface (memorizing) approaches to learning.... Further, it has been repeatedly demonstrated that isolated details are especially readily forgotten, and that information is remembered better and is more useable if students learn it within a broader framework of meaningful interrelationships and understanding. Finally, the knowledge that students accumulate during schooling may be less important than

the learning skills and habits they develop, which can help them to grow and adapt to new needs and experiences throughout their lifetime.[93]

Efforts by experimentalist educators toward building curriculum synthesis during the first half of this century were aimed at such generative and useful learning. Through curriculum synthesis, learners would be better able to see the interrelationships of knowledge and probe more deeply into their studies while also finding their studies relevant to their lives. Once again, without drawing upon the earlier research, contemporary researchers were revalidating what had been well established decades earlier.

TEACHER AS CURRICULUM MAKER

"In the end, the teacher makes the crucial decisions. The quality of the teaching-learning process depends in the last analysis on whether the decisions are made with professional competence by a person shouldering a professional responsibility or whether they are made by an employee following orders, deliberately not becoming involved as an agent responsible for using his own intelligence in the situation."[94] So wrote Margaret Lindsey in 1962. The comment might have been made today, for teachers still must make (and always have made) the crucial minute-by-minute and day-by-day decisions that determine whether students learn what the schools are expected to teach.

Only two parties need be present in the process of curricular implementation: teacher and learner. Only the teacher can supply certain essential conditions for learning—concern about the learner (if this is missing, the learner knows it); enthusiasm (of the teacher) toward the subject matter and in the learning activities; clear explanations; and instruction that is geared to the learner's motivational and achievement level. The principle that teachers are curriculum makers is part of the legacy because it is a fact of educational life.

The problem, as Margaret Lindsey and others have seen clearly, is that the teacher's judgment must be sound—based on the best available knowledge about educational practice. There is simply no substitute for this knowledge, and teachers must act on what they know. No one else can do it for them, for teaching is emergent; it is not a standard set of techniques that can be mandated by state legislatures for every individual child in every classroom. The learner, the other party in the process of curriculum making, is an individual among compeers in the classroom who reflect different as well as common needs and interests. If teachers are to recognize and meet both individual and common needs and interests of learners, they must have the autonomy to make professional judgments.

Such autonomy does not mean working in isolation. A lesson learned through the progressive curricular reforms of the 1920s and 1930s is that teachers need to share their ideas in open communication as a professional faculty. Curriculum articulation and synthesis are not possible when teachers work in isolation. Moreover, the school is a social and intellectual community of shared concerns and responsibilities. Yet teacher isolation continues to be a major impediment to advancing the professional role of the teacher.

Curriculum Making in School and Classroom

The conception that the teacher is a curriculum maker is commonly traced to the curriculum revision movement of the 1920s. For example, according to Cremin, teacher involvement in curriculum improvement began with Newlon's work in Denver.[95] Granted it was then that the teacher became a participant in course construction, working in schoolwide production committees is not the whole of curriculum making. Teachers also (and more commonly) make curriculum in their own classrooms in selecting and using curricular materials.

Teachers do not typically regard themselves as curriculum makers in their daily efforts to find more effective ways of working with individual students and the class as a whole, but nevertheless they are developing the curriculum. They become curriculum makers when they bring into the classroom materials to create a more effective environment for learning, and when they adapt innovations designed by others to their particular students. Teachers must have this broader conception of themselves as curriculum makers; it is essential to their professionalism. Yet they more commonly feel that others make the curriculum.

It is not generally recognized that the idea of the teacher as curriculum maker got its start in the post–Civil War period with the work of Edward A. Sheldon, who saw the curriculum built around object lessons.[96] (Object teaching was described in Chapter 2.) Teachers had to plan ahead of time (as contrasted with hearing children recite from a book) if their pupils were to learn from real experiences with objects. What is extremely important is that object teaching was based on a professional conception of the teacher. Teachers were not technicians; they had to understand the principle on which object teaching was based. As the teacher's manual at Oswego, New York, stressed, teachers were to work out *their own plans and methods.*[97] (The model lessons were just suggestions.) It is this broader conception of teachers as curriculum makers to which we are heirs: Teachers may participate in designing a curriculum for a school or school system, but this more formal activity is only a part of their role as makers of curriculum. In selecting, interpreting, and using available materials, teachers are also making curriculum. Yet unless they have opportunities and commitment to share their problems and successful practices with their colleagues, the possibilities for schoolwide and districtwide curriculum improvement, along with the professionalization of teaching are severely diminished.

Politics Versus Professionalism

The Teacher's Shrinking Space. Although the role of the teacher as curriculum maker is grounded on professionalism, this role has not been reflected in public policy making in recent history. For example, as Mackenzie pointed out in connection with the national curriculum reforms of the late 1950s and the 1960s, the federal government had entered the curriculum scene with a new force in response to the cold war and the space race by funding national curriculum projects in the sciences and mathematics and by funding language laboratories for the teaching of modern foreign languages. At the same time, certain private foundations, such as the Ford Foundation, "set out to reorganize the teaching profession."[98] At the urging of individuals from the industrial-business sector, the federal government also provided funding through the National Defense Education Act of 1958 for bringing the new technology of television, teaching machines, and language laboratories into the classroom. Many school administrators and teachers felt that they had been bypassed in decision-making about curriculum improvement. Indeed, the term "teacher-proof curriculum" was being used by some of the developers of the curriculum packages representing the "new science" and "new mathematics."

Although the failure of the national curriculum reforms of the 1950s and 1960s has been attributed in large measure to the exclusion of teachers from crucial decisions affecting their work,[99] this problem persisted with the statewide minimum-competency testing during the 1970s and with the state-mandated curriculum requirements of the late 1970s and early 1980s. After an extended period during which teachers were experiencing less latitude to function as professionals, by the late 1980's there was some evidence of rediscovering the significance of the teachers's professional role. "Teachers must think for themselves if they are to help others think for themselves, be able to act independently and collaborate with others, and render critical judgment," stated a 1986 report of the Carnegie Forum on Education, as it went on to note that the reforms of the recent past had left teachers with their "work becoming even more rigid, and the opportunities for exercising professional judgment becoming even more limited."[100] The report went on to call for the increased collaborative role of the teacher in curriculum development.

Nevertheless, in looking back over the sweep of events, there is little evidence of "learning from history" where the vital role of the teacher as curriculum maker is concerned. Teachers have not been involved in developing educational policy. The story of policymaking since midcentury is a recital of missed professional opportunities to take an active part in it.

Before midcentury the situation was very different. The public schools had the support of many citizens, and educators played a major role in making policy decisions bearing on the curriculum. Thus many professional educators assumed that if they favored an approach to the curriculum, that was all that was necessary; the public would be satisfied. Yet the issue of public-versus-professional prerogatives in education was looming on the horizon—indeed, it had always been present. However, because of the overconfidence of most professional educators, there was almost no possibility that they would recognize the need to build a joint, mutually enhancing relationship with the public, based on the best interests of the individual and society.

For example, one of the issues raised at a conference of the Joint Committee on Curriculum of the Department of Supervision and Directors of Instruction and the Society for Curriculum Study in the 1930s was how curriculum work should be organized. "Shall we organize for the development of the curriculum as if this were too intricate a process for any but a few very highly trained experts at Washington or your state capital," asked Will French, or should "teachers, principals and supervisors share this responsibility as if it were a part of their regular work?" He observed that the approach to curriculum development inevitably reflected a view of the teacher: "either our belief in having a professionally educated teacher in each classroom or else it should reflect our belief that all we can expect is semi-professional or even skilled-labor ability in the classroom"[101]

Most professional educators evidently assumed that curriculum development would always be in the hands of professionals, and that they need not develop a collaborative relationship with the public to deal with educational problems. This was certainly the feeling in the volume published by the joint committee, which was described by Henry Harap, the chairman, as an "up-to-date summary of (curriculum) thought and practice."[102] In the final review chapter, the approach to curriculum development and the teacher was deemed not to be at issue. There was "consistency of thought" among committee members about the "signs of confusion and curriculum development," wrote Harap, and apparently that was all that mattered. By the late 1980s the problem of teachers as professionals or technicians would become of deep concern to informed educators.

Teacher Professionalism: The Conflicting Current. Deeply entrenched in the legacy, the conception of the teacher as curriculum maker has never left the education literature. The conception has survived the attempts to mechanize teaching in the 1920s, when Franklin Bobbitt led a movement to develop teacher education programs by "scientific analysis."[103] It has survived attempts to make the curriculum "teacher-proof" in the 1960s and the competency-based approach to teacher education in the 1970s—a mechanical approach to teacher education that all but ignored the theoretical principles teachers must use in dealing with classroom problems.

During the latter part of the 1980s, the conflicting current of teacher professionalism began to flow with increased vigor. The idea that teachers must be reflective and deliberative—must know what they are doing and why—received a great deal of attention in the education literature. As Kliebard points out, the idea goes back to the Dewey's laboratory school at the University of Chicago.[104]

Of course, in order to reflect, one must have something to reflect about. When Dewey led teachers' meetings, such questions as the following were raised:

> Is there any common denominator in the teaching process? Here, are people teaching different children of different ages, different subjects; one is teaching music, another art, another cooking, Latin, etc. Now is there any common end which can be stated which is common to all? This is meant in an intellectual rather than a moral way. Is there any intellectual result which ought to be obtained in all these different studies and at these different ages?[105]

Theory was clearly related to practice at the Dewey School, and this was the purpose of reflection. This was all part of what Dewey called the laboratory idea. School practice should be based on principles, and the teacher should be a "thoughtful and alert student of education."[106] In the 1980s "teacher reflection" was in danger of becoming a mechanical process without substance, performed for its own sake and thus in danger of going the way of other educational fads. How one reflects depends on the issue or problem being considered. Scientific methodology is the method for reflection, but it must be stimulated by a profound doubt and a concerted attack on a significant problem.

According to Griffin, if teachers are to function as professionals, there must be "ample opportunities for both formal and informal deliberation around schooling issues, possibilities and dilemmas."[107] This is surely the case, but none of this should cloud the educational leader's recognition that discussion is not necessarily reflection; among professionals one reflects to improve practice in light of principles.

Lessons from the Legacy

As noted earlier, although the curriculum is actually made in the classroom and teachers play the key role, the teacher should not be left in isolation. One lesson from history is that leaving teachers without help and resources does not contribute to their professionalism. We have learned this repeatedly. During the progressive era, when many teachers were expected to develop core curricula without administrative support in providing needed time, consultant expertise, and materials, teachers became overburdened and overwhelmed. During the action-research movement of the 1950s, when teachers were expected to be engaged in practical research and application in solving problems, they floundered without the help of expert consultants. During the 1970s, when teachers were expected to solve their own problems if they could just have centers where they could congregate and pool their collective ideas, the anticipated outcomes never materialized.

What Harap observed in the 1950s is still very much the case: Curriculum development is a continuing cooperative process involving teachers, supervisors, principals, administrative officials, and consultants.[108] With a commitment to the concept of teachers as curriculum makers must go a commitment to giving teachers the kind of help needed to solve curriculum problems.

A second lesson learned is that for any number of reasons teachers do not use the power they actually possess to improve the curriculum. Teachers generally see themselves as being fairly autonomous—as being in control of what is taught and how it is taught—but when it comes to actual practice, they tend to depart very little from a single approach: standing in front of a class—telling, explaining, or lecturing. Thus, although teachers make the curriculum, they are not using their autonomy to implement what they recognize as desirable educational practices. Goodlad found, for example, that teachers do not adjust their teaching approaches to their purposes and the demands of the subject matter.[109] Quite obviously, there are many interconnected problems here: Teacher education, professional socialization, and administrator support are three of critical importance. The teacher education program must include well-supervised opportunities to practice sound educational methods in light of educational principles; the informal social system in the school must support the teacher's efforts to improve the curriculum; principals and supervisors must encourage teachers in their active roles as curriculum makers (and thus influence the social system). As Griffin points out, the teacher's role as curriculum maker is eroded by time constraints, and the principal is in an excellent position to deal with the issue of time, making certain that teachers have the time to engage in assessing curriculum materials and deal with curriculum problems.[110]

In some schools teachers are applying their pedagogical knowledge and improving the curriculum. The fact that some schools as institutions have changed for the better means that it is possible in all schools.

EDUCATION AND SOCIETY: A RETROSPECTIVE OF EVENTS (1956–89)

Selected events in the world of education and society over the past third of our century are presented in Table 6-1. The contrasting columns in the timetable reveal the wide range of events in the stream of our modern human experience. In perspective, we find some events are achievements while others are setbacks or divergences.

On the wider scene, we find television entering virtually all of our homes and coming to exert a dominant influence in the leisure time of the family. We see Martin Luther King, Jr., emerging as a civil rights leader in 1956, the launching of *Sputnik* I and II in 1957, the establishment of the Peace

TABLE 6-1 Timetable of Events in Education and Society: 1956–89

YEAR	EDUCATION	SOCIETY
1956	Physical Science Study Committee (PSSC), the first of the national curriculum-reform projects (discipline-centered) funded by NSF, established; gives priority to the sciences and mathematics in response to the cold war and the space race (1956–68) Arthur E. Bestor: *The Restoration of Learning* Council for Basic Education founded	Dwight D. Eisenhower reelected President; Japan admitted to UN; Martin Luther King, Jr., emerges as civil rights leader; William H. Whyte: *The Organization Man;* oral polio vaccine; Lerner and Loewe: *My Fair Lady* (N.Y.); *Sputnik, I, II* (1957)
1958	National Defense Education Act	European Economic Community (Common Market) established; Khrushchev becomes Soviet Premier; growing tension over school desegregation in South; Boris Pasternak: *Dr. Zhivago* (Nobel Prize); "beatnik movement" spreads from California throughout U.S. and to Europe; Brussels World Exhibition; first studies link TV violence with children's aggression
1959	James B. Conant (1893–1978): *The American High School Today*	Alaska and Hawaii become 49th and 50th states; Fidel Castro becomes Premier of Cuba; Pope John XXIII announces first Ecumenical Council since 1870; Abraham Flexner dies (born 1866); Frank Lloyd Wright dies (born 1869); U.S. Postmaster bans *Lady Chatterley's Lover* from mail (reversed in 1960 by Circuit Court of Appeals)
1960	Jerome S. Bruner: *The Process of Education* A. S. Neill: *Summerhill*	Historic Presidential TV debates (Kennedy and Nixon); John F. Kennedy elected President (youngest); first weather satellite launched (U.S.); Charles Van Doren, Columbia University instructor, arrested with 12 other TV quiz-show contestants for perjury in connection with "rigging" of quiz questions

(cont.)

TABLE *6-1* Timetable of Events in Education and Society: 1956–89

YEAR	EDUCATION	SOCIETY
1961	James B. Conant: *Slums and Suburbs* Lawrence A. Cremin: *The Transformation of the School*	Peace Corps established; U.S. breaks off relations with Cuba; President Kennedy's role in Bay of Pigs fiasco acknowledged; Berlin Wall constructed; Ernest Hemingway suicide (born 1899); President Eisenhower in Farewell Address warns of the growing "military-industrial complex" and of the corruption of the nation's scholars through the "power of money" and federal funding of projects; FCC chairman calls TV a "vast wasteland"
1963	Vocational Education Act of 1963 creates separate full-time and shared-time vocational schools	Civil rights violence in Birmingham, Ala.; Martin Luther King, Jr., arrested; 200,000 "Freedom Marchers" (blacks and whites) demonstrate in Washington, D.C.; President Kennedy assassinated; Lyndon B. Johnson succeeds Kennedy; Barbara Tuchman: *The Guns of August*
1964	Economic Opportunity Act ("War on Poverty," 1964–70); Civil Rights Act	Lyndon B. Johnson elected President, announces "War on Poverty"; escalation of U.S. involvement in Vietnam War; civil rights and anti–Vietnam War demonstrations erupt into sit-ins and violence at the University of California, Berkeley; protests and disruptions follow on other campuses (Columbia in 1968 leading to closing of the campus, and Kent State in 1970), filtering down into high schools; students demand curricular "relevance," resulting in increased electives on current topics; riots in black ghetto sections of U.S. cities (also in 1965, 1966, 1967) leads President Johnson to create National Advisory

TABLE *6-1* Timetable of Events in Education and Society: 1956–89

YEAR	EDUCATION	SOCIETY
		Commission on Civil Disorders; Nobel Prize for Peace: Martin Luther King, Jr.
1965	Elementary and Secondary Education Act National Assessment of Educational Progress British Department of Education and Science requests local educational authorities (school districts) to submit plans for the reorganization of secondary schools along comprehensive lines	Civil rights violence in Selma, Ala.; Martin Luther King, Jr., leads procession from Selma to Montgomery to deliver petition; college students demonstrate in Washington against U.S. involvement in Vietnam War; Medicare Bill signed by President Johnson; riots in Watts section of Los Angeles (35 dead, 4,000 arrested); Max Born: *On the Responsibility of Scientists;* death penalty abolished in Britain
1966	Central Advisory Council for Education (England): *Children and Their Primary Schools* (the "Plowden Report") leads to popularization of the open classroom in the U.S. through Herbert Kohl, *The Open Classroom* (1969), and Charles E. Silberman, *Crisis in the Classroom* (1970) James S. Coleman et al: *Equality of Educational Opportunity*	International Days of Protest (against U.S. policy in Vietnam); *New York Herald Tribune* ceases publication; William Manchester: *The Death of a President;* Mao Tse-tung: *Quotations from Chairman Mao Tse-tung*
1970	Charles E. Silberman (Carnegie Corporation): *Crisis in the Classroom* Ivan Illich: *Deschooling Society*	Student protests against Vietnam War, 4 killed by National Guard at Kent State University (Ohio); reduction of U.S. troops in Vietnam
1973	National Commission on the Reform of Secondary Education (Kettering Foundation): *The Reform of Secondary Education*	Watergate scandal: talk of impeachment of President Nixon, White House aides forced to resign; Vice President Spiro T. Agnew resigns over "payoff charges," succeeded by Gerald Ford; energy crisis in industrial nations precipitated by Arab oil embargo; U.S. Supreme Court gives women unrestricted right to abortion in first 3 months of pregnancy

(cont.)

TABLE *6-1*   Timetable of Events in Education and Society: 1956–89

YEAR	EDUCATION	SOCIETY
1974	Panel on Youth of the President's Science Advisory Committee: *Youth: Transition to Adulthood*	Watergate: White House aides convicted; Presidential involvement in cover-up revealed; President Nixon resigns and is succeeded by Vice President Gerald R. Ford; Ford pardons Nixon
		Carl Bernstein and Bob Woodward: *All the President's Men;* India becomes 6th nation to explode a nuclear device; Alexander I. Solzhenitsyn: *The Gulag Archipelago: 1918–56*
1976	National Panel on High School and Adolescent Education (U.S. Office of Education): *The Education of Adolescents*	U.S. Bicentennial; North and South Vietnam reunited; Jimmy Carter elected President; first women admitted to a U.S. military academy (air force); world's first supersonic passenger service; personal computer
1979	U.S. Department of Education established with Cabinet status; President Carter calls education "our most important national investment"	U.S. and China formally establish relations; nuclear plant accident at Three Mile Island, Pa.; anti–nuclear power demonstrations in Washington, D.C.; over 1 million illegal immigrants apprehended in U.S. (over 90 percent from Mexico); Khomeini seizes rule in Iran and establishes Islamic government; Americans taken hostage in Iran; worldwide gasoline shortage; oil companies make record profits; U.S. ranked 8th among nations in per capita wealth (Switzerland first); first woman (Margaret Thatcher) elected Prime Minister of Britain; first woman elected mayor of Chicago
1982	Mortimer J. Adler: *The Paideia Proposal: An Educational Manifesto* President Reagan calls for return to "the basics" in education; federal	President Reagan reaffirms opposition to gun control; TV film on nuclear holocaust, *The Day After,* viewed by 100 million in U.S. (film condemned as leftist by Moral

TABLE *6-1*   Timetable of Events in Education and Society: 1956–89

YEAR	EDUCATION	SOCIETY
	district judge holds unconstitutional Arkansas law requiring that "creation science" be given equal emphasis in the curriculum where the theory of evolution is taught	Majority); mass rallies in Western Europe oppose nuclear arms; 6 U.S. Congressmen convicted of bribery; best-seller: *In Search of Excellence;* first reports of AIDS
1983	National Commission on Excellence in Education (U.S. Department of Education): *A Nation at Risk: The Imperative for Educational Reform* Ernest L. Boyer (Carnegie Foundation for the Advancement of Teaching): *High School: A Report on Secondary Education in America* Task Force on Education for Economic Growth (Education Commission of the States): *Action for Excellence: A Comprehensive Plan to Improve Our Nation's Schools* National Science Board of the National Science Foundation: *Educating Americans for the 21st Century*	U.S. population: 233 million; prison population double that of 1973; U.S. car production lowest in 20 years; Defense Department items: $17.59 each for bolts costing 67 cents at hardware store, $110 each for diodes available at 4 cents, $92 each for ordinary screws; U.S. Justice Department labels Canadian TV films on nuclear war as "propaganda," resulting in limited showings in U.S. (one film wins Academy Award)
1984	John I. Goodlad: *A Place Called School* Canadian Supreme Court rules that Quebec law restricting availability of English in the school curriculum is unconstitutional	President Reagan reelected (age 73); Reagan visits China; Indira Gandhi, Prime Minister of India, assassinated; Defense Department items: $7,622 each for 10-cup coffee brewers, $171 each for small rechargeable flashlights; AIDS declared top medical priority of U.S. Department of Health
1985	Committee for Economic Development: *Investing in Our Children: Business and the Public Schools* U.S. Supreme Court strikes down Alabama law on daily "minute of silence" in public schools (6-3);	*"Teacher in Space"* program announced by President Reagan; Sharon McAuliffe, 36, New Hampshire junior-high-school teacher, chosen ("first private citizen passenger in space") and contracted by NASA for year-long

(cont.)

TABLE *6-1* Timetable of Events in Education and Society: 1956–89

YEAR	EDUCATION	SOCIETY
	rules (6-3) that school officials or teachers may search students "without probable cause" under "reasonable grounds"; U.S. Secretary Bennett criticizes $1.7 billion federal bilingual education program, saying there is no evidence of child benefit; U.S. Attorney General Meese criticizes U.S. Supreme Court decisions against school prayer and government aid to religious schools (Meese resigns in 1988 under charges of ethical misconduct); high-school graduates in U.S. adult population: 74% as compared to 24% in 1940	speaking tour following flight on space shuttle scheduled for January, 1986 (space shuttle explodes on launching, in 1986, killing McAuliffe and rest of crew; inquiry reveals known design defects caused disaster); UN celebrates 40th anniversary but fails to agree on declaration to mark the event; pregnancy rate of U.S. teenagers more than twice that of other industrial nations; George Gershwin's *Porgy and Bess* performed at the Metropolitan Opera for first time, 50 years after its premier; Defense Department scandals: major contractors suspended and fined for overcharges, false billings, fraud, illegal gifts; Defense Department items: $748 apiece for pliers (under $8 at local hardware store), $435 each for hammers; President Reagan hails "age of the entrepreneur"
1987	Committee for Economic Development: *Children in Need* U.S. and Japan issue separate assessment of each other's school systems: Japanese reformers call for more independent-minded, creative students; U.S. reformers favor more work for students, mastery of skills, and discipline U.S. Supreme Court (7-2) strikes down Louisiana law requiring the teaching of "creation science" in public schools teaching evolution	President Reagan proposes nation's first trillion-dollar defense budget, calls for voluntary prayer in schools and quest for excellence in schools and workplace; West Germany displaces U.S. as world's biggest exporter; TV hearings on U.S. arms scandal involving Iran and Nicaragua; Soviet Premier Gorbachev and President Reagan sign treaty in Washington, D.C., reducing intermediate-range nuclear missiles; TV evangelist sex scandal; scientific advances in superconductivity; insider trading on Wall Street and business-takeover scandals; business schools introduce courses on ethics to counter "creed of greed" in curriculum

TABLE *6-1* Timetable of Events in Education and Society: 1956–89

YEAR	EDUCATION	SOCIETY
1988	William T. Grant Foundation: *The Forgotten Half: Non-College Youth in America*	Boris Pasternak's *Dr. Zhivago* published (post.) in U.S.S.R. (published in the West in 1957; Pasternak won Nobel Prize for Literature in 1958); President Reagan and Premier Gorbachev ratify limited nuclear accords in Moscow; George Bush elected president; U.S. visit by Soviet Premier Gorbachev cut short by earthquake disaster in Soviet Armenia (over 500,000 killed); TV evangelist sex scandals; electronic church becomes big business, with 221 TV and 1,370 radio stations broadcasting mostly religious programs; U.S. Defense Department scandals: Pentagon fraud and bribery investigations, contractor overcharges; U.S. population: over 245 million
	Carnegie Foundation: *An Imperiled Generation: Saving Urban Schools*	
	Allan Bloom: *The Closing of the American Mind*	
	U.S. Supreme Court (5-3) upholds authority of school officials to censor student newspapers (Court holds that student paper is part of the curriculum and not a forum for public opinion)	
1989	President Bush pledges that he will be the "education President"	Continued investigations and convictions for fraud on Wall Street and in defense industry; 150,000 university students march in Beijing, China, in support of democracy and in protest against political corruption; protest in China spreads and is put down by the military with many civilian casualties, arrests, and executions; U.S. celebrates 200th anniversary of inauguration of George Washington as first President; first multicandidate elections in U.S.S.R. since 1917 Revolution: Emporer Hirohito dies (born 1901), leaders of 163 nations attend rites including President Bush; best-sellers: *Chaos* by James Gleick and *Thriving on Chaos* by Tom Peters
	Leading universities introduce ethics courses in MBA programs in wake of Wall Street and business scandals	
	No. 1 best seller: *All I Really Needed to Know I Learned in Kindergarten* (Robert Fulghum)	

Sources: *Facts on File* (New York: Facts on File, Inc.); *Annual Register of World Events* (London: Longman's, Green); Bernard Grun, *The Timetables of History,* rev. ed. (New York: Simon & Schuster, 1979); *The New York Times.*

Corps in 1961, the announcement of the War on Poverty by President Johnson in 1964 (leading to a range of school programs for disadvantaged children and youth), the civil rights movement of the 1960s, the anti–Vietnam War demonstrations on our college campuses, the riots in ghetto sections of our central cities, the Watergate scandal in 1973 (leading to the resignation of a U.S. President for the first time in our history), the right to legal abortion upheld by the U.S. Supreme Court in 1973, the celebration of the U.S. Bicentennial, the widespread use of the personal computer, the decline of the United States and the rise of Japan in global industrial markets, and the rising problem of unethical practices in American business, industry, and financial markets. And we see George Gershwin's *Porgy and Bess* performed for the first time at New York's Metropolitan Opera, fifty years after its premier and after many years of performances at leading opera houses throughout the world.

Many of the social and political events cited above exerted profound influences on the school curriculum. Although the tax conservatives and essentialists appeared to be gaining influence during the late 1940s and early 1950s in their call for "back to basics," the cold war, buttressed by the launching of *Sputnik I,* gave impetus to the national discipline-centered curriculum reforms and the "new math" and "new science" fashioned by university scholar-specialists through grants from the National Science Foundation. New curriculum priorities for mathematics, the sciences, and modern foreign languages were established through the National Defense Education Act of 1958. Unprecedented attention was given to the academically gifted and talented student. The Vocational Education Act of 1963 may have appeared to address the needs of neglected youth, but in providing for the construction of area vocational schools it raised the specter of a divided school system.

The Coleman report of 1966 (*Equality of Educational Opportunity*), a study mandated by the Civil Rights Act of 1964, provided convincing evidence of the deleterious effects of school segregation on black children and youth and provided new impetus for school desegregation.

The aftermath of the "new math" and "new science" found college and high-school students demanding curriculum "relevance" in an era buffeted by civil disorder in our central cities, the war in Vietnam, and the civil rights movement. The response of the colleges and secondary schools was the safety valve of electives on special topics of special interest to special groups. At the elementary level, the open classroom came into vogue. The call for reform at the elementary and secondary levels was "humanizing" the curriculum, but no attempt was made to address the need for systematic curriculum reconstruction. Books appearing on national best-seller lists were urging the schools to adopt a child-centered pedagogy more extreme than anything advocated by the romantic progressivists of the 1920s and 1930s. Paul Goodman's *Growing up Absurd,* published in 1956, and A. S. Neill's *Summerhill,* published in 1960, garnered little attention until the late 1960s, when they were reissued as popular sellers in tune with the radical-romantic counter-reaction. The term "counterculture" became popular among college students, while interest in the occult and "experimentation" with drugs entered the college scene.

The predictable counter-counterreaction was a series of national reports during the 1970s calling for educational retrenchment by reducing the holding power of the high school and reducing the school curriculum to the essential subjects or academic basics. Statewide minimum-competency testing mushroomed, and teachers complied by teaching-to-the-tests.

As we entered the 1980s, there was growing realization that the back-to-basics retrenchment had led to a decline in thinking abilities and in writing skills. Segmental programs were introduced to develop these abilities and skills. A rash of conflicting reports on educational reform appeared during the 1980s, most notably *A Nation at Risk* (1983), issued by the U.S. Department of Education, blaming the schools for the decline of America's historic role in dominating the global economic marketplace. (A quarter of a century earlier, our schools were blamed for the Soviet success in space.) The new threat was the Japanese challenge in the global economy. The American schools were urged to adopt the managerial efficiency know-how of the American business-industrial sector (which went blameless in *A Nation at Risk*).

More moderate studies of our schools during the early 1980s, such as Ernest Boyer's *High School* and John Goodlad's *A Place Called School,* pointed to the need for a coherent curriculum to meet the function of general education in a free society and the need to attune the curriculum to the nature of child and adolescent.

Toward the end of the 1980s, reports were being issued on our neglect of children and youth who were at risk in school and society as the result of economic impoverishment. Quite suddenly in 1987 and 1988 reports appeared on "children in need" and on the "forgotten half"—the population of youth who do not go on to college. But these reports never garnered the attention given to *A Nation at Risk.*

Nevertheless, the chronicle of events over the past third of a century revealed that whenever priority is given to a special population at the expense of other populations, such as the gifted and talented over youngsters at risk, there is bound to be a reaction. The schools of a free society are obliged to serve all the children of all the people by optimizing educational opportunity for all. This was the rallying call of progressive experimentalist educators throughout the twentieth century. A related lesson is that whenever narrow curriculum priorities are established to the neglect of equally needed and honorable school studies, the consequence not only is curriculum imbalance and fragmentation but failure to meet the need for both a common learning and diversified studies for a cosmopolitan pupil population. The social spirit of the school suffers. Such priorities inevitably neglect the nature of the learner (for example, in curtailing the arts in the curriculum), giving us the case of the learner versus the curriculum—a problem addressed by Dewey as we entered the twentieth century. It was then that Dewey prophetically exposed the fallacy of the romanticists in leaving the child and adolescent "free" to determine the curriculum,[111] as was advocated by radical romantics during the late 1960s.

Finally, few educators were facing up to the question of whether our society was being true to itself when the schools were being turned to serving narrow nationalistic or special interests. A free society requires that the schools serve the widest social interest. This is the signal lesson of the American educational experience.

PERSPECTIVE

Ideas from the progressive (experimentalist) education movement have formed the bedrock for present-day educational theory. The experimentalist-progressivists sought to develop in all children self-discipline, social sensitivity, critical and creative thinking, and the ability to solve personal and social problems. Schools with these goals continue to attract parents who want more than the three R's, at least for their own children. Despite curriculum retardation through a skill-drill model of basic education during the late 1970s and early 1980s, knowledgeable educators continued to believe that a rich and balanced curriculum was needed and that inquiry learning lies at the heart of education in a free society.

Unfortunately, inquiry learning became identified with knowledge production in the separate academic disciplines in connection with the curriculum projects for national defense during the 1950s and 1960s, rather than with social problem-solving (as was the case with the core curriculum of the 1930s). In belated recognition that the back-to-basics reductionism of the 1970s and early 1980s had resulted in a decline in thinking ability, the late 1980s were marked by a new emphasis on teaching higher-order thinking skills. However, such efforts were injected segmentally into the curriculum, rather than being made to permeate the entire curriculum. Inquiry had been divorced from action in the curriculum. The recent effort to teach for higher-order thinking skills was not to be confused with Dewey's reflective process, in which thinking culminated in plans of action for solving significant problems and the actual testing of the plans, with the purpose of improving life conditions. In the segmental program to teach higher-order thinking skills, thinking was typically conceived as discrete skills used in dealing with verbal materials. Hence it was closer to the notion of thinking as a mechanical process involving logic, not behavior, that Dewey was trying to get away from. Despite the fact that thinking is not today viewed as a total process, it is nonetheless part of the curriculum legacy.

The curriculum legacy also reveals that learning should be self-impelled by developing the pupil's interest in continued learning, and that the curriculum should be adapted to individual needs as well as to the needs of the social group in the context of fostering democratic social responsibility and optimizing educational opportunity. These principles have been repeatedly violated, especially in our central cities, where "individualized" learning is reduced to mechanical exercises with workbooks, ditto sheets, and programmed instructional materials. In some schools there are children who have never read an entire book whereby they might follow a story line and develop a sense of continuity of ideas.

To deny teachers the autonomy and supportive resources in selecting and adapting curricular materials to the needs of the learners not only mitigates against the teacher as a professional but against the learner's access to a rich and meaningful curriculum. Many of the state-mandated curriculum reforms of the 1980s reflected the attitude of state legislatures, which tended to view teaching as a standard set of techniques that can be applied en masse. Nevertheless, teachers still feel that they have the autonomy to make professional judgments behind their classroom doors. The history of progressive education reveals clearly that professionalism is not synonymous with aloneness; it is based upon a shared and advancing base of knowledge for improved practice in the social setting of the classroom and school. If teachers are to function effectively as curriculum makers in the classroom and school, they must have the needed resources and support services. Denied these conditions, teachers will still make the curriculum—even if it is a poor curriculum. Another lesson from the legacy of the progressive education movement is that teacher education should link improved practices with the theories that undergird such practices along with the most complete research findings.

Finally, the curriculum must be in harmony with the nature of the learner and the ideals of a free society. At one extreme we have witnessed the educational failures of the romantic progressivists, who sought to turn the curriculum over to the "felt needs" and immediate interests of the immature learner. At the other extreme we have witnessed the educational failures of the traditionalists, who have conceived of mind as a vessel to be filled or as a muscle to be exercised through a reductionist drill-skill curriculum in the fundamentals. We have also witnessed the inequities that result when the direction of curriculum reform favors one group at the expense of another. Priorities in curriculum reform must be consonant with the widest public interest so as to serve all the children of all the people as optimally as possible.

The progressive education movement is history, but this history is the legacy of the present. If the lessons of the past are learned, the prospects for progress will be promising.

NOTES

1. Lawrence A. Cremin, *The Transformation of the School* (New York: Knopf, 1961), p. 349.

2. Edgar B. Wesley, *NEA: The First Hundred Years* (New York: Harper & Row, 1957), pp. 154–55.

3. John Dewey, *The School and Society* (Chicago: University of Chicago Press, 1915), p. 149. (First published 1899.)

4. John Dewey, *How We Think* (Lexington, Mass.: D. C. Heath, 1910).

5. John Dewey, *Democracy and Education* (New York: Macmillan, 1916), p. 233–34.

6. Ibid., p. 234.

7. Arthur W. Foshay, "Sources of School Practice," Chapter 7 in *The Elementary School in the United States,* Seventy-second Yearbook, Part II, National Society for the Study of Education (Chicago: University of Chicago Press, 1973), p. 189.

8. Ibid., pp. 188–89.

9. E. D. Hirsch, Jr., "Restoring Cultural Literacy in the Early Grades," *Educational Leadership* 45 (December 1987/January 1988): 68.

10. John Dewey, *Democracy and Education* (New York: Macmillan, 1916), p. 61.

11. Penelope L. Peterson and Susan R. Swing, "Beyond Time on Task: Student's Reports of Their Thought Processes During Classroom Instruction," *The Elementary School Journal* 82 (May 1982): 481–91.

12. John I. Goodlad, *A Place Called School* (New York: McGraw-Hill, 1984), pp. 111–12.

13. H. H. Giles, S. P. McCutchen, and A. N. Zechiel, *Exploring the Curriculum* (New York: Harper & Row, 1942), p. 176.

14. Lou La Brant, "A Word of Protest," *Teachers College Record* 74 (December 1972): 167.

15. Ibid., p. 168.

16. See Robert Glaser, "Variables in Discovery Learning," Chapter 2 in *Learning by Discovery: A Critical Appraisal,* Lee S. Shulman and Evan R. Keislar (eds.) (Chicago: Rand McNally, 1966), p. 23.

17. Jerome S. Bruner, *The Process of Education* (Cambridge: Harvard University Press, 1960), pp. 11–12, 20–22.

18. Jerome Bruner, "The Act of Discovery," *Harvard Educational Review* 32 (Winter 1961): 21–32.

19. Jerome Kagan, "Learning, Attention, and the Issue of Discovery," Chapter 11 in Shulman and Keislar, op. cit., p. 158.

20. M. C. Wittrock, "The Learning by Discovery Hypothesis," Chapter 4 in Shulman and Keislar, op. cit., p. 33.

21. Ibid., p. 42.

22. Lee J. Cronbach, *Educational Psychology,* 3rd ed. (New York: Harcourt Brace Jovanovich, 1977), p. 546.

23. Lyn Corno and Richard E. Snow, "Adapting Teaching to Individual Differences Among Learners," Chapter 21 in *Handbook of Research on Teaching,* 3rd edition, Merlin C. Wittrock (ed.) (New York: Macmillan, 1986), p. 620.

24. Cronbach, *Educational Psychology,* op. cit., p. 457.

25. Glaser, op. cit., p. 18.

26. Henrietta Schwartz, "Unapplied Curriculum Knowledge," Chapter 3 in *Critical Issues in Curriculum,* Eighty-seventh Yearbook of the National Society for the Study of Education, Part I (Chicago: University of Chicago Press, 1988), p. 46.

27. Ibid.

28. Daniel Tanner and Laurel Tanner, *Supervision in Education: Problems and Practices* (New York: Macmillan, 1987), p. 189.

29. Shulman and Keislar, op. cit., p. 189.

30. Jerome S. Bruner, *The Process of Education,* op. cit., p. 14.

31. James B. Conant, *Two Modes of Thought* (New York: Trident Press, 1964), p. 2.

32. Ibid., p. 31.

33. Ibid., p. 95.

34. Benjamin S. Bloom, J. Thomas Hastings, and George F. Madaus, *Handbook on Summative and Formative Evaluation of Student Learning* (New York: McGraw-Hill, 1971), p. 273.

35. Hilda Taba et al., *Teaching Strategies for Developing Children's Thinking* (Palo Alto, Calif.: Institute for Staff Development, 1970).

36. Robert P. Green, Jr., "U.S. History Today: Back to the Basics the Right Way," *The Social Studies* 69 (July-August 1978): 170.

37. Irving Morrissett, Preface to *The Current State of Social Studies: A Report of Project SPAN* (Boulder, Colo.: SSEC Publications, 1982), pp. vii–xii.

38. David Van Clear and Charles W. Funkhouser, "Inquiry, 'Oz,' and Populism," *Social Education* 51 (April/May 1987): 282.

39. Wayne Welch et al., "The Role of Inquiry in Science Education: Analysis and Recommendations," *Science Education* 65 (January 1981): 33.

40. Pinchas Tamir, "Stability and Change in Inquiry Orientation of High School Biology Teachers," *Educational Research* 28 (February 1986).

41. Welch et al., op. cit., p. 33.

42. Paul D. Hurd et al., "Biology Education in the Secondary Schools of the United States," *The American Biology Teacher* 42 (October 1980): 388–410.

43. Arthur W. Foshay, "How Fare the Disciplines?," *Phi Delta Kappan* 51 (March 1970): 351.

44. John Dewey, *Experience and Education* (New York: Macmillan, 1963), p. 87. (First published 1938.)

45. William J. Bennett and Edwin Delattre, "Moral Education in the Schools," *The Public Interest* no. 50 (Winter 1978): 81–89.

46. Herbert M. Kliebard, "Fads, Fashions and Rituals: The Instability of Curriculum Change," Chapter 2 in *Critical Issues in Curriculum,* Eighty-seventh Yearbook, Part I, National Society for the Study of Education (Chicago: University of Chicago Press, 1988), pp. 16–34.

47. Dewey, *Democracy and Education,* op. cit., p. 148.

48. Hilda Taba, *Curriculum Development: Theory and Practice* (New York: Harcourt, Brace, 1962), p. 289.

49. Terence J. Crooks, "The Impact of Classroom Evaluation Practices on Students," *Review of Educational Research* 58 (Winter 1980): 463, 464.

50. Linda Hamrick and Harold Harty, "Influence of Resequencing General Science Content on the Science Achievement, Attitudes Toward Science, and Interest in Science of Sixth Grade Students," *Journal of Research in Science Teaching* 24 (January 1987): 15–25.

51. B. F. Skinner, "Programmed Instruction Revisited," *Phi Delta Kappan* 68 (October 1986): 108–9.

52. Benjamin S. Bloom, *Stability and Change in Human Characteristics* (New York: John Wiley, 1964).

53. John W. Atkinson and Norman T. Featherstone, *A Theory of Achievement Motivation* (New York: John Wiley, 1966).

54. Jean Piaget, *The Origins of Intelligence in Children,* trans. by Margaret Cook (New York: International Universities Press, 1952).

55. Taba, *Curriculum Development: Theory and Practice, op. cit., p. 308.*

56. Thomas J. Shuell, "Individual Differences: Changing Conceptions in Research and Practice," *American Journal of Education* 94 (May 1986): 372.

57. Ibid.

58. Ibid.

59. Lyndon B. Johnson, "A Message from the President," in *Contemporary Issues in American Education* (Washington, D.C.: U.S. Office of Education, 1965), p. 6.

60. Ibid., p. 5.

61. Ibid.

62. Shuell, op. cit., pp. 357–58.

63. Benjamin S. Bloom, *Human Characteristics and School Learning* (New York: McGraw-Hill, 1976), p. 213.

64. Ibid., p. 214.

65. Lester F. Ward, *Dynamic Sociology* vol. 2 (New York: Appleton, 1883), p. 602.

66. Jeannette Veatch, "Return to Reason; Individualized Reading," in Malcolm P. Douglass (ed.), *Claremont Reading Conference, 1987* (Claremont, Calif.: The Claremont Reading Conference Center for Developmental Studies, 1987), p. 178.

67. A. Harry Passow, "Issues of Access to Knowledge: Grouping and Tracking," Chapter 9 in *Critical Issues in Curriculum,* 87th Yearbook of the National Society for the Study of Education, Part I (Chicago: University of Chicago Press, 1988), p. 205.

68. R. Freeman Butts and Lawrence A. Cremin, *A History of Education in American Culture* (New York: Holt, Rinehart and Winston, 1953), p. 443.

69. Passow, op. cit., p. 209.

70. Jeannie Oakes, *Keeping Track: How Schools Structure Inequality* (New Haven, Ct.: Yale University Press, 1985), p. 30.

71. Lawrence A. Cremin, "The Problem of Curriculum Making: An Historical Perspective," in *What Shall the High Schools Teach?,* 1956 Yearbook of the Association for Supervision and Curriculum Development (Washington, D.C.: Association for Supervision and Curriculum Development, 1956), pp. 17–18.

72. Goodlad, op. cit., pp. 155–56.

73. Ibid., p. 155.

74. Passow, op. cit., p. 223.

75. "Drive Launched to Put 'Real Books' in Classrooms," *TC Today* 15 (Spring/Summer 1988): 8.

76. John B. Carroll, "A Model of School Learning," *Teachers College Record* 64 (May 1963): 723–33.

77. Bloom, op. cit., p. 4.

78. Lee J. Cronbach, "Comments on Mastery Learning and Its Implications for Curriculum Development," in Elliot W. Eisner (ed.), *Confronting Curriculum Reform* (Boston: Little, Brown, 1971), p. 53.

79. Benjamin S. Bloom, "New Views of the Learner: Implications for Instruction and Curriculum," *Educational Leadership* 35 (April 1978): 571–73.

80. Benjamin S. Bloom, "A Response to Slavin's Mastery Learning Reconsidered," *Review of Educational Research* 57 (Winter 1987): 508.

81. National Commission on Excellence in Education, *A Nation at Risk* (Washington, D.C.: U.S. Department of Education, 1983).

82. See for example, John R. Lucy, "Curriculum Revision: Who Will Provide the Leadership?," *National Association of Secondary School Principals Bulletin* 70 (November 1986): 85–87.

83. Cited in *The Chronicle of Higher Education,* Vol. 34 (July 20, 1988), pp. 1, A-14.

84. Ernest L. Boyer, *A Quest for a Common Learning: The Aims of General Education* (Washington, D.C.: Carnegie Foundation for the Advancement of Teaching, 1981); National Institute of Education, *Involvement in Learning: Realizing the Potential of American Higher Education* (Washington, D.C.: U.S. Department of Education, 1984); Association of American Colleges, *Integrity in the College Curriculum* (Washington, D.C.: The Association, 1985).

85. Richard Clark, "Who Decides? The Basic Policy Issue," Chapter 8 in *Critical Issues in Curriculum,* Eighty-seventh Yearbook, Part I, National Society for the Study of Education (Chicago: University of Chicago Press, 1988), pp. 175–204.

86. Philip W. Jackson, "Mainstreaming Art: An Essay on Discipline-Based Art Education," *Educational Researcher* 16 (August-September 1987): 39, 42.

87. American Association for the Advancement of Science, *Science for ALL Americans, Summary Report, Project 2061* (Washington, D.C.: The Association, 1989), pp. 5, 10, 11.

88. BSCS *Journal* 1 (April 1978): 1.

89. Ernest O. Melby, "A Critique," Chapter 22 in *Child Development and the Curriculum,* Thirty-eighth Yearbook, Part I, National Society for the Study of Education (Bloomington, Ill.: Public School Publishing Co., 1939), pp. 439–40.

90. Dwayne Huebner, "Implications of Psychological Thought for the Curriculum," in Association for Supervision and Curriculum Development, *Influences in Curriculum Change* (Washington, D.C.: The Association, 1968), p. 28.

91. James B. Macdonald, "Curriculum Development in Relation to Social and Intellectual Systems," Chapter 5 in *The Curriculum: Retrospect and Prospect,* Seventieth Yearbook, Part I, National Society for the Study of Education (Chicago: University of Chicago, 1971), p. 105.

92. Lawrence A. Cremin, *Public Education* (New York: Basic Books, 1976), p. 48.

93. Crooks, op. cit., p. 467.

94. Margaret Lindsey, "Decision-Making and the Teacher," in A. Harry Passow (ed.), *Curriculum Crossroads* (New York: Bureau of Publications, Teachers College, Columbia University, 1962), p. 39.

95. Cremin, *Transformation of the School,* op. cit., pp. 299–300.

96. Elwood P. Cubberley, *Public Education in the United States* (Boston: Houghton Mifflin, 1947), p. 390; see also Daniel Tanner and Laurel Tanner, *Supervision in Education: Problems and Practices* (New York: Macmillan, 1987), pp. 32–35.

97. Elizabeth Mayo, *A Manual of Elementary Instruction, for Infant School and Private Tuition, 1860;* cited in Lois Coffey Mossman, *Changing Conceptions Relative to the Planning of Lessons* (New York: Teachers College Press, 1924), p. 4.

98. Gordon N. Mackenzie, "Politics of Curriculum Change," in *Curriculum Crossroads,* op. cit., p. 79.

99. Ford Foundation, *Annual Report* (New York: The Foundation, 1973), p. 3.

100. Carnegie Forum on Education and the Economy, *A Nation Prepared: Teachers for the 21st Century* (New York: Carnegie Corporation, 1986), pp. 25, 26.

101. Will French, "Signs of Confusion and Resulting Issues," in Henry Harap (ed.), *The Changing Curriculum* (New York: Appleton-Century, 1937), pp. 21, 22.

102. Henry Harap (ed.), *The Changing Curriculum,* op. cit., p. vi.

103. Franklin Bobbitt, "Discovering and Formulating the Objectives of Teacher Training Institutions," *Journal of Educational Research* 10 (October 1924): 189.

104. Herbert M. Kliebard, "Fads, Fashions, and Rituals: The Instability of Curriculum Change," Chapter 2 in *Critical Issues in Curriculum,* Eighty-seventh Yearbook, Part I, National Society for the Study of Education (Chicago: University of Chicago Press, 1988), p. 25.

105. Katherine Camp Mayhew and Anna Camp Edwards, *The Dewey School: The University School of the University of Chicago 1896–1903* (New York: Appleton Century, 1936), p. 368.

106. John Dewey, "The Relation of Theory to Practice in Education," in *The Relation of Theory to Practice in the Education of Teachers,* ed. Charles A. McMurry, Third Yearbook, Part I, National Society for the Scientific Study of Education (Bloomington, Ill.: Public School Publishing Co., 1904), p. 15.

107. Gary A. Griffin, "Leadership for School Improvement: The School Administrator's Role," Chapter 11 in *Critical Issues in Curriculum,* Eighty-seventh Yearbook, Part I, National Society for the Study of Education (Chicago: University of Chicago Press, 1988), p. 256.

108. Henry Harap, "Curriculum Trends at Mid-Century," Eleventh Annual Delta Pi Epsilon Lecture, Chicago, Illinois, December 19, 1952 (Cincinnati, Ohio: South-Western Publishing, 1953), p. 10.

109. John I. Goodlad, *A Place Called School* (New York: McGraw-Hill, 1984), pp. 101–29.

110. Griffin, op. cit., p. 254.

111. John Dewey, *The Child and the Curriculum* (Chicago: University of Chicago Press, 1889).

SELECTED REFERENCES

Association for Supervision and Curriculum Development. *Influences in Curriculum Change.* Washington, D.C.: National Education Association, 1968.

———. *A New Look at Progressive Education.* 1972 Yearbook. Washington, D.C.: National Education Association, 1972.

———. *Improving Teaching.* 1986 Yearbook. Alexandria, Va.: The Association, 1986.

Bell, Daniel. *The Reforming of General Education.* New York: Columbia University Press, 1966.

Bloom, Benjamin S. *Human Characteristics and School Learning.* New York: McGraw-Hill, 1976.

Bower, Gordon H. and Ernest R. Hilgard. *Theories of Learning.* Englewood Cliffs, N.J.: Prentice-Hall, 1981.

Boyer, Ernest L. *High School: A Report on Secondary Education in America.* New York: Harper & Row, 1983.

Bruner, Jerome S. *The Process of Education.* Cambridge: Harvard University Press, 1960.

———. *Toward a Theory of Instruction.* Cambridge: Harvard University Press, 1966.

Cremin, Lawrence A. *The Transformation of the School.* New York: Knopf, 1961.

Dewey, John. *How We Think.* Lexington, Mass.: D. C. Heath, 1910.

———. *The School and Society.* Chicago: University of Chicago Press, 1915. (Originally published in 1899.)

———. *Democracy and Education.* New York: Macmillan, 1916.

———. *Freedom and Culture.* New York: Putnam, 1939.

Giles, H. H.; McCutchen, S. P.; and Zechiel, A. N. *Exploring the Curriculum.* New York: Harper & Row, 1942.

Goodlad, John I. *A Place Called School.* New York: McGraw-Hill, 1984.

Inglis, Alexander. *Principles of Secondary Education.* Boston: Houghton Mifflin, 1918.

Lazerson, Marvin; McLaughlin, Judith; McPherson, Bruce; and Bailey, Stephen K. *An Education of Value.* New York: Cambridge University Press, 1985.

Marshall, Leon C., and Goetz, Rachael M. *Curriculum-Making in the Social Studies,* Report of the Commission on the Social Studies of the American Historical Association, Part 13. New York: Scribner, 1936.

National Commission on Excellence in Education. *A Nation at Risk: The Imperative for Educational Reform.* Washington, D.C.: U.S. Department of Education, 1983.

National Society for the Study of Education. *Child Development and the Curriculum,* Thirty-eighth Yearbook, Part 1. Bloomington, Ill.: Public School Publishing Co., 1939.

————. *The Curriculum: Retrospect and Prospect,* Seventieth Yearbook, Part I. Chicago: University of Chicago Press, 1971.

————. *The Elementary School in the United States,* Seventy-second Yearbook, Part II. Chicago: University of Chicago Press, 1973.

————. *Critical Issues in Curriculum,* Eighty-seventh Yearbook, Part I. Chicago: University of Chicago Press, 1988.

Piaget, Jean, and Inhelder, B. *The Growth of Logical Thinking from Childhood to Adolescence.* New York: Basic Books, 1958.

Prescott, Daniel. *Emotion and the Educative Process.* Washington, D.C.: American Council on Education, 1938.

Robinson, James Harvey. *The Humanizing of Knowledge.* New York: George H. Doran Co., 1924.

Schwab, Joseph J. *College Curriculum and Student Protest.* Chicago: University of Chicago Press, 1969.

Shulman, Lee S., and Keislar, Evan R., eds. *Learning by Discovery: A Critical Approach.* Chicago: Rand McNally, 1966.

Taba, Hilda. *Curriculum Development: Theory and Practice.* New York: Harcourt Brace Jovanovich, 1962.

Tanner, Daniel, and Tanner, Laurel. *Supervision in Education: Problems and Practices.* New York: Macmillan, 1987.

7

Ideals Old and New

"History deals with the past, but this past is the history of the present," wrote Dewey, for the present reflects the heritage of the struggles of the past.[1] In the same vein, the struggles of the present set the stage for the future.

In recent years there has been a great deal of popular and professional writing on the future to the extent that the field has been termed futurism. Much of this writing has been quite fantastic—a kind of crystal-ball gazing coupled with utopianism. The record of utopian schemes and visions in our history reveals how far off the mark they are when they are fashioned in isolation from the conditions of the times and in absence of any concerted effort to reshape and correct any wanting conditions. In other words, the future is shaped by what is being done here and now, in the time frame of our current history.

While history should give us perspective, philosophy should provide us with prospect. As a regulator for the testing of ideas in action and as a compass for setting our present course of action, philosophy is more than mere academic speculation.

The different uncertainties of life, the different diagnoses of the causes and proposals for dealing with difficulties in life, and the conflict of interests among groups result in competing philosophies, noted Dewey. "One would not expect a ruling class living at ease to have the same philosophy of life as those who were having a hard struggle for existence." He went on to define philosophy as the "general theory of education," for he viewed education as the supreme human interest in which all other problems come to a head.[2] Yet although his own philosophy had been most fully expounded in *Democracy and Education,* Dewey noted that "I do not know what philosophic critics, as distinct from teachers, have ever had recourse to it. I have wondered whether such facts signified that philosophers in general, although they are themselves usually teachers, have not taken education with sufficient seriousness for it to occur to them that any rational person could actually think it possible that philosophizing should focus about education as the supreme human interest."[3]

Competing philosophies reflect conflicting conceptions concerning the nature of the learner, the nature of society, and the organization of knowledge and its functions in the making of the curriculum. In recognizing the significance of philosophy in these connections, Bode wrote: "if the younger generation is to achieve 'participation' in our social life the emphasis in curriculum construction and in teaching must be placed on social outlook, on reflective consideration of what constitutes a good life in the social order."[4] In effect, we need to understand how competing philosophies present conflicting conceptions of the good person leading the good life in the good social order, and how the school and the curriculum are expected to contribute to these ends. Philosophy, then, serves as a compass in determining the curriculum.

FROM TRADITIONALISM TO PROGRESSIVISM— THE TRANSFORMATION OF THE CURRICULUM

By the latter part of the nineteenth century the American experience had witnessed such severe breaks with European educational and social traditions that, in historical perspective, it seems inevitable that a genuinely American educational philosophy should emerge to meet the expansive prospects for the twentieth century. The seeds for the new philosophy were being sown not only in academia, but in our literature and daily life. In *The Prince and the Pauper* (1882), Mark Twain exposed the difference between privilege and penury as mainly an accident of birth coupled with environmental conditions. In *A Connecticut Yankee in King Arthur's Court* (1889), Twain portrayed the American character as being in control of circumstances through scientific explanation and practical application, as opposed to being controlled by superstition, happenstance, and blind authority.

Darwin's *Origin of Species* (1859) and the subsequent advances in science during the latter part of the nineteenth century rocked the very foundations of the old supernatural explanations and displaced them with naturalistic explanations of human nature and the universe.

During the last two decades of the nineteenth century, the waves of immigration were not only rising dramatically but reflected the far more diverse geographical and cultural origins of people seeking opportunities not available in the Old World. The agricultural revolution reduced human drudgery in subsistence farming, giving great impetus to urbanization. The great pluralism of the American population gave fuller justification to the wisdom of those who had been engaged in the long struggle for the American public secular school.

Advances in scientific thought concerning human nature and the universe buttressed the democratic social conception of a humanity committed to progress through the unleashing of intelligence, as opposed to the old traditions and the imposition of authority. The new view was embodied in Lester Ward's *Dynamic Sociology* (1883) and later in the works of John Dewey, who systematically examined the need to reconstruct the school curriculum in accord with the dynamic nature of knowledge and the ideals of a democratic society. Before discussing the impact of Dewey's experimentalist philosophy on the curriculum, a brief examination of the forces of traditionalism is presented.

From Absolutism to Experimentalism

As discussed earlier, the dominant strain of ideas on the function of the school brought over from Europe to colonial America was rooted in theocentric traditionalism: education for salvation. Hence the curriculum was directed at religious indoctrination (with the teaching of reading designed to promote a knowledge of the scriptures). Although it is beyond the purview here to examine in any detail the profound and extended influences of Christian traditionalism on the school curriculum, one finds that textbooks in the public schools of the late nineteenth century continued to refer to God, God's will, and man's soul.

Decades later (1925), what came to be called "the world's most famous court trial" found high-school biology teacher John T. Scopes on trial for having violated a Tennessee statute prohibiting the teaching of evolution. To this day, the theater play and motion picture dramatizing the Scopes trial are prohibited from being presented in some public schools around the nation.

Throughout the 1980s leading Christian fundamentalists sought to bring "creationism theory" into the school science curriculum on an "equal" footing to counter the "Godless" theory of evolution, despite repeated setbacks in the courts. The late Richard Hofstadter was clearly premature when he wrote in *Anti-intellectualism in American Life* (1962) that "Today the evolution controversy seems as remote as the Homeric era to intellectuals in the East."[5] In fact, the evolution-creationism controversy in the school curriculum was so rampant during the 1980s that the California State Curriculum Development Commission reported in 1985 that it was unable to find a science textbook for the junior-high grades that gave adequate treatment to evolution and other topics of "controversy."[6]

In his only autobiographical work, "From Absolutism to Experimentalism," Dewey related that when he was completing his undergraduate studies during the late 1870s, "Teachers of philosophy were at that time, almost to a man, clergymen" and the "supposed requirements of religion, or theology, dominated the teaching of philosophy in most colleges."[7] But by the late nineteenth century, the philosophy of idealism, largely influenced by the German philosophers (Hegel, Schelling), replaced the theistic influence with a kind of nonsectarian spirituality that held that the moving force in the universe is spiritual rather than physical (ideas rather than matter).

With the trend toward nonsectarian education in an increasingly pluralistic society and with the idealistic tenet of nonsectarian spirituality, idealism replaced Christian traditionalism without confrontation, for both views were rooted in the dualism that held spiritual man above the physical universe. As indicated, the spiritual grounding of idealism gave emphasis to the creative social force of humanity.

Idealism continued to dominate American philosophical thought into the early years of the twentieth century, when the time became ripe for the synthesis of the uniquely American experimentalist philosophy. Nevertheless, the progressive efforts to transform the school and the curriculum met with great conflict, which has continued to this day.

TRADITIONALISM AND THE CURRICULUM—PRESERVATION AND TRANSMISSION

Perennialism or Classical Humanism

During the early decades of the twentieth century, the philosophy of perennialism or classical humanism, drawing upon idealism and faculty psychology, was explicated as a systematic educational position. Embracing the dualism that sets mind above the physical and biological universe, the classical humanists or perennialists held that the sole purpose of education is the cultivation of mind through the study of permanent truths to be found in the classical studies.

Curriculum Dualism. The perennialists held that in the classical or permanent studies, knowledge is external and absolute, as opposed to practical and modern studies—such as the natural sciences, social sciences, vocational education, health and physical education—which treat knowledge as dynamic and inextricably connected with social change and growth. The perennialists or classical humanists viewed the curriculum as properly centered on the classical literary works of the Western world and on classical language—the traditional liberal education.

At the elementary-school level the fundamentals were to serve as the foundation for the classical studies. No attention need be given to the nature and interests of the learner, since the immature learner is not a valid consideration when fashioning the curriculum.

Mental Discipline

Not only did the perennialists regard the interests of the learner as ephemeral, but they held that the discipline of the mind requires rigorous exercise and any consideration of student interests leads only to "soft pedagogy." Mind was to be regarded as a muscle to be strengthened through exercise or as a vessel to be filled. The fact that individuals are endowed with minds of different capacities meant only that their intellectual brew should differ only in quantity and not in quality. Hence the curriculum was to be the same for all. The research findings of behavioral science, which have long refuted such a notion of mind, are given virtually no credence by contemporary perennialists, whose philosophic system is based upon a priori truths concerning human nature and the nature of knowledge.

Permanent Studies

As the twentieth century wore on, the perennialists or classical humanists spoke less of the spiritual or supernatural quality of humanity, but they continued to embrace the classical literary studies as the means to strengthen the powers of reason to equip the student with the eternal verities that are valid for any time and place. In the words of the late Robert M. Hutchins, writing about the purpose of education as being focused on the elements of our common human nature,

> These elements are the same in any time or place. The notion of educating a man to live in a particular time or place, to adjust him to any particular environment, is therefore foreign to a true conception of education.
>
> Education implies teaching. Teaching implies knowledge. Knowledge is truth. Truth is everywhere the same. Hence education is everywhere the same.[8]

Although Hutchins served powerfully as chancellor of the University of Chicago over many years (1929–50), the undergraduate curriculum developed at Chicago never did exemplify Hutchins' Great Books program or a traditional liberal arts program. Instead, the College of the University of Chicago organized its curriculum around broad fields for general education that included interdisciplinary studies in the humanities, social sciences, and natural sciences—with the subject matter often focused on themes and pervading problems.

General Education Versus Traditional Liberal Education

Recognizing the inadequacy of the perennialist tradition for liberal education, leading American colleges during the 1930s used the term *general education* to signify the common core of undergraduate studies in place of liberal education. General education took the illiberal out of liberal education by opening the core undergraduate requirements to interdisciplinary curricular designs, problem-focused studies, and more progressive approaches to the curriculum. A parallel transformation occurred at that time in the secondary-school curriculum, reflecting advances in our understanding of the nature of the learner, heightened concern for the pervasive need to relate the curriculum to the wider democratic social interest, and growing recognition of the need for curriculum articulation and synthesis. Where traditional liberal education had been concerned with transmission of the cultural heritage for a select population, general education was concerned with cultural transformation for a free society through universal secondary education and open-access higher education.

Nevertheless, perennialists continued to hold for basic education in the elementary school, the fundamental academic studies and literary classics of the Western world in the secondary school, and the old literary tradition of liberal education in the college.

Human Nature and Knowledge. Perennialist philosophy virtually ignores the findings of the behavioral sciences concerning human nature and the advances in knowledge wrought by the natural sciences; hence one is apt to regard perennialism as a quaint relic of a bygone era. But perennialism or classical humanism continues to have influential adherents. Like its handmaiden, essentialism ("back to basics"), perennialism gains resurrection during periods of social and educational retrenchment. Contemporary perennialists still hold to an outmoded concept of mind based upon the long-discredited faculty psychology.

In his widely read critique of the American high school published in 1984, Theodore Sizer, a former headmaster of Phillips Academy (Massachusetts), stated: "For centuries, concerned scholars have asked what knowledge is most worthy, what schools should provide for the discipline and furniture of the student's mind, the skills he requires, and the substantive knowledge he should grasp."[9] In 1828, President Jeremiah Day reported to the Yale faculty that the "two great points to be gained in intellectual culture are the *discipline* and the *furniture* of the mind; expanding its powers, and storing it with knowledge."[10]

Educational Elitism. Although Hutchins was a strong proponent of universal secondary education, many contemporary perennialists such as Sizer embrace the elitism of their predecessors, who viewed formal education beyond the elementary school as a privilege rather than a right. For the masses, "mastery of the minima" would be sufficient. In the words of Sizer, "Compulsory attendance in an educational institution should cease when a young citizen demonstrates mastery of the minima, and most young citizens should master these minima before senior high school. . . . High school would be an opportunity, not an obligation."[11]

Regarding the accessibility of schooling for the masses and the curricular offerings of the school, perennialists hold to the aphorism that "less is more," and they contend that the true process of learning is almost necessarily painful. "There is hurt in learning," contends Sizer, "and it is difficult to persuade someone to hurt himself."[12]

Teaching Methods and the Curriculum

Along with the essentialists, perennialists place great emphasis on drill at the elementary level. In recent times they have drawn an analogy in seeing the incessant drills in coaching sports as the appropriate drill-skill repertoire of the classroom teacher.

Mortimer Adler's *Paideia Proposal* (1982) classified the appropriate mode of teaching into three categories: didactic instruction (telling and explaining) for the acquisition of organized knowledge; development of learning skills through coaching and drill; and Socratic questioning for enlarged understanding of ideas and values. (Adler took the term paideia from the Greek, meaning the "bringing up of the child.") Oddly, Adler dedicated his proposal to Horace Mann and John Dewey, along with Robert Hutchins.

The Learner and the Curriculum. The perennialist refusal to consider the nature of the learner in developing the curriculum is reflected in *The Paideia Proposal.* Instead of seeing childhood and youth as distinct phases of human development requiring uniquely appropriate learning experiences for effective growth, childhood and youth are regarded as obstacles to be gotten over with as quickly as possible. "Youth itself is the most serious impediment—in fact, youth is an insuperable obstacle to being an educated person," declares the Proposal. The Proposal goes on to call for twelve years of basic schooling for all, capped by the Socratic study of great literary works and other works of art. This kind of learning "aims at raising the mind up from a lesser or weaker understanding to a stronger and fuller one," declares Adler, and the "art of the teacher depends on the teacher's understanding of how the mind learns by the exercise of its own powers," declares Adler, as though the mind exists as a separate entity.[13]

The Paideia Proposal cites Dewey in expressing its opposition to vocational education, failing to acknowledge that Dewey was attacking the traditional narrow training for social predestination, while he was calling for vocational education to enhance the individual's social power and insight.[14] The Proposal calls for a one-track curriculum of basic schooling over twelve years, implying that a comprehensive curriculum is undemocratic because it separates students into tracks.

However, from Dewey to Conant, it was shown how a comprehensive curriculum would be fashioned to meet the common needs of all youth while also ministering to their special needs. Although *The Paideia Proposal* was widely discussed, its influence on the schools was relatively limited despite its appearance at a time when the call was for a return to more fundamental values and a fundamental curriculum.

The Great Divide. At midcentury, Conant had succinctly described the divide between the traditionalists and progressivists regarding the function of the school and its curriculum:

> Roughly speaking, the basic argument about general education turns on the degree to which the literary and philosophical traditions of the western world, as interpreted by scholars and connoisseurs before World War I, should be the basis of the education of *all* American youth. The watershed between two fundamentally opposed positions can be located by raising the question: For what purpose do we have a system of public education? If the answer is to develop effective citizens of a free country, then we seems to be facing in one direction. If the answer is to develop the student's rational powers and immerse him in the stream of our cultural heritage, then we appear to be facing in the opposite direction.[15]

This divide was to be reflected in the educational and popular literature of the 1980s, when the schools came under renewed attack by leading perennialists.

Curricular Reductionism.   Perennialism and essentialism tend to be resurrected during periods of educational and social retrenchment. During 1987 and 1988, two relevant books appeared on the national best-seller lists: *The Closing of the American Mind,* by Allan Bloom, attacked our schools and colleges for the decline of the traditional liberal arts; and *Cultural Literacy,* by E. D. Hirsch, Jr., offered a compendium of factual "knowledge" in history, literature, geography, and government as a "fast-food" indicator of the well-educated individual.

During the period from 1983 to 1988, William J. Bennett, previously chairman of the National Endowment for the Humanities, served as Secretary of Education in the Reagan Cabinet and used that office to expound the perennialist cause for the school and college curriculum. Throughout the history of the office of U.S. commissioner or secretary of education, the individual in that post almost invariably favored a progressive philosophy attuned to the great expansion of popular education and the need for modernizing the curriculum in accord with the demands of a changing society. As a perennialist, Bennett was an exception, but he took office at a time of educational retrenchment. His call for redirecting the elementary-school curriculum back to the fundamental skill subjects and the secondary-school curriculum to the fundamental academic disciplines garnered little opposition from school leaders, who had been battered by several years of curricular reductionism through "back to basics."[16]

But when Bennett attacked the colleges for allowing the study of Western civilization (the humanities) to lose its central place in the undergraduate curriculum, a storm of controversy arose. The storm reached its peak in 1988, when Bennett attacked the Stanford faculty for yielding to politics when it revised the undergraduate core requirements in the classics of Western literature so as to include contemporary literature and non-European culture.[17] In a report issued when he chaired the National Endowment for the Humanities, Bennett had called on the colleges to restore the humanities to the central place in the curriculum, and he described the humanities as a "body of knowledge and a means of inquiry that convey serious truths, defensible judgments, and significant ideas. Properly taught, the humanities bring together the perennial questions of human life with the greatest works of history, literature, philosophy, and art."[18]

Academic-Nonacademic Dualism. Although the perennialists or classical humanists concede a place for science in the curriculum as a fundamental academic discipline, it is the humanities that are nonpareil. And while the perennialists make some concessions to "nonacademic" subjects, such subjects are relegated to electives that are restricted in number. Their bias against practical, vocational, and contemporary studies is an artifact of Ancient Greek civilization, when work was for the slave whereas the ideal education of the freeman was the cultivation of the intellect. The metaphysical doctrine, developed by Plato and Aristotle, that rational knowledge is derived from a higher source than experience is anchored in perennialism. Although experimental science demolished this doctrine, perennialism continues to hold to the traditional dualisms of contemplation versus action, mind versus body, intellect versus emotion, cultural studies versus vocational studies, knowledge versus experience, and so on.

Humanities Versus the Sciences. Perennialists see the humanities as the study of the great achievements of Western civilization as exemplified by the great classics in literature and the arts. But are not the great human achievements also attributable to the advent of modern science and science as a mode of inquiry? To the perennialist, who extolls the classical studies as exemplifying the permanent truths, science must be relegated to a separate and lesser knowledge culture, for science holds nothing sacred except its modes of inquiry; it holds to no absolute truths and sees the physical and biological universe as constantly evolving.

Where permanence is the guiding word for the perennialist, growth and change are the qualities of the natural world as seen by the progressivist. It would take the American philosophy of pragmatism and its orchestration into the philosophy of experimentalism by Dewey in the twentieth century to explicate the import of science for educational theory and to give science its due recognition as a system of inquiry that has revolutionized civilization.

Whatever efforts are expended in embracing the sentiments for a return to the past, they are bound to be fruitless exercises, for the discoveries of science cannot be undiscovered. In the old scheme, observed Dewey, knowledge signified precisely and exclusively the turning away from change to the changeless. "In the new experimental science, knowledge is obtained in exactly the opposite way, namely through deliberate institution of a definite and specified course of change."[19]

Essentialism

In response to the rising industrialism of the nineteenth century in England and the United States, it was deemed necessary that the schools provide instruction in the fundamentals, or three R's, for children of the working classes. According to Bernal, the "new working class needed enough acquaintance with the three R's to do their jobs properly, and provision for teaching them was reluctantly provided on the cheapest possible basis. But there was all the more reason for seeing that the education of the masses did not go too far, and that it introduced no unsettling ideas."[20]

Literacy. The great waves of immigrants in the United States spanning the early decades of the twentieth century witnessed the call for literacy through the three R's in our city schools. Efforts by progressivists to provide a richer and more complete curriculum for all children were attacked by conservative business leaders and others as unnecessary and as "frills" in the curriculum. Dewey sharply criticized such views as antidemocratic when he wrote in 1917 that

> He who is poorly acquainted with the history of the efforts to improve elementary education in our large cities does not know that the chief protest against progress is likely to come from successful business men. They have clamored for the three R's as the essential and exclusive material of primary education—knowing well enough that their own children would be able to get the things they protest against. Thus they have attacked as fads and frills every enrichment of the curriculum which did not lend itself to narrow economic ends. Let us stick to business, to the essentials, has been their plea, and by business they meant enough of the routine skills in letters and figures to make those leaving the elementary school at about the fifth or sixth grade useful to *their* business, irrespective of whether pupils left school with an equipment for advance and with an ambition to try to secure better social and economic conditions for their children than they themselves had enjoyed.[21]

Although we have come a long way since the time when Dewey leveled his attack against such narrow vested interests, the call for "back to basics" has been a recurrent one throughout the twentieth century.

Reaction Against Progressivism. In reaction against the progressive curricular reforms in the elementary and secondary schools during the first two decades of the twentieth century, a number of educators during the 1930s contended that the schools must refocus the curriculum on the recognized academic subjects and on the fundamental skills. A leading figure expounding the essentialist view was William C. Bagley of Teachers College, Columbia University. In historical perspective, Bagley's criticisms seem quite moderate in contrast to the criticisms of modern-day essentialists.[22] In Bagley's time a romantic branch of progressivism had indeed gone to extreme in child centeredness and laissez-faire pedagogy, which, incidentally, came under Dewey's criticism as well.

Essentialism gained impetus after World War II, when it was found appealing to tax conservatives, who opposed the great expansion of school facilities to meet needs that were neglected through the decade of the Great Depression, the war years, and the efforts to provide for the school population explosion as a result of the postwar baby boom. Leading essentialists also sought to capitalize on the cold war and space race in promoting their curricular prescriptions.

Training the Mind. Perhaps the most systematic explication of the essentialist position at midcentury was the widely debated book *The Restoration of Learning* (1955), written by Arthur Bestor, a history professor at the University of Illinois. Bestor contended that the school's exclusive task lies in training the intellect and that this can be accomplished only by delimiting the curriculum to the fundamental academic studies of English (grammar, literature, and composition), mathematics, science, history, and modern foreign languages. (Social studies would be replaced entirely by history, and credit would be disallowed for nonacademic electives.) He proceeded to restate the essentialist position that the schools were being sidetracked from the exclusive task of training the intellect by seeking to meet the personal-social needs of children and youth through a comprehensive curriculum embracing the development of salable skills (vocational studies), health, democratic citizenship, and worthy use of leisure time (for example, the studio arts and other "nonacademic" studies are nonessentials, or curricular frills).

Ignoring the research to the contrary, Bestor reiterated the essentialist position that efforts to integrate or synthesize the curriculum below the college level are misguided on the ground that such synthesis arrives only after the student "has marshalled the array of separate intellectual powers" through the separate organized academic subjects.[23] Hence curriculum synthesis lies in the province of higher education, contended Bestor (with the consequence that over half our pupil population would be denied an integrated curriculum except for a single integrated course in the senior year of high school).

Essential Versus Nonessential Studies. In attacking the vocational and practical studies, Bestor resorted to ridicule and distortion. "The West was not settled by men and women who had taken courses in 'How to be a pioneer,'" wrote Bestor, as if to imply that the West was won by historians and literati.[24] He proceeded to call for the use of standardized tests for pupil ability grouping and promotion. Such tests would also be used at the completion of compulsory schooling to dramatize that the continuance of one's education is not a right but a "privilege bestowed upon the meritorious and the energetic."[25]

After *Sputnik I,* Bestor sought to expound his essentialist curricular prescriptions as the remedy for our nation's alleged failure to beat the Soviets in the space race. However, the limelight of school criticism shifted to Admiral Hyman G. Rickover, who proceeded to expound his essentialist views at congressional hearings, in the popular press, and even in some educational journals. Rickover's curricular prescriptions and his notion of mind and mental discipline were essentialist to the core, as revealed in these words:

> For all children, the educational process must be one of collecting factual knowledge to the limit of their absorptive capacity. Recreation, manual or clerical training, etiquette, and similar know-how have little effect on the mind itself and it is with the mind that the school must solely concern itself. The poorer a child's natural endowments, the more does he need to have his mind trained.... To acquire such knowledge, fact upon fact, takes time and effort. Nothing can really make it "fun."[26]

The notion of mind as a sponge, vessel, or muscle is shared by essentialists as well as perennialists, who also see the educative process as necessarily painful. To go back to Aristotle, "youths are not to be instructed with a view to their amusement, for learning is no amusement, but is accompanied with pain."[27] Presumably the effective curriculum is to be administered like good medicine. Both the perennialist and essentialist see the proper curricular prescription at the elementary level as consisting of mastery of the basic skills and factual information. Both favor the reinforcement of this learning in the secondary school through the traditional academic studies, although the perennialist would place more emphasis on the Great Books and classical languages and less on the laboratory sciences and the modern approaches to disciplinary knowledge. The emphasis on the basic skills, rote learning, and drill at the lower levels of schooling, coupled with the mechanistic conception of mind, finds an ally in behavioristic psychology in the elementary school.

Academic Versus Comprehensive High School.   Both the perennialist and essentialist see the secondary school as a purely academic institution, although many of them have favored a dual system of secondary education with separate academic and vocational high schools. For example, Rickover attacked the American comprehensive high school and advocated that we adopt the traditional dual system of European schooling. If the choice is between democracy and efficiency, we must choose efficiency. In Rickover's words,

> One cannot argue the issue of comprehensive schooling versus separate secondary education on a philosophical basis. But one can argue it on the basis whether the country really has a choice as between efficient education—that is, separate schools above the elementary levels—and pure "democratic" education which insists on the inefficient time-wasting comprehensive high

school. In my opinion, we no longer have that choice. We must opt for efficiency.[28]

In the face of powerful sentiments to abandon the comprehensive high school, it took the prestige and moderation of James B. Conant to save this American institution through his influential report of 1957, *The American High School Today*. Although Conant is often portrayed as an essentialist, his advocacy of a comprehensive curriculum and of the comprehensive high school belie such a portrayal. His report contained some elements of essentialism, but on balance his recommendations were eclectic. In other instances he had endorsed experimentalist documents for curriculum reform, such as when he chaired the Educational Policies Commission at the time it issued its revised report, *Education for ALL American Youth—A Further Look* (1952). Moreover, he was later to retract his stance in utilizing standardized tests for gauging school achievement and determining college admissions. "I recognize the multiplicity of examinations and am ready to support a proposal for more emphasis on school records and less emphasis on examinations," stated Conant.[29]

The Disciplinary Doctrine. In the wake of the cold war and the space race, Bestor's essentialist criticisms and prescriptions for curriculum reform were virtually eclipsed as the curriculum priority shifted to the sciences and mathematics. The National Science Foundation proceeded to support national curriculum reforms in the sciences and mathematics. The National Defense Education Act of 1958 provided federal funds for instruction in the sciences, mathematics, and modern foreign languages, new instructional media, and guidance and testing programs principally for discovering and developing the talents of our most academically able pupils. A new curriculum priority and hierarchy was created. History and the literary studies were neglected—not to mention the arts and vocational education.

Educators in the social studies sought to imitate the discipline-centered approaches taken in the sciences by shifting their focus to the social sciences, but this only added to the further congestion of the curriculum. The nature of the learner was recast in the form of a miniature adult scholar working to advance knowledge in the disciplines along the line of the university scholar-specialists.

Leading disciplinary advocates held that the chief if not the sole criterion for including any subject in the school curriculum is whether that subject is recognized as an academic "discipline." Theorists propounding the discipline-centered curriculum reforms appeared to be promoting a new brand of essentialism without embracing the old concept of mind. "The first principle is that the content of instruction should be drawn entirely from the fields of disciplined inquiry" as developed by "organized communities of specialists," contended Joseph Schwab. Five years later, Schwab was to shift his position in response to the wave of student protest and demand for curricular "relevance." In 1969 he added the criterion of practicality to the curriculum and the need to include the arts in revealing the relations among areas of the curriculum. "Pervasive specialism unexamined creates in students the illusion from which we all suffer to some degree—the illusion that subject matters as now distinguished are inevitable products of natural divisions," wrote Schwab.[30] As a biologist, Schwab should have been aware of the shortcomings of the discipline's doctrine from the start, since biology is a broad field in which scientific knowledge is highly interrelated.

Counterreactions. Instead of seeking curricular synthesis, the response to the demand for "relevance" was a shift to extreme pupil-centered approaches in the elementary school and a myriad of elective options in our secondary schools and colleges. This occurred in the wake of growing opposition to our heightened engagement in the Vietnam War at a time when civil rights and poverty were the key domestic issues.

A brief effort was made during the early 1970s under the leadership of the U.S. commissioner of education to promote career education in our elementary and secondary schools on the ground that we had been giving excessive emphasis to the academic side of the curriculum and college preparatory studies, with the consequence that we were creating "academic snobbery."[31] But this effort was short-lived as the reaction against the student-centered curricular concessions resulted in the demand for a return to the traditional values of authority, discipline, respect, and academic standards. The term *new basics* appeared in reference to the standard but "beefed-up" academic subjects required of all, to which was added computer literacy. Coupled with the call for higher standards through standardized achievement tests for pupil sorting and grouping, high-school graduation, and college admission, the new basics would enable our nation to meet the Japanese challenge for supremacy over world markets and would restore our leadership role among nations. This was the message, loud and clear, from the report *A Nation at Risk* (1983), issued by the National Commission on Excellence under the auspices of the U.S. Department of Education.[32]

Various documents calling for school reform during the late 1980s advocated cultural literacy, scientific literacy, computer literacy, and other segmented forms of literacy.[33] In historic perspective, this would appear to be a curious use of the term literacy. Instead of seeing these functions of the curriculum as an integral part of general education, they were segmentally inserted into the curriculum along with the fundamental skills as the new basics.

Curriculum Isolation and Congestion. From the historic record it can be predicted that as long as the response to the narrowness of the old basic education is to inject additional segmental studies into the curriculum without reconstructing the curriculum as an interdependent whole, the school will suffer from curriculum congestion. Each subject will be treated in isolation and in competition with other subjects for due recognition. Special interests will determine which new subjects will be inserted or given priority over other subjects at a particular time. The counterreaction to the multiplicity of subjects will be a call for a return to the fundamentals. "Back to basics" then once again becomes the simple solution and gains wide appeal, especially at times of social conservatism. Essentialism has its day once again. As Dewey prophetically observed,

> When it is perceived that after all the requirements of a full life experience are not met, the deficiency is not laid to the isolation and narrowness of the teaching of the existing subjects, and this recognition made the basis of reorganization of the system. No, the lack is something to be made up for by the introduction of still another study, or, if necessary, another kind of school. And as a rule those who object to the resulting overcrowding and consequent superficiality and distraction, usually also have recourse to a merely quantitative criterion: the remedy is to cut off a great many studies as fads and frills, and return to the good old curriculum of the three R's in elementary education and the equally good and equally old-fashioned curriculum of the classics and mathematics in higher education.[34]

Eclecticism

Torn between traditionalist and progressivist views on the curriculum, some educators have sought to bring elements from both sides together. Such efforts have tended to result in a kind of admixture rather than a coherent and unified rationale for the curriculum. Probably the most thoughtfully and eloquently formulated eclectic statement on the school and college curriculum was the Harvard Report, *General Education in a Free Society,* issued in 1945 at the behest of James B. Conant, then president of Harvard. "Education can therefore be wholly devoted neither to tradition or experiment," stated the report. "It must uphold at the same time tradition and experiment," and "though common aims must bind together the whole educational system, there exists no one body of knowledge, no single system of instruction equally valid for every part of it."[35]

Compromise Versus Resolution.   The chief problem with the eclectic lies with the many irreconcilable conflicts between the traditionalist and progressivist conceptions of the nature of the learner and views on the curriculum. For example, the conceptions of mind as seen by the traditionalist and progressivist are so radically opposed that no compromise is possible. Such differences in the conception of mind make for radically different curriculum prescriptions and modes of teaching. Where the experimentalist-progressivist draws on the best available evidence from the advancing body of educational research, the traditionalist holds to a priori truths concerning the nature of the learner and the formulation of the curriculum. Thus the eclectic position represents compromise rather than resolution. Since each eclectic borrows different elements from the conflicting philosophies, there is no unified eclectic position that could be called a philosophy. Because the eclectic draws upon many traditionalist tenets, the outlook tends to be conservative.

Another highly influential eclectic document was Conant's *The American High School Today*, issued in 1959 at the height of the cold war and the space race. As mentioned, Conant embraced the democratizing function of the comprehensive high school, but his conception of general education was a list of traditional academic course requirements. Although he opposed curricular tracking, he favored ability grouping, subject by subject, based upon standardized tests. Except for a senior course on problems of American democracy, to be heterogeneously grouped, Conant made no case for curricular correlation or synthesis. His support of vocational education in the high school was powerfully expressed, although his recommendations for the academically talented students carried far more weight with school boards and school administrators in the wake of *Sputnik I.*

Another example of an eclectic document, *High School: A Report on Secondary Education in America* by Ernest L. Boyer, was issued in 1983 by the Carnegie Foundation for the Advancement of Teaching. Although Boyer's report avoided the accusatory and condemnatory language characteristic of so many of the reports on school reform during the 1980s, he failed to support the comprehensive high school. He addressed the democraticizing function of the American high school, yet he endorsed a nationwide network of federally supported residential academies in science and mathematics for elite students. He criticized the bookkeeping device of the Carnegie unit in inventorying academic credits and addressed the need for curriculum integration through common learnings, yet he proposed a standard list of courses and credits by "academic units" required for graduation—units virtually identical to Carnegie units.

In addition to the list of academic courses required for graduation, Boyer recommended that all students take a half-unit course in the arts (which he classified under "language"), in technology, in health, in a seminar on work, and in a senior independent project. He addressed the great problem of dropouts and youth unemployment, yet he focused on the weaknesses of existing programs of vocational education in the comprehensive high school (without showing how the federal-state supported programs might be strengthened). Instead, he proposed "elective clusters" for exploration of career options for the noncollege-bound students. In short, where the Conant report served to save the comprehensive high school and the comprehensive curriculum, the Boyer report, issued a quarter of a century later, was willing to scrap this uniquely American invention in favor of a general academic high school geared mainly to serving the precollege population. Yet both reports were eclectic in orientation and prescription, containing many contradictory elements in the quest for compromise.

PROGRESSIVISM AND THE CURRICULUM— GROWTH AND TRANSFORMATION

Although progressive education grew out of a vast humanitarian movement in the United States extending from the latter nineteenth century to the mid-twentieth century, its roots can be traced to the ideas of such figures as Benjamin Franklin, Thomas Jefferson, Horace Mann, and others who viewed public education as the key to the advance of American democracy.

Over the years, many traditionalists have cast progressive education as a singular movement and have sought to portray it as a permissive pedagogy based upon a romanticized notion of the learner. It has been indiscriminately labeled *life-adjustment* education, as though the agenda of progressive education was to perpetuate conformance to the status quo.[36] As a pluralistic and complex movement, progressive education came to be distorted by some of its professed disciples as well as by its most vociferous critics. A brief examination of the division and conflict among the various schools of progressive education is offered in the section that follows in order to separate experimentalist ideas from romanticism on the one hand and reconstructionism on the other.

Progressive education as a movement may be seen as having collapsed after World War II in the wake of McCarthyism, the cold war, and the space race. Yet, as Cremin observes, so many progressive educational reforms had become accepted practice by midcentury that an irreversible transformation was effected in the schools.[37] Born from the very idea of progress and the ideal of a democratic society, progressive educational thought and practice could not be denied as long as progress and democracy were taken seriously.

Experimentalism

The Idea of Progress and the Distribution of Knowledge.   The systematic explication of the idea of progress and the significance of universal public education in the making of a progressive, democratic society can be found in the writings of sociologist Lester F. Ward. In his classic work *Dynamic Sociology* (subtitled *Applied Social Science*), published in 1883, Ward noted that the dynamic, evolutionary forces of the natural world require a dynamic conception of knowledge. But where evolution in nature is a meandering process, human progress depends upon the development and application of intelligence for improving the human condition.

"The supposed intellectual inequality is greatly exaggerated," contended Ward. The key problem is access to knowledge, and a cardinal principle of a democratic society is education as a social function through universal public education (for females as well as males). The great chasm between the intelligent and the ignorant in society was caused by inequality of educational opportunity. Ward observed that where evolution rests upon the power of the environment to mold the organism, education is a quality of the environment that can be designed to develop human potentials for improving the life of the individual and the life of society.[38]

Three Universal Curricula.   Ward stressed that society suffers when it regards the scientific attitude as the exclusive province of the science specialist (who may, in reality, be unscientific in the narrowness of social outlook and pursuits beyond his specialty). The leading tests, or criteria, for determining what knowledge is most important for all is the test of relative *generality* and relative *practicality*. The first universal curriculum for the school should be aimed at general and practical knowledge. The second universal curriculum should provide for even greater generality and practicality, while embracing many interchangeable (interdependent) branches. The third universal curriculum should be directed at advanced studies, elected by the student with the guidance of the teacher, for life pursuits (specialization). Ward viewed education not only as a means but as itself an end in that it should serve to enable the individual to grow in the understanding and in the intelligent control of experience.[39]

In answer to social reformers who contend that the solution to social inequity resides in the redistribution of wealth, Ward noted that "they are working at the roof instead of at the foundation of the structure which they desire to erect."[40] For Ward, the foundation rests with the diffusion of knowledge through universal education, whereby intelligence would be developed and directed at individual and social improvement.[41]

Ward's passionate belief in the power of the environment and the school as a planned environment in releasing intelligence for a progressive and democratic society was to find expression in Dewey's experimentalist philosophy. "He anticipated John Dewey," wrote Commager, "and supplied him with a scientific basis for much of his educational philosophy."[42] Unfortunately, as Cremin observed, Ward was "massively ignored" in his lifetime.[43]

Pragmatism.   Dewey's experimentalist philosophy also took roots from the progressive American philosophy of pragmatism developed by two contemporaries of Ward, mathematician Charles Peirce (1839–1914) and psychologist William James (1842–1910). As with Ward, they rejected the doctrine of absolute or a priori truths of the traditionalists and held that truth derives from the scientific investigation of ideas through the test of consequences. A priori truths are static, and are imposed or derived by authority or dictate, rather than by independent thinking. "Science is dynamic. Whatever it touches is transformed."[44]

To the pragmatist, no knowledge is above or beyond natural explanation. In his views on psychology, James applied Darwin's biological principles in conceiving of mind as an evolutionary development in bringing the human species toward successful adaptation to environment. This organic conception of mind laid the basis for rejecting the traditionalist doctrine of mental discipline, with its notion of mind as a muscle to be exercised or as a vessel to be filled with information or facts. Ward, too, had attacked this "crude assumption that the brain is a hollow sphere." As Ward commented, "The fact is that the lowest town gossip has a larger number of items of information stored away in his brain than Humboldt ever had. It requires no greater effort to know something important than something unimportant."[45]

A Uniquely American Philosophy. Dewey not only drew upon the progressive ideas of pragmatism, but he orchestrated it into the uniquely American philosophy of experimentalism. When Dewey's work *Democracy and Education* appeared in 1916, Walter Lippmann described it as the "mature wisdom of the finest and most powerful intellect devoted to the future of American civilization."[46]

In his classic study *An American Dilemma* (1944), Swedish social economist Gunnar Myrdal paid tribute to Dewey and other American progressivists in recognizing the power of the environment and the changeability of human beings long before these ideas came to be expressed in the social sciences.

> Research in, and discussion of, education is prolific. In America, pedagogy anticipated by several generations the recent trend to environmentalism in the social sciences and the belief in the changeability of human beings. It gave a basis for the belief in democratic values and expressed the social optimism of American liberalism.
>
> .... The marriage between philosophy and pedagogy in Dewey and his followers has given America the most perfected educational theory in modern times. America has, therefore, seen more of enterprising and experimental progressive redirection of schools than has any other country.[47]

Myrdal was so struck by the compelling faith in public education shared by Americans that he regarded it as a "principal conclusion of the American Creed"[48]—a conclusion that was so powerfully embraced and perpetuated by the experimentalists.

Dualisms Demolished. Dewey's chief ideas and contributions have been treated extensively in earlier chapters, so that it is only necessary here to summarize and elaborate briefly on his work. Throughout his writings, Dewey sought to demolish the dualistic and oppositional tenets of the traditional philosophies: mind versus body, intellectual development versus character development, knowing versus doing, intellect versus emotion, theoretical versus practical knowledge, logical versus psychological knowledge, scientific versus humanistic studies, culture versus vocation, labor versus leisure, mind versus matter, nature versus nurture, individuality versus society, method versus subject matter, discipline versus freedom, interest versus intellect, experience versus knowledge, scientific versus artistic, ends versus means, and so on.

Such dualisms, noted Dewey, which had infected Western philosophy as a legacy of a prescientific age, stemmed from the ideas of the ancient Greek philosophers, who viewed practical activity as the province of the slave, whereas sheer contemplation above the material world was the exclusive and elevating province of the freeman or master. Hence liberal education came to be held as true education as opposed to practical studies. The ancient Greek dualisms and bias came to be inherited in Christian thought and perpetuated in modern Western philosophy, which, as a consequence, failed to benefit from the revolutionary system of scientific inquiry and failed to contribute to modern democracy in a scientific age, contended Dewey.

Humanizing the Curriculum Through the Modern Studies. Dewey held that the old static conception of knowledge ran counter to the dynamic nature of knowledge as conceived through scientific inquiry. Traditional philosophy had failed to come to grips with the "deepest problems of common humanity," and had failed to recognize that the curriculum "is humanized in the degree in which it connects with the common interests of men as men." The consequences, noted Dewey, were conditions in the curriculum that "infect the education called liberal with illiberality."[49]

Hence Dewey laid the ground for general education in place of traditional liberal education. He stressed the necessary continuity and interdependence between general education and vocational education in a free society (as opposed to vocational training for conformance to the machinery of the existing industrial order). In a modern democratic society, thinking man and working man are one and the same. Dewey contended that the curriculum should not be made up of divided and specialized subject matters, but should be reflectively formulated, coherently designed, and meaningfully attuned to the growth of the learner and to the improvement of existing community life. "A curriculum which acknowledges the social responsibilities of education must present situations where problems are relevant to the problems of living together, and where observation and information are calculated to develop social insight and interest."[50]

General Education in an Age of Specialism. Experimentalist educators not only pointed to the need for curriculum articulation in the face of an expanding and diversified curriculum that had grown out of the age of specialism and the diverse interests of a polyglot population, but to the need for coherence in a common curriculum for general education. Throughout the first half of the twentieth century, notable efforts were undertaken in schools and colleges to redesign the common curriculum. By midcentury, experimentalists, along with moderately conservative educators, were voicing great optimism over the prospects for general education in the secondary school and college as the means for advancing "unity through diversity." In the words of F. Champion Ward of the University of Chicago, "In the nation, 'general education' is at last in vogue. Its principles bid fair to become the operative educational theory of the remainder of this century."[51]

But specialism and special-interest education were to win out in the college and university, while the schools tended to look to the academic side of the curriculum for basic education and preparation for college. Nevertheless, during the closing years of the 1980s there was a growing rediscovery of the need to reconstruct the curriculum in the school and college to meet the persistent need for general education. In their quest for a common learning amid the growing diversified studies, experimentalist educators early in this century had a telling vision of the needed "unity through diversity" in a free society.

Method of Intelligence. The very organization or systematization of knowledge is evidence that it has been subjected to intelligence or methodized, contended Dewey; consequently, method is never outside of subject matter. The supreme educational method in a free society is the method of intelligence or problem-solving through reflective thinking. In essence, it is exemplified in the modes of scientific inquiry for problem solutions in all areas of the curriculum, and not just in science as a specialized subject matter. Such a method has a clear moral purpose: to free intelligence and to combat ignorance, bias, blind authority, and superstition.

Inquiry and Consequences. Dewey criticized the old ideal that the pursuit of knowledge for its own sake is good in itself. Intelligence and knowledge must be directed at the illumination of consequences relevant to existing social conditions. This was the hard lesson learned by the theoretical physicists who split the atom. In the words of the Nobel laureate Max Born,

> In the operation of science and its ethics a change has taken place that makes it impossible to maintain the old ideal of the pursuit of knowledge for its own sake which my generation believed in. We were convinced that this could never lead to any evil since the search for truth was good in itself. That was a beautiful dream from which we were awakened by world events.[52]

Born was not expressing his disillusionment with science but was pointing to the need for science and rationality to be directed at the human condition.

Two Cultures. More than half a century earlier, Dewey had warned that when science is divorced from social and moral consequences, its discoveries are in danger of being misused for the barbarism of a prescientific age. And he repeatedly attacked the humanists for their aloofness from science and warned of the dangers of the two-cultures split as "knowledge divided against itself."[53] The two-cultures divide continues to be perpetuated to this day by the humanists or perennialists and by some existentialists. "All that is human, all that is of concern to us, lies outside natural science," declares Allan Bloom in *The Closing of the American Mind* (1987)—revealing the closed mind of the perennialists.[54]

Science Versus Scientism in Curriculum Making. Dewey is also erroneously linked with those who sought to reduce education to quantifiable measurements.[55] Dewey viewed such reductionist efforts as scientism rather than scientific. He repeatedly held that there must be no divorce between qualitative ideas and quantitative treatment, and that the former must always guide the latter. The outcome of scientific methods is not uniformity or standardization but the liberation of individuals by enabling them to see new problems, devise new procedures—thereby making for diversification rather than for set uniformity.[56]

In 1927, Boyd Bode directly criticized the efforts being made to work out educational problems quantitatively without a wider democratic social vision. Referring to those engaged in such measurements, Bode wrote:

> Education, for them, is still a matter of training in skills and in the passive acceptance of prevailing standards, which is wholly in the spirit of the aristocratic tradition. No account is taken of the fact that the individual must either be fitted to become a cog in the social mechanism, or else must be educated according to some notion of how this mechanism is to be changed. To suppose that the work of education can be carried on effectively without reference to the larger issue is plain self-deception. There is no such thing as being neutral.[57]

Democracy and 'isms. Dewey's vision of democracy has been caricatured as an effort to restore our society to the spirit of the New England town meeting.[58] But it was Dewey who stressed that such a model was inadequate to contemporary life because the older publics in local communities were largely homogeneous, rather than cosmopolitan, and were relatively static.[59] The dynamic conditions of contemporary life in a free society required a philosophy attuned to the idea of progress. Yet he warned against progressive education being reduced to an 'ism, for 'ism implies a certain set of fixed doctrines. This was the pitfall of traditional philosophies, with their absolute truths and appeal to authority as opposed to the open system of scientific inquiry. Hence 'ism is inimical to experimentalist thinking, held Dewey as he warned the progressivists against falling prey to 'isms.

> Those who are looking ahead to a new movement in education adapted to the existing need for a new social order, should think in terms of Education itself rather than in terms of some 'ism about education, even such an 'ism as "progressivism." For in spite of itself any movement that thinks and acts in terms of an 'ism becomes so involved in reaction against other 'isms that it is unwittingly controlled by them. For it then forms its principles by reaction against them instead of by a comprehensive constructive survey of actual needs, problems, and possibilities.[60]

Dewey's warning was issued at a time when the nation was in the depths of the Great Depression and when a number of progressivists were impatient with the experimentalist approach. As reconstructionists, they were calling for a bolder and more direct educational attack on social problems so as to build a new and truly democratic social order. Dewey's warnings against 'ism also applied to the narrowness of the romantic progressivists, whose prescriptions were child-centered to the extreme. In connection with Dewey's warning against 'ism, it is acknowledged that 'ism as indication of a fixed doctrine does not apply to experimentalist theory, since such theory rejects absolute and a priori truths.

Reconstructionism

Although reconstructionist ideas are found in the historic stream of utopian writings, the Great Depression galvanized the consciences of many progressivists who called for a more direct attack on social problems through the agency of the public schools. To the reconstructionists, experimentalist ideas were too "neutral" or indirect at a time of social crisis, when a more direct ideology was required for correcting social ills and building a new and truly democratic social order. Indeed, many progressive schools of that day, and even today, adopted progressive practices for their own clientele without embracing the wider democratic social vision for other people's children.

Dare the School Build a New Social Order?   In a series of electrifying speeches delivered in 1932 to various educational associations, George S. Counts of Teachers College challenged progressive educators to address the great crisis of the times, fashion a new vision of human destiny based upon social welfare, and channel the public schools to the task of giving the rising generation the means toward realizing such a vision.

Counts acknowledged that the school is but one of many formative social agencies, but he held that this should not deter progressive educators from harnessing the powers of the school for social reconstruction. Nor should progressive educators fear the "bogies of imposition and indoctrination" as far as the function of the school is concerned, contended Counts.[61]

The Indoctrination Issue.   In *Democracy and Education* Dewey had pointed to the necessary continuity between ends and means. Democratic ends require that the schools employ democratic means through reflective inquiry into social problems. Dewey's response to the indoctrination question was that it was out of the question in the schools of a free society. Dewey, Bode, and other experimentalists pointed out that there was all the difference in the world between prescribing beliefs and in identifying problem areas for reflective consideration of issues and solutions on the part of the learner. As noted in chapter 5, in an address before the NEA in 1934, Dewey stressed that it would be revolution enough if educators were to recognize the reality of social change and to act upon that recognition in the schools.[62] In *Experience and Education* (1938), as cited earlier, Dewey warned progressive educators against 'isms even in the form of progressivism in the building of a new democratic social order.

In reply to the contention that the experimentalist commitment to the method of intelligence is too neutral in an era of great social change and conflict, Dewey pointed out that the freedom of intelligence was indeed the most powerful ally of progress and democracy. Hence the commitment to the method of intelligence implies a social orientation that is not neutral; yet it is the most powerful means of combating indoctrination, intimidation, and suppression. "An intelligent understanding of social forces given by the schools is our chief protection," Dewey maintained. "There are difficulties enough in the way of the schools obtaining the power to promote this understanding ... and it alone will give educators concerned with a new social orientation a herculean task to perform."[63]

Hence the implementation of experimentalist principles and practices in the curriculum would, in itself, constitute a revolutionary transformation. It would open the curriculum to the reflective examination of alternative ideologies, however controversial. It would defeat censorship and would seek to develop autonomously thinking citizens in the context of democratic social responsibility.

Utopian Visions. Although reconstructionism never became a main current for educational reform, one cannot deny that American society has not fully used the best available knowledge in attacking the pervasive problems of poverty, social disaffection, crime, hunger, disease, unemployment, the environment, international conflict, human rights, and the like. According to Brameld, a vast body of knowledge-achievement resources are waiting to be used if only we release them to solve these pervading problems through organized worldwide democratic machinery.

However, there is a troubling strain of utopianism in the reconstructionist vision. Brameld viewed the masses as the "great reservoir of strength for tomorrow's education. Here, indeed, is the fountainhead of all other utopian potentials presently emerging." Few progressivists would quarrel with this great faith in universal education as a bulwark for democracy. But Brameld saw the schools taking on the direct task of social redirection. "The immediate task before the (teaching) profession is to draw upon this strength and thus to strengthen control of the schools by and for the goal-seeking interests of the overwhelming majority of mankind," argued Brameld.[64]

This raises the question not only as to whether our society would allow the profession to exercise such control, but whether such control would truly be in the interests of a democratic society. History is replete with utopian schemes for education and society. However admirable and noble the utopian visions of the reconstructionists, their prescriptions are preformulated and directed by an enlightened elite. To use Mumford's words, such an elite are the "accredited ministers of progress." Mumford had pointed out that despite the ofttimes use of the word freedom by utopians, the "pervasive character of all utopias is their totalitarian absolutism, the reduction of variety and choice, and the effort to escape from such natural conditions or historical traditions as would support variety and make choice possible." And, although their ends may be labeled democratic, "almost all utopias emphasize regularity, uniformity, authoritarianism, isolation, and autarchy."[65]

The fact that reconstructionist prescriptions do not preclude indoctrination in the schools raises the question as to whether reconstructionism embraces a kind of political absolutism that Mumford was concerned about.

Romanticism

As early as 1902, Dewey had warned against the extreme child centeredness being advocated by some reformers in the name of the "new education." Just as the "old education" had invidiously misconceived of childhood "as something to be got away from as soon as possible and as much as possible," there was the danger that the new education would romanticize childhood and would leave the direction of the curriculum to the present interests of the child. As a consequence, continued Dewey,

> The child is expected to "develop" this or that fact or truth out of his own mind ... without being supplied any of the environing conditions which are requisite to start and guide thought.... It is certainly as futile to expect a child to develop a universe out of his own mere mind as it is for a philosopher to attempt that task.[66]

Romantic Naturalism.   The romantic conception of the child as a source of immature goodness has its origins in the romantic naturalism of Rousseau. In his iconoclastic *Émile* (1762), Rousseau offered such aphorisms for the upbringing and education of the child as,

> We can do much, but the chief thing is to prevent anything being done.
>
> Reverse the usual practice and you will almost always do right.
>
> Young teacher, I am setting before you a difficult task, the art of controlling without precepts, and doing everything without doing anything at all.
>
> Let the child do nothing because he is told; nothing is good for him but what he recognizes as good.

Although Rousseau tempered his romantic view of the child with a call for "well-regulated liberty," with the means of curiosity being "rightly directed," his romantic vision of the child prevailed. Yet he did recognize the need for a curriculum. "The real object of our study is man and his environment," wrote Rousseau. "Let him (the pupil) not be taught science, let him discover it."[67]

Science and Sentiment. As discussed shortly, some radical school reformers of the 1960s went so far as to dismiss the importance of a curriculum in the education of the child. It will be recalled that the child-study movement in the United States during the 1890s began as an effort to induce educational reform through the scientific study of the child. However, romantic progressivists came to conceive of a child-centered curriculum dominated by sentiment rather than science. As an officer of the Child-Study Division of the NEA declared at the organization's annual meeting in 1900, "Better is it to know nothing of the plant's structure and functions, but to love in order to gain knowledge. Better still that love and knowledge should kiss each other."[68]

The authoritarian educational practices of the times gave justification for the romantic progressivists in seeking to kindle in teachers more humane, affectionate, and empathic attitudes toward children. But their belief in the centrality of child life in the curriculum led them to regard immediate felt interests and spontaneous activity indulgently as achievements rather than as means toward intellective and social growth.

To this day, Dewey's name is invoked with Rousseau's by some perennialists and essentialists for having promulgated an educational scheme where books are of little importance.[69] But in *The School and Society* (1899), Dewey had made a diagram of his ideal school in which the library is at the center in unifying the intellective resources for illuminating all practical activities.

Radical School Reform. The era of social protest and student activism beginning in the mid-1960s brought forth a host of best-selling books advocating radical romantic schemes of schooling. Few reader's of A. S. Neill's *Summerhill* were aware that his school in England served only from forty-five to sixty pupils. Neill expounded a romantic notion of the innate goodness and wisdom of the child and the thesis that the child will best flower forth if left to his or her own devices:

> Well, we set out to make a school in which we should allow children to be themselves. In order to do this, we had to renounce all discipline, all direction, all suggestion, all moral training. . . . All it required was what we had—a complete belief in the child as a good, not evil being. . . .
> My view is that the child is innately wise and realistic. If left to himself without adult suggestions of any kind, he will develop as far as he is capable of developing.[70]

Neill denied the need for a formal curriculum, but he explained that university entrance examinations made it a necessary concession to offer traditional academic subjects at Summerhill. "Books are the least important apparatus in a school," declared Neill, and "Most of the school work that adolescents do is simply a waste of time of energy, of patience. It robs youth of its right to play and play and play."[71]

   The attacks on education by radical romanticists attracted a wide read-
ership and became particularly appealing to student activists on our college
campuses during the late 1960s. One of the most popular authors for the
radical college students was Paul Goodman, who declared that the "purpose
of elementary pedagogy, through age twelve, should be to delay socialization,
to protect children's free growth," and "We must drastically cut back formal
schooling because the present extended tutelage is against nature and arrests
growth."[72] However, Goodman's followers were not prepared to cut back
their own formal schooling nor that of their own children. They were apparently referring to other people and to other people's children in a disguised
elitism under the banner of radical progressivism. Goodman argued that the
chief means of learning and teaching for the masses should be incidental
education, as opposed to a preconceived curriculum, in taking part in the
ongoing activities in society. While he held that "many of our youth, both
poor and middle class, might be better off if the system did not exist, even if
they had no formal schooling at all," he later revealed his elitism by justifying
academic schools for the academically able, who would be "unencumbered
by the sullen bodies of the others."[73]
   The idea of incidental learning based upon the child's felt interests and
the rejection of a preplanned curriculum permeated the best-selling literature of the times. "We cannot know, at any moment, what particular bit of
knowledge or understanding a child needs most," wrote John Holt. "Only he
can do this." Hence the very idea of a planned curriculum is deemed invalid.

> The idea of the curriculum would not be valid even if we could agree what
> ought to be in it. For knowledge changes. Much of what a child learns in
> school will be found or thought, before many years, to be untrue.... Since
> we can't know what knowledge will be most needed in the future, it is sense-
> less to try to teach it in advance....
>   Learning is not everything, and certainly one piece of learning is as good
> as another.[74]

   The romanticist notion that freedom resides in allowing the learner to
pursue his or her spontaneous interests was repeatedly attacked by Dewey
as fallacious, for freedom resides in the intelligent direction of choices and
the intelligent control of experience. "Direct immediate discharge or expression of an impulsive tendency is fatal to thinking, contended Dewey. "Genuine freedom, in short, is intellectual; it rests in the trained *power of
thought*.... To cultivate unhindered unreflective external activity is to foster
enslavement, for it leaves the person at the mercy of appetite, sense, and
circumstance."[75]
   During the late 1960s, alternative schools embracing romanticist ideology appeared. But they soon faced a crisis of reality, as in the case of other
forms of protest schools in the past, and soon were either disbanded or
moved toward more conventional approaches. The historic record reveals
that not only do alternative schools suffer from a short life, but they tend to

serve a special clientele and they are conceived as a way of avoiding to come to grips with the need to improve the existing public schools.[76]

Existentialism

Although the roots of existentialism can be traced back to the nineteenth century in the ideas of the Danish theologian Søren Kierkegaard (1813–55) and the German philosopher Friedrich Nietzsche (1844–1900), it found a modern following after World War II through the writings of such men as Jean-Paul Sartre, Albert Camus, and Gabriel Marcel.

In reaction to an age of impersonal technology and alienation in an indifferent universe, the existentialist turns to subjective introspection to find the meaning of human existence. The individual cannot find such meaning in the rational world of science but must turn inward to a world of private aestheticism of existential thought. By finding the meaning of his own existence, the individual discovers the authentic self and achieves a full awakening of his or her spontaneous human powers.

A Literary Movement. The plight of the lost individual in an uncaring universe became an overwhelming theme in literature after midcentury, as many literary intellectuals were attracted to existentialism and the rejection of the rational world of science.

During the latter 1960s, existentialism became vastly appealing among radical segments of the college populace, who saw themselves engaged in a struggle to become free of rational constraints through an attack on the repressions and inadequacies of our dominant social institutions. Hence one could engage in the private aestheticism of existential thought while also actively engaging in a revolt against the established authority of our modern institutions, including the university, which are allegedly bent on the suppression of selfhood. (Interestingly, the students engaged in this revolt did not choose to free themselves from the university by leaving it.)

One of the leading gurus in the counterculture movement was Theodore Roszak, a professor of history who took heart from what he saw as the "great negation of reason" and the rejection of science by the college generation of the 1960s in favor of the transcendental mysticism and occultism of our neolithic prehistory. "Myth and occult tradition have more to tell us than science or scholarship ever will," wrote Roszak.[77]

Strains of Romanticism. Existentialism has been largely a literary movement, and existentialists have not developed a unified or systematic rationale for the curriculum. Nevertheless, their wide and varied criticisms of traditional education and their prescriptions for school reform closely resemble those offered by the romantic naturalists and radical romanticists.

To the existentialist, the route to knowledge is personal, and the function of education is to help the individual find the meaning of personal existence. Since the child is born into a "world of meaninglessness," the child should be left to extract possibilities without compliance. The school, therefore, must be an environment in which the "full exercise of the spontaneous human self is the avenue to authenticity as a person." Educators must extricate the child from the "crushing overload of social controls" so as to release the powers of the self.[78]

Neither the standard curriculum of essential subject matters nor the experimentalist focus on reflective thinking for problem-solving is adequate to the task. The pupil is to be given the widest latitude possible in determining the curriculum. "Let the student 'appropriate' to himself any knowledge he studies," advises Kneller. Some existentialists such as Kneller follow Rousseau in recommending that schools be abolished altogether, with each youngster being under the personal tutelage of a teacher for an "I" and "Thou" dialogue.[79]

In the few instances where it was claimed that existentialist schools were created, these schools were invariably small and private, catering to an exclusive or relatively homogeneous clientele, and the curriculum in these schools tended to be indistinguishable from the schools of the romantic naturalists. For example, a description of one self-styled existentialist school stated that there were no required courses, assigned groups, prescribed number of classroom hours, grades, or evaluations. Instead, emphasis was given to "learning through self-motivation and self-regulation," "equal status of all pursuits," "evaluation through self-criticism," "teaching based on interest," "spontaneous formation of learning groups," and "teacher retention based on student demand"—with four-year-olds having an equal vote with faculty in general school meetings. The descriptions of the school were pregnant with romantic idealizations of the child. "The most self-directed students appeared to be the four-to-six-year-olds. They were busy all day long and did not seem to require direction or supervision."[80]

Whatever form the existentialist curriculum might take, there remains the nagging question of how it is possible for a child to find the meaning of his or her own existence when education is focused on spontaneous self-interests. And there is the question of how it is possible to remake civilization, as the existentialists claim is their goal, when the existentialist prescription is personal and independent of social means. This is one of the contradictions of existentialism.

Negation of Science and Rational Thought. Perhaps the most serious contradiction and danger in existentialism lies in its tenet that freedom is to be gained by the rejection of science and its system of inquiry, for the history of science reveals that science has been the greatest ally in freeing intelligence. In rejecting science, the existentialists unwittingly serve the cause of anti-intellectualism. To hold that the inner world is separate and even opposed to the natural world invites a kind of escapism into unreality and mysticism. The interest in existentialism by the college generation of the latter 1960s also witnessed segments of the college population turning to the mysticism of Oriental religions, to the occult, and to the drug culture.

In *Human Nature and Conduct* (1922), Dewey prophetically warned that when science and technology are divorced from moral concerns, when the methods of science are not employed to illumine the wider social intelligence, the consequence is the perpetuation of the most brutal side of technology, coupled with the retreat from intelligence into an unreal sanctum of a so-called inner mind:

> For the neglect of sciences that deal specifically with facts of the natural and social environment leads to a side-tracking of moral forces into an unreal privacy of an unreal self.... Each sign of disregard for the moral potentialities of physical science drafts the conscience of mankind away from concern with the interactions of man and nature which must be mastered if freedom is to be reality. It diverts intelligence to anxious preoccupation with the unrealities of a purely inner life.... The masses swarm to the occult for assistance. The cultivated smile contemptuously. They might smile out of the other side of their mouths if they realized how recourse to the occult exhibits the practical logic of their own beliefs. For both rest upon a separation of moral ideas and feelings from knowable facts of life, man and the world.[81]

In denigrating science, existentialists tend to make a caricature of scientific thinking as coldly neutral, and they proceed to blame science and technology for the political misuses of science and technology. "The best available evidence has nothing to do with morality or human fulfillment," argues Maxine Greene as she holds with Roszak that "We need only recall the testing that led to the A-bomb and the H-bomb, to extermination camps, to nerve gas, to napalm." Greene points to the Nazi death camps as an example of the "application of scientific knowledge to mass extermination," revealing her confusion in taking political decision-making as science.[82]

The fact that an evil act can be systematically planned and executed rationally does not mean that such an act is the logical outcome of rational thought. The act is irrational and an outcome of evil political ideology. The "problem" of how to exterminate a people is not a problem of science any more than is the problem of how to assassinate a U.S. President. To pose such a problem in the first place is indicative of irrational forces at work. The conception of an evil act originates with evil personal, social, or political motives—not with the motives of science.

"The eye sees many foul things and the arm and hand do many cruel things. Yet the fanatic who would pluck out the eye and cut off the arm is recognized for what he is," wrote Dewey. To Dewey, "It is a curious state of mind which finds pleasure in setting forth the 'limits of science.' For the intrinsic limit of knowledge is simply ignorance." Where there is ineptitude among those who misuse science, "its removal lies in rectification of its use, not in the abuse of the thing used."[83]

In making the case against science and rational thought, existentialists fail to explain why the existential antirationalism of Nietzsche and Heidegger could find compatibility with the antirationalism of Nazi Germany. When existentialists hold that the "best available evidence has nothing to do with morality or human fulfillment," the implication is that we should not guide our thoughts and actions according to the "best available evidence." Such a view would appear to open the way to the thinking of a prescientific age, warned Jacques Monod, the Nobel Laureate biologist. For it was an abiding commitment to the " best available evidence" through science that put humanity in control of its destiny, as opposed to being under the control of unexplained forces or authoritarian dictate. If, as the existentialists claim, humanity exists in an uncaring universe, that is all the more reason why humanity must not retreat to a primitive tradition ignorant of science or aversive to science, maintained Monod. For the very ethic of knowledge wrought by science gives humanity the freedom to choose; human destiny is not spelled out *for* humanity, but *by* humanity. This ethic is fundamental to education in and for a democracy.[84]

The caricature of science as a coldly rational and objective knowledge domain is laid to rest in these words by Einstein:

> Whoever has undergone the intense experience in this domain (science) is moved by profound reverence for the rationality made manifest in existence. By way of the understanding he achieves a far-reaching emancipation from the shackles of personal hopes and desire, and thereby attains that humble attitude of mind toward the grandeur of reason incarnate in existence, and which, in its profoundest depths, is inaccessible to man. This attitude, however, appears to me to be religious, in the highest sense of the word....
>
> The further the spiritual evolution of mankind advances, the more certain it seems to me that the path to genuine religiosity does not lie through the fear of life, and the fear of death, and blind faith, but through striving after rational knowledge.[85]

SOCIAL EFFICIENCY AND SOCIAL CONTROL

From the turn of the century through the years immediately after World War I, increasing attention was being given to the democratic prospect in the United States. Such figures as Lester Ward, Edward Ross, and John Dewey had pointed out that the critical factor for a democratic society is the extent to which the intelligence of the public is developed and released so as to exercise control over conditions, rather than being controlled by them. This, in turn, would make social improvement on a vast scale possible, making for real social efficiency. But it would require that education, indeed universal public education, become an active factor in this transformation.

Drift Versus Social Efficiency for Democratic Social Improvement

Lester Ward attacked the widely accepted belief that mediocrity is the normal condition of society and that the endowment of capacity for achievement is relatively rare. Ward contended that the great potential for achievement and, therefore, social improvement rests with the wide release of opportunity and "emancipation from the current beliefs on the subject." This release of human potentials through education and progressive legislation would improve human productivity along with the more equitable distribution of benefits, thereby making for real social efficiency for social improvement. Ward ended *Applied Sociology* (1906) with these words: "Thus all the varied streams of benefit would unite in securing the twofold end of increasing the sum total of social efficiency and social improvement." In earlier writings, Ward had pointed out that instead of allowing the social system to drift, education should be made an active factor in developing human intelligence for the control of conditions and the progressive improvement of society.[86]

Ross and Dewey went to great pains to point to the difference between social control (and social efficiency) in the older pyramidal societies of privilege and imposition as contrasted to a democratic society, with its wide release of human potentials through popular education. Unfortunately, the concepts of social efficiency and social control, which appeared widely in the educational literature between 1900 and 1920, came to be portrayed by educational historians mainly in their invidious meanings. To this day, the one-sided aspect of social efficiency and social control is promulgated by some writers on the history of the school curriculum.

Misinterpretation and Misconstruction of Social Control and Social Efficiency

In his history of the American high school (1964), Edward A. Krug interpreted social control and social efficiency as a narrow doctrine of imposition on the individual, and he proceeded to link the *Cardinal Principles* report (1918) with promulgating this doctrine, which, according to Krug, had been promoted by the sociologist Edward Ross in his book *Social Control* (1901). Unfortunately, recent works on the history of the curriculum have followed Krug in portraying Ross, along with the *Cardinal Principles* report, as promoting the role of the school for inculcating this narrow version of social control and efficiency.[87]

The Two Sides of Social Control. Ross had actually identified two sides of social control: the traditional side of the old pyramidal society, which holds to an outmoded curriculum and imposes obedience to the status quo, and the side attuned to the idea of progress and social opportunity necessary for a democracy. In Ross' words,

For a pyramidal society putting a severe strain on obedience, the safest and best education is one that wears away the energy of youth in mental gymnastics, directs the glance toward the past, cultivates the memory rather than the reason, gives polish rather than power, encourages acquiescence rather than inquiry, and teaches to versify rather than to think. It is natural that teachers in meeting such requirements should construct a system that favors the humanities rather than the sciences, literature and language rather than history, and the forms of literature rather than the substance.[88]

Ross then went on to relate how all this was changed by the great democratic upheavals and the demand for an enlightened public. Yet he noted that the almost exclusively intellectual cast for education was largely retained. But he pointed out that the "successful working of democratic government is making ever greater demands upon the intelligence of the common man, and the disposition to educate for citizenship at the public expense is ever more marked."[89]

Again, in Ross' words,

The old societies dreaded change. So they sought to run each generation into conventional moulds, and were worried if any traces of individuality still remained. Our Western societies, on the other hand, have embraced the idea of progress and made it a part of their tradition. In the faith that the present will be surpassed, they would prepare their youth to initiate, or at least to welcome, progress.[90]

But Ross cautioned that we would be very far wrong to conclude that the control function in modern educational policies has been thrust aside. Ross stressed that despite the differences between the old societies and the new in regard to the functions of public education, the old function of external control remains. And he proceeded to illustrate this old function with a quote from Daniel Webster's portrayal of the public school (from Webster's Plymouth oration) as a "wise and liberal system of police, by which property and the peace of society are secured."[91] Ross observed that, in sharp contrast, the contemporary scene was marked by a clamor for a secular civic and moral education to replace the social controls of the old education. "Just what shape this new education will take, no one can say," wrote Ross before the turn of the century. "But it will not be merely one more branch of study like ethics or civics. . . . It will seek not so much to fix certain principles by authority, as to suggest directly actions and feelings and modes of viewing conduct."[92]

Need for a New Kind of Social Efficiency and Control

Ross was calling for a new kind of social control for a modern democracy in the form of social insight and the power of enlightened self-direction through popular education. Instead of imposition of moral controls by authority and preachment, principles and actions would be revealed directly through the curriculum and in the life of the school. But the path, cautioned Ross, would not be easy. Again, in Ross' words:

> When we note the enormous resources and high centralization of a first-class educational system; when we consider that it takes forcible possession of the child for half the time during its best years, and submits the little creature to a curriculum, devised more and more with reference to its own aims and less and less to the wishes of the parent; when we consider that the democratic control of this formidable engine affords no guarantee that it will not be used for empire over minds,—we may well be apprehensive of future developments.

Ross then concluded that a kind of checks and balances would be needed to protect and promote the spiritual freedom in this educating modern state through vigorous association with other free institutions to "forbid the undue ascendancy of the control organization of society."[93]

Unfortunately, Ross' analysis of the two-pronged aspect of social control was miscast by Krug and recent curriculum historians in the traditional suppressive vein that Ross had so vigorously attacked. Thus Ross is frequently quoted as having advocated free education as an "economical system of police," when Ross was actually quoting from Daniel Webster in portraying the view of the function of schooling by the old order—a view, maintained Ross, that was no longer tenable for a modern, free society.[94]

Ross had clearly embraced Ward's idea of progress for the growth of a free society, and he dedicated his book *Social Control* to Ward, who was his uncle by marriage. Ross was dismissed from his professorship at Stanford for the radically progressive ideas he put before his students. Apparently, his enemies at that time understood his messages on social control better than many contemporary historians. In his autobiography, Ross was to recount how he feared that his writings on social control would be used by conservatives to ruin him. He was to find a more congenial setting for his ideas at the University of Wisconsin.

Social Control and Efficiency for the Release of Human Potentials. As with Ross, Dewey addressed the two sides of social efficiency and control: the traditional side of imposition and subordination versus the progressive side of utilization through the extension of opportunity throughout the populace. In 1916 he wrote:

> The opposing emphasis took the form of a doctrine that the business of education is to supply precisely what nature fails to secure; namely, habituation of an individual to social control; subordination of natural powers to social rules.... It is a fact that we must look to the activities and achievements of associated life to find what the development of power—that is to say, efficiency—means. The error is implying that we must adopt measures of subordination rather than of utilization to secure efficiency. This doctrine is rendered adequate when we recognize that social efficiency is attained not by

negative constraint but by positive use of native individual capacities in occupations having a social meaning. . . .

When social efficiency as measured by product or output is urged as an ideal in a would-be democratic society, it means that the depreciatory estimate of the masses characteristic of an aristocratic community is accepted and carried over. But if democracy has a moral and ideal meaning, it is that a social return be demanded from all and that opportunity for development of distinctive capacities be afforded all. The separation of the two aims in education is fatal to democracy; the adoption of the narrower meaning of efficiency deprives it of its essential justification.[95]

Social Efficiency and the *Cardinal Principles* Report

The 1918 report of the NEA Commission on the Reorganization of Secondary Education, *Cardinal Principles of Secondary Education,* clearly and repeatedly embraced the democratic side of social efficiency as utilization as opposed to subordination. Noting that the secondary school, like other social institutions, tends to be conservative, the report addressed efficiency in a democracy in terms of the school developing "in each individual the knowledge, interests, ideals, habits, and powers whereby he will find his place and use that place to shape both himself and society toward ever nobler ends." The report echoed Dewey's message in "protest against any and all plans, however well intended, which are in danger of divorcing vocation and sociocivic education." The curriculum common to all "should kindle social ideals and give insight into social conditions and into personal character as related to these conditions," and the student should "realize that democracy itself is an ideal to be wrought out by his own and succeeding generations." Clearly, then, the report called for the school to develop in the individual the social insight and power to control his or her own destiny in the context of democratic social responsibility.[96]

Prototype of Democracy. The *Cardinal Principles* report went on to advocate a unitary school structure through the coeducational comprehensive high school as opposed to a divided system. "In short, the comprehensive high school is the prototype of a democracy in which various groups must have a degree of self-consciousness as groups and yet be federated into a larger whole through the recognition of common interests and ideals."

Through constants, a common curriculum would be provided for all, while variables would allow for the pursuit of differentiated specialized studies to meet vocational needs and for advanced work in special fields, along with free electives to meet special interests.

In criticizing the separate specialized high schools (academic and vocational), the report held that the comprehensive high school would provide for joint association of youth from different backgrounds while providing curriculum flexibility so that the student need not be locked into an inappropriate or unwise choice of curriculum. Opportunity to pursue higher education should be open to students who have undertaken vocational studies and not merely to the few who conform to the traditional requirements for college entrance. The report went so far as to call for compulsory education to age eighteen at a time when only about one out of every nine youngsters was graduating from high school.

At the time the report was being written, there were powerful influences favoring the establishment of a dual system of secondary education in the United States along the lines of European nations. As a result of the report, the federal Smith-Hughes Act of 1917 was implemented to provide for vocational education primarily through the agency of the comprehensive high school rather than the separate vocational high school. With the exception of our largest cities and certain other scattered instances, our nation had opted for a unitary school structure through the agency of the comprehensive high school.

Misconstruction of the Report. Thus the kind of social efficiency embraced in the *Cardinal Principles* report was not expressed in the "depreciatory estimate of the masses characteristic of an aristocratic society," to use Dewey's words, but that "opportunity for development of distinctive capacities be afforded all."

Butts and Cremin (1953) accurately viewed the *Cardinal Principles* report as signaling a radical change in looking to the high school as a place for educating *all* American youth, as opposed to the selective European tradition, and in revealing the need for a comprehensive curriculum to meet a comprehensive range of educational functions within a unitary school.[97] However, other educational historians were to seize upon the concept of social efficiency in the narrow sense of isolation and imposition, and they proceeded to attach this narrow meaning to the use of the term in the *Cardinal Principles* report.

In his history of the high school (1964), Krug cast the *Cardinal Principles* report as a perverse document for the promotion of the narrow and restrictive side of social efficiency. He proceeded to interpret the concept of differentiated curricula as serving the function of social efficiency through the separation of students by social and economic backgrounds, ignoring the repeated emphasis in the report against such isolation and discrimination.[98]

Other writers in educational history have followed Krug in portraying the *Cardinal Principles* report as promoting a "social-sorting function" by means of curriculum tracking through differentiated curriculums in the comprehensive high school.[99] But the report of 1918 showed how such a diversified curriculum would be flexible, and how a sense of democratic unity could be developed through the constants that constitute the common curriculum for general education. Like the modern land-grant university, the comprehensive high school was envisioned in the *Cardinal Principles* report as serving both the common and specialized needs of a cosmopolitan student population.

Belief in Democracy. To the traditionalists the *Cardinal Principles* report is seen as egalitarian and anti-intellectual in ministering to the needs of youth beyond cultivating the powers of the mind. In the words of Richard Hofstadter,

> The report is breathless with the idealism of the Progressive era and the war—with the hope of making the educational world safe for democracy and bringing a full measure of opportunity to every child. Our secondary education, the commission argued, "must aim at nothing less than complete and worthy living for all youth"—thus far had education gone beyond such a limited objective as developing the powers of the mind.[100]

Today one finds some leading figures in intellectual circles who see something naive in those who, in the past, held a strong belief in democracy.[101] Somehow, such a belief is unsophisticated in today's world. But the contemporary world reveals a continuing struggle for human rights and opportunities, and the school is still seen as a key agency in this struggle. The historic record reveals that progress has been made when people are seen in terms of their possibilities, not their limitations.

"As a Key Fits a Lock." James B. Conant repeatedly expressed his belief that the comprehensive high school is the chief means of forwarding the idea of unity based on diversity in the American democratic society. And he viewed the *Cardinal Principles* report as the signal document that catalyzed the revolution in secondary education.

In tracing the significance of the *Cardinal Principles* report of 1918, Conant pointed out that he was struck by the ways in which the ideas in the report, along with those of Harvard professor Alexander Inglis in *Principles of Secondary Education* (1918) and the writings of John Dewey, fit the new problems of the times "as a key fits a lock."[102] Conant noted that Inglis undoubtedly was an influential member of the NEA Commission on the Reorganization of Secondary Education, which issued the *Cardinal Principles* report of 1918, and that the report and the text authored by Inglis corresponded on virtually all points.

On the other hand, Krug made only passing reference to Inglis as having been a member of the commission and its committees. Instead, he dwelled upon Clarence Kingsley, a teacher of mathematics in the Brooklyn public schools who chaired the commission. Krug proceeded to describe the report as "Mr. Kingsley's Report."[103] In following Krug, Kliebard states that "Kingsley was to engineer, almost single-handedly, the *Cardinal Principles* Report," and he makes no mention of Inglis.[104]

Conant described his encounter with the report and the writings of Inglis and Dewey in these words:

> Reading Professor Inglis' volume in the light of what has been happened since was to me a fascinating experience. One saw a revolution through the eyes of a revolutionary . . . or at least a reform through the eyes of a reformer; one noted the current appraisal of those social changes that made imperative certain pedagogical reforms. But, in addition, one reads an account of a process which was still going on and learns what the progressive educators at the time of World War I were predicting about the future. Reading the 1918 Report of the NEA Commission on the Reorganization of Secondary Education affords something like the same experience. . . . Professor Inglis was a member of the NEA Commission and, I judge, an influential member. Certainly his book and the Report agree on all essential points.
>
> . . . . As I read the NEA Report, Professor Inglis' volume, and the writings of John Dewey before 1920, I am struck with the way the new ideas fit the new problems as a key fits a lock.[105]

Will French opened his study on general education in the American high school by showing the parallels between the positions taken in 1918 by Alexander Inglis in *Principles of Secondary Education* and those in the *Cardinal Principles* report of 1918, and in their call for a "common integrating program of education in high school."[106] Those who have chosen to see the *Cardinal Principles* report as "almost entirely Kingsley's own production" and as a scheme for the narrow efficiency of social isolation and predestination, have ignored the evidence to the contrary.[107] The themes of educational opportunity and unity through diversity, through a common and comprehensive high school, ring loud and clear in the *Cardinal Principles* report and in the writings of Alexander Inglis and other progressivists in the second decade of the twentieth century. At the memorial ceremony at Harvard commemorating Alexander Inglis (1879–1924) upon his untimely death, it was pointed out that "He played a commanding part in the work of the Commission on the Reorganization of Secondary Education" and, as a member of the commission's Reviewing Committee responsible for preparing the final report, "Inglis and his associates frequently changed the original judgments and always improved them."[108]

The Comprehensive High School as Prototype of Democracy

In his study of general education in the high school, published in 1957, Will French noted that the intervening years since the issuance of the *Cardinal Principles* report of 1918 had found that the purposes of secondary education as stated in the report "have been affirmed and reaffirmed in complementary statements by various professional and lay groups, until now there is almost unanimous acceptance of such purposes in determining what the high school curriculum should be."[109] At midcentury, Butts and Cremin reached this conclusion regarding the transformation of the high school since the time of the *Cardinal Principles* report: "Whatever the inadequacies and difficulties that still remained in the newer conception of secondary education for all youth, most educators were convinced that the gains outweighed the losses and that no retreat was possible or desirable."[110]

Conant's Faith.   Throughout his mature years, Conant repeatedly expressed his abiding belief in the comprehensive high school. In tracing its origins, Conant viewed it as the "creation of a prolonged surge of sentiment of the American people," and he concluded,

> I should call it a surge of noble sentiment. But my use of the adjective may only betray the fact that I was not only alive, but young, in the period when the waves of hope for humanity were running high.
>
> I must confess as I have reviewed the educational history of that period, I find my faith and optimism returning. So I venture to close ... with a prophecy. If the free world survives the perils that now confront it, I believe historians in the year 2059 will regard the American experiment in democracy as a great and successful adventure of the human race.... They will regard the American high school, as it was perfected by the end of the twentieth century, not only as one of the finest products of democracy, but as a continuing insurance for the preservation of the vitality of a society of free men.[111]

Conant was to include in his autobiography four speeches that he had made throughout his illustrious career (he actually had several illustrious careers—as a scientist, Harvard president, U.S. ambassador, and educational statesman). Of these four speeches, two were on public education, with one being devoted entirely to the comprehensive high school under the title "Unity and Diversity in Secondary Education."[112] While his faith in the comprehensive high school never wavered, he was to express apprehension as to its future when there is failure to recognize its contribution in helping keep our society open and free. In 1970 he wrote:

> I am an advocate of the comprehensive high school, but I must admit that the future of this institution is far from certain in the United States. It is strange that the enthusiasm for an American invention is so limited in this country just at the time when other nations are beginning to explore applications of the basic idea.... Are the high schools of the United States to be so designed so to be effective means of forwarding the idea of unity based on diversity in a democratic community, or is the comprehensive concept to be given at best only lip service? Far more than the nature of our schools is involved in the answer to this question. The entire structure of our nation may be at stake—possibly even its survival as an open society of free men.[113]

Conant's fears appeared justified. While the comprehensive high school had survived the hysteria of the early years of the space race, it was under attack during the late 1960s and early 1970s by radical critics from the left who called for alternative schools and the curtailment of formal schooling for the noncollege population.[114] In the 1970s federal reports called for the replacement of comprehensive high schools by academic high schools for the academically able, and separate specialized, part-time schools for noncollege-bound youth.[115] During the same period, studies were undertaken to support a national policy of lowered investment in schooling.[116] Whether these developments were symptoms of a kind of hardening of the arteries of the young nation could only be determined by the response of the public, which continued to hold onto the belief in education and in a unitary school structure serving comprehensive functions.

As the 1980s were coming to a close, one could not find any voices such as Conant's. Contemporary historians were not dealing kindly or fairly with the evolution of this unique institution and its contributions to American life. The fact that over the years it was so viciously attacked by both those of the extreme right and left would appear to signal that it has been regarded as a powerful institution of our society. Indeed, it had become so ingrained in our culture that efforts to change the structure of our school system through alternative schools and through separate vocational schools have been met with resistance at the grassroots level. With an increasing number of other advanced democratic nations discovering the comprehensive secondary school as the key to advancing educational opportunity, it appeared that the rediscovery of this institution by American historians and educators was overdue.

PERSPECTIVE

The idea of progress has guided the progressive redirection of American education in the twentieth century. Figure 7-1 portrays the conflicting currents between progressivism and traditionalism over the past century. Despite the ebb and flow between conservative and progressive forces which continue to this day, the belief in education, as Myrdal pointed out, remains a principal conclusion of the American Creed.

When Conant wrote about the "revolutionary transformation of the American public school," he was referring not only to the great extension of educational opportunity for all the children of all the people through progressive educational reforms during the twentieth century, but to the American invention of a unitary school system and the expansion of the curriculum to include the modern studies.[117] American progressive educators had recognized the inadequacies and dangers of delimiting the curriculum for the masses to the mere basics for the purpose of literacy to fit the needs of the industrial system. For a free society it was necessary that the curriculum provide for a common universe of discourse, understanding, and competence through general education in place of mere basic education.

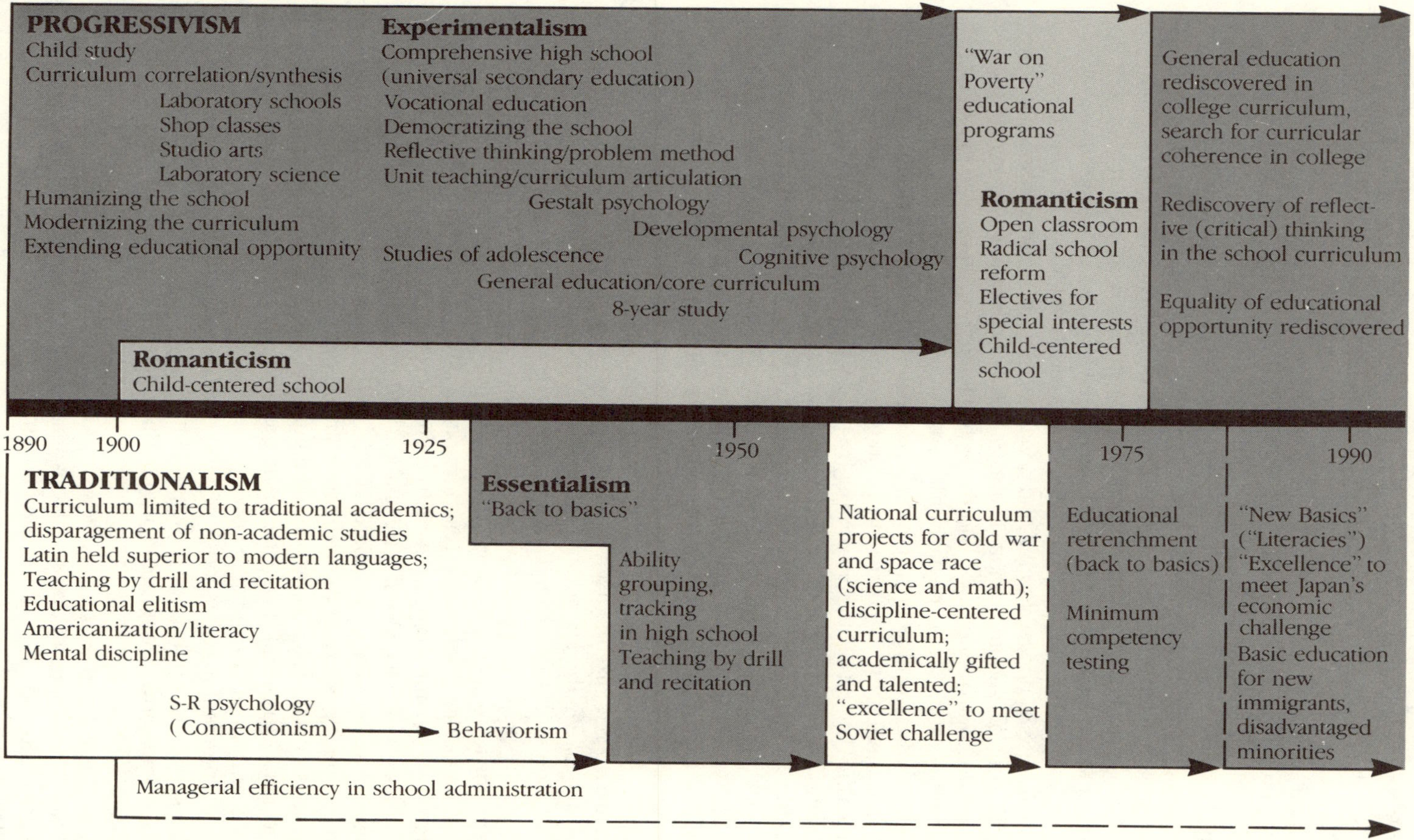

PROGRESSIVISM
Child study
Curriculum correlation/synthesis
Laboratory schools
Shop classes
Studio arts
Laboratory science
Humanizing the school
Modernizing the curriculum
Extending educational opportunity

Experimentalism
Comprehensive high school (universal secondary education)
Vocational education
Democratizing the school
Reflective thinking/problem method
Unit teaching/curriculum articulation
Studies of adolescence
General education/core curriculum
8-year study

Gestalt psychology
Developmental psychology
Cognitive psychology

"War on Poverty" educational programs

General education rediscovered in college curriculum, search for curricular coherence in college

Rediscovery of reflective (critical) thinking in the school curriculum

Equality of educational opportunity rediscovered

Romanticism
Child-centered school

Romanticism
Open classroom
Radical school reform
Electives for special interests
Child-centered school

1890 1900 1925 1950 1975 1990

TRADITIONALISM
Curriculum limited to traditional academics; disparagement of non-academic studies
Latin held superior to modern languages;
Teaching by drill and recitation
Educational elitism
Americanization/literacy
Mental discipline

S-R psychology (Connectionism) ⟶ Behaviorism

Managerial efficiency in school administration

Essentialism
"Back to basics"
Ability grouping, tracking in high school
Teaching by drill and recitation

National curriculum projects for cold war and space race (science and math); discipline-centered curriculum; academically gifted and talented; "excellence" to meet Soviet challenge

Educational retrenchment (back to basics)
Minimum competency testing

"New Basics" ("Literacies")
"Excellence" to meet Japan's economic challenge
Basic education for new immigrants, disadvantaged minorities

Figure 7-1. Main Currents and Countercurrents Affecting the Curriculum: 1890—Present.

At the same time, American progressive educators recognized the need for the secondary school to meet the diversified needs of a polyglot population through studies providing for specialization (college preparatory and vocational education), enrichment, and exploration. No longer would the high school be an exclusively college-preparatory institution, with its curriculum determined by the colleges. They saw the needed transformation of the curriculum in terms of the growing democratic conscience and in connection with advances in knowledge concerning the nature and development of children and adolescents. They envisioned a new concept of social efficiency: the release of human potentials through the widest extension of educational opportunity, as opposed to the traditional doctrine of efficiency through external controls and imposition. They conceived of education as growth in the power to control one's own life through intelligence, as opposed to blind authority, habit, dictate, or happenstance.

Yet the road has been rocky. Throughout the twentieth century, many school administrators, curricularists, and business leaders continued to embrace the concept of efficiency through a production model of schooling with all kinds of externally imposed controls. The struggle for general education continues in the face of pressures to reduce the curriculum to the basics or to specialized knowledge production to meet narrow nationalistic interests, as opposed to the widest public interest. Educational reforms are undertaken in favor of one side of the curriculum against another side, or in favor of one pupil population over another. The consequence has been that the curriculum is seen in the opposition between academic and practical studies, the failure to recognize the necessary interdependence of studies, and the opposition between the learner and the program of studies.

The succession of educational reforms by reaction and counterreaction raises the persistent question at various times as to why there is failure to learn the lessons of our historic past. Some historians may bemoan the repetitive reworking of ideas and reappearance of developments. Some may portray these seeming repetitions as recurrent cycles, or some may see these shifts between educational retrenchment and progress in terms of the metaphor of the pendulum. A superficial analysis of the situation may tempt one to see the resolution at the midpoint. But the pendulum resting at the midpoint is at stasis. Moreover, the pendulum follows a single plane of movement, whereas social change occurs in the vital interaction of different forces in different planes simultaneously.

Progress, then, depends upon the capacity to build upon our cumulative knowledge so that our present is better than our past. "The true starting point of history is always some present situation with its problems," observed Dewey.[118]

Ideals taken seriously serve as a compass to gauge the direction of our means. The testing of our educational means and consequences against our highest and widest social ideals will determine the extent to which our society is true to itself.

NOTES

1. John Dewey, *Democracy and Education* (New York: Macmillan, 1916), p. 251.

2. Ibid., pp. 382, 383.

3. John Dewey, "From Absolutism to Experimentalism," in George P. Adams and William P. Montague (eds.), *Contemporary American Philosophy,* vol. 2 (New York: Russell & Russell, 1930), p. 28.

4. Boyd H. Bode, "Education at the Crossroads," *Progressive Education,* vol. 8 (November 1931), p. 548.

5. Richard Hofstadter, *Anti-intellectualism in American Life* (New York: Knopf, 1962), p. 129.

6. California State Department of Education, *News Release* (December 10, 1985), p. 3.

7. Dewey, "From Absolutism to Experimentalism," op. cit., p. 15.

8. Robert M. Hutchins, *The Higher Learning in America* (New Haven: Yale University Press, 1936), p. 67.

9. Theodore R. Sizer, *Horace's Compromise* (Boston: Houghton Mifflin, 1984), p. 89.

10. "Original Papers in Relation to a Course of Liberal Education," *American Journal of Science and Arts* 15 (January 1829): 300.

11. Sizer, op. cit., p. 88.

12. Ibid., pp. 9, 89, 159.

13. Mortimer J. Adler, *The Paideia Proposal* (New York: Macmillan, 1982), pp. 53, 61.

14. Dewey, *Democracy and Education,* op. cit., p. 372.

15. James B. Conant, *Education in a Divided World* (Cambridge: Harvard University Press, 1949), pp. 74–75.

16. William J. Bennett, *James Madison High School* (Washington, D.C.: U.S. Department of Education, 1987); *James Madison Elementary School* (Washington, D.C.: U.S. Department of Education, 1988).

17. James Atlas, "The Battle of the Books," *The New York Times Magazine* (June 5, 1988), pp. 24–26, 72–74.

18. William J. Bennett, *To Reclaim a Legacy* (Washington, D. C.: National Endowment for the Humanities, 1984), p. 8.

19. John Dewey, *The Quest for Certainty* (New York: Capricorn, Putnam, 1960), p. 84. (First published 1929.)

20. J. D. Bernal, *Science in History,* vol. 4 (Cambridge, M.I.T. Press, 1971), p. 1149.

21. John Dewey, "Learning to Earn," *School and Society* 5 (March 24, 1917): 332.

22. William C. Bagley, *Education and Emergent Man* (New York: Nelson, 1934).

23. Arthur Bestor, *The Restoration of Learning* (New York: Knopf, 1956), p. 60.

24. Ibid., p. 80.

25. Ibid., p. 354.

26. Hyman G. Rickover, "European Vs. American Schools," *Phi Delta Kappan* 40 (November 1958): 61.

27. Aristotle, *Politics, Great Books of the Western World,* vol. 9 (Chicago: Encyclopedia Britannica, 1952), p. 544.

28. Hyman G. Rickover, *American Education—A National Failure* (New York: Dutton, 1963), p. 89.

29. *The New York Times,* November 3, 1967, p. 50.

30. Joseph J. Schwab in Stanley Elam (ed.), *Education and the Structure of Knowledge* (Chicago: Rand McNally, 1964), p. 7; *College Curriculum and Student Protest* (Chicago: University of Chicago Press, 1969), p. 241.

31. Sidney P. Marland, Jr., "Career Education Now," address at the Annual Meeting of the National Association of Secondary School Principals, Houston, Texas, January 23, 1971.

32. National Commission on Excellence in Education, *A Nation at Risk* (Washington, D.C.: U.S. Department of Education, 1983), pp. 5–7, 24.

33. National Science Board, *Educating Americans for the 21st Century* (Washington, D.C.: National Science Foundation, 1983), p. 52.

34. Dewey, *Democracy and Education,* op. cit., p. 289.

35. Report of the Harvard Committee, *General Education in a Free Society* (Cambridge,: Harvard University Press, 1945), pp. 51, 79.

36. Hofstadter, op. cit., Ch. 13, "The Road to Life Adjustment."

37. Lawrence A. Cremin, *The Transformation of the School* (New York: Knopf, 1961), pp. ix, 352–53.

38. Lester F. Ward, *Dynamic Sociology,* Vol II (New York: Appleton, 1883), pp. 598, 602, 632–32; Laurel N. Tanner and Daniel Tanner, "Environmentalism in American Pedagogy: The Legacy of Lester Ward," *Teachers College Record* 88 (Summer, 1987), pp. 537–47.

39. Ward, ibid., pp. 492, 502–4, 621–22, 625–33.

40. Ibid., p. 597.

41. Ibid., p. 497.

42. Henry Steele Commager, *The Search for a Usable Past* (New York: Knopf, 1967), p. 258.

43. Cremin, op. cit., p. 98.

44. Ward, op. cit., p. 497.

45. Ibid., p. 571.

46. Walter Lippmann, "The Hope of Democracy," *New Republic,* vol. 7 (July 1, 1916), p. 231.

47. Gunnar Myrdal, *An American Dilemma* (New York: Harper & Row, 1962), p. 883. First published 1944.)

48. Ibid., p. 709.

49. Dewey, *Democracy and Education,* op. cit., p. 352.

50. Ibid., pp. 225–26.

51. F. Champion Ward et al., *The Idea and Practice of General Education* (Chicago: University of Chicago Press, 1950), p. v.

52. Max Born, "What Is Left to Hope For," *Bulletin of the Atomic Scientists* 20 (April 1964): 2.

53. John Dewey "Science as Subject-Matter and as Method," *Science,* vol. 31 (January 1910), p. 127; *The Public and Its Problems* (New York: Holt, 1927), pp. 174–75.

54. Allan Bloom, *The Closing of the American Mind* (New York: Simon and Schuster, 1987), p. 356.

55. Elliot W. Eisner, *The Educational Imagination,* 2nd ed. (New York: Macmillan, 1985), p. 10.

56. John Dewey, *The Sources of a Science of Education* (New York: Liveright, 1929), pp. 12, 27.

57. Boyd H. Bode, *Modern Educational Theories* (New York: Vintage, 1927; first published by Macmillan), p. 234.

58. Harry S. Broudy, *The Real World of the Public Schools* (New York: Harcourt, 1972), p. 172.

59. Dewey, *The Public and Its Problems,* op. cit., pp. 135, 139.

60. John Dewey, *Experience and Education* (New York: Macmillan, 1938), pp. vi–vii.

61. George S. Counts, *Dare the School Build a New Social Order?* (New York: John Day, 1932), p. 7.

62. Boyd H. Bode, "Education and Social Reconstruction," *The Social Frontier,* vol. 1 (January 1935), p. 22; John Dewey, "Education and Social Change," *The Social Frontier,* vol. 3 (May 1937), p. 235; "Education for a Changing Social Order," in *NEA Addresses and Proceedings,* 1934, pp. 744–52.

63. John Dewey, "The Teacher and His World," *The Social Frontier,* vol. 2 (January 1935), p. 7.

64. Theodore Brameld, *Patterns of Educational Philosophy* (New York: Holt, 1971), p. 519.

65. Lewis Mumford, *The Pentagon of Power* (New York: Harcourt, 1970), pp. 210–11.

66. John Dewey, *The Child and the Curriculum* (Chicago: University of Chicago Press, 1902), pp. 15–16, 18.

67. Jean Jacques Rousseau, *Émile* (London: Dent, 1911), pp. 9, 58, 84, 141.

68. Thomas P. Bailey, "Some Difficulties of Child-Study," *NEA Proceedings* (Chicago: University of Chicago Press, 1900), p. 583.

69. E. D. Hirsch, *Cultural Literacy* (New York: Vintage, Random House, 1987), pp. 119, 120.

70. A. S. Neill, *Summerhill* (New York: Hart, 1960), p. 4.

71. Ibid., p. 25.

72. Paul Goodman, *New Reformation* (New York: Random, 1970), p. 86.

73. Ibid., p. 88.

74. John Holt, *How Children Fail* (New York: Dell, 1964), pp. 176, 177, 179.

75. John Dewey, *How We Think* (Lexington, Mass.: Heath, 1933), pp. 87, 90.

76. Daniel L. Duke, *The Retransformation of the School* (Chicago: Nelson-Hall, 1978).

77. Theodore Roszak, *The Making of a Counter Culture* (New York: Doubleday, 1969); *Where the Wasteland Ends (New York: Doubleday, 1972), p. 372.*

78. Van Cleve Morris, "Existentialism and the Education of Twentieth-Century Man," in Stan Dropkin et al. (eds.), *Contemporary American Education* (New York: Macmillan, 1970), pp. 258, 260.

79. George F. Kneller (ed.), *Foundations of Education,* 3rd ed. (New York: Wiley, 1971), pp. 259, 264.

80. Arnold J. Rosenberg, "Educational Existentialism in the Sudbury Valley School," *Educational Leadership,* vol. 30 (February 1973), p. 481.

81. John Dewey, *Human Nature and Conduct* (New York: Holt, 1922), pp. 10–11.

82. Maxine Greene, *Teacher as Stranger* (Belmont, Calif.: Wadsworth, 1973), pp. 103, 129.

83. John Dewey, *Individualism Old and New* (New York: Capricorn, 1962), pp. 97, 98. (First published 1929.)

84. Jacques Monod, *Chance and Necessity* (New York: Vintage, 1972), pp. 170, 180; Daniel Tanner, "Knowledge Divided Against Itself," *Bulletin of the Atomic Scientists* 39 (March 1983): 34–38.

85. Albert Einstein, *Out of My Later Years* (New York: Philosophical Library, 1950), pp. 29–30.

86. Lester F. Ward, *Applied Sociology* (Boston: Ginn, 1906), p. 339; *Dynamic Sociology,* op. cit., pp. 631–33.

87. Edward A. Krug, *The Shaping of the American High School* (New York: Harper & Row, 1964), pp. 274, 276, 393; Barry M. Franklin, *Building the American Community* (London: Falmer, 1986), pp. 90–94; Herbert M. Kliebard, *The Struggle for the American Curriculum* (Routledge & Kegan Paul, 1986), pp. 93, 112–15, 127–28.

88. Edward A. Ross, *Social Control* (New York: Macmillan, 1901), p. 172.

89. Ibid.

90. Ibid., p. 173.

91. Ibid., p. 174.

92. Ibid., p. 177.

93. Ibid., pp. 178–179.

94. Franklin, op. cit., p. 19; Joel Spring in Clarence J. Karier, Paul Violas, and Joel Spring, *Roots of Crisis* (Chicago: Rand McNally, 1973), p. 31.

95. Dewey, *Democracy and Education,* op. cit., pp. 138–39, 142.

96. Commission on the Reorganization of Secondary Education, *Cardinal Principles of Secondary Education* (Washington, D.C.: U.S. Bureau of Education, 1918), pp. 7, 9, 14, 16.

97. R. Freeman Butts and Lawrence A. Cremin, *A History of Education in American Culture* (New York: Holt, 1953), p. 592.

98. Krug, op. cit., p. 276.

99. Joel Spring, *The Sorting Machine* (New York: David McKay, 1976), p. 58.

100. Hofstadter, op. cit., p. 336.

101. *The New York Times,* September 29, 1988, p. C21.

102. James B. Conant, *The Child, the Parent, and the State* (Cambridge: Harvard University Press, 1959), p. 93.

103. Krug, op. cit., pp. 378–406.

104. Kliebard, op. cit., p. 112.

105. Conant, *The Child, the Parent, and the State,* op. cit., pp. 92–93.

106. Will French, *Behavioral Goals of General Education in High School* (New York: Russell Sage, 1957), pp. 1–2.

107. Krug, op. cit., p. 384.

108. *Alexander Inglis 1879–1924. In Memoriam.* Cambridge: Harvard University Press, 1925, pp. 8, 33.

109. French, op. cit., p. 22.

110. Butts and Cremin, op. cit., p. 505.

111. James B. Conant, *The Child, the Parent, and the State,* op. cit., pp. 102–3.

112. James B. Conant, *My Several Lives* (New York: Harper & Row, 1970), pp. 665–70.

113. James B. Conant in Alvin C. Eurich (ed.), *High School 1980* (New York: Pitman), pp. 73, 80.

114. Goodman, *Compulsory Mis-education,* op. cit.; Edward Z. Friedenberg, *Coming of Age in America* (New York: Vintage, 1967), p. 250–51, 257.

115. National Panel on High School and Adolescent Education, *The Education of Adolescents* (Washington, D.C.: U.S. Office of Education, 1976); Panel on Youth of the President's Science Advisory Committee, *Youth: Transition to Adulthood* (Chicago: University of Chicago Press, 1974); Daniel Tanner, "Splitting up the School System," *Phi Delta Kappan* 61 (October 1979): 92–97.

116. Christopher Jencks, *Inequality* (New York: Basic Books, 1972); Daniel Tanner, "The Retreat from Education—For Other People's Children," *Intellect* 102 (January 1974): 223–25.

117. Conant, *The Child, the Parent, and the State,* op. cit., p. 84.

118. Dewey, *Democracy and Education,* op. cit., p. 251.

SELECTED REFERENCES

Adler, Mortimer J. *The Paideia Proposal: An Educational Manifesto.* New York: Macmillan, 1982.

Aikin, Wilford M. *The Story of the Eight-Year Study.* New York: Harper & Row, 1942.

Bell, Daniel. *The Reforming of General Education.* New York: Columbia University Press, 1966.

Bennett, William J. *To Reclaim a Legacy: A Report on the Humanities in Higher Education.* Washington, D.C.: National Endowment for the Humanities, 1984.

Bestor, Arthur. *The Restoration of Learning.* New York: Knopf, 1956.

Bloom, Allan. *The Closing of the American Mind.* New York: Simon and Schuster, 1987.

Bode, Boyd H. *Modern Educational Theories.* New York: Macmillan, 1927.

Boyer, Ernest L. *High School: A Report on Secondary Education in America.* New York: Harper & Row, 1983.

Boyer, Ernest L., and Levine, Arthur. *A Quest for a Common Learning.* Washington, D.C.: Carnegie Foundation for the Advancement of Teaching, 1981.

Bronowski, Jacob. *The Origins of Knowledge and the Imagination.* New Haven: Yale University Press, 1978.

Butts, R. Freeman, and Cremin, Lawrence A. *A History of Education in American Culture.* New York: Henry Holt and Company, 1953.

Callahan, Raymond E. *Education and the Cult of Efficiency.* Chicago: University of Chicago Press, 1962.

Caswell, Hollis L., ed. *The American High School: Its Responsibility and Opportunity.* Eighth Yearbook of the John Dewey Society. New York: Harper & Row, 1946.

Chamberlain, Dean, et al. *Did They Succeed in College?* New York: Harper & Row, 1942.

Commission on Humanities, Rockefeller Foundation. *The Humanities in American Life.* Berkeley: University of California Press, 1980.

Commission on the Reorganization of Secondary Education. *Cardinal Principles of Secondary Education.* Washington, D.C.: U.S. Bureau of Education, 1918.

Conant, James B. *Education in a Divided World.* Cambridge,: Harvard University Press, 1949.

———. *The Child, the Parent, and the State.* Cambridge,: Harvard University Press, 1959.

———. *Shaping Educational Policy.* New York: McGraw-Hill, 1964.

Counts, George S. *Dare the School Build a New Social Order?* New York: John Day, 1932.

Cremin, Lawrence A. *The Transformation of the School.* New York: Knopf, 1961.

———. *The Genius of American Education.* New York: Random House, 1965.

———. *Public Education.* New York: Basic Books, 1976.

———. *American Education: The Metropolitan Experience, 1876–1980.* New York: Harper & Row, 1988.

Dewey, John. *The School and Society.* Chicago: University of Chicago Press, 1899.

———. *The Child and the Curriculum.* Chicago: University of Chicago Press, 1902.

———. *Democracy and Education.* New York: Macmillan, 1916.

———. *The Quest for Certainty.* New York: Capricorn Books, 1929.

———. *The Sources of a Science of Education.* New York: Liveright, 1929.

———. *How We Think,* rev. ed. Lexington, Mass.: D. C. Heath and Company, 1933.

———. *Experience and Education.* New York: Macmillan, 1938.

———. *Freedom and Culture.* New York: Putnam, 1939.

Dewey, John, and Dewey, Evelyn. *Schools of Tomorrow.* New York: Dutton, 1915.

Dykhuizen, George. *The Life and Mind of John Dewey.* Carbondale: Southern Illinois University Press, 1973.

Educational Policies Commission. *Education for ALL American Youth—A Further Look.* Washington, D.C.: National Education Association, 1952.

Glass, Bentley. *The Timely and the Timeless.* New York: Basic Books, 1970.

Hofstadter, Richard. *Anti-intellectualism in American Life.* New York: Knopf, 1962.

Hutchins, Robert M. *The Higher Learning in America.* New Haven: Yale University Press, 1936.

Inglis, Alexander. *Principles of Secondary Education.* Boston: Houghton Mifflin, 1918.

Krug, Edward A. *The Shaping of the American High School.* New York: Harper & Row, 1964.

Myrdal, Gunnar. *An American Dilemma.* New York: Harper & Row, 1964.

National Commission on Excellence in Education. *A Nation at Risk: The Imperative for Educational Reform.* Washington, D.C.: U.S. Department of Education, 1983.

National Society for the Study of Education. *General Education in the American College.* Thirty-sixth Yearbook, Part II. Chicago: University of Chicago Press, 1939.

———. *General Education.* Fifty-first Yearbook, Part I. Chicago: University of Chicago Press, 1976.

———. *Modern Philosophies of Education.* Fifty-fourth Yearbook, Part I. Chicago: University of Chicago Press, 1955.

Ravitch, Diane. *The Revisionists Revised.* New York: Basic Books, 1977.

———. *The Troubled Crusade: American Education 1945–1980.* New York: Basic Books, 1983.

Report of the Harvard Committee. *General Education in a Free Society.* Cambridge: Harvard University Press, 1945.

Rickover, Hyman G. *American Education—National Failure.* New York: Dutton, 1963.

Rugg, Harold O. *Foundations for American Education.* Yonkers-on-Hudson, N.Y.: World Book, 1947.

Seguel, Mary L. *The Curriculum Field: Its Formative Years.* New York: Teachers College Press, 1966.

Silberman, Charles E. *Crisis in the Classroom.* New York: Random House, 1970.

Snow, C. P. *Two Cultures and the Scientific Revolution.* New York: Cambridge University Press, 1959.

Tanner, Daniel. *Secondary Education: Perspectives and Prospects.* New York: Macmillan, 1972.

Tanner, Daniel, and Tanner, Laurel. *Curriculum Development: Theory into Practice,* 2nd ed. New York: Macmillan, 1980.

Thomas, Russell. *The Search for a Common Learning.* New York: McGraw-Hill, 1962.

Van Doren, Mark. *Liberal Education.* Boston: Beacon Press, 1959. (First published 1943.)

Ward, F. Champion, et al. *The Idea and Practice of General Education.* Chicago: University of Chicago Press, 1960.

Ward, Lester F. *Dynamic Sociology.* New York: Appleton and Company, 1883.

———. *Applied Sociology.* Boston: Ginn & Company, 1906.

Weinberg, Alvin M. *Reflections on Big Science.* Cambridge: M.I.T. Press, 1967.

White, Morton. *Science and Sentiment in America.* New York: Oxford University Press, 1972.

Whitehead, Alfred N. *The Aims of Education.* New York: Macmillan, 1929.

Wirth, Arthur G. *Education in the Technological Society.* Scranton, Pa.: International Textbook Company, 1972.

INDEXES

Name Index

Adams, George P., 369*n*.
Addams, Jane, 20–21, 23, 28*n*., 127–128, 146*n*.
Adler, Mortimer J., 312, 333, 369*n*., 373*n*.
Aikin, Wilford M., 27*n*., 228, 230–231, 265*n*., 266*n*., 268*n*., 373*n*.
Allen, Ann Taylor, 56, 84*n*.
Allen, Jerome, 90, 142*n*.
Aristotle, 278, 335, 338, 370*n*.
Atkinson, John W., 287, 322*n*.
Atlas, James, 369*n*.
Ayres, Leonard, 184–185, 208*n*.
Ausubel, David P., 179–180, 208*n*.
Babbidge, Homer D., Jr., 82*n*.
Bachman, Frank, 132–133, 146*n*., 147*n*., 201
Bacon, Francis, 50, 62, 278
Bagley, William C., 9, 161, 196, 205*n*., 259, 336, 369*n*.
Bailey, Stephen, 269*n*., 326*n*.
Bailey, Thomas P., 371*n*.
Baker, G. Derwood, 206*n*.
Baker, James H., 68
Barnard, Henry, 40, 43, 76, 77, 83*n*., 85*n*.
Barnes, Emily Ann, 207*n*.
Beard, Charles, 4–6, 8, 21–22, 26*n*., 28*n*.
Becker, Carl, 17, 27*n*.
Bell, Daniel, 325*n*., 373*n*.
Bell, Howard M., 258
Bell, Terrel H., 28*n*.
Bennett, William J., 314, 322*n*., 334–335, 369*n*., 373*n*.

Berman, Barbara, 183, 208*n*.
Bernal, J. D., 336, 369*n*.
Bestor, Arthur, 25, 28*n*., 252–253, 261, 267*n*., 268*n*., 309, 337–338, 369*n*., 373*n*.
Blaine, Anita McCormick, 113
Bloom, Allan, 315, 334, 348, 373*n*.
Bloom, Benjamin S., 10, 28*n*., 279, 287, 290, 295–296, 301, 321*n*., 322*n*., 323*n*., 325*n*., 371*n*.
Bobbitt, Franklin, 180–183, 187–192, 200, 203, 208*n*., 209*n*., 210*n*., 215–216, 306, 324*n*.
Bode, Boyd H., 10, 28*n*., 153, 157, 159, 161, 185, 192, 204*n*., 205*n*., 208*n*., 210*n*., 221, 258, 264*n*., 328, 348, 369*n*., 371*n*., 373*n*.
Bonser, Frederick G., 173, 206*n*., 207*n*.
Born, Max, 347, 370*n*.
Bourne, Randolph, 132, 146*n*.
Bower, Gordon H., 211*n*., 325*n*.
Bowers, C. A., 264*n*., 268*n*.
Boyer, Ernest L., 247, 267*n*., 313, 317, 323*n*., 325*n*., 342, 373*n*.
Brameld, Theodore, 264*n*., 350, 371*n*.
Brickman, William W., 15–16, 27*n*.
Briggs, Thomas H., 118, 145*n*.
Bronowski, Jacob, 374*n*.
Brookover, Wilbur B., 46, 83*n*.
Broudy, Harry S., 371*n*.
Broyler, C. R., 207*n*.
Bruner, Jerome S., 177–178, 207*n*., 265*n*., 275, 278, 309, 320*n*., 321*n*., 325*n*.

Subject Index

A

Absolutism, 329–330
Academic disciplines, 339
  mental discipline and, 177
  structure of, 178
  transfer of learning and, 177, 178, 180
Academic-nonacademic dualism, 335
Academic studies, 125, 136, 139, 291, 332, 337, 340
  mental discipline and, 174–176, 337
  nonacademic studies and, 233–234, 337
  vocational studies and, 177, 234, 268
Academically gifted and talented, 107, 179, 316, 339, 342, 367
Academy, 31, 32–33, 50, 62–65, 74, 75, 81, 124, 134, 135
Achievement, evaluation of, 170–171
Achievement testing, 170–171, 283. *See also* Minimum-competency testing; Standardized tests
Action-research movement, 307
Activism, 283
Activities, purposeful, 130, 159, 160, 161, 162, 202
Activity analysis, 124, 163, 188, 189, 190, 196, 203. *See also* Job analysis
Activity curriculum, 154, 155–157, 158, 159, 160, 161, 165, 238–240, 263
Activity movement, 154–157, 238
Adjustment, 248, 249
Adolescence, 115, 117. *See also* Youth education

Adult education, 127
Affective education, 285–286, 287
Affective-existential stream, 283
Agricultural education, 128, 158, 159
Aims. *See* Educational aims; Educational objectives
Alabama curriculum program, 236, 237, 313
Alternative schools, 178, 282, 353–354, 366
American Association for the Advancement of Science, 163, 299, 300
American Council on Education, 225, 242, 256, 258
American Creed, 22, 345, 366
American Education Fellowship (AEF), 225, 261, 262
American educational conscience, 134, 135
American Educational Research Association (AERA), 162
American Historical Association, 4
American Institute of Instruction, 40, 47
American Journal of Education, 40–41, 47, 54, 76
American language, 36, 75
American Progressivism, 125–126, 141, 178, 215
American Revolution, 31, 33, 35, 39, 80, 135, 290
American Society of Equity, 128
American Youth Commission, 242–243, 256, 258
Americanization, 126, 367